INVASION OF THE THIRD REICH

End of Operation Eclipse: Field Marshal Bernard Montgomery signing Articles of Surrender. (*Imperial War Museum*)

INVASION OF THE THIRD REICH

WAR & PEACE

OPERATION ECLIPSE

PATRICK DELAFORCE

AMBERLEY

For my sweet wife
with very many thanks for her help with this book.

First published 2011

Amberley Publishing
Cirencester Road, Chalford,
Stroud, Gloucestershire, GL6 8PE

www.amberleybooks.com

British Library Cataloguing in Publication Data.
A catalogue record for this book is available from the British Library.

ISBN 978-1-84868-948-0

Typesetting and Origination by Amberley Publishing.
Printed in Great Britain.

Contents

Foreword   8

Introduction: The British Liberation Army   9

1   Hitler's Crumbling Third Reich   21
2   Making War   33
3   Bleak Mid-Winter: Longstop in the Ardennes   47
4   Hobart's Terrible 'Funnies'   65
5   Bleak Mid-Winter: Operation Blackcock   75
6   Betuwe: The 'Island' Campaign   90
7   Reichswald Battles: Operation Veritable   101
8   Reaching the Rhine: Operation Blockbuster   131
9   Capturing Arnhem: Operations Destroyer and Anger   147
10   Weapons of Revenge   162
11   Rhine Crossing Battle: Operation Plunder   168
12   Airborne Attack: Operation Varsity   182
13   Affairs of State   190
14   Over the Rhine   195
15   Battle for the Teutoburger Wald   202
16   T-Force: 'Thieving Magpies'   215
17   Bergen-Belsen Concentration Camp   220
18   Operation Forrard On to Bremen   233
19   Capture of Bremen: Operation Clipper   244
20   *Alpenfestung*: Göbbels' Hoax   261
21   Capture of Hamburg   265
22   Racing the Russians to the Baltic   278
23   Admiral Dönitz's 'Fourth Reich'   300

24 Final Surrender: Operation Eclipse 309
25 Liberation of *Festung* Holland 330
26 Liberation of Denmark 362
27 Liberation of *Festung* Norwegen 381
28 Liberation of POW Camps 398
29 Freedom for Hitler's Slaves 408
30 Retribution: War Crimes Tribunals 420

Appendices
A The Holocaust and the Death Camps 427
B Hitler's Nuclear Option 430
C Operation Unthinkable 436

Bibliography 438
Acknowledgements 439
Glossary 440
Index 444

The last defenders – Hitler decorating Hitler Youth who won the Iron Cross in battle, 30 March 1945.

The Pursuit and the Channel Ports

'The Pursuit and Channel Ports.' By the end of 1944, the British Liberation Army had reached the frontiers of the Third Reich.

Architects of victory in Operation Eclipse: Field Marshal Bernard Montgomery with Major General Adair (Guards Armoured) left, Lt General Horrocks (30 Corps Commander) right and Major General 'Pip' Roberts (11th Black Bull Armoured) extreme right. (*Imperial War Museum*)

Foreword

This book is the sequel to *The Rhine Endeavour*, which documented the events of September 1944, when the British Liberation Army liberated 20 million of Adolf Hitler's victims – French, Belgian and Dutch. Poised on the borders of the Third Reich, within five months a further 20 million civilians of Holland, Norway, and Denmark, and a multitude of Allied prisoners of war and Displaced Persons (DP), were rescued in Operation Eclipse.

The British Liberation Army brought fearful war, peace, justice and retribution. This is the story of Monty's young soldiers – Patrick Delaforce was one of them – who helped end the ignoble Third Reich.

The author (on right), troop leader with 13 RHA in Kiel, May 1945, who fought in the five major battles in Operation Eclipse.

The British Liberation Army

This is the story of Operation Eclipse – the grand design – the plan for the British Liberation Army (BLA), as part of the Allied Command (Americans, Canadians, French and Poles), to invade and conquer the Third Reich in 1945.

By the end of 1944 much had been achieved. Operation Overlord, the invasion into German-defended Normandy, after eleven weeks of attritional fighting during which battlefield casualties averaged 7,000 a day, had been an outstanding success. Hitler had sent his best panzer troops, SS divisions and Hitler Jugend in and they were outnumbered, outgunned, smashed by the Allied air forces, pulverised by the massed artillery and not even the Normandy *bocage* defensive terrain could save them.

The Great Swan followed. General 'Blood and Guts' Patton raced through Brittany and headed for Paris. Very politely, General de Gaulle's French troops were allowed in first. In Operation Anvil dozens more American divisions swept up the Rhône valley to strengthen Eisenhower's huge Allied army.

Next came the British Great Swan, when General Montgomery's four armoured divisions, 7th Desert Rats, 11th Black Bull, the Guards and the Poles, swept north for 250 miles through western and northern France into the Low Countries.

September 1944 was the 'zenith' month for the BLA. Le Havre was captured in a classic all-services battle in Operation Astonia. The Desert Rats and the Poles liberated Ghent, Lille and all the northern French towns; famous names of the Great War all fell. The Guards Armoured thrust into Brussels for the untold, unimaginable joy of liberation. The 11th Armoured Division, in which the author served, with a lot of help

9

Field Marshal Bernard Montgomery led the British Liberation Army to victory in Operation Eclipse. (*Imperial War Museum*)

from the Belgian Liberation Army, captured the greatest prize of all – Antwerp city and its huge, great dockland.

It was too good to be true!

Euphoria reigned. All the field marshals and generals joined in a litany of great expectation: 'War will be over by Christmas,' 'On to Berlin.' The liberated citizens of France, Belgium and some in Holland said of their German conquerors, 'Hitler kaput.'

In the autumn of 1944 Alan Moorehead, the intrepid Australian war journalist, wrote:

> It was a most dangerous period of delay. Every hour, every day, the German morale was hardening. As the broken remnants of the Fifteenth and Seventh Armies struggled back to the Reich they were regrouped into new formations [kampfgruppen]. Anything and everything served at this desperate moment. Submarine crews were put in the line as infantry; the German water-police were mobilised; there was a brigade of deaf men who presumably received their orders in deaf and dumb language. There was a whole division of men who suffered from stomach ailments and had to be served with special bread.

Throughout the Reich every officer and man on leave was summoned back to his post. Extraordinary prisoners were collected – near-sighted clerks who had left their city offices three weeks before; men with half-healed wounds, even cripples and children of fifteen or sixteen [about to join the dreaded Hitler Jugend]. It was a makeshift hotch-potch army, an emergency army put in simply to hold the gap, simply to fight for time while the German generals reorganised on a sounder basis. Little by little a crust was formed along the valley of the Rhine from the Swiss border to the Zuyder Zee.

On 6 December 1944 Prime Minister Churchill wrote to President Roosevelt:

> The time has come for me to place before you the serious and disappointing war situation which faces us at the close of the year ... The fact remains that we have definitely failed to achieve the strategic object which we gave our armies five weeks ago. We have not reached the Rhine in the Northern part and most important sector of the front. We shall have to continue the great battle for many weeks before we can hope to reach the Rhine and establish our bridgeheads. After that again, we have to advance through Germany.

By the beginning of December 1944, the official statistics for the rosters of the German Feldheer (armed forces strength) showed over 10 million soldiers able and probably willing to fight and die for their Führer. This included the Luftwaffe, Navy, coastguards, police, the new Volks-grenadier divisions, the Volksturm (Home Guard), convalescent units, sweepings from the German prisons, multitudes of 'pressed' men or 'volunteers' from the east (Ost-truppen), Poles, Czechs, Rumanians, Russians and the rather dangerous SS 'foreign' turncoats from the occupied territories. They all joined in – France, Belgium, Holland, Italy, and the Vikings from Scandinavia – providing young, dedicated men who, as renegades, knew what their future would be if captured. Probably there would have been a British SS unit or two if Operation Sealion had been successful.

The comparative failure of Operation Market Garden in September had been caused by many factors. Undoubtedly the main cause was the astonishing skill and resolution of the German field commanders who marshalled aggressive defences to thwart Field Marshal (from 1 September) Bernard Montgomery's huge army thrusting into the centre of Holland.

Hitler's generals – Model (left) confers with Student, Bittrich and Harmel.

Liddell Hart, the distinguished military expert, interviewed many of Hitler's commanders immediately after the end of the war and wrote: 'The German generals of this war were the best-finished product of their profession – anywhere. They could have been better if their outlook had been wider and their understanding deeper. But if they had become philosophers they would have ceased to be soldiers.' Any student of history who reads Field Marshal Michael Carver's comments in his memoirs on the many British generals he served with or under will agree. The German generals were far better than the vast majority of the Allied generals. Sad, but true!

Although some of Hitler's *festung* fortress commanders were mediocre, most of them defended their ports with great tenacity. Indeed, Dunkirk was so well protected that it was deemed pointless to grind the defenders down and they eventually surrendered at the end of the war – totally undefeated! Old von Rundstedt, certainly Field Marshal Model ('Hitler's Fireman'), Bittrich and Student, who commanded the Parachute Army, were probably more experienced and capable than most of the Allied generals. General von Zangen, for example, created a German 'Dunkirk'

Monty and his generals: Dempsey (on his left), Crerar (on his right), Thomas (on his far right) and 'Pip' Roberts (behind his right shoulder). Behind Monty are Scottish generals wearing Tam o'Shanters.

by skilfully extracting the bulk of the 15th Army from the Pas de Calais north and across the river Scheldt, at night, not only into safety but to add to the German defences in Holland. He wrote:

> Therefore, I order commanders, as well as the National Socialist indoctrination officers, to instruct the troops in the clearest and most factual manner on the following points: Next to Hamburg, Antwerp is the largest port in Europe …
>
> After overrunning the Scheldt fortifications, the English would finally be in a position to land great masses of material in a large and completely protected harbour. With this material they might deliver a death blow to the north German plateau and to Berlin before the onset of winter.
>
> In order to pretend that the battle of Antwerp is unimportant and to shake the morale of its defenders, enemy propaganda maintains that the Anglo-American forces already possess sufficient ports which are intact, with the result that they are not at all dependent on Antwerp. That is a known lie. In particular, the port of Ostend, of which the enemy radio speaks frequently, is completely destroyed. Current delays in the enemy's conduct of the war are attributable in great measure to the fact that he still must bring all his supplies through the improvised facilities of Cherbourg. As a result, he has even had to lay a temporary oil pipe-line from these to the interior of France …

In his last speech, Churchill said again, 'before the storms of winter we must bring in the harvest in Europe'. The enemy knows that he must assault the European fortress as speedily as possible before its inner lines of resistance are built up and occupied by new divisions. For this reason he needs the Antwerp harbor. And for this reason, we must hold the Scheldt fortifications to the end. The German people is watching us. In this hour, the fortifications along the Scheldt occupy a role which is decisive for the future of our people. Each additional day that you deny the port of Antwerp to the enemy and to the resources that he has at his disposal, will be vital.

(Signed) VON ZANGEN

General of the Infantry

Hitler, Göring and Göbbels had between them conjured up a huge army despite the staggering losses on the Russian front, in North Africa, and in Normandy, which still numbered over ten million men. Göring's Parachute Army from Luftwaffe sources was young, fanatical and seemed happy to fight and die for the Third Reich. It was deployed immediately opposite the BLA, and in the late autumn of 1944 often won the day. The SS troops were the *crème de la crème* of Hitler's forces, but unfortunately they left a long trail of atrocities behind them. The author saw one at Breendonk fortress south of Antwerp, where the Belgian SS and German Gestapo had tortured, maimed and executed anyone who might be part of the Resistance and, of course, the Jewish population.

Other disquieting factors were that the German armies had recovered from Normandy and were fighting in hastily assembled kampfgruppen in the polders and Peel country of Holland with great vigour and audacity. By contrast the BLA, with limited sources of manpower due to its immense losses of mainly 'Poor Bloody Infantry' (PBI) in Normandy, had had to disband over twenty formations, including the magnificent 50th Tyne-Tees Northumbrian Division. As the Luftwaffe was in almost total decline, the need for the anti-aircraft regiments in every one of Montgomery's divisions was now deemed not to be essential. Many of the anti-tank artillery regiments in every division were less vital, as Tigers, Panthers, Leopards and the host of Teutonic panzers had suffered immense losses. And the survivors were fighting desperately on the Eastern Front to keep Stalin's hordes at bay, so tens of thousands of young men in khaki swapped jobs for a much more dangerous one and joined 3rd British, 15th Scottish, 43rd Wessex, 49th Polar Bears,

Battlegrounds of France, Belgium, Holland, into Germany.

51st Highland and 53rd Welsh divisions who were desperate for reinforcements.

The balance of power between the Allies had been swinging inevitably away from Prime Minister Churchill and the British contribution to winning the war. True, the Royal Navy and the RAF were performing miracles practically every single day, but on land it was a different matter.

On the Eastern Front 410 Russian and German divisions were battering each other with staggering losses on both sides. But on the Western Front 'only' 120 divisions were locked in combat. At the end of 1944, Hitler had 133 divisions at war in Russia, 76 in north-west Europe, 24 in Italy, 10 in Yugoslavia and 17 lurking in the wings in Norway and Denmark.

General Eisenhower then had a total of 79 US and French divisions under his command (49 infantry, 26 armoured and 4 airborne). Field Marshal Montgomery had 12 British, 3–5 Canadian, some who had arrived from Italy, and one Polish division.

At their few 'Great Power' meetings, Churchill's influence was waning, President Roosevelt was ailing and was soon to die, and Josef Stalin made promises without intending to honour them. His agenda was quite straightforward: bloody revenge on Hitler's wicked Operation Barbarossa and the maximum of communist influence and power in the

15

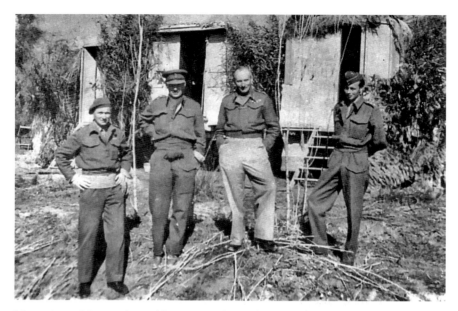

Monty (second from right) and his ADCs in front of three war caravans.

Baltic States and Eastern Germany, including the capture of Berlin and poor Poland, for whom many years back – or so it seemed at the time – Britain and France went to war.

Josef Stalin stated cynically, but accurately: 'England provided the time, America provided the money and Russia provided the blood.' With a huge population of 190 million, against the 80 million of the Third Reich, it was clear that Stalin could accept huge losses of men and territory until, with much help from 'General Winter', the tide turned. The failure to take Moscow and Stalingrad and the battles of Kiev and Kursk would soon prove decisive. In the Second World War, Russian military losses were about 11 million, and Nazi losses 3.8 million. Even worse, about 23–26 million Soviet citizens died, one way or another, during the war. Millions more endured wounds, hardship, loss of homes and land, and captivity in Germany.

By contrast the USA service deaths in all theatres of war numbered 405,399 and those of the British numbered about 190,000.

There were still terrible tribulations lying ahead of the BLA: the thunderbolt in the Ardennes, and operations Blackcock, Veritable, Blockbuster, Anger, Varsity and Plunder. There were painful landmarks

21 ARMY GROUP

PERSONAL CHRISTMAS MESSAGE
FROM THE C-IN-C

(To be read out to all troops)

1. The forces of the British Empire in western Europe spend Christmas 1944 in the field. But what a change has come over the scene since last Christmas.

The supreme Battle of Normandy carried with it the liberation of France and Belgium.

Last Christmas we were in England, expectant and full of hope ; this Christmas we are fighting in Germany.

The conquest of Germany remains.

2. It would have needed a brave man to say on D day, 6 June, that in three months we would be in Brussels and Antwerp : having liberated nearly the whole of France and Belgium ; and in six months we would be fighting in Germany : having driven the enemy back across his own frontiers.

But this is what has happened.

And we must not fail to give the praise and honour where it is due :

" *This was the Lord's doing, and it is marvellous in our eyes.*"

3. At Christmas time, whether in our homes or fighting in the field, we like to sing the carols we learnt as children ; and in truth, this is indeed a link between us and our families and friends in the home country : since they are singing the same verses. The old words express exactly what we all feel today :'

" *Glory to God in the highest, and on earth peace, good will toward men.*"

That is what we are fighting for, that is what we desire : on earth peace, good will toward men.

4. And so today we sing the Christmas hymns, full of hope, and steadfast in our belief that soon we shall achieve our hearts' desire.

Therefore, with faith in God, and with enthusiasm for our cause and for the day of battle, let us continue the contest with stout hearts and with determination to conquer.

5. And at this time I send to each one of you my best wishes and my Christmas greetings.

Wherever you may be, fighting in the front line, or working on the lines of communication or in the ports, I wish all of you good luck and a happy 1945. We are all one great team ; together, you and I, we have achieved much ; and together, we will see the thing through to the end.

6. Good luck to you all.

B. L., Montgomery
Field - Marshal
C-in-C 21 Army Group.

Belgium.
Xmas, 1944

Monty's Christmas message.

on the way. The appalling concentration camp of Bergen Belsen, the difficult battle to capture Bremen, and the seizure of ruined Hamburg, but among all the trauma of daily armed confrontation was the fact that the BLA succeeded in bringing peace and liberation to nearly 20 million of Hitler's victims: most of Holland, aided by the Canadians and Poles; the sovereign countries of Denmark and Norway; the liberation of vast numbers of prisoners of war; and several million (out of six million) nomadic displaced persons. These slaves of the Hitler regime worked in the factories, on the farms, and in the defences of Germany. Poor devils – many of them knew not how or where to go. The many Russian 'serfs' faced a dangerous future if they returned to their native country. But they were, or would be by May 1945, freed from Nazi captivity.

Unbeknown to the Allied leaders on New Year's Day 1945, there were three great moral hazards ahead of them. Chapter 25 chronicles the long, unhappy final year, when most of the Dutch citizens were starving. Seyss-Inquhart, the German Reichskommissar for the Netherlands, deliberately created the *Hongerwinter* of 1944–45. The Dutch royal family and government in exile pleaded for the Allies, who in Market Garden had fought and controlled a sizeable part of the country, to finish the job. But Seyss-Inquhart was already destroying polder-dykes and flooding prosperous sectors and was threatening even more. And Field Marshal Montgomery and Eisenhower too, decided that the whole purpose of Operation Eclipse – the destruction of the Third Reich – was paramount. So Holland starved! Operation Manna, a humanitarian food relief programme, was finally agreed in late April 1945.

Among the millions of displaced persons roaming Germany during 1945 were over two million captured Russian prisoners of war. On release many of them were frightened of being repatriated; to be a prisoner of war in the peculiar Russian mindset was considered to be treasonable.

The Allied commanders in the West were confronted with this terrible dilemma. There was no reason to believe that, on their return, the vast majority would be sent arbitrarily to the hated *gulags*. The Geneva Convention rules were that third party prisoners of war were to be returned to their homeland.

When finally the Allied Commission had to organise some stable law and order in the defeated Third Reich, with every major city and town destroyed, the best candidates able to obtain order out of chaos were all loyal, dedicated Nazis, although many of course denied that. The millions of German prisoners of war were 'screened'. The vast majority were released in a short time, a small minority were charged with war crimes and tried, and another small minority, including a future president, were allowed to continue supervising their fellow countrymen, albeit peacefully. It was difficult to imagine the same thing happening if Operation Sealion had succeeded. Britain would have been under the jackboot and all their leaders permanently in prison camps or dead and buried!

Retribution was also a moral issue. Proven war criminals should face justice in appropriate tribunals under international law, which should, above all, be seen to be eminently fair. Nuremberg was unique in its scale and was observed by the press of the world. Justice was seen to be done. There were also minor war crimes tribunals in Hamburg and Luneberg, which are covered in this book. The author was a junior officer in 3rd RHA, Desert Rats, at the time and was one of three officers who combined jury and judicial duties, advised by an eminent Judge Advocate General. In Hamburg, several dozen 'minor' war criminals, mostly prison guards, were tried and sentenced. Later, just before his twenty-second birthday, he witnessed, as one of fifty official British Army of the Rhine (BAOR) officers, Mr Albert Pierrepoint, the official British hangman, in action in Hameln.

This book is about the way in which the citizen-army of Great Britain, the BLA, emerged from the slough of despondency in Holland, smashed, slowly and very painfully, through the Siegfried Line, defeated Hitler's armies west of the Rhine, and fought five river crossing battles to reach the Baltic just before Stalin's Cossack army marauders. On the way they stormed the vital port of Bremen and captured Hamburg.

They brought peace and liberation to most of Holland, to Denmark, to Norway, to tens of thousands of Allied prisoners of war, and succour for some of the millions of nomadic homeless and displaced persons, effectively slaves of the Nazi regime. The BLA forced a corridor about 100 miles wide and thrust ahead some 250 miles. The German army claimed in 1918/19 that they had not been defeated, as at the Armistice they withdrew to the Fatherland. The author's father fought them in Flanders fields and then became a member of the BAOR. His son did exactly the same thing some twenty-five years later. The main difference was that for the first time ever the German country was invaded and conquered, 'Alles kaput.'

Above: Liberation.

Left: Freedom.

Below: Retribution.

CHAPTER ONE

Hitler's Crumbling Third Reich

One of the greatest mysteries of the twentieth century was how a motley collection of not very intelligent German street brawlers, led and totally dominated by one man, could take most of Europe and threaten the rest of the world with brutal war. Adolf Hitler (1889–1945), an Austrian misfit and loner, with a slight education, no family genes of note and no political background, created the infamous Third Reich by sheer determination, confidence, willpower, deviousness and luck. It was incredible that a brave, undistinguished Great War corporal, who never fired a gun in anger, and was distinctly not officer material, should encourage, organise and control the world's most brilliant fighting force, and control them from one of his twenty headquarters until the sordid end.

William Shirer was a determined American CBS journalist resident in Berlin in the late 1930s and into the start of the Second World War who witnessed the Führer's activities for several years. He attended a colossal Nuremberg rally for the Nazi faithful. There were 30,000 people in the great Luitpold Hall, tens of thousands packing the narrow streets to get a glimpse of Hitler and watch the goose-stepping military might, and half a million at the Zeppelin Meadow. Shirer wrote:

> You have to go through one of these to understand Hitler's hold on the people, to feel the dynamism in the movement he's unleashed and the sheer, disciplined strength the Germans possess. And now – as Hitler told the correspondents yesterday – the half-million men and women who've been here during the week will go back to their towns and villages and preach the new faith with new fanaticism.

Hitler rewarding his youth troops. Hitler 'Jugend' in the making!

Back in Berlin I tried to sort over my first impressions of Adolf Hitler. In looks and appearance he was rather different from what I had expected. In Nuremberg, except during the traditional hysterical outbreak against the Bolsheviks and the Jews, he did not look or behave like the mad, raging, brutish dictator I had been reading about and which he had proved himself to be by his merciless massacre of the SA leaders and political opponents less than three months before.

His face was rather common. It was coarse. It was not particularly strong. Sometimes, when he obviously was fatigued from the long speeches, the hours spent in reviewing his troops, it appeared flabby.

All through the week in Nuremberg, where I often sat or stood but a few feet from him in the stands, I tried to size up the features of the man. He was about five feet, nine inches tall and weighed around 150 pounds. His legs were short and his knees turned in slightly so that he seemed to be a bit knock-kneed. He had well-formed hands, with long, graceful fingers that reminded one of those of a concert pianist, and he used them effectively, I thought, in his gestures during a speech or when talking informally with a small group.

His nose betrayed the brutal side of him. It was straight but rather large and broadened at the base, where thick nostrils widened it. It was the coarsest feature of the face. Perhaps it was to soften it that he grew his famous Charlie

Chaplin mustache. His mouth was quite expressive, and it could reflect a variety of moods.

It was the eyes that dominated the otherwise common face. They were hypnotic. Piercing. Penetrating. As far as I could tell, they were light blue, but the color was not the thing you noticed. What hit you at once was their power. They stared at you. They stared through you. They seemed to immobilize the person on whom they were directed, frightening some and fascinating others, especially women, but dominating them in any case. They reminded me of paintings I had seen of the Medusa, whose stare was said to turn men into stone or reduce them to impotence. All through the days at Nuremberg I would observe hardened old party leaders, who had spent years in the company of Hitler, freeze as he paused to talk to one or the other of them, hypnotized by his penetrating glare. I thought at first that only Germans reacted in this manner. But one day at a reception for foreign diplomats I noticed one envoy after another apparently succumbing to the famous eyes. Martha Dodd, the vivacious young daughter of the American ambassador, had told me a day or two before I left for Nuremberg, to watch out for Hitler's eyes. 'They are unforgettable,' she said. 'They overwhelm you.'

His oratory also was overwhelming. at least to Germans. It held them spellbound. At Nuremberg I grasped for the first time that it was Hitler's eloquence, his astonishing ability to move a German audience by speech, that more than anything else had swept him from oblivion to power as dictator and seemed likely to keep him there.

The words he uttered, the thoughts he expressed, often seemed to me ridiculous, but that week in Nuremberg I began to comprehend that it did not matter so much what he said but how he said it. Hitler's communication with his audiences was uncanny.

Hitler was a great gambler, not for money but for the highest stakes of war. In 1940 and 1941, every gamble came off: brave Poland was over-run in weeks; at Munich Hitler had walked all over Neville Chamberlain; 'Weser Exercise' swallowed up Denmark and Norway; 'Fall Gelb' swamped Holland, Belgium and France when Europe's largest army simply imploded and the famous Maginot Line was bypassed at both ends.

In December 1940 William Shirer in Berlin wrote: 'When I left, German troops, after their quick and easy conquests of Poland, Denmark, Norway, Holland, Belgium and France, stood watch from the North Cape to the Pyrenees, from the Atlantic to beyond the Vistula. Britain stood alone. Few doubted that Hitler would emerge from the conflict as the greatest conqueror since Napoleon. Not many believed that Britain would survive.' Soon Yugoslavia and Greece followed and were over-run.

The great gambler had called 'heads' every single time and had guessed right. But his luck started to run out. 'Tails' it was as Rommel's German and Italian armies surrendered in North Africa. The aerial battle over Britain had not been won.

Soon hubris set in. The world lay at the Führer's feet. His well-trained Wehrmacht and Luftwaffe were all-conquering. In his book *Mein Kampf* he had spelt out his objectives for all the democracies to read. Of course, the Führer, the architect of the Third Reich, which would last for a thousand years, was locked into his own private cuckoo-land of make-believe unblemished by reality. On every front – Italy, Russia and north-west Europe – his ten million strong warriors were in disarray.

If he had not committed two acts of lunacy, perhaps three, the world, and certainly Europe, would have had an unprecedented era of despair, violence and little hope. Operation Barbarossa was utter madness. The evil Joseph Stalin had absolutely no intention of invading Germany – for all sorts of excellent reasons. The second act – vainglorious and stupid in spades – was the declaration of war against the United States to show some unnecessary solidarity with his far-flung allies in Japan. President Roosevelt had spent several years being converted, persuaded and cajoled by Winston Churchill into stepping up 'commercial' help (such as fifty decayed, obsolete destroyers), to help and incidentally, bankrupt his distant ally. A formal declaration of war was what Churchill desperately needed, but Roosevelt's voting public would never have allowed it.

These were the two obvious mistakes. The third and perhaps just as deadly is shown in Appendix B: 'Hitler's Nuclear Option.' If Hitler had not been told that all his very, very eminent nuclear physicists were Jewish, and therefore 'sub rosa' unreliable and untrustworthy, his race for the ultimate vengeance weapon could, maybe would, have been achieved.

At the Führer's naval conference on 8 July 1943, Grand Admiral Dönitz advised Hitler that two new types of submarine had been designed, which would revolutionise the war at sea. These new *Die Boot* could travel as fast *under* water as on the surface. They could operate submerged for prolonged periods without having to come up to charge their batteries. Dönitz said: 'Entirely new possibilities are introduced by permitting U-boats to approach a convoy quickly. They could also take swift evasive action at 15 knots underwater instead of being obliged to surface. This will make the enemy's present anti-submarine defence entirely ineffectual.' Dönitz was delighted. Hitler was delighted and Albert Speer was told to grant top priority to the construction of these new U-boats. Dönitz's team reckoned a minimum of 17 months was needed. Speer was confident that by not building prototypes and testing them, he could reduce the time required by half. By December 1943 a full-scale mock-up of each model had been built and the first electro U-boats would be ready by the spring of 1944.

Despite providing his existing fleet with better defensive radar, heavier anti-aircraft armament and a new acoustically guided torpedo, Dönitz knew that for every ship his U-boats sank the Americans were building four new Liberty vessels. The Allied long-range air patrols were becoming more effective and the British Royal Navy convoy systems were better protected.

Allied bombing caused delay to Speer's production. A Type XXI prototype was destroyed in Kiel harbour and many of the subcontractors lacked the necessary skill and precision required. Even the new Schnorkel, which allow batteries to be recharged without surfacing, had many technical problems. Nevertheless, in mid-1944 Dönitz still had well over 400 serviceable U-boats.

By early 1945, 128 new electro U-boats, not the 245 planned, were ready for sea trials. Bletchley Park's Ultra machine had detected clues about Dönitz's new dangerous 'toys', so from the end of 1943 the construction yards had been bombed and the shallow waters of the Baltic had been mined.

The famous war correspondent, Chester Wilmot, pointed out in his majestic *Struggle for Europe* that because Grand Admiral Dönitz was pushing the claims of his new electro U-boats, which required the deeper waters of the Gulf of Danzig, Memel, East Prussia and the Courland Pocket in western Latvia for their trials, Hitler felt compelled to leave forty *vital* Wehrmacht divisions to defend the eastern Baltic shores from Konigsberg northwards from the Russian Red Army. Even though in February 1945 Dönitz had 450 U-boats – 'the largest number that Germany had ever possessed', he told the Führer – the formidable thrust by the BLA reached Kiel harbour in time to ensure that the electro U-boats and two-men midget submarines were captured.

So Hitler's dreams of lethal new victory weapons, V-1s, V-2s, the ME jet fighters, the new U-boats, and his half-hearted efforts with an atomic

Battered ruins of Cleves.

bomb, had all failed. They would have been nightmares – fortunately, they were mainly thwarted by the interdiction by the Allied air forces.

The Führer must have realised by February that his vaunted Vengeance weapon [*vergeltungswaffe*], conducted by Flak Regiment 155, had not brought Britain to its knees. 15,000 V-1s, the noisy, pilotless and grossly inaccurate monoplane, which was targeted on London and Antwerp, had caused terror on a limited scale. About 6,000 of them had not reached their targets. Next came the V-2, a liquid-fuelled rocket travelling at supersonic speed, which was impossible to intercept, unlike the V-1 which could be shot down or even gently nudged. The 5,000 V-2s with the same one-ton high explosive warhead failed to break the British spirit. Indeed, there was evidence that Bomber Harris's obliteration of every major town in Germany had failed to break the German collective will to force a regime change.

Albert Speer had worked production miracles in the battered Third Reich. Hitler made his architect friend Armaments Minister in 1942, and he became second only to Hitler himself as a power on the home front. Skoda factories at Pilsen produced panzer tanks. Two million French POWs worked in the mines and on the farms to release German manpower for the armed services. A further 7.8 million slave labourers were made to work in the Ruhr. Factories went underground to escape the bombing or were rebuilt outside the towns. Oil came into the Reich from Romania. Synthetic oil production, despite Bomber Harris' 1,000 bomber raids on the target, remained steady at between 4 and 5 million tons each year, peaking at 5.7 million in 1943. Tank production rose from 6,000 in 1942, to 12,000 in 1943. Averaging over 30 million tons in 1941, coal production averaged over 250 million tons in 1944. It was incredible!

Hitler ruled his generals and *festung* fortress commanders with an iron fist. Even portly Field Marshal Hermann Göring, the Luftwaffe boss and nominally No. 2 in the Nazi hierarchy, was petrified of Hitler. Göring's promises to destroy the British RAF in Operation Sealion, which had ended in dismal failure, meant that he was never fully trusted again. Several field marshals committed suicide. Operation Valkyrie, the assassination plot in July 1944, had made Hitler even more paranoid. His remaining top generals, Model, von Rundstedt, Kesselring, Guderian and Kettel stayed faithful even though they knew that many of the orders they received were impossible to carry out. They tried their best.

First 'Hitler's Fireman', Field Marshal Model:

14 October 1944
ORDER OF THE DAY
Soldiers of the Army Group!
The battle in the West has reached its peak. On widely separated fronts we must defend the soil of our German homeland. Now we must shield the sacred soil of the Fatherland with tenacity and doggedness ... *The Commandment of the hour is: None of us gives up a square foot of German soil while still alive.*

Every bunker, every block of houses in a German town, every German village must become a fortress which shatters the enemy. That's what the Führer, the people and our dead comrades expect from us. *The enemy shall know that there is no road into the heart of the Reich except over our dead bodies ...*

Egotism, neglect of duty, defeatism and especially cowardice must not be allowed room in our hearts. *Whoever retreats without giving battle is a traitor to his people ...*

Soldiers! Our homeland, the lives of our wives and children are at stake!

Our Führer and our loved ones have confidence in their soldiers! We will show ourselves worthy of their confidence.

Long live our Germany and our beloved Führer!
MODEL
Field Marshal

Then there followed another message to the troops:

I expect you to defend Germany's sacred soil with all your strength and to the very last. The homeland will thank you through untiring efforts and will be proud of you.

New soldiers will arrive at the Western front. Instil into them your will to victory and your battle experience. All officers and NCOs are responsible for all troops being at all times conscious of their great responsibility as defenders of the Western approaches. Soldiers of the Western Front!

Every attempt of the enemy to break into our Fatherland will fail because of your unshakeable bearing:
Heil the Führer!
VON RUNDSTEDT
Field Marshal

So through the combined efforts, threats, and bullying by Hitler's formidable coterie, Himmler, Göbbels and Göring, the strength towards the end of 1944 was Wehrmacht and Waffen SS 7,536,946; Luftwaffe 1,925,29; and Kriegsmarines 703,066 – a total of 10,165,303.

Heinrich Himmler, Hitler's terrible henchman, who organised the 'Final Solution', the supervision of the destruction of Jewry, not only in the Reich but also in every occupied country, had taken over command of the 'Home Army' in Germany after the failed assassination attempt on 20 July.

In the autumn of 1944, a document called 'Enemy War Aims' was officially propagated across the Third Reich by Himmler.

In May 1944 the Soviet Union offered a plan to her Allies whereby all members of the German forces would be made prisoners-of-war and organised into labour battalions for forced labour in the Soviet Union. The USA as well as England agreed to the proposal without restrictions.

On top of that, the USA demanded that the geographical unity of Germany be dissolved by running corridors through it, which would be inhabited by non-Germans. They intend to distribute these sectors to 'a population with more peaceful tendencies' while making Germany defenceless and enslaved.

To destroy German national pride, a complete understanding exists between Moscow, London and Washington.

(a) They will not make peace with Germany, but will continuously occupy the country.

(b) They intend to intermarry Germany women with members of the occupying forces.

(c) German children will be educated after separation from their parents ...

The will to destroy is not directed against National Socialism but, without any doubt, against the entire German nation.

Whoever does not fulfil his duty to the utmost during the coming weeks and months is helping to make these war aims of the enemy a terrible reality.

And to his SS troops Himmler sent this brutal message:

Reichsführer SS 10 September 1944

Certain unreliable elements seem to believe that the war will be over for them as soon as they surrender to the enemy.

Against this belief it must be pointed out that every deserter will be prosecuted and will find his just punishment. Furthermore his ignominious behaviour will entail the most severe consequences for his family. Upon examination of the circumstances they will be summarily shot.

(Signed) HIMMLER

Many thousands of the Reich SS had been forced to surrender in Normandy. The survivors were now warned.

The arch-propagandist, Dr Joseph Göbbels, had a very difficult task – on every front in late 1944 the great armies of 1940, 1941, 1942 and 1943 were in full retreat. The homeland had been bombed to destruction, the enemy were nearing the borders. Milton Shulman, who interviewed most of the key German commanders immediately after the end of the war, wrote:

And when the commanders had paused for breath, Göbbels and his propaganda boys stepped in to continue pumping into the dazed and weary body of the German soldier the synthetic stimulants of fear and faith which alone could keep him resisting. But the propaganda line had undergone a change since the early days of the invasion. Then the emphasis had been on hope – the promise of secret weapons and secret armies which would suddenly appear to crush the Allies in one violent cataclysm. The secret weapons had come and gone and yet the shadow of defeat was closer and darker than it had ever been before. The promise of secret weapons now had to be soft-pedalled. The emphasis was now on fear – fear of the destruction of Germany, of the rape of its womanhood, of the vengeance of the Russian Bolsheviks. Hammering on these themes like some mad musician at an organ, Göbbels pulled out all the stops, reaching a Wagnerian crescendo of frenzied hysteria. One typical example of the propaganda efforts used to frighten or shame the German soldier into staying in the line was a leaflet entitled 'The Watch on the Rhine'. Over the picture of a medieval German warrior, complete with flowing cloak, chain-armour and enormous sword, standing guard on the Rhine, the following words, amongst others, were written:

Comrade, the enemy means to outflank the West Wall at the very point where we are and to cross the Rhine into Germany!

Shall our people, shall our families, have suffered five years in vain?

Shall they suffer misery and starvation amid the ruins of our cities in a conquered Germany?

Do you wish to go to Siberia to work as a slave?

What do you say about it?

Never shall this happen.

Never shall the heroic sacrifices of our people prove in vain!

> Therefore, everything depends now on your courage! The struggle against an enemy who at the moment is still superior is tremendously hard. But for all of us there is no other way out than *to fight on with knives if need be*.
>
> It is better to die than to accept dishonour and slavery!
>
> It is better to be dead than a slave!
>
> Therefore – keep the watch on the Rhine steadfastly and loyally.

Nevertheless, Hitler's Third Reich was crumbling!

The vast majority of the BLA poised on the frontier of the Third Reich – poised to break and enter a strange, hostile land – had never visited Germany before, and almost certainly had never met any Germans socially. The front line soldiers had encountered the SS and the Hitler Jugend and did not like what they saw. They and their families had suffered almost five years of total war, perhaps in the many towns blitzed by the Luftwaffe. They thought they knew quite a lot about Hitler, his revolting gang and 'Lord Haw-Haw', the renegade British radio 'comic'. Almost certainly they knew little about the appalling butchery of the Jews (and many others) in the extermination and concentration camps.

Alan Moorehead wrote in *Eclipse*:

> For most of us it was our first experience of Germany itself, the first time we had come into contact with large numbers of German civilians and seen the way they lived and dressed and carried themselves. It was the beginning of an immensely complicated relationship between ourselves and the defeated, a story that kept changing its plot ... As soon as you discovered evil and malice in one place you were immediately confronted with kindness and genuine innocence in another ... No matter where you went, or what you did, was placed against the unending tragedy and physical ruin of the country.

The black, brutal, sinister side of the Third Reich was hidden from the vast majority of the BLA and from most of the journalists. The appalling atrocities enacted at Auschwitz, Buchenwald, Belsen and Dachau were only discovered in the last few dying weeks of the war. In the excellent book *War Report, Despatches: D-Day to VE Day*, BBC war correspondents – Robert Reid on Buchenwald, Richard Dimbleby on Belsen, and Ian Wilson on Dachau – write about their firsthand on-the-spot visits to those hells on earth. The appendix on the camps at the end of this book is not for the faint-hearted. It is the testimony to the lasting shame of Hitler's Third Reich.

Total war – destruction of the Third Reich.

CHAPTER 2

Making War

Ahead for the BLA lay several set-piece 'Monty' attacks planned down to the last detail. Overwhelming close air support (CAS) by Typhoon cab ranks and colossal barrages, and under that shelter – a hideous, noisy umbrella – infantry supported by tanks, flails, Crocodiles and petard-throwing AVREs would make their slow, very careful advance.

However, it often failed to work out quite as planned!

The War Office's 'Current reports from Overseas' secured reports made at the time by eminent German military commanders. One from the Italian front noted:

> The conduct of the battle by the Americans and English was, taken all round, once again very methodical. Local successes were seldom exploited … British attacking formations were split up into large numbers of assault squads commanded by officers. NCOs were rarely in the 'big picture', so that if the officer became a casualty, they were unable to act in accordance with the main plan. The result was that in a quickly changing situation *the junior commanders showed insufficient flexibility.* For instance, when an objective was reached, the enemy would neglect to exploit and dig in for defence. The conclusion is: as far as possible *go for the enemy officers.* Then seize the initiative yourself.

The Panzer Lehr, the finest German armoured division in Normandy, under General Fritz Bayerlein, in an intelligence report noted that:

> … a successful break-in by the enemy was seldom exploited in pursuit. If our own troops were ready near the front for a local counter-attack, the ground was immediately regained. Enemy infantry offensive action by night is limited

South Lancashires advance on Venray during 'Operation Aintree', November 1944. *(Imperial War Museum)*

Infantry of 3rd British Division move up. Mine sweeping on the right, tank support on left. *(Imperial War Museum)*

to small reconnaissance patrols … It is better to attack the English who are very sensitive to close combat and flank attack at their weakest moment – that is, when they have to fight without their artillery.

A British corps commander in the Italian campaign wrote:

The destruction of the enemy was most easily achieved when we managed to keep him tired and in a state of disorganisation, which resulted in unco-ordinated defence and lack of food, petrol and ammunition. We were undoubtedly too inelastic in our methods when faced with changing conditions. After six weeks of mobile fighting, during which the enemy never launched anything bigger than weak company counter-attacks, we still talked too much about 'firm bases' and 'exposed flanks'.

Time and time again the German defenders held their front line with a minimum of strength, but with many observation posts to bring down heavy defensive nebelwerfer 'stonks'. The thin defensive line protected by substantial minefields absorbed the huge Allied bombardments. At the second or third stage in their defensive tactics the German commanders sent small patrols behind Allied positions forcing the British to defend their flanks.

German infantry attack.

German defenders prepare ambush for British troops. (*Imperial War Museum*)

The PRO/WO208/393 has another German report: 'The British infantryman is distinguished more by physical endurance than by special bravery. The impetuous attack, executed with dash, is foreign to him. He is sensitive to energetic counter-attack.'

Max Hastings, in his superb book *Overlord*, wrote:

Again and again a single German tank, a handful of infantry with an 88mm gun, a hastily mounted attack, stopped a thoroughly organised Allied advance dead in its tracks. German leadership at corps level and above was often little better than that of the Allies and sometimes markedly worse [perhaps obeying a foolhardy order from their Führer?] But at regimental level and below, it was superb. The German army appeared to have access to a bottomless reservoir of brave, able and quick thinking colonels commanding battlegroups and of NCOs capable of directing the defence of an entire sector of the front.

Every army, since warfare was chronicled in the Old Testament, has had the front line soldiers claiming bitterly that their weaponry, uniforms and rations were inferior to those of the enemy.

However, apart from the Allied artillery, which was highly regarded and feared by the opposition, in every single field the German armoury

British armour and infantry.

was more effective. Take tanks: Tigers and Panthers or Shermans and Cromwells. Take machine guns: Spandaus and Schmeissers or Brens and Stens. A German infantry company *carried* sixteen machine guns compared to the British nine and the American eleven. Take the German panzerfaust (the finest infantry anti-tank weapon of the Second World War) or the Heath Robinson PIAT. Take mortars: the British 2-inch and 3-inch weapons were reliable but slow. The German infantry division usually had twenty 120mm mortars, which could hurl a 35-pound bomb (compared to the famous British 25-pounder gun) a distance of 6,000 yards.

The Allied PBI hated and feared the nebelwerfer, the five-barrelled projector whose bombs were fitted with a brilliantly conceived siren, causing it to wail as it flew through the air, which had an effect on those who heard it, often more penetrating than its explosive power. Nebelwerfers came in three sizes: 150mm (75-pound bomb, 7,300-yard range); 210mm (248-pound bomb, 8,600-yard range); 300mm (277-pound bomb, 5,000-yard range). Each of the five regiments of these – the bulk of them concentrated in the British sector in Normandy – contained sixty or seventy projectors, some of them track mounted.

The large, cumbersome, lethal dual-purpose 88mm AA/anti-tank gun ruled the armoured battlefields and brewed up all Allied tanks in its sights.

German Panzer Mk 5, or Panther.

88mm dual-purpose gun.

Nevertheless Allied rations were regarded as much superior to captured liverwurst and other delicacies. After all 'an army marches on its stomach'!

General Brian Horrocks, the best corps commander in the BLA, despite a lacklustre performance in Operation Market Garden, commanded 30th Corps, which in Operation Veritable in February 1945 mustered 200,000 men-at-arms. He wrote sympathetically about the PBI:

> This battle was a particularly good example The 53rd Welsh Division and, further south, the 51st Highland Division were fighting their way through that sinister black Reichswald Forest. Their forward troops would very often consist of two young men, crouching together in a fox-hole, both of whom had long since come to the conclusion that the glories of war had been much over-written. They were quite alone for they might not be able to see even the other members of their own section and all around them was the menace of hidden mines.
>
> It is this sinister emptiness that depresses them most – no living thing in sight. During training, officers and NCOs had been running round the whole time, but they cannot do it now to anything like the same extent, or they won't live long. Our two young men are almost certainly cold, miserable and hungry, but they are at least reasonably safe as long as they remain in their fox-hole. But they know that soon they will have to emerge into the open to attack. Then the seemingly empty battlefield will erupt into sudden and violent life. When that moment arrives they must force themselves forward with a sickening feeling in the pit of their stomachs, fighting an almost uncontrollable urge to fling themselves down as close to the earth as they can get. Even then they are still alone amidst all the fury: carrying their loneliness with them.

Later on in this book, the chapter on Operation Plunder describes Montgomery's military thrust into the heart of Germany, destined eventually for the Baltic and the liberation of Denmark and Norway. He called it, in his inimitable style, 'cracking around' in Germany. His armoured divisions had perfected the Great Swan through the Low Countries. This was to be the Great German Swan. The author's division was the *schwerpunkt*, the main driving force.

Field Marshal
Bernard Montgomery
with Lt General Horrocks
(30 Corps Commander) right.
Detail of picture on page 7.
(*Imperial War Museum*)

2nd Battalion Grenadier Guards Armoured in the Great Swan. (*Imperial War Museum*)

In a BBC radio broadcast Wynford Vaughan-Thomas described the Great Swan accurately as he watched 11th Armoured Division:

Out on the flanks of our advance go our recce cars [Inns of Court Daimler armoured cars]. Their job is not so much to fight as to find out where the enemy is, and they keep watching the side roads while the regimental group [battle group of, for instance, 3rd Royal Tank Regiment and 4th Battalion King's Shropshire Light Infantry – the author's usual group] is pushing up the main axis [usually called the Centre Line], the road we've chosen for our advance. This group has in the lead perhaps a squadron, perhaps two, of tanks [changed each day to diminish the risk of sudden death] and with a squadron [in fact, infantry platoons] actually riding on the tanks or else carried in their own carriers [Bren or armoured half tracks] are the infantrymen of the armoured division [besides the KSLI, the 1st Herefords or 3rd Monmouths] especially trained to work with the tanks. The tanks of the regimental group HQ [with Lt Colonel Robert Daniel DSO, the author's CO] follow close behind and not so very far behind them come the guns of the group, mobile 25-pounders [Sexton Ram SPs built in Canada, weighing 32 tons, crew of six under a sergeant, maximum speed 36 mph]. There's a gunnery officer [Forward Observation Officer, FOO, usually a Captain RHA] up with the forward elements ready to call up his guns by radio the moment they are needed. [A 'troop' target of four guns; a 'battery' target of eight guns; or, with the colonel's blessing, a 'regimental' target of 24 guns.] So the forward tanks [usually Shermans, occasionally Cromwells] start up the road. When you watch them as I did from a hill overlooking the whole seemingly deserted countryside they seem to probe and stop and hesitate around corners, moving by little fits and starts, for being in the lead tank is one of this war's most uncomfortable jobs. The officer [or sergeant] in that lead tank has got to make absolutely certain, before he moves, that the house up the road, say, is not hiding an anti-tank gun [the deadly 88mm dual purpose gun is a large, free-standing brute that certainly could not be installed inside a house], or that the woods on either side do not contain fox-holes [slit trenches] with the Germans [often young lads of 15 or 16] manning bazookas [cheap, one-shot, hand held, deadly up to 50 yards]. If all is clear then he radios down the line and the column moves on to its next bound. But if the enemy opens up then the flexible structure of the regimental [battle] group allows the commander to decide exactly how he should deal with the opposition. It may be that it's only a small and extremely frightened flak unit [with one or more 88mm guns] firing one round for form's sake before surrendering. The tanks can deal with that roadblock by blasting away at it [the new Comet tank had a 17-pounder gun; the Sherman had a 75mm gun with a lighter shell]. But the defenders may be made of sterner stuff. Then the infantry may have to dismount and work around the road block to outflank it, while tanks and the 25-pounders give them fire support. The regimental group can in some cases call up our fighter-bombers [usually Typhoons. The radio call was 'Limejuice', followed by a specific map reference. A squadron of Typhoons was called a 'Cab Rank'] to hit the strong-point before they move to the attack. And it may take an hour or so [besides the luxury of the Cab Rank, one alternative was to have available one or more AVRE (Armoured Vehicles Royal Engineers) Churchill tank with a bombard spigot bomb, nicknamed 'the Flying Dustbin', which could destroy most 'fortifications' at up to 200 yards]. Small-scale fighting before the roadblock is smashed and the spearhead probes forward again. So when you watch it on the ground our advance seems no wild race but rather a series of little actions fought along the road almost in fits and starts.

In a curious sort of way the Great Swan was a fairly civilised form of warfare. Casualties on both sides were fairly light. Relatively little damage was done to the villages and small towns along the armoured divisions' centre line.

11th Armoured tanks approaching Antwerp.

However, the more traditional Montgomery set-piece grand slam operation was another matter; a long intense bombardment, initially perhaps by the RAF or USAAF, followed by a huge artillery barrage involving 25-pounder regiments, medium artillery, even heavy artillery and occasionally the Canadian rocket 'flying mattress', all fairly skilfully directed at the enemy defences identified by RAF photography. Then a combination of infantry and armour set off, each offering mutual support; the PBI 'leaning on the barrage', i.e. keeping as close as possible to the shells falling just ahead so that the defenders would keep their heads down. It was all textbook stuff. The only problem was, certainly in a dozen battles in Normandy, that the Germans knew what was coming by observation, listening to radio traffic, and sometimes by Luftwaffe photography. So, in the night they pulled back 90 per cent of their troops to secondary defences perhaps a quarter or half a mile further back, and thus avoided annihilation.

Montgomery, for all sorts of sensible military and humanitarian reasons, wished to retain his finite resources. But inevitably, fighting Hitler's experienced storm troopers, casualties were heavy. The Public Record Office in Kew has an interesting document (PRO WO106/4348) about two British divisions, which identifies statistics of officer and other rank casualties in the north-west European campaign. Predictably 69 per cent occurred during an attack; 23 per cent in defence; and 8 per cent on patrols. Shelling by guns and particularly mortars accounted for 57 per cent, 35 per cent by machine-guns or rifles, and 6 per cent by mines. Infantry platoon leaders and also infantry company commanders each accounted for about 30 per cent, and their commanding officers for a surprising 18 per cent. Since there were infantry battalion commanders in their late twenties, perhaps this is understandable. Again predictably, close-quarter fighting (within a quarter of a mile) accounted for 40 per cent, then 18 per cent at long range, and 13 per cent during the unhappy time forming up for attacks. A British infantry company officer who landed on D-Day, June 1944 had a 90 per cent chance of being a casualty during the 11 months' war; a 20 per cent chance of being killed, and a 70 per cent chance of being wounded. Other ranks had a 14 per cent chance of being killed, and a 62 per cent chance of being wounded. The casualty figures for the whole front line infantry and most of the armoured units during the campaign showed well over 100 per cent of casualties, with reinforcements and 'recycled' casualties coming back for more!

The BLA spent much time and lost many lives trying to capture the key pivotal town of Caen. Eventually High Command asked for the

Allied air forces to 'take out the town', which they did. The vast bulk of the German defenders had left during the night and thousands of French citizens were killed. Unfortunately, this happened very frequently. In the long campaign in Holland, hundreds of Dutch civilians were killed by pre-attack bombardments. In his diary, Lt General Brian Horrocks wrote that during Operation Veritable he felt compelled to order/ask the RAF to bomb Goch and Cleves, key German towns in the Reichwald. In his book *A Full Life*, he admits to feeling guilty that such attractive old towns should be obliterated along with their inhabitants. Later on, the major city of Bremen was 70 per cent destroyed by bombing, but it still needed four British divisions fighting hard for several days to take the place. Hamburg, an even larger city, was destroyed by a firestorm caused by bombing, which killed 30,000 inhabitants. The mayor was allowed to surrender the city to the Desert Rats without a fight.

And so it went on – every city and most large towns in Hitler's Third Reich were reduced to rubble, including of course, Dresden and Berlin.

The ruins of a German city.

Battleground on the German border. Each square shows a specific German or Allied division.

Towards the end of the war Churchill and most of the Allied generals wanted the joint American and British forces to get to Berlin – symbolically – before the Russians did. Eisenhower consulted with his generals and presumably with SHAEF and asked for their assessment of probable Allied casualties. The consensus was 100,000. Eisenhower arbitrarily decided, without reference to Churchill or Montgomery (but perhaps in consultation with the powerful General Marshal in Washington) that those losses were not acceptable. Ironically, Josef Stalin had no intention of allowing the Western Allies to take Berlin. He did not care if the Red Army lost 100,000, a quarter or half a million casualties – which they did!

Stalin ordered Marshal Zhukov to capture Berlin. It required two gargantuan armies involving 2.5 million troops, 6,250 tanks and 7,500 aircraft to achieve their object. The losses to the Red Army, to the German defenders, and to the inhabitants were unbelievably high.

This author saw many of the shattered villages and small towns in Normandy, battered Bremen (briefly), Hamburg and Kiel. Amid the devastation, the survivors had cleared the streets of rubble, found 'lodgings' in the cellars, and managed to get drinking water and some food in from the countryside. Hans Schmidt-Isserstedt, the gifted conductor of the Hamburg Rundfunk Orchestra, had assembled his orchestra – most

Winter Warfare: white-painted Sherman tanks and marching infantry. (*Imperial War Museum*)

of it anyway – and within a month of the end of war was making superb music for the members of the new British Army of the Rhine!

The moral dilemma of the time had faded. Bomber Harris, RAF supremo, started token bombing of Berlin in 1940. Hitler had upped the stakes with the Baedecker blitzes and when his paratroops, panzers and Stukas invaded Holland, the Luftwaffe obliterated Rotterdam and threatened to do the same to Amsterdam, The Hague and every other city. Bomber Harris was responsible for 1,000 bomber raids. Hermann Göring retaliated with the London blitz, which this author experienced during his school holidays in the West End. The East End and the docks were blown to pieces, as was the open plan Sloane Square tube station, where 250 people were killed. The terrifying aerial battles, tit for tat, went on and on. The end result was the race for nuclear power and the atom bomb; Appendix B details 'Hitler's Nuclear Option'. The Führer believed to the bitter end that his Vengeance weapons, V-1s and V-2s would so cow the British people that Churchill would be forced to sue for peace.

The BLA and those sturdy Cinderella War warriors, Crerar's Canadians, eliminated perhaps 90 per cent of the Vengeance weapon sites. The few surviving sites were in north-west Holland and caused little damage. These weapons were pointless – they could not possibly hit strategic military targets. In effect, they were mechanical suicide bombers targeting everybody and nobody, inflicting awful casual atrocities wherever they landed. The Third Reich will be forever remembered for the Holocaust and for other monstrosities, and the Vengeance weapons should be included in that long list.

CHAPTER 3

Bleak Mid-Winter: Longstop in the Ardennes

Towards the end of Operation Overlord, as the German armies were caught in the Argentan-Falaise corridor, Adolf Hitler started planning for a massive counter-attack, the like of which had not been seen before. The audacious plan was initially called 'Wacht am Rhein' ('watch on the Rhine'), a purely defensive move if the Allies heard about it. His next step was to conjure up the manpower to achieve this secret plan. Hermann Göring proffered his private army of relatively unemployed Luftwaffe ground crew and pilots and summoned a startled Kurt Student, a superb warrior, to head the new 1st Parachute Army, which by 1 December had over 30,000 tough young Nazi fanatics longing to fight and die for their Führer. On 18 October 1944, Hitler announced a gigantic *levée en masse* of the entire German people, ordering every able-bodied man to the defence of the Fatherland.

Anti-aircraft flak units fought as infantry; garrison troops were brought down from Finland, Norway and Denmark; conscripted prisoners of war and the despised 'Ost' troops appeared in their thousands. The Kriegsmarines were first-class opponents and Hitler formed from scratch about thirty brand new Volksgrenadier divisions, which were sent into the line with a few weeks' training. So that was how the Fatherland, in desperate straits by the end of 1944, had over ten million mustered soldiers.

Hitler's proclamation declared that in every district of the greater Reich a German Volkssturm would be set up, comprising every man between the ages of sixteen and sixty capable of bearing arms. These units would be led by the most capable organisers and leaders of 'the well-proven bodies of the party, the SA, the SS, the National Socialist Motorised Corps and the

Hitler Youth'. Although the Volkssturm would not wear uniforms, merely arm-bands with the words 'Deutscher Volkssturm', they were nevertheless soldiers within the meaning of the army code. Service in the Volkssturm was to have priority over duty in any other organisation, and the formation, training and equipment of the Volkssturm was to be the responsibility of the SS Reichsführer Heinrich Himmler. 'The Volkssturm will be sent into the field according to my instructions by the Reichsführer,' ordered Hitler.

'Every mile that our enemies advance into Germany,' said Himmler in a speech accompanying this proclamation, 'will cost them rivers of blood. Every house, every farm, every ditch, every tree and every bush will be defended by men, women and children ... Never and nowhere must or may a man of the Volkssturm capitulate ...'

Brave words, however, were not enough to turn this untrained citizenry into soldiers overnight. It takes training, weapons and time to make a soldier. The Volkssturm could be given very little of each. By the turn of the year its members were still only civilians with arm-bands. The following letter, dated 11 January 1945, written by an old man to his son in the army, might well have been written by one of Britain's Home Guard after Dunkirk:

Every German male up to the age of 60 is liable for service, as is well known. Those who are unfit for military service and those who had been discharged from the Forces are included, if they are fit for office or similar work. ... As we have no equipment or weapons, training presents considerable difficulties, especially during the present weather. Last Sunday week, as we were practicing description of terrain, judging distances and deployment in extended order beside and behind the water-tower (with the high tank), our men suffered very much from the cold. Another point is that the drill is new even for the old soldiers of the last war, whilst many of our men have never been soldiers before. There is need, therefore, for a considerable amount of patience, skill, and above all, time, in order to achieve definite results. Last Sunday we had an army-training demonstration team here, to give our men their first glimpse of the present-day infantry weapons and to explain them in general terms. Much water will have to flow down the Lengenfeld Brook before we receive our own fire-arms and are allowed to take them home.

However, time was the one thing that both the Volkssturm and von Rundstedt did not have.

Wacht am Rhein: by Christmas Day Hitler's three armies had made their furthest advance towards the River Meuse.

Hitler's daring master plan was then called '*Herbstnebel*' or 'Autumn Mist' because it was essential that the operation took place in the worst possible weather to minimise the Allied air forces' 'Jabos'. So D-Day was fixed for 16 December. In 1940, Hitler's armies bypassed the French Maginot defence lines, with their *schwerpunkt* in the Belgian Ardennes. Despite all his generals' advice this is what he did a second time. Two huge Panzer armies, backed by a third Wehrmacht in great secrecy, were assembled and burst upon several scattered US infantry divisions. Ultra at Bletchley Park had picked up a dozen clues, but no senior SHAEF officer pieced them together.

Hitler had assembled this colossal army and its commander was his old, solid, cautious von Rundstedt. No Allied intelligence officer would connect him with an audacious, perhaps foolhardy operation such as Autumn Mist!

In October 1945 Alan Moorehead wrote:

The Rundstedt plan was one of the most imaginative and daring proposals of the war. He [Hitler] resolved to put his fresh and secret Sixth Panzer Army straight through the Ardennes Forest and then, having crossed the Meuse, it would proceed straight to Brussels and Antwerp. The possibilities were endless. To begin with, Eisenhower's forces would be cut in half. Four Allied armies: the Canadian, the British, the 9th US and most of the 1st US, would be bottled up in Holland and Belgium. With Antwerp taken they had no escape route by the sea. Their only hope would be to fight their way south into France, abandoning their vast system of dumps and many, many thousands of guns, tanks, workshops and men. There was even some doubt as to whether the trapped armies could put up much resistance. Once Antwerp fell they had no other supply port. Within a week (so the German planners argued) we might have exhausted our shells. This plan ... was not so fantastic as it sounds.

Moorehead outlined the other key factors. No information available, thus confusion would happen; the German generals knew the Ardennes terrain well; low Allied morale; no point in taking risks if the end of the war appeared to be so soon; the quality and size of Rundstedt's strike forces; the possible renaissance of the Luftwaffe. 'All of these factors together ... and you must concede that Rundstedt had a reasonable hope of so cutting up Eisenhower's armies that they would not recover for many months to come ... Yes anything might happen if the Reich got through intact to the summer of 1945. They might even propose a separate peace to Russia. Hitler might say to Moscow, "Look you see the Allied position in the west is hopeless. Let us come to an agreement and finish the war."'

The Battle of the Bulge became one of the famous (six-week) campaigns of the Second World War. It was America's greatest land battle of all time and the BLA only had a small part to play in it. It was won after attritional fighting in snow, ice, fog, swamps and misery. The GIs, with immense support from the combined air forces – when the skies eventually cleared – won the day.

Field Marshal Montgomery reacted quickly and Lt General Horrocks was ordered to get his 30th Corps in place post-haste to guard all the key towns with bridges across the river Meuse, specifically at Dinant, Namur and Liège. The 6th Airborne Division was back in the UK, but by Boxing Day the 3rd and 5th Parachute Brigades were in place around Rochefort and Grupont.

Both the American and the British press were complaining bitterly that Field Marshal Montgomery had committed no British troops to fight alongside the Americans in the Ardennes. Lt General Horrocks'

Right: Field Marshal Bernard Montgomery inspects 6th (British) Airborne Division with Major General E. L. Bols and senior officers, 16 January 1945. (*Imperial War Museum*)

Below: Desert Rats troops produce home comforts for a slit trench, Christmas 1944.

30th Corps, or most of it, had been guarding the vital bridges over the river Meuse since 21 December – a front of 25 miles. For a week 30th Corps acted as an efficient longstop in case the panzers did succeed in reaching the Meuse. With adequate fuel supplies they would have done. Horrocks did not want to cross in force east of the river, which would move them across the American lines of communication. Montgomery urgently required his key 30th Corps for the next phase of 21st Army Group's advance into Germany for Operation Veritable. However, when General Harmon, encouraged by General Hodges, attacked and defeated the German 2nd Panzer Division, Montgomery ordered 30th Corps to cross at Dinant and over a second new bridge at Chanley. The author's armoured brigade of 11th Armoured Division included 3rd Royal Tank Regiment at Dinant, 2nd Fife and Forfar Yeomanry at Namur and 23rd Hussars at Givet. 8th Rifle Brigade actually guarded the three vital bridges.

On Christmas Eve, 3rd RTR were in action against the reconnaissance troops of 2nd Panzer Division and destroyed two Panthers, a Mk IV, a half-track and a scout car. Trucks loaded with ammunition and fuel were satisfactorily blown up. On Christmas Day the veteran 51st Highland Division was detached south of the Meuse near Liège as a reserve to the US 1st Army.

On 5 January, Chester Wilmot sent out his BBC War Report:

British troops are fighting alongside the American First Army in our counter-offensive against the western end and the northern flank of the German salient in the Ardennes. It was British armour and infantry which captured the two villages south of Rochefort on Wednesday and yesterday another British force joined in the attack on the Americans' right. East of Marche they pushed the Germans back nearly a mile with a series of thrusts into the hills along a five to six mile front ... When the Germans broke through in the first weekend of their offensive Field Marshal Montgomery at once brought British divisions south in case the Americans needed them and as the German threat developed, the roads leading back into Belgium were packed with British convoys day and night. It was remarkable how quickly and efficiently we moved thousands of troops with all their guns, tanks, ammunition and engineering supplies. The Belgians lined the roads and cheered the Tommies as the convoys moved towards the new front ... The combined Allied attack brought disaster to the Germans' division thrusting west from Rochefort. Its leading elements were within sight of the Meuse but at Ciney and Celles the British and Americans caught them ... we've counted lying there derelict 81 German tanks, 7 assault guns, 74 other guns and 405 vehicles.

One of Hitler's surprises was the Luftwaffe Operation Bodenplatte, a colossal one-day 'strafe' involving a thousand planes which smashed up dozens of Allied aerodromes and wrote off several hundred planes. It was a thunderclap on New Year's Day 1945. The author was in Brussels when their onslaught savaged three airfields early in the morning, within a mile of him.

On 3–4 January the 53rd Welsh Division, two battalions of the British 6th Airborne Division and the 29th Armoured Brigade were all in action in the combined Allied counter-attacks around Foy-Notre-Dame. Horrocks' attack as right-flank protection to the US 7th Corps was in two prongs. Armour (29th Armoured Brigade early in December had been issued with superb, brand new British-made Comet tanks, equipped with 76mm gun and quite formidable. At panic stations on 18/19 December they had to leave their new toys and retrieve their beat-up Shermans from a tank depot near Brussels) and paratroops

Sherman tanks in the Ardennes.

would attack the German defence line facing north-west along a high ridge eight miles from St Hubert, and also secure, in a mainly infantry attack, crossings over the river Ourthe and cut the vital Rochefort-St Vith road. The villages of Sorinnes and Boiselles were found clear. 61st Reconnaissance and a dashing Belgian SAS unit patrolled eastwards; Hans-sur-Lesse and Tellin were clear but St Hubert and Bure were firmly held. The armour and 7th and 13th Parachute battalions of 5th Parachute Brigade were tasked with the capture of Bure and Wavreille and exploitation to Grupont and Forrières. 3rd Parachute Brigade occupied the area around Rochefort.

Major Jack Watson, CO 'A' Company 13th Parachute Battalion, later wrote:

We reached the start line and looked down on the village which was silent. However, the enemy knew that we were there and were waiting for us. As soon as we broke cover, we came under heavy fire – I looked up and saw the branches of the trees above me being shattered by machine-gun fire and mortar bomb splinters. The enemy had set up sustained fire machine-guns on fixed lines and these pinned us down before we had even left the start line. This was the first time that I had led a company attack and after a few minutes I had lost about a third of my men. We were held up for about a quarter of an hour because of the dead and wounded amongst us but we had to get going.

We were some four hundred yards from the village and so, as quickly as I could, I got a grip of my company and gave the order to advance. Whatever happened, we had to get into the village as quickly as possible. On the way we suffered more casualties, including my batman. One of my men was hit by a bullet which ignited the phosphorous grenades that he was carrying. He was screaming at me to shoot him. He died later.

We reached the village and took the first few houses, in one of which I installed my company headquarters. At this stage I was unaware that B Company was also suffering badly in its attempt to take the high ground, having come under fire from tanks and artillery. Bill Grantham had been killed on the start line, along with one of his platoon commanders. Lt Tim Qinser and Company Sergeant Major Moss, his company second in command and one of the other two platoon commanders, had been wounded. The only surviving platoon commander, Lt Alf Largeren, led the remainder of B Company to their objective. Unfortunately he was killed later in the day whilst clearing a house in which there was an enemy machine-gun position.

Once the company was in the village, it was very difficult to find out exactly what was happening. I got my platoon commanders together to make sure that their platoons were secure and to give them orders for moving forward to start clearing the rest of the village. It was a most peculiar battle because we would be in one house, with my company headquarters and myself on the ground floor, when my radio operator would suddenly tell me that there were enemy upstairs. In other instances, we were upstairs and the enemy were downstairs!

We were suffering heavy casualties as we advanced, clearing each house in turn. Eventually we reached the crossroads in the middle of the village by the old church. I had kept the commanding officer informed as to our progress and he decided to move C Company up to support us. However, by that time the enemy had decided to send in some of their Tiger tanks and they were now firing at us, demolishing some of the houses in the process. I moved from one side of the road to the other, drawing their fire. One of the tanks opened fire on me and the next thing I knew was that the wall behind me was collapsing. At that point one of my PIAT teams came running up and opened fire on the tank, destroying its tracks. They were extremely brave.

The battle went on like this all day. The enemy counter-attacked but we managed to hold them. They forced us back and then we in turn advanced again. It became very difficult to keep the men awake because they were exhausted and had not eaten a hot meal all day. During that night, the fighting continued non-stop with us firing at the Germans and them firing back and shelling us. When we had told Battalion Headquarters that we were up against armour, C Squadron of the Fife and Forfar Yeomanry was sent forward to support us. A troop approached the village first but the leading tank was blown up by a mine. The remaining tanks then tried to approach from another direction and reached the village but one was knocked out. Three tanks stayed with us during that night but by the following morning all of them had been knocked out. The problem was that the Shermans were no match for the Tigers and by the end of the battle 16 of them had been put out of action. We were also reinforced by C Company of the 2nd Battalion of the Oxfordshire and Buckinghamshire Light Infantry, under Major Johnny Granville, because my own company was by then down to one platoon in strength.

During the following day, 5 January, we were subjected to five further counter-attacks which were supported by enemy armour. However, by that time we had a field regiment and a medium battery in support and started giving the enemy a hard time too. They responded to our shelling by trying to blast us out of Bure with their own artillery. Luckily, however, most of my men had experienced heavy shelling in Normandy and thus knew what to expect.

I instructed Major Johnny Granville to move his men forward beyond my own positions in order to find out what was happening. As his company advanced, the enemy counter-attacked again with two Tiger tanks in support. We beat them off and then everything went quiet. At that point I decided that it was now high time that we secured the other half of the village, along with C Company and Major Granville's company, and cleared the Germans out of all the houses. This we did, with much hand-to-hand and close-quarter fighting going on all day.

By about 2100 hours that night we had finally taken the whole village, with my company overcoming the last enemy position. We established ourselves in defensive positions but that same night received orders to withdraw. We later discovered that 7th Parachute Battalion had made an approach from a different direction and, meeting little opposition, had taken Grupont. As a result, we ourselves did not have to go any further. In the very early hours of the following day, 6 January, I assembled my very tired and very wet company and withdrew to Tellin. The battalion had suffered casualties which totalled seven officers and 182 soldiers. Of these, about 68 men had been killed, of whom about half were my company. They were buried in a field in Bure by our padre, the Reverent Whitfield Foy, a few days later.

Lt Edward Harte, 23rd Hussars, wrote:

A Squadron moved out from Beauraing, then to Wellin and Tellin. The awkward top-heavy Shermans skated about on the icy roads like a stampede of drunken elephants. First Sergeant Huthwaite's tank went up on a mine; next Sergeant Roberts' was bazooka'd and he was killed. When we reached Bure four more tank crews were killed. The Germans clung to the houses and ruins, hid in cellars and catacombs, fighting and sniping to the end. There followed an afternoon of very bitter fighting in the village which was in a hollow and the main street was littered with bodies, both Airborne and Germans. Stanley Goss with his troop gave magnificent support but both his support tanks were knocked out by a Tiger.

The 53rd Welsh Division arrived on New Year's Eve. Their 160th Brigade relieved 2nd US Armoured Division in the Marche area and 158th Brigade relieved 2nd US Armoured Division on the river Lesse near Houyet and Ciergnon. Eventually a 13-mile front was held between Houyet and Aye. There was thick snow on the ground and icy, dangerous roads. The

Highland Light Infantry regimental band, about forty strong, came out for a jolly visit over Hogmanay and soon found themselves in the line where they could see *live* Germans within 200 yards! Their two gunner regiments, 83rd Field at Fromville and 133rd at Rochefort, were soon in action. Along the roads lay wrecks of German vehicles of all sorts abandoned, burnt and shattered, but also many American anti-tank guns over-run by the enemy and shot up at close quarters. CSM Cullen, 4th Welch Battalion, noted: 'We were moving across a long viaduct with a concrete balustrade along each side when we saw tanks coming down the road towards us. They were American and in a real state of panic. Crewmen were standing with their heads visible in the turrets and were shouting that the Krauts were behind them. The tanks were moving faster than they should have been on the icy surface.' One Sherman, by mistake, crushed a Welsh rifleman to death, pinning him to the side wall. 'Later we found that the American tanks were supposed to be there to provide us with support in establishing new positions.' The main opposition ahead was the remnant of 116th Panzer Division with six battalions, each reduced to about 300 men backed by some tanks, SPs and mortars. Elements of 9th Panzer Division were in the south-west sector opposite Marche. 53rd Welsh Division then took part in a four-day battle to capture Rendieux-le-Bas, Waharday, Grimbiemont, and the line of the river Hedrée.

There is a detailed account of the very difficult attacks against the 2nd Monmouthshires, 1st East Lancashires, 6th and 7th Royal Welch Fusiliers, 4th Welch, the Oxfordshire and Buckinghamshire Light Infantry and the Manchesters in *Red Crown and Dragon*. There are two interesting accounts, the first by Major A. J. Lewis, 4th Welch, which was tasked with the capture of Authiers de Tailles:

> The rough mountains would have made the going hard in any case, but snow, ice and the cold made the going even worse. There was no cover and the icy, cold wind seemed to whip right through our bodies. The attack was made [supported by 144 RAC tanks] in the face of heavy machine-gun and artillery fire and many were the deeds of outstanding heroism. One private soldier [Private J. A. Strawbridge] after being hit was seen to carry back wounded on five occasions before inevitably being hit again and mortally wounded. A lance corporal with his lower arm blown off continued to lead his section in attack until the objective was gained. How could the enemy withstand such courage! Neither soldier received any award for gallantry.

The Welsh 53rd
Division advance
towards Hotton,
9 January 1945.
(*Imperial War
Museum*)

British Shermans
of 29th Armoured
Brigade (11th
Armoured Division)
advance towards
Hotton, 9 January
1945. (*Imperial War
Museum*)

The second account is in the diary of Lt Colonel Crozier, CO of the 1st Manchesters:

> Jan 1: 71 Brigade at Marche taking over from the Americans C Company. Move with 158 Brigade and take over on the left. Jan 2: All companies had a dreadful day trying to get their carriers up, some only making one mile in eight hours, roads covered with ice. Temperature dropped. Very cold. Jan 3: Moved HQ to Sinsin-Granite, 8 miles NW of Marche. Jan 4: Attack today went well in spite of considerable enemy opposition and very bad weather conditions. Several enemy counter-attacks including Tiger tanks. Snowing all day, about three inches on ground. Going very bad. C Company abandoned their carriers and carried their [MMG] guns and ammo up two miles of hillside. Jan 5: 2 Mons after several attacks failed to take their objective on the left and this pm the general [Ross] decided to switch the attack to the right and centre. Nothing gained all day and enemy counter-attack this evening against 7 RWF met with some success. Heavy snow in the hills and frosts south of Marche and Hotton. Jan 6: Last night's counter-attack postponed our attack. Jan 7: Very successful battle today, all objectives taken. Division is now on high ground N of Marche-Rendieux road. Our infantry casualties fairly heavy.

Indeed, the division suffered well over a thousand battle casualties in their week of fighting, plus several hundred cases of frostbite. Although the Airborne Division, fresh out of the UK, arrived with white camouflage winter clothing, the Welsh PBI were issued with theirs *after* the Ardennes campaign! Having taken Waharday and cleared the road blocks on the road to Rendieux-le-Bas, the 53rd Welsh Division went into reserve on 11 January in the Liège area and was replaced by the 51st Highland Division.

Arriving on 7 January in the Ardennes, the 'Highway Decorators' were in action at dawn on 9 January. Their first objective was the high ground west of La Roche, 30 miles east of Dinant and 15 miles north-west of Bastogne. The Scotsmen had a good supply of 'weasels', little tracked vehicles that could move across snow without bogging down. The supporting tanks of 33rd Armoured Brigade had special gripping snow studs fitted to their tracks. Major Martin Lindsay, acting CO of 1st Gordons, visited the RWF battalions that were holding the front until relief on 9 January. They recommended a *constant* supply of dry socks and hot tea! By nightfall Warizy, Cheoux, Hodister and Lignièrie were

Troops of the 5th Seaforth Highlanders of 51st Division move through Hotton in Ram Kangaroos in January 1945.

51st Highland Division in Hotton on the way to La Roche (*Imperial War Museum*)

captured or occupied. The Derbyshire Yeomanry's armoured cars led the Black Watch into Hampteau and at dawn on the 11th into La Roche. Pte Stan Whitehouse, B Company 1st Black Watch, recalled: 'We occupied La Roche village littered with German corpses from an artillery shelling. In the sub-zero temperature the bodies looked fresh and still alive. We were ordered to deal with SS men still holding out.' In front of the men of B Company, two platoon commanders were shot by snipers. 'Once again we were without an officer. Platoon commanders were snipers' prime targets, a lesson we had learned in Normandy, but a new breed of officers coming through made the enemy sharpshooters' task so much easier by flaunting themselves in the front line with map boards, binoculars and other trappings of rank.' The Highlanders pushed on to Hives, Lavaux, Thimont and Roupage. 152nd Brigade was sent over the hills to occupy Halleux and Vecmont. Divisional HQ moved to Rendeux Haut to control the final phases of the battle. The enemy, from 3rd Panzergrenadier Division and 116th Panzer, were now retreating fast to keep pressure on the Bastogne defenders. But they left small rearguards, snipers, mines and booby traps to delay the Scotsmen. With 32 degrees of frost, Bren guns froze up and armoured car and tank engines had to be run to avoid seizing up. By 15 January, at the end of their battle, 5th Black Watch had lost six killed in action, thirty wounded and forty-two sick and out of action with frostbite and exposure to the intense cold. On 10 January, Genes and Ronchamps were occupied. Major H. Decker, a gunner FOO with 5th Seaforth and a former bookmaker, had laid odds against 'his' Scots capturing Mierchamps. From Ronchamps much of the mile-long road to Mierchamps was heavily mined and there was a blown bridge on the way over the little river Brouze. Up a winding road through thick woods and over a ridge to the village where many panzergrenadiers were lying in wait, odds of 50:1 looked about right. However, Decker with his artillery regiment laid on a thundering barrage and by 1900 hours, to everyone's surprise, 180 half-frozen panzergrenadiers defending Mierchamps were in the bag.

The advance went on. 2nd Seaforth attacked and captured Ronchamps but suffered casualties from heavy shelling. Spandaus, mortars and Panthers caused casualties to the Argylls trying to capture Beaulieu. On 13 January, they not only took Beaulieu but Lavaux and Cens as well. Major Martin Lindsay: '13 January was an unlucky, unpleasant day.' From La Roche, 1st Gordons were ordered to go through Hubermont and then occupy Nisramont. The score of panzergrenadiers in Hubermont put up a fight; and 'friendly fire' from the Black Watch inadvertently wounded Lt David Scott-Moncrieff. Panther tanks in Nisramont knocked out four 'friendly' tanks and SPs; Frank Philips, their gunner FOO was badly wounded. Every Gordon's vehicle was shot at by the hostile Panthers and Major Martin's men suffered twenty casualties. On 14 January, it was the end of the battle for the Highland Division when they linked up with 84th US 1st Infantry Division advancing northwards. Two days later the US 1st Army and the US 3rd Army met at Houffalize, seven miles east of Nisramont. Monty's British 'longstop' troops had suffered 1,400 casualties including 200 killed in action in their three weeks of minor battles closing out the very tip of Wacht am Rhein. They had helped to push back the panzer forces almost 40 miles from Dinant. Ewen Traill, the padre with 1st Gordons, always of his own choice went into battle as a non-combatant with one or other of the rifle companies. He said, 'What a small degree there was between sticking it out and breaking down. When going forward, it only needed one man to shout, "This is murder, I'm getting out" and he would take half a dozen with him.' The margin between success and failure was narrow, with tired troops and war-weary NCOs who did not feel up to taking the responsibilities of officers.

The war correspondent for the *Sunday Times*, R. W. Thompson, noted the beauty of the snow-covered Ardennes hills, but 'with every mile forward, this loveliness becomes a menace and a horror to fight with all the energy each man can muster ... up every hill the troops are manhandling the heavy trucks trying to gain a wheel grip even with chains. Here and there the tracked vehicles slither hopelessly to subside deep into the ditches ... But all the time bulldozers are working, clearing and breaking up the snow and ice to powder and civilians are smashing away with picks and shovels while every man with a spade digs down to the earthy roadside banks beneath the snow to shovel soil for the wheels that must grip ... their ears are blasted constantly by shock as heavy guns roar and splash the white world with bursts of flame.'

The most controversial event that occurred during the Battle of the Bulge was not when General Eisenhower felt compelled to ask Field Marshal Montgomery to take temporary command of two American armies. That decision was logical because the German hammer blow of ten panzer divisions with 2,000 tanks and SP guns had split the American

The harsh winter of 1944–45.

defences down the middle and somebody had to give them sensible orders. Since Monty and Ike had been exchanging 'words' for several months on policies and priorities, it was very much to Eisenhower's credit that he asked Montgomery to take command of General Simpson's US 9th Army and General Hodge's 1st Army on the north-east flank of the battle. This Monty proceeded to do, efficiently and very politely and tactfully so that the two American generals could have no complaint. However, after the battle was over he obviously caused deep umbrage in interviews when discussing '*tidying*' up the defensive lines and writing: 'I am enjoying a very interesting battle, but one ought to burst into tears at the tragedy of the whole thing'. The conference on 7 January was a disaster for public relations.

In any case it ended as a great American victory. However, the history books rarely mention that the ferocious battle lasted for *six weeks*, to the end of January 1945; that General 'Blood and Guts' Patton wrote in his diary on 4 January just after the 6th US Armoured Division was severely mauled, 'We can still lose this war'; that Winston Churchill took such a grave view of the probable outcome that on 6 January he begged Josef Stalin to advance by a week a major winter campaign (which he did) to take the pressure off the Ardennes (Hitler immediately sent reinforcements to the Eastern Front); that Major General 'Slim Jim' Gavin, the highly experienced GOC of the 82nd US Airborne Division wrote: 'We are training our [airborne] men to drive tanks and tank destroyers, since our armoured supporting people frequently abandon their vehicles when threatened in an attack. If our infantry would fight this war would be over by now ... American infantry just simply will not fight. No one wants to get killed. Our artillery are wonderful and our air corps not bad, but the regular infantry – terrible.'

Nevertheless in the wicked winter conditions of deep snow, icy winds, icy roads and often thick fog the American GIs rallied. The skies brightened and the Allied fighter-bombers ruled the battlefields and very, very slowly the three great German armies, by the end of January and after six weeks of ferocious fighting, were back where they started.

Wacht am Rhein had not succeeded. The losses on both sides were hideous – between 80,000 and 90,000 each.

The Ardennes struggle had ensured that General Eisenhower would take even fewer risks. His nerve had been badly shaken. It took seven weeks for Eisenhower's armies to recover their balance after the shock of the Ardennes Battle of the Bulge. The Führer's most formidable forces, 5th and 6th Panzer Armies, were mauled and unable to oppose Marshal Zhukov and his Russian forces in the Vistula offensive early in 1945. General Horrocks, in his book *A Full Life* wrote:

> The Germans had failed primarily because they had underestimated the fighting qualities of the American front-line troops. The American divisions had weathered this unexpected storm most creditably, but their losses had not been light ... The German losses in men and material were, however, much more serious because, unlike the American, they could not be replaced. In the words of Manteuffel himself: 'The cost was so great that the offensive failed to show a profit. The last German reserves had suffered such losses that they were no longer capable of affecting the situation either on the western or eastern fronts.'
>
> The effect on the morale of the German troops was disastrous. After the Ardennes all hope of winning the war had gone. Disillusionment and bitterness now began to creep in.

CHAPTER 4

Hobart's Terrible 'Funnies'

Percy Cleghorn Stanley Hobart, known to his family as Patrick and to the British Army as Hobo, was a remarkable man. He had many claims to fame. He was the only man in the world to have created and formed three magnificent fighting formations. In late 1938, he raised more or less from scratch Britain's first armoured division. The 7th Armoured fought in all the turbulent North African campaigns, winning three Victoria Crosses in the process. However, Hobo, who was the most experienced tank man in the British Army, was booted out of the army in late 1939 by a 'Junta' of cavalry generals and joined Churchill's Home Guard as a corporal. Rescued by Churchill personally, he was then entrusted with the formation and training of the 11th Armoured Division, to which the author belonged – this time mainly in Yorkshire. The Hobart family had a bull as part of their escutcheon and a rampant black bull with red hooves, horns, nose etc., duly appeared. Destined to sail with the division to North Africa, Hobart failed his medical test. Churchill then secured for his protégé the responsibility for creating a brand new concept – a military zoo of either very dangerous or very useful animals!

The 79th Armoured Division – the Germans were not fooled by the British Army's apparent luxury of quite so many divisions – became by far the largest armoured division in the world, with 21,000 soldier-engineers. It never fought in any battle as a division, not even as brigades, but usually as regiments or squadrons. It also had the insignia, in a triangle, of a thoroughly bad-tempered bull, black, white and dark orange. In fact Hobart's brief was, 'Your formation will be trained primarily in their special roles and secondly as normal tank formations'. Every 'Funny', as they were christened by the army, had to have an offensive characteristic.

Hobart's crest for his 79th Armoured division.

Crocodile flame-thrower with trailer, in action north of Schilberg during Operation Blackcock. (*Imperial War Museum*)

The most fearful zoo animal was the Crocodile flame-thrower, which in 1940 was assembled by the Lagonda car company with technical assistance from the Anglo-Indian Oil Company. A variety of prototypes were created, including the RNR Cockatrice, which was designed for airfield defence against enemy air force troops. In 1941, the 7th Buffs were converted from infantry into the 141st Regiment Armoured Corps (RAC) and with 7th RTR and 9th RTR formed 31st Armoured Brigade. The British-made Churchill infantry-support tank Mk VII had a flame nozzle, which replaced the hull-mounted machine-gun, so its main 6-pdr gun could still be used. A trailer was towed, which carried 400 gallons of diesel oil mixed with tar. Fuel consumption was 4 gallons per second. The duration of a flame shot at a target was only one or one and a half seconds. In the armoured trailer were also bottles of nitrogen for pressurising the fuel, which passed through a pipe fitted under the hull of the tank. The pipe was protected by an armoured shield. The most effective flame range was 90 yards and the maximum 120 yards. It took a minimum of one and a half hours to refuel and usually 15 minutes to 'pressure up', but less in an emergency. The equipment (trailer, nozzle, piping and controls) was manufactured in kit form for the Royal Electrical and Mechanical Engineers (REME) to convert or replace in the field. Eight hundred kits were manufactured. By the end of the war, three regiments of Crocodiles were in action: the Buffs, 1st Fife and Forfarshire Yeomanry and the 7th RTR. Each regiment had sixty Crocodiles and the Buffs only had theirs ready a few days before D-Day in June 1944. The vast majority of infantry commanders were unfamiliar with the flame-throwing concept. At close range they were lethal on enemy pill-boxes, strongpoints, occupied houses, Spandau positions and trenches. They could burn most woods, except those with thick foliage, and the flame could burn on water and across most canals.

Lt Andrew Wilson of the Buffs, author of *Flame Thrower*, describes how he first encountered a Crocodile demonstrating its ferocity:

> The crew manipulated a system of valves and gauges. Instead of the co-driver's MG there was now an ugly little nozzle with two metal tongues above it like the points of a sparking plug. There was a continuous hissing and ticking from the trailer. A little burst of fire, like a struck match above the nozzle, tested the spark and the tank began to move forward. It went towards the first target, a concrete pill-box. Suddenly there was rushing in the air, a vicious hiss. From

the front of the tank a burning yellow rod shot out. Out and out it went, up and up with the noise like the slapping of a thick leather strap. The rod curved and started to drop, throwing off burning particles. It struck the concrete with a violent smack. A dozen yellow fingers leapt out from the point of impact searching for cracks and apertures. All at once the pill box was engulfed in fire – belching, twisting, red-roaring fire. And clouds of queer-smelling grey-black smoke ... the rod went clean through an embrasure, smacking, belching, roaring.

Quite terrifying! Their weakness was the necessity for close-quarter action and the infantry being supported had to assault the enemy position as quickly as possible after flaming to obtain the maximum demoralising effect. The battle of 's-Hertogenbosch, Operation Guy Fawkes, at the end of October 1944, was a great success for the 53rd Welsh Division and the Desert Rats. Major R. N. Deane, A Company 2nd Monmouths, wrote: 'The thing which most added a new element to the atmosphere of Modern War was Flame. The place at which flame-throwers were principally used during this successful three-day set-piece attack was in the advance on the dykeland village of Bruggen ... there I first saw Modern War closely resemble what I imagine Medieval Hell was thought to be like.'

The Americans were shown most of Hobart's 'Funnies' before Operation Overlord and were reluctant to accept them. However, in the difficult siege of the great port of Brest in Brittany the defenders in the key citadel showed absolutely no signs of surrendering. So General Omar Bradley asked for some Crocodiles to help reduce Fort Montbarey and its 250-strong diehard garrison. A deep moat, an anti-tank ditch plus casemented fortress walls, many guns, three lines of defences and a minefield full of large naval shells combined to make an assault very difficult. Major Nigel Ryle's B Squadron of the Buffs was loaned to General D. H. Gerhardt's investing forces. The Buffs travelled on huge Diamond T tank transporters. The amazing battle that followed is related in *Churchill's Secret Weapons*. Bravery and dash were successful and on 18 September the garrison of 30,000 surrendered; praise was heaped on the Buffs. Generals Simpson, Sands and Gerhardt all wrote commendations; they were featured on the BBC and in *Life* magazine; and they were showered with thirteen Silver and Bronze Stars. The Buffs spent a few days unofficial UK leave and so

AVRE 'bombard' tank with menacing Spigot Mortar Bombard, known as the 'flying dustbin' petard. Ideal for destroying enemy strong points at 100 yards' range. (*Imperial War Museum*)

Sherman flail tank (Crab) crosses the river Orne during operations in July 1944; their mine sweeping saved many lives. (*Imperial War Museum*)

noticeably enjoyed themselves that they were known, forever, as 'the Playboys'.

The second most ferocious 'Funny' was the AVRE Churchill Mk III or IV tank, with a specially designed 290mm calibre Petard spigot mortar with a fire rate of two or three of these huge mortar bombs per minute. The 40-pound projectile housed a 26-pound hollow charge bomb nicknamed 'flying dustbin'. It had an effective range of 80 yards and the spigot was fixed to the 6-pdr gun mantlet. The spare Besa machine-gun was removed to permit stowage of engineering equipment and spare flying dustbins. The hinged hatches over the co-driver's position were removed and the aperture sealed with a steel plate in which a sliding hatch was fitted through which the petard was loaded. The AVRE Churchill's weight was about 40 tons and the crew consisted of the commander, driver, demolition engineer, wireless operator, mortar gunner and the co-driver, who was also the mortar loader.

The 1st Assault Brigade RE consisted of 5th, 6th and 42nd Assault Regiments, usually farmed out a troop at a time. The Churchill tank was made to be extremely versatile and alternative 'Funny' specialities were as follows.

On the back could be carried a huge brushwork paling fascine of which Julius Caesar would have been proud. It was ideal for filling deep ditches and bomb craters, quickly, efficiently and cheaply. The fascines were about 8 feet in diameter and 12–14 feet long. Alternatively a bobbin log 'carpet' could be carried to lay over treacherous muddy ground.

Or a small box iron girder bridge could be carried for laying across streams and minor rivers that did not require a large Bailey (meccano-type) bridge that would take sappers many hours to assemble. It was known as the SBG Assault Bridge.

The Skid Bailey Bridge was pulled or towed to span a 60-foot wide river – it was used in Operation Blackcock, the capture of Bremen and other actions.

A mobile Bailey 'Scissors' bridge was pushed forward by the Churchill tank, disengaged and then mounted by the AVRE to drop the second half in place.

An armoured sledge was towed behind an AVRE, bringing up to the front line heavy engineering gadgets, including explosives.

The Germans were extremely skilled in laying giant defensive minefields, usually of round flat Teller mines, which could obliterate a

Infantry into battle in Kangaroos on the way to 's-Hertogenbosch. (*Imperial War Museum*)

man and knock out any armoured fighting vehicles (AFVs). The author's FOO Bren gun carrier went up on a double Teller mine in the Dutch Peel country, which destroyed the carrier and the unfortunate driver.

The answer was the Sherman Mk V 'Crab' flail tank, which must have saved the lives of hundreds of sappers, pioneers and PBI. General Irwin Rommel had four *million* mines laid along the French coastline defences!

The first flail was a Matilda tank of 42nd RTR, known as a Scorpion and it was deployed in the desert battles including at Alamein. Major W. R. Birt, 22nd Dragoons, who had sorrowfully left their cavalry horses behind and regretfully exchanged their normal Sherman tank assault role for flails, wrote:

> The principal problems in the use of the flail: (1) to maintain a straight and accurate path to the objective when the tank driver was completely blinded by the swirling chains; (2) to direct three tanks together through a minefield clearing a path of mines wide enough for the follow-up infantry and tanks; (3) to protect the flailing tanks during 15–20 minutes as they crawled [at 1½ mph]

A flail tank in burning Arnhem. (*Imperial War Museum*)

their slow, undeviating way in the face of enemy gunners where most of their own gunners were blind.

The loud jangling noise, the thick dust storm, the exploding mines were nevertheless an awe-inspiring frightening sight to the defenders.

Major General Hobart realised that a major task was that of transporting armoured and fighting carriers of the PBI towards and close to the *schwerpunkt* of their assault. So a magnificent zoo soon appeared: Buffaloes with a Mk II or III Churchill stripped of its turret, cupola and main gun, which could carry thirty fully equipped infantry, or a Bren, or Universal carrier and crew of a Weasel or Jeep, or a 6-pdr anti-tank gun, or a 25-pdr gun and crew, or an Airborne bulldozer or 4 tons of cargo. They had three or four 30-inch machine-guns or a 20mm Polsten cannon. They had a speed of 7 knots on or in water hazards, or 25 mph on land. There were 600 Buffaloes in Hobart's zoo and they were very popular with the PBI. They were noisy so movements were usually made at night. Terrapins were eight-wheeled trucks that could carry 8–10 infantry.

The clever Canadians had built Sherman-style AFVs, which included the Sexton SP 25-pdrs (in the author's regiment) and the turretless Rams, used to carry infantry in Operation Totalise. So Hobart introduced the Kangaroos to 49th RTR in December 1944 and quite quickly 250 vehicles were constructed. They could take a section of eight armed PBI fairly safely at speed into battle. Indeed, every infantry formation in the BLA was hooked on Kangaroos, or if 'swimming' was required, Buffaloes.

The German defenders everywhere were dismayed by the sudden arrival of the British *Schwim-Panzers*, Sherman gun tanks carefully fitted with dual-duplex (DD) steerable propellers. They travelled (swam) at 4 knots and had a high waterproof canvas screen to keep water out. The defenders of the city of Bremen were noticeably disheartened when a DD Sherman attack was launched on them. Once General Montgomery saw the DD tanks in their trials at Linney Head in Pembrokeshire, he decided they would lead the Allied forces ashore on D-Day. In the water they looked like harmless rubber boats. Of the 122 DD tanks launched from their LCTs, 83 landed ashore safely and went into action. The Americans, General Eisenhower in particular, liked the idea, but launched their fleet not 4,000 yards out, but 6,000 yards out in a rough sea, which was asking for trouble. Of the thirty-nine DD tanks that were swamped, the majority were from 749th US Tank Battalion.

Hobart's fecund mind also produced the Bullshorn, Conger, General Wade, Goat, Great Eastern, Lobster, Porpoise, Rhino, Rodent, Snake, Tapeworm, Weasel (an amphibious Jeep) and Wasp (a small flame-thrower on a Universal carrier).

In December 1944, Hobart set up 557th Assault Training Regiment at Gheel in Belgium. It became the Assault Training and Experimental Establishment RE. New problems were the wooden German Schu mines; more sophisticated tank bridges; improved multi-barrelled smoke shell dischargers (vital in operations Veritable and Varsity); indestructible Canadian rollers pushed in front of tanks to clear mines; tapeworm anti-mine devices; a Crocodile to scorch and burn *mined* areas; a Weasel mine-clearer for use against Schu mines; ARKS; log and other carpets; and a tankdozer (a bulldozer mounted on a tank).

Major General Hobart was one of the heroes of the Second World War. In the First World War, he won the DSO and the OBE, was mentioned

Order of Battle – 79th Armoured Division.

six times in despatches, was wounded, captured by the Turks, rescued by a Rolls Royce armoured car unit, and later became *the* tank expert in the British Army. Even Brigadier Michael Carver, the thrusting armoured commander *par excellence* in the Second World War, wrote of Hobo, 'we exercised under the eagle eye of the fierce brigade commander, the great 'Hobo', Percy Hobart. He was a merciless trainer who drove us all hard and overlooked no detail, his intensity matched by his keen interest in all ranks under his command. He was universally respected, admired and served with enthusiasm.' Carver thought Hobo was also 'a bully'!

CHAPTER 5

Bleak Mid-Winter:
Operation Blackcock

Operation Shears had been planned to take place in December, but the Ardennes Wacht am Rhein caused delay, so it became Operation Blackcock and was duly launched by General Ritchie's 12th Corps in mid-January. Two German divisions, 176th and 183rd Wehrmacht, with much artillery, SP assault guns and paratroop units in support, held a substantial triangle on the Belgian-German borders. They held a line 12 miles north-south between Sittard-Maeseyck-Heinsberg-St Odilienberg-Roermond. On the west side ran the river Maas and Juliana Canal and on the east the river Roer. However, running parallel to the start line was a long, winding river 20 feet across called the Saeffeln and Vloed Beeks, which would cause problems.

General Ritchie's plan for Blackcock was in three phases. The Desert Rats (7th Armoured) on the left flank would strike north-east from Bakenhoven towards Roermond, via Susteren, Echt, Montfort and Linne. Parallel on their right would be 8th Armoured Brigade (Red Fox) and 155th Brigade of 52nd Lowland Division. From Susteren they would sweep east to Heide and the wooded, swampy area known as the Echterbosch. The third phase on the right/east flank was for the rest of 52nd Lowland and 43rd Wessex Wyverns to clear a deep triangle into Germany with Breberen, Scherwalden Rath, inside the Siegfried Line and just north of the key town of Heinsberg, a mile from the river Roer.

The German defenders had had plenty of time to lay huge minefields. In reply Major General Hobart's great team of 'Funnies' would provide Sherman flail tanks (Crabs) to deal with the mines; Crocodile flame-throwers to deal with pill-boxes and defended buildings; and scissor bridges mounted on Churchill tanks to cross streams, small

75

rivers and major bomb sites. If the visibility was reasonable, which it was not, the RAF would supply Typhoon fighter bomber support. Lt Colonel Dallmeyer, CO of the Lothians and Borders (flails) was the 'Funny' adviser to the Desert Rats and the 52nd Lowland. He allocated 'horses for courses': for instance the Buffs Crocodile flame-throwers, A Squadron to the Desert Rats and B Squadron to the Lowlanders; and his own Crabs, A Squadron to 8th Armoured Brigade, B Squadron to the Queens infantry brigade (of 7th Armoured), and C Squadron to 52nd Lowland. Captain Harry Bailey was a tough troop commander who had flamed his way from the Normandy beaches and possessed a sense of humour in his macabre expertise. As described by him the 141st (RAC), the Buffs, Crocodiles had had their Churchill flame-throwers 'tricked out in their cute snow camouflage whitewash on the hull and little frocks from parachutes draped round their darling little turrets. Now they looked chic and *distingué.*'

General Ritchie, like all of Montgomery's corps commanders, always had access to considerable artillery support. For Blackcock he had eight field 25-pdr and six medium and heavy regiments on call.

The Desert Rats Queen's Brigade soon reached Susteren after a scissors bridge over the Vloed Beek at Bakenhoven had been put in place by the

Desert Rats AFVs are painted white for snow warfare before Operation Blackcock.

Churchill AVREs. Thick fog caused confusion to friend and foe as both sides wore white snow smocks. Major John Evans with 1/5th Queens infantry won the DSO in the two-day fight for Susteren, which was depicted by the war artist Bryan de Guingeau in the *London Illustrated News* of 17 February. Their attack from the west took place in pitch darkness and in thick mud. Evans wrote:

> We heard a guttural shout and a single shot was fired. We then adopted our usual tactic of rushing in screaming and shouting, firing from the hip. We ran through the forward part of the town taking about 37 prisoners and not suffering a single casualty … At dawn we discovered three enemy tanks in the town. There were no 6-pdr A/Tank guns. Our own tanks had failed to reach us because of the dykes, drainage ditches and soft ground. There followed some desperate fighting with the tanks demolishing corner street properties on top of our men. Corporal Dolly knocked the track off one tank with a Piat for which he later received the Military Medal. I fired my captured Schmeisser – two short bursts at two tank commanders in their open turrets. It was obvious we were in for a long day and would suffer many casualties.

The acting CO, Major Jack Nangle, arranged that the corps artillery would shell the village to try to knock out the tanks. During the shelling and counter-shelling, Evans was badly wounded and Lt Stone was killed. It was a shambles, but the company held its position in spite of thirty-nine casualties, including all the officers, and twenty-nine Queens were taken prisoner. Against that, forty enemy prisoners were taken and at least that amount killed. Fewer than forty men survived that day. Captain John Franklyn and all the platoon commanders were killed. John Evans was the only officer to survive, although he had two sets of wounds and eventually his left arm was amputated. B Squadron 1st RTR finally managed to cross the Beek and come to the assistance of the survivors of B Company; in the mopping up next day they took another seventy-seven prisoners. Peter Roach describes 1st RTR's start to Operation Blackcock:

> We moved off [from Stadtbroek near Sittard on the 16th] on ice-covered roads and in a thick fog which held up the attack and gave us time to whitewash our tanks as some sort of camouflage. With the daylight [on the 17th] came a thaw which though slight turned the tracks to quagmire. Slowly we made our way

forward but the main advance down the centre got bogged down. All through the late afternoon we sat near a stream which the engineers and Pioneer Corps were trying to bridge under constant mortar and shell fire.

In the Susteren battle, 1st RTR lost seven tanks to bazooka teams and anti-tank guns.

The 11th Hussars had put a patrol into Oud Roosteren, which was later captured by 6th KOSB under command from 52nd Lowland Division. Lt Alan Parks, with C Squadron 1st RTR, wrote: 'My orders were to take my troop and capture the small village of Heide, just NE of Susteren, across a railway line as A and B Squadrons were moving north to Echt and Schilberg.' Later C Squadron 1st RTR with the 2nd Devons and flame-throwing Crocodile Churchill tanks, pushed north to capture Ophoven and the western sector of Echt, taking 100 prisoners. The historian of the Devons described the operation:

> In thaw and thick fog at 1630hrs on Jan 17th, the dyke bridges came under heavy shellfire which delayed the tanks. When they got across our carriers had to be hitched to them. In the snow, slush, sniping, across minefields and despite MG and 75mm fire the two columns moved off. Each column consisted of a mobile screen of two troops of 1 RTR tanks, a section of Bren gun carriers, a section of assault Pioneers, then two more troops of tanks, our infantry company in [armoured] Kangaroos, a section of Norfolk Yeomanry SP A/Tk guns, a section of 3-in mortars, a 6-pdr A/Tk section, a RE recce party and the RHA FOO. Major Overton took D Company on the right towards Schilberg. In the villages Nazi slogans were painted on the walls, 'We will never capitulate.'

'Snatch' Boardman wrote in *Tracks in Europe*: '1RTR pushed into Echt and soon met heavy resistance from well-placed A/Tk guns and bazooka men. They lost a number of tanks. The Skins were to pass through Echt and supported by 1/5 Queens, to capture and hold Montfort.' The Germans had several SPs and anti-tank guns in Echt and Schilberg, a mile to the east. By 18 January the 2nd Devons and 1st RTR had taken Echt, Hingen and Schilberg, but three miles north-east St Joost was well defended. Captain Bill Bellamy, 8th Hussars, noted:

> Meanwhile the battle in St Joost itself became fiercer and fiercer. It was a desperate struggle between first-class British troops and one of the toughest

18 January, 1 RTR
and 2nd Devons
capture Echt.

of the German parachute regiments – Hübners. Early on the morning of the
21st another attack was mounted on St Joost. Once again B Squadron under
Wingate Charlton fought with great gallantry in support of the infantry. Thick
fog reduced visibility to less than 100 yards. Richard Anstey and Douglas
Ramf were ordered to take their two troops, retrace the route of the previous
day and find a way round St Joost to outflank it from the east. I was sent to
the bridge in Hingen to act as a forward wireless link if needed. The tanks
clattered off into the dense fog and all went well for some minutes. Then I
heard Richard shout over the wireless 'Two SPs to our front – engaging', and
at the same time I heard the crack of three shots from tank guns, followed by a
series of shots, then silence. [Two of Richard's and one of Douglas's tanks had
been knocked out by three Mark IV 75mm SP guns.] I had an extraordinary
view of St Joost and could see and hear the noise of the battle. It sounded and
looked to be terrifying, flames, smoke, continuous machine-gun and rifle fire,
the crack of tank guns and the whistle and crump of artillery shells.

The three lost tanks were recovered the next day, as well as a Sherman
Firefly from the cellar of a farmhouse!

By nightfall the DLI's fourth attack – D Company plus Crocodiles, 8th
Hussars tanks and A Company 1st RB – had taken the gutted little town.

Hübner later admitted that one of his companies had been destroyed, another almost so.

Although sixty prisoners and three SPs were captured, the losses to the Durhams and RB had been heavy. Most of the several hundred German troops killed were inside the houses or down in their cellars. It was a savage and bitter battle in which Lt Colonel C. A. Holliman DSO, CO 5th RTR and a Desert War veteran, was killed. The Durhams licked their wounds and stayed around Posterholt on the river Roer, temporarily under the command of US 16th Corps. In deep mud they were bombarded by rocket shells which left craters 10 feet wide and 5 feet deep. There they stayed until 21 January, when they retired to Weert in Holland for their first rest since landing in Normandy, in the previous June.

Operation Blackcock still had some way to go, as there were four more defended villages north-east of Echt/Schilberg that had to be cleared: Montfort, nearby Aandenberg, Paarlo and St Odilienberg.

The Skins were ordered to pass through Echt and, supported by 1/5th Queens, to capture and hold Montfort, which had been heavily bombed by the RAF. But C Company 1st RB, commanded by Lt Dawson Bates, reached Aandenberg just north of Montfort, where they spent a hectic 24 hours until relieved first by the Queens, then by the Devons. Corporal 'Snatch' Boardman of the Skins wrote of this action: 'Many bridges were found to have been destroyed but since they spanned narrow gaps they were replaced by scissor bridges though this slowed the pace. The Recce squadron was ordered to relieve 8th Hussars at a stream half a mile from Montfort.'

It was late afternoon on 22 January when the bridge was finally in position and 4th Troop B Squadron crossed. Supported by C Company 1st RB, they moved forward to capture Aandenberg. Montfort presented an eerie sight after the heavy RAF bombardment, with the light from the burning houses and the reflection off low cloud of the searchlights, nicknamed 'Monty's Moonlight'. The troop edged forward and into a desperate battle with the German paratroopers, with the crackle of small arms fire, shouting and the crash of mortar bombs. At 2200hrs the 1/5th Queens arrived on C Squadron tanks and joined the all-night battle.

In the morning, on 23 January, 5th RTR and 2nd Devons finally cleared Montfort, arriving from the wooded western sector, with the Skins, 1/5th Queens and 1st RB moving down from the northern suburbs. Under the ruins lay 270 Dutch civilians killed by the bombing. It had been a two-

21 January 1945. Troops on the right flank of the attack moving north-eastward through Saeffelen and the German village of Hongen.

day battle to clear Aandenberg and Montfort. Even the wood clearing on the 25 January cost 1/5th Queens a further sixteen casualties.

The Skins spent 24–26 January mopping up around Montfort, which was occupied by 1st RB. On the 26th, the final advance to clear the Maas-Roer 'Sittard' triangle continued. To the right, with the objective of Posterhout, a village five miles east, went 1st RTR and 1/5th Queens. In the centre, heading north to take St Odilienberg, were the Skins and 2nd Devons. On the left (west) 8th Hussars supported 1st Commando Brigade to take Linne. 1st Commando Brigade, with 5th RTR, carried out some combined patrols along the Maas near Linne, Heide and 'Bell' island from 25 to 28 January, in which Lance Corporal Harden RAMC won the VC.

Norman Smith, 5th RTR, returning from UK leave noted: 'The Big Freeze came to an end in the first week of February. The Commandos did a good mopping up job and the Maas was crossed by infantry in little boats (some men, incredibly, swimming in the icy water to get the wounded back). A big barrage was put down [on 24 January] while they got the interlinking Bailey bridges across the river for our tanks to go over.' This was in the operation against 'Bell' island on the far bank of the Maas.

81

Lt Hugh Craig-Harvey of the Skins related his experience during the battle for St Odilienberg:

> A set-piece attack by two troops of C Squadron. I commanded First troop and Henry Woods Fourth Troop plus two companies of the Devons, Flail and Crocodile flame-throwers from the Lothians and Border Horse. Since the Americans were expecting to take over the area the following day – and since this was the only serious battle being fought that day (the 26th) a great number of senior British *and American* officers came to watch … We had been issued with aerial photographs. Why I was not sure, because the village only had two streets and was bounded on the east side by the river Roer.

Craig-Harvey was blown up four times in the five-hour battle. Teller and the wooden Schu mines were everywhere, often under snow. And enemy mortars and machine-guns across the river Roer, which flowed through St Odilienberg, made life unpleasant. Meanwhile, three miles south 1/5th Queens and 1st RTR moved on briskly, and on the same day Posterhout had been secured. By 29 January, the Queens had occupied Paarlo and Holst, south of Posterhout. The Queens were involved in a sharp action at Paarlo. When on the night of the 29th/30th A Company was sharply counter-attacked by fifty enemy in assault boats backed by shelling and mortaring, Derrick Watson wrote: 'The ground was frozen hard so we abandoned the idea of digging in, so Lt Max Baker, a Canloan officer with 8 platoon, occupied a large 4-storey house in the main street overlooking the river.' And Verdon Besley recalled: 'Late in the evening there was a sudden barrage and then a terrific bang upstairs and two men were brought down blinded by a bazooka. Corporal Dennis took them to the cellar for safety.' Verdon was then carrying out a spirited battle from the top of the stairs dodging bullets and grenades, retaliating with both while Dennis did the same from the cellar. Rescue was at hand by a Czech officer known better as Robert Maxwell, who with Derrick Watson and Corporal John Melmoth relieved the beleaguered garrison. The RHA and 1st RTR tanks in support gave the retreating Germans a noisy send-off. The Queens received seven casualties, took ten prisoners and caused many 'hostile' casualties. In March, Monty presented MCs to the two Maxies (Baker and Maxwell) for their part in the Paarlo fracas. On the next day, 31 January, the remaining bridge over the Roer at Vlodrop, south of Roermond, was blown up and Operation Blackcock came to an end – fifteen days and nights of constant fighting against a determined foe, with horrible weather and minefields everywhere.

The Desert Rats, after their sustained brilliance in North Africa, had a difficult time in Normandy and their success in Operation Blackcock helped restore their pride – and fame!

Major General Hakewill Smith's 52nd Lowland Division had arrived late in the day for Operation Eclipse. They originally had been trained for mountain warfare with the object of rudely disturbing Hitler's forces in Norway. Then they were retrained as air-portable – infantry landing in Dakotas on a captured airfield and deploying very rapidly indeed. Third time lucky, they arrived in September to help the Canadians and the marine commandos to capture the key island of Walcheren, whose occupants were preventing Antwerp harbour from being opened. At 0630hrs on 18 January the 4/5th Battalion Royal Scots Fusiliers of 156th Brigade started from Tuddern, just north-east of Sittard with the objective of Waldfeucht in the wooded, hilly, but also swampy Echterbosch region six miles north-east of Sittard. The Saeffeln Beck, the 20 foot-wide stream with a high bank on one side and marshy patches along its course, was lined with minefields on both sides. No tank, flail, Crocodile, AVRE, Wasp or Weasel could be of help. However, the Canadian Rocket Battery fired four massive salvoes in support, which helped the Fusiliers to cross, despite heavy casualties. The 6th Cameronians had the same problems, but 11,000 smoke shells screened Hongen. Fusilier Dennis Donnini won the Victoria Cross in Stein. Although wounded several times, he threw grenades, rescued another wounded Fusilier, took up a Bren gun and charged the enemy, firing all the time, until he was killed.

Soon Havert, Lindstein and Heilder were captured. The 5th Battalion Highland Infantry suffered forty-three casualties and captured ninety enemy, and the 6th Cameronians suffered equally taking Breberen and Nachbarheid. Bocket fell to 6th HLI; it was the key to open the way to Waldfeucht.

The Lowlanders had the support of the well-trained 8th Armoured Brigade, who were largely frustrated by the streams, minefields and swamps. However, the armour got across a Bailey bridge and 2,000 yards of open, snow-covered country leading to Breberen. Their accurate shooting wrecked the enemy strong points and helped the Lowlanders immensely.

The taking of Waldfeucht was achieved by 155th Brigade under Brigadier MacLaren, but their armoured Kangaroos could not get into major action. 4th KOSB were faced by those rare beasts – Tiger tanks, five of them lurking around Koningsbosch. On 21 January, 5th KOSB encountered them in Echterbosch. Their intrepid anti-tank platoon sited their 6-pdr guns and at close range, 100 yards, destroyed two of them. The Borderers got into Waldfeucht but were heavily counter-attacked. A Tiger tank did a lot of damage to 5th KOSB until 4th KOSB appeared in the evening. There was a bitter little action supporting 5th KOSB of the Lowland Division around Waldfeucht, as a strong German counter-attack came in. Three inches of snow had fallen and three Tiger tanks loomed up in the mist 100 yards away. In the town square the infantry of both sides were slogging it out. A Tiger knocked out a Hussar Sherman and panzerfaust fired from the top floor of houses knocked out two more Shermans. KOSB casualties were heavy. Two more Shermans were knocked out, again by panzerfaust. By midday the enemy had retaken three-quarters of the town and by the end of the day 13/18th Hussars had lost twenty tanks, the last five to concealed 88mm guns.

Within three days, 156th and 157th Brigades had made progress along the central axis, and 155th on the north-west flank.

The task of seizing Heinsberg, a key town of 5,000 inhabitants, was allotted to 155th Brigade. The RAF had flattened it, and 7/9th Royal Scots

Battle for St Joost, 20/21 January, by 1st Rifle Brigade, 8th Hussars and Durham Light Infantry.

Havert, captured in January 1945 by 5th Highland Light Infantry.

The attack on Heinsburg by 4th King's Own Scottish Borderers.

and 4th KOSB advanced by night into the outskirts. When tanks of 8th Armoured and the trusted Crocodiles had arrived by the 24th, they managed to keep and hold the town despite heavy gunfire from the Siegfried Line.

The Lowland Division, which included 'Pontius Pilate's Bodyguard' (the Royal Scots) and 'Hell's Last Issue' (Highland Light Infantry) had done well in appalling battle conditions. The division had lost 101 killed in action, 752 wounded and 258 sick, who were evacuated. The divisional artillery had fired more than 100,000 rounds of 25-pdr ammunition. At Hongen, in Germany, they were the first British division to set up their headquarters in the Third Reich. And for some strange reason a Moscow communiqué of the day credited the Lowlanders with the fifty hamlets, villages and towns captured in Operation Blackcock.

The unhappy Wessex Wyverns, after decimation in Normandy, acute problems in Operation Market Garden, five weeks garrisoning 'the Island', and Operation Clipper, the joint operation to capture Geilenkirchen with the American 84th (Railsplitters) Division, were spending December recovering. In the panic when Wacht am Rhein appeared on 16 December, a small task force went south to help guard the three bridges over the river Meuse.

In early January 1945, Major General Thomas took over temporary command of 30th Corps when Lt General Horrocks went on sick leave to the UK.

Brunssum was the centre of the Wyverns' social activities: NAAFI, ENSA, hot baths (vital!) at the mining pitheads, snowball fights with the Dutch children, even romantic attachments. It was a quiet period before the next storm and certainly the Wessex Wyverns had encountered many storms and were to encounter more. In Operation Blackcock the division was given three objectives: Hart, Jug and Kettle.

Prime Minister Churchill, who had views on every aspect of war and peace, also had them on the codewords for military operations. He forbade any codeword that implied levity! He said that it was humiliating for any of the British Army to risk their lives for a *frivolous* objective. So the Wyverns' objectives had mundane names, but of course they were indisputably dangerous.

130th Brigade was responsible for Operation Hart, the capture of Langbroich and Waldenrath, and for the second part of Jug, 129th Brigade for the first part of Jug, i.e. Wetterach, and 214th Brigade for Kettle, Randerath, on the far eastern flank.

On 20 January, 4th Somersets captured Schummer Quartier and then walked into Langbroich unopposed and 5th Wiltshires took over Breberen from 52nd Lowland. The next day 4th Dorsets travelled in style in armoured Kangaroos against Schier Waldenrath. On the next day the Hampshires took Putt and helped by Crocodiles did a 'pepperpot' barrage and captured Waldenrath. That was the end of Operation Hart.

Operation Jug followed on the 23rd, with 4th Wiltshires starting from Birgden in Kangaroos, dressed in white to blend with the snow – painted gas capes, bedsheets and snow suits – on their way to take Straeten. Their back-up was formidable: Crocodiles, flails, SP A/Tk guns (there were still Tigers roaming around) and Churchill tanks of the Grenadier Guards. 4th Somersets were tasked with taking Scheifendahl, a desolate area of farmland, featureless and covered with a thick carpet of frozen snow. Corporal Doug Proctor noted: 'Each section was to have its own Kangaroo but as usual, chaos reigned. Only sufficient arrived to transport one company [not the whole battalion].' Next came Erpen, over 1,500 yards of open country. Lt Sydney Jary reported: 'An extraordinary sight silhouetted by the setting sun on a ridge about 2,000 yards away was a long column of 150 German troops. Behind us a platoon of

Some of the prisoners captured during operation Blackcock being escorted to the POW cages.

8th Middlesex Vickers MGS firing special Mk VIII long-range ammo engaged them. I could see the Germans scatter in panic.'

Every British division had a specialist regiment, often the Middlesex, the Kensingtons or the Manchesters, who were support troops with 3-inch mortars which could fire a heavier mortar bomb much further than the standard 2-inch mortar. They also had medium machine guns (MMG) which were far superior to the infantry Bren gun. The cheap little unreliable Sten was ideal only for close-quarter fighting.

The 8th Middlesex was the MMG and heavy mortar regiment of the Wessex Wyverns. Corporal Don Linney recalled: 'We set up our Vickers MMGs for a really big barrage. Behind us was a troop of Welsh Guards [in Churchill tanks of 6th Independent Guards tank brigade] who treated us to a rendition of beautiful choral singing with many of the Welsh favourites ending with "Guide me, Oh thou great Jehovah" to the stirring tune Cwm Rhondda.'

The Wyverns on the eastern flank closed in on the river Roer with small actions in Schleiden, Utterath, Aphoven, Schafhausen, Hullhoven, Dremmen and Porsein – all probably mentioned in another Moscow communiqué!

In front of Schafhausen was a wide, flat valley through which the river Roer flowed. It became a No Man's Land with snipers by day and patrols at night.

Lt John McMath, signals officer of 5th Wiltshires, described the classic attack on Utterath:

Carried in Kangaroos under the usual huge barrage; together with the Bren carriers and troop of Churchill tanks there were over 100 armoured vehicles, surged forward over the flat open snow-covered fields. They looked like a mighty fleet of warships. At this fearful spectacle the enemy gave in at once. Utterath was captured, 80 prisoners taken and only one casualty suffered. Then the small villages of Baumen and Berg were taken. [Later] L/Corporal Holloway with his section removed 126 Reigel mines from frozen ground. On 26 January the enemy sent over pornographic leaflets in shells!

Brigadier Essame's 214th Brigade in reserve prodded their way through minefields to Nirm, Kraudorf and Randerath without undue trouble. Hart, Jug and Kettle were accomplished. When Major General Ivo Thomas, the fearsome divisional commander, returned from

Operation Blackcock.

commanding 30th Corps, he would have been pleased with the way the Wyverns, without him, had made mincemeat of the unfortunate 183rd and 176th Wehrmacht divisions.

The fine armoured regiments of the Red Fox 8th Brigade – 13/18th Hussars, Sherwood Rangers Yeomanry and 4/7th Royal Dragoon Guards – had a very difficult time in Operation Blackcock. They could rarely venture off the icy roads and tracks because they would get bogged down immediately. There were minefields everywhere. Often the bridges would not take the weight of a Sherman. The enemy deployed 88mm anti-tank guns, SP guns, often Tigers, and more frequently, the deadly close-quarter bazooka.

CHAPTER 6

Betuwe: The 'Island' Campaign

In every serious war since time began there has been an area between two opposing armies denied to both sides. In the First World War of 1914–18, No Man's Land was often scores of miles long between one side's barbed wire defences and the other's equivalent defence. For weeks, sometimes months, efforts were made to break the deadlock, always with large, utterly futile casualties. Artillery fire was meant to destroy the wire to allow passage through for the poor bloody infantry (PBI). In the north-west European campaign for over *six months* a No Man's Land existed in the Betuwe. This was the Dutch name for 'the Island', a large rectangle north-south between Nijmegen and Arnhem, two substantial towns ten miles apart. In the centre was the small town of Elst. The Wettering Canal bisected the Island, running some 20 miles west-east through Zetten, Valberg, Homert, just north of Elst and meandering south-east towards Haalderen. The northern boundary was the Lower Rhine running west-east from Wageningen, Randwijk, Renkum, Meteren, Driel, Arnhem, then south past Huissen to the junction with the river Waal, which winds itself through Nijmegen with its two vast bridges, road and rail, west past Oosterhout to Druten, and parallel to the river Maas heading for the North Sea.

The No Man's Land was an area of about 150 square miles and the military issue was simple. The aggressive German forces under Field Marshal Model wished to drive the Allied defenders out of the south of the Island. And come what may they wanted to destroy the vital Nijmegen bridges.

Nearly all the British infantry divisions at one stage or another garrisoned the Island, and for two months post Market Garden so

The Island.

did the US 101st Airborne Division. It was no arena for armour as the Guards Division would remember sadly from their Rhine endeavour in September 1944. The ingenious Major General Percy Hobart had naturally designed amphibious war machines. The Buffalo fought and carried infantry, the DUKW carried, and both swam if they had to. They were joined by the Terrapin and Weasel (See Chapter 5).

The Dutch *verdronken* (drowned) land and the manmade polders indicated the very high water table. Slit trenches quickly filled with water. Artillery platforms had to be carefully strengthened and shored up. Farms and civilian houses were at a premium to the defenders, and fairly easy targets for the attackers.

A Buffalo. See page 72.

Captain Athol Stewart described the plight of the PBI in the Dutch polder land:

Do you know what it is like? Of course you don't. You have never slept in a hole in the ground which you had dug while someone tried to kill you ... a hole dug as deep as you can as quick as you can ... the site given you by an officer who isn't as much interested in your comfort as in putting you where you can kill Germans. It is an open grave and yet graves don't fill up with water. They don't harbour wasps or mosquitoes [as in Normandy] and you don't feel the cold clammy wet that goes into your marrow! At night the infantryman gets some boards, or tin, or an old door and puts it over one end of his slit trench, then he shovels on top of it as much earth as he can scrape up nearby. He sleeps with his head under this, not to keep out the rain but to protect his head and chest from airbursts. Did I say sleeps? Let us say, collapses. You see the infantryman must be awake for one half of the night. The reason is that one half of the troops are on watch and the other half are resting, washing, shaving, writing letters, eating or cleaning weapons; that is if he if not being shot at, shelled, mortared or counter-attacked or if he is not too much exhausted to do it.

When he is mortared or shelled he is deathly afraid and in the day-time he chain smokes, curses, or prays, all of this lying on his belly with his hands under his chest to lessen the pain from the blast. If it is at night smoking is taboo. If there are two in the trench they sit one at each end with their heads between their knees and make inane remarks ... such as 'That one landed on 112 Platoon', or they argue as to the type of the shell. If the enemy are coming the soldier has to stay above ground and does not notice the shelling much. He is too busy trying to keep the enemy away. A trench is dug just wide enough for the shoulders, as long as the body and as deep as there is time. It may be occupied for two hours or two weeks. The next time you are near some muddy fields after rain take a look in a ditch. That is where your man lives!

Because of the dominance in the skies of the Allied air force, the Germans became masters of the night. Food, rations, drink and supplies of ammunition came up to the front often in horse-drawn carts. Reinforcements came up and replaced the front-line troops. The wounded were taken back to relative safety and the dead buried. But above all the Germans usually fought better at night than the Allied troops. Their patrols were more frequent and usually more dangerous. They always intended to dominate No Man's Land.

The battle arena of the Island was low-intensity fighting; none of Monty's grand set-piece attacks. A PBI section would encounter a hostile PBI section. The British would radio back for help – quick help – from their divisional MMG and heavy mortar regiment. Captain Michael Bayley was a troop commander with the 2nd Kensingtons and his sketches illustrate perfectly life and death on the Island.

Winter on the Island with the 2nd Kensingtons. (*Michael Bayley*)

Patrol boat in the Dutch polders. (*Imperial War Museum*)

Corporal Barnett's fighting patrol on the Island. (*Imperial War Museum*)

Patrolling activity during the winter months was intense on both sides and there were frequent clashes. There were four types of patrol: *Reconnaissance* patrols were sent out to gain information without fighting for it, including efforts 'to capture a prisoner by stealth' in order to find out details of his unit; *Fighting* patrols were usually of 10–12 men, on occasions up to platoon strength, whose object was to capture or destroy enemy positions and certainly to obtain prisoners and information; *Contact* patrols had to establish communications with 'friendly' flanking units; and *Standing* patrols, up to platoon strength, occupied protective positions forward of the main defences to give warning of impending attacks. Such patrols were prepared to fight, but not at all costs! The Germans were usually highly skilled at having relatively weak forward positions on which the open barrages would fall, i.e. defence in depth.

On 8 December 1944 the 25th German Army in Holland flooded the greater part of the Island, the Betuwe. The 51st Highland Division and the 49th Division, the Polar Bears, were both under the command of General Crerar's Canadian Army. It was always known that from 1 November onwards under conditions of high water in the rivers Waal and Lower Rhine, the enemy could swamp the area by breaching dykes at the eastern end of the Island. So Operation Noah was planned. One contingency was that the Germans would combine flooding with renewed attempts to destroy the great Nijmegen road bridge. Problems would concern the civilian refugees, livestock and military traffic control. On 2 December, dykes were blown north of Elst and also west of Arnhem. Most of the marching troops came off rowing storm-boats, as did civilians, but herds of cattle and civilians had priority and retired southwards in good order.

Field Marshal Model and General Kurt Student's determined army of kampfgruppen, bolstered by experienced young paratroopers, a Dutch SS battalion, and remnants of SS panzer divisions, were determined to recapture Nijmegen if possible and certainly to destroy the huge road bridge there. Much ingenuity was deployed by the British to protect the bridge and by the Germans to destroy it! Floating mines, expert frogmen with explosives, floating boats or rafts with mines or explosives, occasional Luftwaffe sorties and one-man submarines were all deployed. Brockforce was the name of the special force under Lt Colonel D. V. G. Brock, consisting of the 2nd Kensingtons, whose medium machine-gun and 3-inch mortar regiment was a vital part of the Polar Bears Division defending the crucial Nijmegen road bridge. Their rifle marksmen, with great pleasure, shot anything that moved in the river, mostly pieces of wood, wreckage, hen-coops, anything that might harbour an explosive. A comprehensive floating boom was constructed several hundred yards upriver of the bridge, covered by searchlights (known as 'Monty's Moonlight') at night, plus MMG and mortars.

On 13 January 1945, there was much anxiety for Brockforce. The wreckage lying in the river at the railway bridge was shattered by an explosion at 0300 hours. It was an attack by three midget submarines. One beached on the north bank of the river Waal and the crew were killed by shelling. Another was hit by artillery fire and blew up, and the third was heavily engaged, turned round, dived and disappeared. They carried mines or torpedoes, and also large floating logs with mines lashed to them – 12 feet long and 2 feet in diameter. Despite being hit by 40mm shells, the logs did not blow up and the mines had to be defused. Nevertheless, it was a brave effort by the Boche frogmen. The defenders were now christened HMS Brockforce.

Sgt Bill Hudson of the 757th Field Company RE remembered:

> The three RE Field Corps took their turns to operate the 'Woolwich Ferry' across the Waal. It was a Class 9 close support raft running to a scheduled timetable. Lt Oglesby was our 'Skipper'. The main channel was fairly narrow, but about one third of the strip on either side was made over flooded fields and farmland with houses, barns, fence poles protruding out of the water. Our many other jobs included laying booby traps for 2nd Essex, and anti-personnel mines for 2 Glosters, demolishing a footbridge at Wettering canal, dismantling a 50 ft Bailey bridge at Slijk-Ewijk, and constructing a hot baths unit.

Zetten was a medium-sized village six miles north-west of Nijmegen. It was rather unusual, for in mid-January a company of the 1st Leicesters held nine houses at one end and the Germans a dozen houses at the north end. Company HQ had two houses which were linked to each platoon by wireless and line. The gunner FOO and mortar platoon fire controller were both based at company HQ. Suddenly, early in the morning of the 18th, twelve companies of paratroopers – two or three battalions – attacked the Leicesters on their way to capture and destroy the Nijmegen Bridge. They had crossed the Lower Rhine during the night and supported by bazookas, mortars and Spandau fire, a furious battle was started. Reinforcements from the Leicesters, the 2nd Gloucestershires and a troop of Canadian Sherman tanks were sucked into the fighting. Zetten was lost until Major General MacMillan, who had taken over from 'Bubbles' Barker on 30 November, got fed up and on 20 January sent the 2nd South Wales Borderers and the 2nd Essex to recapture Zetten. Altogether the battle for Wetten lasted four days and the Polar Bears had 220 casualties, but they captured 400 paratroopers and accounted for another 300 killed or wounded. The 2nd Kensingtons fired 300,000 mortar bombs in support and the artillery regiments a similar amount. The battle was fought in blinding snow and bitter cold, and cases of frost-bite needed treatment. The Germans fled across the Wettering Canal to the hamlet of Indoornik, which was immediately flattened by Typhoons, artillery and mortars. The 'Nijmegen Home Guard' had done rather well! But the Germans still held the villages of Elden, Driel, Huissen, Heteren and Angeren.

Divisional gunners with 25-pdrs were based on both sides of the river Waal, although flooding of gun pits was a great problem. Their forward observation officers (FOOs) were in the villages of Bemmel, Haalderen, Elst, Valberg, Andelst and Zetten, aloft in church steeples or on the first or second floor of any suitable building. Much of the time the No Man's Land or lagoons were covered in snow or ice and patrols wore snow suits. Patrols of varying strengths laid mines, booby traps and tried to take a prisoner for unit identification. Many patrol clashes were fought at night and 'naval engagements' were fought in flimsy canvas assault boats. The success of a patrol often depended on captured goats, sheep, pigs or chickens!

The usual tour of duty was four weeks in the line and two weeks of rest in Nijmegen. The Dutch families were splendidly hospitable and dances, concerts, cinemas, parties and above all, the bath units, were available.

The winter frost went on until 6 February, and the huge 2nd Army offensive to clear the rivers Maas and Rhine started two days later. Most units disliked the eastern sector around Haalderen. Lt A. A. Vince of the 2nd Essex recalled:

> We agreed that it was the worst sector to look after. On the right ran the river Waal well above ground level and contained by a 'bund'. The only road was under small arms fire and approach had to be made by the Jeep track made out

of rubble from the destroyed houses. Whether the ground was frozen or feet deep in black mud, it was impossible to dig and one had to fight from the ruins of buildings and from cellars. Not a house remained whole and almost every room was fortified with sandbags and chests filled with dirt. In the small slits where windows used to be, there was a weapon of some kind with the safety catch permanently at fire and a finger always on the trigger. The few houses not defended were mined and the unwary patrol from either side rarely left such a building in one piece. Contact with the enemy was as little as 100 yards. The whole battalion area could be, and was, swept by Spandaus and other weapons. The little clusters of wrecked buildings earned their own names such as 'Rotten Row', 'Sniper's Alley' and 'Spandau Joe the Third'.

Lt Colonel Hart Dyke, who commanded the Hallamshires (York and Lancaster Regiment), described his front line between Andelst and Zetten:

Starting from right to left along the Wettering canal were the isolated farms of Het Slop and de Taart, then Talitha Kumi on the far bank of the river, on the main road Zetten – Indornik – Randwijk. On the left was Hemmen, where there was a castle, two houses and a demolished bridge. The Hallams put out strong patrols on 10 February across the Wettering.

The Polar Bears were ordered to patrol even more offensively to simulate a coming divisional advance, to mislead the enemy, thus drawing off reinforcements from the main 2nd Army battle in the Rhineland and west of the Siegfried Line. Brigadier Gordon ordered the Hallams to occupy the De Hoeven farm, 6,000 yards ahead from Zetten. The Dutch SS troops in front knew their patch only too well and the Hallams had several disasters. One section's assault boat was blown up on a mine causing ten casualties, mostly fatal. Another platoon, twenty-nine strong, of B Company was trapped and all its members killed, wounded or taken prisoner. On 11 March the 2nd SWB relieved the Hallams.

The Island was garrisoned for four months by the Polar Bears who were not required to take part in Operation Veritable and the breaking of the Siegfried Line. Lt Colonel C. D. Hamilton, the CO of the 7th Duke of Wellington's (from Yorkshire) recalled:

The 'I' staff headed by Captain 'Wrecker' Tris Bax published the first issue of the *Yorkshire Pud* – a digest of world and battalion news, with cartoons which, through snow or battle, has come out every day since. At the end of February we had another six-day break off the Island at Druten where a taxi service of V-1 bombs overhead made a rest period more harassing than usual. I wonder if GHQ realise that in a 'rest' period as they are so charmingly called, one works twice as hard. We now discovered that 220 days of the 250 since D-Day had been spent in the line. We have taken more Boche prisoners than we had lost in casualties and since D-Day had travelled almost 700 miles. We were still to be the Nijmegen Home Guard.

Fusilier Ken West, a signaller with A Company of the Royal Scots Fusiliers, in his book *An' It's Called a Tam-o'-Shanter*, had a number of anecdotes. Part of his diet included cheese and marmalade sandwiches, which, toasted over a charcoal and cow muck fire, produced a flavour beyond description. He, and others, listened to Glenn Miller on the American Forces network: 'The song "American Patrol" would come over the airwaves and instantly we would hear the machine-gunners firing in time to the music. Brrup, ti, brrup, ti, brrup, brrup and so on right through the song.' Ossie, their cook, a swarthy Geordie of about thirty, had devised a special jerry can cooker. His porridge, bangers, and powdered-egg omelettes and apple tarts were regarded with much favour. They saw a screaming whining plane over Bemmel. 'We could see the sleek silver belly of its fuselage. "It got no bloody propeller an' it's arsehole's on fire," was one inspired comment.' It was not a V-1 or a V-2 but a brand new ME 262, the first operational jet plane in the world. In their pastorie (church) the Scots Fusiliers repaired the smashed organ with tape and chewing-gum. Ben Brenner, a peacetime cinema organist, played 'Bells Across the Meadow', 'Silent Night' and 'The First Noel'. At the Wintergardens, most big American films were shown, including Bing Crosby and Bob Hope in the 'Road' series; Laurence Olivier in *Henry V* was also very popular.

When Captain Murray MC reported a party of fifty-seven enemy passing through an orchard and the brigade stood to, he was afterwards nicknamed 'Heinz'. There were no beans and no enemy, but certainly fifty-seven trees and possibly a goat or two. When the great thaw came, twenty dead Germans and three dead British soldiers were discovered buried deep under the snow.

Every night the Polar Bears listened on the radio to 'Mary of Arnhem', who had a nice cultured voice with a friendly approach. Radio Hilversum gave the war news as seen through German eyes, often mentioning British towns (pubs and dance halls) damaged by V-1 and V-2 bombs.

In April the 'Nijmegen Home Guard' rejoined their comrades of the BLA. In the autumn of 1944, they had liberated the large Dutch towns of Roosendaal, Tilburg and Breda. For the final months of the war the Polar Bears would take a major part in the liberation of northern Holland.

A few miles west of the main Island battleground, the indomitable 11th Hussars, the Cherry Pickers, had spent many dreary, cold, wet weeks in and around Dutch and Belgian farmhouses and hamlets. This is Lt Brett-Smith's description of Moerdijk in early February 1945. It had a world-famous mile-long bridge, road and railway side by side, a great engineering feat, which had been blown up by the retreating Germans at the end of 1944:

Moerdijk was an exception even here, for it was nothing more than a shambles, with not one house untouched by fire, shot or bomb. The only signs of life were the cats – rangy, furtive animals who would suddenly streak across the street from one ruin to another. Of the German occupation there was little enough sign – a destroyed SP on the main street, an AA gun near the convent, and one grave – a rough affair with four empty shell-cases to mark the corners and the usual scrap of paper in a bottle, the cross made by nailing two bits of packing case together. From the tower of the convent you could see as far as the fine church of Dordrecht on a clear day, and all the village spires and windmills and red-roofed hamlets in between stood out in a vivid and colourful landscape when the sun was shining. On the far bank there were a number of white pillboxes manned by the enemy who sometimes got over-confident and sunned themselves on the grass nearby or watched their rations and ammunition coming up in little carts. Occasionally we registered a direct hit on these pillboxes but they were too strongly built to yield to our small mortar-bombs. Still it no doubt shook all the occupants and may have done some harm to the careless ones. But the chief memory of Moerdijk remains the dead village itself – the upturned piano in a front garden, riddled with bullet holes, the grave grey statue of St Francis of Assisi behind the convent gazing unseeingly at a pile of empty bully-tins, an old Ford car lurching on its rims in a charred garage, its tyres nothing but grey ashes. Moerdijk was strangely reminiscent of the villages in Normandy: there was the same smell of death, the same incongruous but terrible destruction.

CHAPTER 7

Reichswald Battles: Operation Veritable

When war was declared in late 1939, a sweet, funny little song became popular: 'We're going to hang out our washing on the Siegfried Line.' Nobody knew for certain where the Siegfried Line was – presumably in Germany facing the formidable French Maginot Line.

The British Liberation Army had always known that sooner or later Monty would ask them to break through the Siegfried Line, which Milton Shulman describes so vividly:

The ... factor that was instrumental in saving the German armies in the West in the Fall of 1944 was the Siegfried Line. The construction of this well-publicized system of fortifications had begun in 1936 immediately after the reoccupation of the demilitarised Rhineland, and had been feverishly worked upon until the fall of France in 1940. Closely following the 1939 German frontier, the line extended approximately 350 miles from the Swiss border opposite Basle to the junction of the Belgian, Dutch and German borders at München-Gladbach. From there north to Cleve little had been accomplished in the way of deep concrete shelters, and at this end the line rather tapered off into a series of isolated bunkers and field fortifications.

The Siegfried Line varied in depth, strength and effectiveness from place to place along its entire length. Thus, in the area of the Saar where it was at its strongest, it achieved a depth of nearly three miles. Forts were scattered in profusion in this sector, attaining a density of about 40 forts per 1,000 square yards. In contrast to this, the line along the Rhine from Karlsruhe to Basle was only about a half-mile deep and contained only two rows of forts. In the area of Aachen, where the Allies had first reached this belt of fortifications, the Siegfried Line consisted of two thin strings of forts with little density or depth.

The forts themselves were of different designs, but they were usually manned by either machine-gun or anti-tank gun crews, and sited to produce a closely interlocked zone of fire. The roofs and walls were built of cement some five feet thick, and their average size was about 35 feet by 45 feet. The normal complement of men for such forts was about ten, and they lived a damp and cold existence in them. When a battle was at its height, it was considered suicide to vacate one of these bunkers, because Allied artillery and mortar fire was centred on the entrances. Not daring to leave their shelters, even for the purpose of relieving themselves, unbearable sanitary conditions were soon added to the other discomforts of the inmates.

Although no new work had been done on the Siegfried Line after May 1940, and a large amount of the wire had been removed and the mines lifted in the intervening years, this system of fortifications still presented a formidable barrier in the Fall of 1944.

When the Allies crossed the Seine in the early Fall of 1944 engineers and construction troops were rushed to the German frontier in a feverish effort to renovate and improve the long-disused fortifications. From the Fatherland every able-bodied man was hurried forward to be ensconced in the cement bunkers and there they were exhorted to stem the impending invasion of the Reich. The Siegfried Line was now Germany's last hope. On 15 September Field Marshal von Rundstedt issued the following concise order:

1. The Siegfried Line is of decisive importance in the battle for Germany.
2. I order:
   The Siegfried Line and each of its defensive fortresses will be held to the last round and until completely destroyed.
3. This order will be communicated forthwith to all headquarters, military formations, battle commanders and troops.

Note the wording of this order – 'to the last man' had been replaced by the more practical 'to the last round'. And from behind their hastily occupied concrete forts these new troops, fighting well on their own soil, managed to check an immediate invasion of the Fatherland. But it is extremely unlikely that their efforts would have been of much avail had Allied supplies been able to keep up with Allied armoured columns.

The BLA was to be tasked with breaking into and through the northern 14-mile stretch of the Siegfried Line. The first objectives were the two medieval German towns of Cleve and Goch, then through the great Reichswald Forest south to the river Maas, thence to Wesel on the Rhine.

This story does not attempt to do justice to the Canadian divisions of General Crerar's fine army, who fought equally horrible actions in Operation Veritable, many of them nautical, in the battlefields flooded by the German defenders.

Part of General Dwight Eisenhower's 'broad front' strategy – no *schwerpunkt* for him – was for Field Marshal Montgomery's British and Canadian forces to clear and occupy the area between the Rhine and Maas rivers. Planning had started in November 1944. The first plan was called 'Siesta', to clear the Island eastward to the Pannerdensch canal, but it was thwarted when the Germans flooded most of the area. General Horrocks then made another plan, called 'Wyvern', for his 30th Corps, which was handed over to General Crerar's Canadian Army staff. It then became 'Valediction', and was for a south-east advance against two German divisions, the 84th and 190th Wehrmacht infantry. Then Hitler's sudden onslaught in the Ardennes delayed everything and in the New Year 'Valediction' became 'Veritable', which General Horrocks described in *A Full Life*:

> We resumed our interrupted preparations for the Reichswald battle. 30 Corps was lent to the 1st Canadian Army for this operation, designed to destroy all German forces between the Rhine and the Meuse. It was to be a two-pronged affair. We, the northern prong, were to attack in great strength on 8th February. Then, when all the German reserves were on the move north to meet this threat, the southern prong, General Simpson's 9th US Army, would cross the river Roer and advance towards us.
>
> The German forces would thus be caught in a vice. If they elected to fight west of the Rhine they would be destroyed and fewer German troops would be available to counter our thrust into the Reich itself. If they decided to withdraw back over the Rhine, 21st Army Group would be right down on the bank poised to make a crossing anywhere along its length, the primary object of the Rhineland battle.
>
> In theory a perfectly straightforward plan, but not quite so easy as it looked. All operations fought by armies are largely influenced by the shape of the ground and also by weather conditions. None more so than this one.

Above: The 'dragons teeth' of the Westfall – Siegfried Line. (*Harrison Stanley, 111-CC-109298-4-129-46*)

Left: Field Marshal Montgomery, General Horrocks and Prince Bernhard of the Netherlands outside 30th Corps headquarters before the Reichswald Battle, February 1945.

Opposite above: The capture of the Reichswald Forest and Cleve, February 1945.

B Company 2nd Argyll & Sutherland Highlanders aboard their 'big friends' in Kranenburg, 8 February 1945, at the start of Operation Veritable, in which 15th Scottish Division suffered over 1,500 casualties.

Troops of 154th Highland Brigade move into the Reichswald on the opening day of the operation. A heavy bombardment of the forest had blasted the positions of the German 84th Division and the going was relatively easy. Resistance stiffened the next day when the enemy bolstered his defences with high-calibre troops. (*Imperial War Museum*)

Churchill tanks bogged down in the mud in the Reichswald, February 1945.

Right: Buffalo with PBI
in Kranenburg on their
way to Cleve, February
1945.

Below: AVRE supports
53rd Welsh Division night
attack in Reichswald
Forest, 9 February 1945.
(*Birkin Haward*)

43rd Wessex Wyvern Division advancing through Kranenburg to Cleve, 9 February 1945.

Horrocks then went up to the front line and:

I saw in front a gentle valley with small farms rising up on the other side and merging into the sinister blackness of the Reichswald (German forest), intersected by rides but with only one metalled road running through it. North of the forest ran the main road from Nijmegen to Cleve – that is from Holland into Germany. North of this again was the low-lying polder land which had been flooded by the Germans and looked like a large lake with the villages – built on slightly higher ground – standing out above the water. To the north flowed the broad expanse of the Rhine. The Germans were holding the far bank. South of the Reichswald was more low-lying ground which ran down to the river Meuse. This was completely dominated by the southern edge of the forest. The British 2nd Army held the other side of this river. We were therefore faced with a bottle-neck between the forest and the polder land and this had been heavily fortified in depth by the Germans. Moreover the whole area was lousy with mines.

This was really the outpost position of the Siegfried Line which lay 3,500 yards to the east and consisted of an anti-tank ditch, some concrete emplacements, barbed-wire, mines and so on. Furthermore the small Rhineland towns such as Cleve and Goch had been made into hedgehogs, fortresses prepared for all-round defence. The cellars in the houses of all these German frontier towns had been specially constructed for battle – concrete basements with loop-holes and so on, a further example of the careful German preparations for war. Further east still was one more lay-back position called the Hochwald. So the German defences were in considerable depth.

We had to get through this bottle-neck before we could break out into the German plain beyond and the key to the bottle-neck was the high ground at Nutterden. This was the hinge of the door which led to the open country. The front was held by one German division, the 84th, supported by about 100 guns, but we estimated that there were approximately three infantry and two panzer divisions in reserve which could be brought into the battle pretty quickly.

But Crerar and Horrocks were up against all sorts of problems. The first was the great skill of General Alfred Schlemm, who in November 1944 had been transferred from the Italian front to take over from General Kurt Student commanding the 1st Parachute Army. They held a sector of the Western front with four divisions, from the junction of the rivers Rhine and Maas to Roermond. Milton Shulman interviewed all of the surviving German generals at the end of 1945. He wrote:

Nazi race purists would have had an embarrassing few moments attempting to explain the presence of Alfred Schlemm on an Aryan General Staff. For with his rather short body, his broad Slavic face, his large, bulbous nose and his dark, almost chocolate skin, he looked the antithesis of what Hitler and Rosenberg would have us believe was the true German type. He had been General Student's Chief-of-Staff at Crete, had led a corps at Smolensk and Vitebsk in 1943, and had been responsible for containing the Allied bridgehead at Anzio in Italy in January 1944. His record, coupled with an orderly mind and a keen grasp of tactical problems, placed him amongst the more able generals still available in the Wehrmacht. The contrast between his non-Teutonic physical appearance and his undoubted military ability may not be very significant, but it is interesting.

Schlemm immediately ordered his troops to build a series of defensive lines. The first forward line was held by light troops, whose purpose was to slow down the Allied attack, giving time for his reinforcements to be rushed into place. So in front of the usual thundering artillery barrage that predictably started Operation Veritable on 8 February was General Heinz Fiebig's hapless 84th Infantry Division, which consisted of two regiments: the 1062nd Grenadier and 1051st Grenadier covering the edge of the forest, and the 1052nd Grenadier defending the Rhine flood plain to the north. Two immediate reserves were the Sicherungs

Battalion Munster (elderly Home Guard) and 276th Magen (stomach) Battalion with chronic digestive problems. However, the more powerful 2nd Parachute Regiment defended General Fiebig's sector astride the Hekkens-Nijmegen road, parallel to the little river Niers. General Schlemm's armour was 655th Heavy Anti-tank Battalion with thirty-six assault SP guns. Further back were 180th (Klosterkemper) Wehrmacht Division; Erdmann's 7th Parachute Division, near Geldern; Maucke's 15th Panzer Grenadier Division; the 346th Panzer Loser (Steinmuller Division); and finally General Heinrich Freiherr von Lutwitz's very dangerous 47th Corps. The latter had about ninety tanks between them belonging to 116th Panzer and 15th Panzergrenadier Divisions. Schlemm's second defence line was east of the Reichswald on the axis Rees, Cleve and Goch, and his third and final line ran from Geldern, through the Hochwald via Xanten to Rees. Two miles at the northern end, four miles at the southern end, was the Siegfried Line just east of the only respectable road bisecting the Reichswald.

The second problem was the weather and the effect it had on the battlegrounds, as General Eisenhower reported:

> ... the weather conditions could hardly have been more unfavorable, January had been exceptionally severe, with snow lying on the ground through the month, and when the thaw set in at the beginning of February, the ground became extremely soft and water-logged, while floods spread far and wide in the area over which our advance had been planned to take place. The difficulties thus imposed were immense, and the men had sometimes to fight waist-deep in water ... Under such conditions it was inevitable that our hopes for a rapid break-through should be disappointed, and the fighting soon developed into a bitter slogging match in which the enemy had to be forced back yard by yard.

The BLA had fought on difficult battlefields before: the *bocage* countryside in Normandy, in the Dutch polders on the Island, in the swampy Peel country – but now they were confronted with the huge Reichswald Forest. Colonel Stacey, the Canadian military historian described it:

> Much of the country between the Rhine, Waal and the Maas was open and gently undulating, largely arable, some small woods and suitable for armoured warfare. Just inside the German frontier, the west edge of this rolling plain,

was the Reichswald, a large irregular forested area, eight miles west to east and four miles wide. A dozen miles to the east, the approach to Xanten was barred by the Hochwald and the Balberger Wald forming a belt of woods, one to three miles deep and six miles north to south. The trees in these State forests were young pines four to seven feet apart in rectangular blocks divided by narrow rides. Two paved roads crossed the Reichswald north to south converging on Hekkens. None ran from west to east, so military traffic depended on one-way tracks along sandy rides. The river Niers, swollen by flooding with bridges blown, flowed west along the southern boundary from Goch to Gennes on the Maas.

The logistics for Operation Veritable were formidable. At their peak, the manpower that needed feeding was 476,193, including civilian labour and prisoners. So before the start a stockpile of 2,318,222 rations was built up! For the necessary artillery fire plans 1,471 25-pdr HE shells were needed *per gun* in addition to the 250 rounds carried by each regiment. The RASC brought up huge bulk shipments of petrol. Fifty companies of engineers, three road construction companies and twenty-nine pioneer companies were all fully employed maintaining the few roads and many dirt tracks. These crumbled under the heavy rain, some deliberate hostile flooding and the weight of 30-ton tanks and SP guns.

General Harry Crerar, whose Canadian Army had battled so long and so bravely in the clearance of the Scheldt estuary, which resulted in the opening of the port of Antwerp, now faced a great challenge. Field Marshal Montgomery had entrusted him with temporary command initially with 15th Scottish, 51st Highland and 53rd Welsh Divisions, part of General Horrocks' 30th Corps. The second stage would bring under command 43rd Wessex Wyverns, 52nd Lowland and the Guards Armoured Divisions. The Canadian divisions involved were 3rd Division, who would be waterborne and clear the enemy from isolated fortified villages which had been stranded by rising flood waters on the northern flank, and the 2nd Division, also on the northern flank outside the Reichswald on relatively dry land.

The battleground for Operation Veritable was triangular in shape with Nijmegen as the north-west apex, and Wesel as the principal objective 25 miles east-south-east, via Cleve, Calcar and Xanten. The south-east attack followed the line of the rivers Maas and Niers, with objectives of Goch, Weeze, Kevelaer and Geldern.

Allied information showed that the German reserves which would probably appear during Veritable were 47th Corps under General von Luttwitz. This still-powerful formation included General Plocher's 6th Parachute Division, General von Waldenburg's 116th Panzer Division and General Mauke's 15th Panzergrenadiers. Immediately south was General Meindel's 2nd Parachute Corps with 7th Parachute, 8th Parachute and Fiebig's 84th Wehrmacht. Two more Wehrmacht infantry divisions, the 180th and 190th, were guarding the line south of Weeze to the south of Venlo.

The British Army was outstanding in many ways, for instance its code words for operations and objectives. In Veritable, the planners had decided that Goch was Bangor, Cleve was Wigan, the Reichswald Forest was Repton, and Nuttenden was Ratby. The various report lines were Vindictive, Ramillies, Malaya, Lion, Resolution, Repulse, Temeraire, Valiant, Howe, Kentucky, Virginia etc. Possibly the naval words related to the many flooded battle zones needing amphibious carriers. The official passwords, which everybody forgot, were: D-1 Father Thames, D-Day Virgin Snow, D+1 Silver Ring, D+2 Sour Grapes and D+5 Simple Simon. Just in case Veritable was extended, the spare code words were Plum-Duff and Short-Odds. When 51st Highland Division was advancing on Goch via Hervost, Grafenthal and Asperden, there were six strong pillboxes to be seized, which were called Shem, Ham, Japhet, Faith, Hope and Charity.

General Eisenhower had planned a vast pincer movement. Operation Grenade was an ambitious plan for General Simpson's US 9th Army to capture no fewer than seven dams over the river Roer in the heart of the Westwall/Siegfried Line. But German engineers blew the dam machinery and destroyed the discharge valves. The result was a steady and very powerful flow of water that would create a long-lasting flood along the river Roer, preventing further progress by the Americans. So Field Marshal von Rundstedt immediately sent further divisions north to reinforce General Schlemm's defences and Eisenhower sent two divisions north to replace the 52nd Lowland and 11th Armoured Divisions who joined in Veritable. The Scots became the right (western) flank attack advancing south-east parallel to the river Maas.

It was planned that Operation Veritable should have three separate phases: clearing of the Reichswald and securing the line Gennep-

Asperden-Cleve; capturing the axis Weeze-Udem-Calcar and Emmerich; breaking through the Hochwald 'lay-back' defence lines and securing up to the line Geldern-Xanten.

That still left the bitter triangle from Wesel west to Xanten, south-west to Geldern, with General Alfred Schlemm's troops fiercely defending the approaches into Wesel.

General Horrocks wrote:

> The success of Veritable depended on two things. First, obtaining complete surprise, and secondly on the weather. If the Germans got wind of our attack they would move up their reserves before the battle started. But the weather exerted the biggest influence of all, because the ground was frozen hard, and if only the frost would hold until 9 February, our tanks and motor transport would be able to go everywhere across country without any difficulty. I had no doubt at all that under these conditions we should break out very quickly into the plain beyond and I hoped secretly to bounce one of the bridges over the Rhine.
>
> Surprise would not be easy. An enormous concourse of men, tanks, vehicles and guns had to be moved into the outskirts of Nijmegen and the woods nearby unknown to the Germans. This involved the most intricate staff work. By day the roads must remain empty, showing just an occasional vehicle – the normal traffic, in fact. But as soon as it got dark, feverish activity began. Vehicles, almost nose to tail, came out of their hide-outs and started moving up. Thirty-five thousand vehicles were used to bring up the men and their supplies. One million, three hundred thousand gallons of petrol were required. Five special bridges had to be constructed over the Maas. One hundred miles of road must be made or improved. An intricate traffic control system had to be set up involving 1,600 military police, and each unit was given the most exact timing.

Veritable was eventually fought by most of the BLA. Horrocks' 30th Corps had 200,000 men of war, supported by 1,400 artillery guns – 25-pdrs and mediums plus every type of Hobart's 'Funnies' – Crabs, Crocodiles, AVRE Petards and, for crossing the flooded areas, Kangaroos and Buffaloes. The RAF bombed Cleve and Goch to pieces on the night of 7 February with further heavy raids on Emmerich, Calcar, Udem and Weeze.

General Horrocks continued:

> So I decided to attack with five divisions in line, from right to left, 51st Highland, 53rd Welsh, 15th Scottish, 2nd and 3rd Canadian. Behind were the 43rd Wessex and Guards Armoured Divisions ready to pass through and sweep down the Rhineland.
>
> The first essential was to smash through the 84th as quickly as possible and get the high ground, the hinge, before the Germans could bring up their reserves. It was a race for Nutterden, but at the same time I had to clear the Reichswald itself, otherwise the Germans could have concentrated troops there and struck at my communications. Moreover, I wanted the road running through it because I knew how difficult it would be to supply a large modern army with all its complicated needs along one road.

Initially progress of Veritable was slow, partly due to the fact that it rained for the first eight days. But 15th Scottish captured Kranenburg and 53rd Welsh took the Brandenberg 'feature', 300 feet above sea level, on the way to Geldenberg and Wolfsberg. General Fiebig's 84th Division was overwhelmed, 1,200 prisoners were taken, and six out of fourteen battalions were destroyed as 51st Highland advanced deep into the Reichswald Forest.

Lt Colonel B. A. Pearson, CO 8 Royal Scots (14 Brigade) and Lt Colonel de Wilton, 2 Gordons (227 Brigade) consult a map on the way to Cleve, 10 February 1945.

A Churchill tank from 147th Regiment RAC makes a path through the Reichswald on 10 February. The forest was thought to be impenetrable to armour, but tank crews found a way through the forest by deducing that if the trees were small enough they could be pushed over and if they were too large for this, then they were wide enough apart to pass between. The use of armour in the middle of such densely wooded area came as a shock to the Germans. (*Imperial War Museum*)

Left: the quick-release coupling which retained the fascine in place on the AVRE.
Right: A close up of a Petard mortar with a 'Flying Dustbin' displayed alongside.

A Weasel and DUKW on their way to Cleve through Kranenburg which was flooded by the Germans when they destroyed the Rhine bank further upstream.

Men of the 2nd Gordon Highlanders from 227th Brigade, 15th Scottish Division, wait in their Kangaroos outside the town of Kranenburg for the drive forward to Cleve. (*Imperial War Museum*)

2nd Gordon Highlanders pass knocked-out German AFVs, advancing from Donsbruggen towards Cleve, 11 February 1945.

R. W. Thompson, the *Sunday Times* correspondent, noted: 'The battlefield has become practically a naval action. The tops of houses, the turrets of derelict tanks, smitten tree trunks and branches or telegraph poles and all the fearful garbage of war gave shape to all this desolation of water. Otherwise it might almost have been the sea.' Horrocks' XXX Corps troops referred to themselves as the Water Rats (as opposed to the Desert Rats). At night they looked for islands of mud for their 'laagers'.

The Germans had seeded all the approaches with mines – Tellers for the AFVs and halftracks, and wooden-cased Schu mines, practically undetectable, which would blow a soldier's leg off. Many mines were linked to others and many were booby-trapped with smaller mines buried underneath the Tellers. The SS had a nasty trick of booby trapping dead bodies, theirs and those of the Allies. The author can vouch for this personally as he saw it in the Dutch Peel country.

On the second day, 9 February, as the 51st Highland Division advanced through Breedeweg, north of Grafwegen, another axis advanced through Bruik and a third north of Bruik – all heading into the heart of the Reichswald Forest.

Lt Colonel James Cochran, OC, noted:

One long slog through this forest with desperate and often hand to hand battles by the infantry night after night. The ammunition and supply columns did wonderful work in replenishing the units up one axis, which after the first day's fighting became a sea of mud and water, of signals linesmen working day and night to keep the main axis and its satellite arteries clear ... the great spirits of the Jocks of the infantry battalions which kept them on top of these desperate German soldiers, Hitler Youth and paratroops fighting as infantry and also like demons, never gave them any rest and dislodged them from one defence position after another.

It took the Highland Division three days of hard fighting to clear Gennep, Heyen and Kessel.

Further north, 53rd Welsh pushed two miles east to Stoppelberg, the highest point in the Reichswald, overlooking Materborn. 15th Scottish cleared Schottheide with 6th KOSB in Kangaroos, 2nd Gordon Highlanders were nibbling at Nuttenden, and 8th Royal Scots seized Esperance Hill. Lt Ross Le Mesurier, a brave Canloan officer whose Scout platoon was attached to 5th Camerons wrote:

Without tank support which had become bogged down, machine-gun, snipers and mortars took their toll throughout the morning of the 9th. My head was creased by a bullet, then a piece of shrapnel hit my back. Later on another fragment hit my upper left arm, which stiffened up. The day dragged on, progress was slow and darkness came early. It also started to rain. Our company wireless operator was badly wounded, in great pain, his uncontrolled moans seemed to draw gunfire. My company commander, Major Donald Callender, yelled out, 'For God's sake, Ross, do something'. The wind was blowing towards the Germans, so I cocked a phosphorous grenade to throw it. It was hit by a bullet or a piece of shrapnel and burst in my face which was covered with blobs of burning goo ... I rubbed handfuls of snow mixed with mud on my face to stop the burning. Some Germans began advancing towards us. Our firing forced them to go to ground. A few of us charged them firing from the hip. My Sten gun jammed, so I freed my shovel. They started to run and we chased them. I hit one with the shovel blade in the neck. He hit the ground in a heap. I swung at another but he ducked and it glanced off his shoulder.

A day in the life of an infantry officer ended the next day when the Seaforths relieved the Camerons and Le Mesurier was evacuated to hospital in Ghent. On the Materborn feature the German 7th Parachute Division resisted with great force around Bresserberg. General Horrocks wrote:

> An entirely different type of operation was carried out by the 44th Brigade of the 15th Scottish. Their task was to breach the northern extension of the Siegfried Line, consisting of anti-tank ditches, mine-fields, concrete emplacements and barbed-wire entanglements. Not one single man was on his feet. The officers controlling the artillery fire were in tanks. The leading wave of the assault consisted of tanks with flails in front beating and exploding the mines to clear passages through the mine-fields. Then came tanks carrying bridges and fascines on their backs to form bridges over the anti-tank ditch. The next echelon was flame-throwing tanks to deal with the concrete pill-boxes, and finally infantry in cut-down tanks, i.e. with the top taken off, called Kangaroos.

By the second night Horrocks' 30th Corps had captured 2,700 prisoners and the following day Field Marshal von Rundstedt ordered: 'Cleve must be held at all costs.'

The Taking of Cleve

Eric Codling, 8th Middlesex, noted:

> We had a visit from Major General Thomas [GOC Wyverns] complete with riding breeches, boots and a large peaked cap. He presented Military Medals won and then explained to us that he was in the dog-house with Monty because the last job [the taking of Cleve] we did was a complete balls-up and he hoped *we* would make a better job of things next time. We almost felt sorry for him but at our level we did not know what he was on about. Apparently the Germans withdrew and the two brigades [both from 43rd] ended up firing at each other! Something must have gone horribly wrong for the General to come and commiserate with us!

Lt General Horrocks wrote:

> General Crerar had asked me, "Do you want the town of Cleve taken out?" By taking out he meant, of course, totally destroyed. This is the sort of problem

with which a general in war is constantly faced, and from which there is no escape. Cleve was a lovely, historical Rhineland town. Anne of Cleves, Henry VIII's fifth wife came from there. No doubt a lot of civilians, particularly women and children were living there ... After all the lives of my own troops must come first. So I said "Yes".'

The RAF shattered Cleve and when 129th Brigade leading the Wyverns tried to bypass it by a road to the south, they lost their way in the rubble, fallen buildings and enormous bomb craters, and ended up in the centre of town, in the dark. The fire fight in difficult street fighting at night ended with friends firing vigorously on friends: 129th Brigade Wessex on 214th Wessex and probably Wessex on Scotsmen as well, since 15th Scottish were tasked with capturing Cleve from the west! To be fair to General Horrocks, he admitted his error: 'I unleashed my first reserve, the 43rd Wessex which was to pass through the 15th Scottish and burst out into the plain. This was one of the worst mistakes I made in the war ... caused one of the worst traffic jams of the whole war. In spite of me, the 15th Scottish and the 43rd Wessex forced their way into the shattered ruins that had once been Cleve and some very hard fighting took place.'

Horrocks optimistically had hoped to capture Cleve on the first day in order to wheel southwards and take Goch.

From Monty downwards British generals were nearly always almost grotesquely optimistic with their military plan. It took two days difficult fighting by 15th Scottish to capture Cleve on 11 February. The old, spiteful enemy, 7th Parachute Division under General Erdmann, had turned up to bolster the defences of Cleve and 6th Parachute Division under General Lt Plocher was lurking a few miles away.

Colonel Mutussek, the garrison commander of Goch, the western cornerstone of the Siegfried Line, had 180th and 190th Wehrmacht Infantry Divisions and 2nd Parachute Division under his command – all part of General Straube's 86th Corps. 116th Panzer Division was defending the northern approaches and 15th Panzergrenadier Division was defending the Forest of Cleve, just north-west of Goch. Unfortunately, they put up a staggering defence, which it took four divisions of General Horrocks' 30th Corps to subdue, despite every possible combination of bombardments and death from Hobart's terrible 'Funnies'.

Infantry from the 2nd Seaforth Highlanders of the British 51st Division advance through the Reichswald. In the background a Churchill Crocodile flame-thrower tank rumbles forward ready to deal with a strong point that the battalion encountered during the advance. (*Imperial War Museum*)

The 15th Scottish Division advancing through Cleve, which was severely damaged when Bomber Command attacked the town with Blockbuster bombs instead of the incendiary bombs General Horrocks had requested, February 1945.

The Guards Armoured Division resting prior to the advance on Goch, February 1945.

British infantry preparing to advance to Goch, 16 February 1945.

82nd Assault Squadron RE AVREs with assault bridges and fascines during a night attack, Operation Supercharge, near Goch. (*Birkin Haward*)

A jeep carrying wounded passes through Goch on the way to a First Aid post.

Operation Veritable, 8 February 1945.

Lt General Horrocks, Field Marshal Montgomery and Major-General Barber, GOC 15th Scottish Division, confer during Operation Veritable.

The Oxfordshires and Buckinghamshires move up to do battle in the Reichwald on board a 'big friend'.

German POWs captured in Operation Veritable.

The Capture of Goch

After the capture of Cleve the next few days were spent slowly consolidating and keeping up relentless pressure on General Schlemm's forces, as General Horrocks recalled:

> From now on the battle developed into a slogging match as we inched our way forward through the mud and rain. It became a soldier's battle fought most gallantly by the regimental officers and men under the most ghastly conditions imaginable. It was a slog in which only two things mattered, training and guts, with the key men as always the battalion commanders. The Germans rushed up more guns and more divisions. Eventually we were opposed by more than 1,000 guns, 700 mortars and some ten divisions; they were certainly fighting desperately to prevent our getting to their famous Rhine. Slowly and bitterly we advanced through the mud supported by our superb artillery.
>
> Historians may well in the future pass over this battle as dull but it was far from dull for the front-line soldiers. As I went round day after day I marvelled at the stoicism of these youngsters. They were quite unmoved by the fact that they were the cutting edge of a vast military machine stretching right back through bulging lines of communication to war factories in the United Kingdom.
>
> The strain to which the soldier of to-day is subjected is far, far greater than anything experienced by his grandfather or his great-grandfather.

On 13 February, the sixth day of Operation Veritable, Field Marshal von Rundstedt issued the following order of the day to the German Armies:

> Soldiers of the Western Front.
>
> The enemy is on the march for a general attack on the Rhine and the Ruhr. He is going to try with all the means in his power to break into the Reich in the west and gain control of the Ruhr industry. You know what that signifies so soon after the loss of Upper Silesia. The Wehrmacht would be without weapons, and the home country without coal.
>
> Soldiers, you have beaten the enemy in the great battles of the autumn and the winter. Protect now your German homeland which has worked faithfully for you, for our wives and our children in face of the threat of foreign tyranny. Keep off the menace to the rear of the struggling Eastern front, so that it can break the Bolshevist onslaught and liberate again the German territory in the East.

My valiant fellow-combatants. The coming battles are going to be very hard but they demand that we stake our utmost. Through your perseverance the general attack of the enemy must be shattered. With unshakeable confidence we gather round the Führer to guard our people and our state from a destiny of horror.
VON RUNDSTEDT
Field Marshal

General Major Wolfgang Mauke's 15th Panzergrenadier Division was positioned south of Cleve between the square Forest of Cleve and the Reichswald. General Major Siegfried von Waldenburg's 116th Panzer Division moved towards Bedburg east-south-east of Cleve and was soon locked in battle with Thomas' 43rd Wessex Wyverns, who had taken Trippenberg. 4th Wiltshires lost 200 casualties in three days fighting. Eric Codling, 8th Middlesex, was there. 'Next task to secure escarpment overlooking Goch from the north. A bitter struggle against a fanatical enemy. DF rained down and continued for what seemed an eternity. Soon the German fire shifted to the slowly advancing infantry, slowly advancing but much reduced in numbers. Difficult to climb out of our refuge – a sure sign of "bomb-happiness". First real evidence of long-term effects of months of action whittling away the reserves of courage that we had enjoyed at the beginning of the campaign. The bank balance was running out.' On the 15th, 4th Dorsets confronted Kampfgruppe Hutze. Wally Caines was the radio operator in the scout car of the adjutant, Captain Richards:

1000hrs objective three small villages on a crest overlooking the outskirts of Goch. The German paras opened up with all they had. Spandaus and every sort of weapon. They had dug into the ground floor of the houses in the first village, concealed themselves excellently. Shells and mortars rained down and both company COs, Majors Symonds and Gill, were wounded in the afternoon. By now Jerry was falling back. Very few prisoners were taken. The boys had no intentions over worrying about that.

Colonel George Taylor, the much-decorated CO of 5th Duke of Cornwall's Light Infantry, noted: 'four battalion attack. 1st Worcesters on the right, 7 Somersets on the left, 5 DCLI and 4 Somersets would exploit southwards to get on the high ground overlooking Goch.'

Starting from the hamlets of Blacknik and Berkhovel, General Thomas planned to capture Pfalzdorf, Imigshof, Bermanshof and Schroenshof and then to cut the main road from Goch north-east to Calcar. General Horrocks wrote:

> The turning-point came on 16 February, when the 43rd Wessex Division carried out a brilliant 8,000 yards advance which brought them to the escarpment overlooking the fortified town of Goch, which was subsequently captured by the Jocks of the 51st Highland and 15th Scottish Divisions. At this time my right flank was very much a Scottish army. The 52nd (Lowland Division) were on the extreme right and one of the regiments supporting the attack on Goch was that magnificent medium artillery regiment The Scottish Horse.
>
> On the right of the 15th Scottish were the 53rd Welsh Division who disappeared into the Reichswald itself where they were to spend one of the most unpleasant weeks of the whole war owing to the difficulty of movement up the narrow boggy rides. [One of them was called 'Chewing Gum Alley', which Churchill would have vetoed!] They fought their way steadily forward against increasing German opposition. This was the division which, in my opinion, suffered most. For nine days without ceasing they edged their way ahead. The narrow rides made tank support almost impossible and they were constantly being faced by fresh German reserves. [The battle for the Asperberg feature by the Niers river two miles north of Goch lasted two whole days, 14–16 February.]
>
> They never faltered and on 18 February they reached their objective, the east edge of the forest, having suffered 5,000 casualties – 50 percent of the total lost by this division during all these operations in Europe. The 18th of February is a day of which Wales has every right to be proud.

Alastair Borthwick describes in his book *Sans Peur, 5th Seaforth in WW II* how the 51st Highland Division attacked Goch through Asperden: 'We watched as several mattresses of rockets went over, each weighing ten pounds, equivalent to a medium 5.5-inch shell. They made a sound like rushing water as three mattresses each with 300 rockets passed overhead into Asperden.' The enormously thick 60-foot square concrete pillboxes in the Siegfried Line were heaped over with earth. 'Infantry and supporting arms dealt with the trenches outside. The casement was the weak point but even 17-pdr anti-tank shells simply bounced off. But AVRE Churchill tanks with a 40-lb "dustbin" bombard thrown by a petard would blow the steel shutters out of the casemate. Then a Crocodile would come up, squirt unignited fuel through the casemate for half a minute, and then fire one ignited squirt after the rest. The garrison died instantly and horribly. Quite soon the German defenders realised that their supposedly "impregnable" Siegfried Line pillboxes had become a death trap.'

The Allied air forces and artillery concentrations had destroyed most of Goch. The streets were blocked to tanks and wheeled traffic and the house debris was ideal cover for snipers, Spandaus and bazooka teams. The enemy were well dug-in, in gardens, behind buildings and in cellars. 1st Gordons suffered 140 casualties, 5/7th Gordons 133, Argyles 121, Black Watch 125, 2nd Seaforth 141.

On 21 February Veritable was over – all the objectives, including Goch, captured.

During Veritable the Canadians earned two Victoria Crosses (Sgt Aubrey Cousins and Major Tiltson). They lost 379 officers and 4,935 men as well as many non-battle casualties. But General Horrocks' 30th Corps lost 770 officers and 9,600 men. Most were lost in the final week of February. The general hospitals in Louvain, Brussels and Bruges were crammed full with the casualties.

Lt General Horrocks wrote:

> During the course of this horrible battle nine British and Canadian divisions supported by a vast array of artillery had been under command of 30 Corps. We had smashed our way through carefully prepared enemy defensive positions under the most unpleasant conditions possible. No one in his senses would wish to fight a winter campaign in the flood plains of north-western Europe, but there was no alternative. We had encountered and defeated three panzer, four parachute and four German infantry divisions. We took 16,800 German prisoners. Enemy casualties were about 75,000 against 15,634 suffered by us. This was unquestionably the grimmest battle in which I took part in WWII.

The third volume of Colonel C. P. Stacey's official history of the Canadian Army, *The Victory Campaign*, notes: 'Let no one misconceive the severity of the fighting during those final months. In this, the twilight of the gods, the defenders of the Reich displayed the recklessness of fanaticism and the courage of despair. In the contests west of the Rhine in particular they fought with special ferocity, rendering the battle of the Reichswald and the Hochwald grimly memorable in the annals of this war.'

The poet Alan Seeger wrote in his poem '*Rendezvous*': 'But I've a rendezvous with Death / at midnight in some flaming town'. In and around Goch, Welshmen, Scots and Wessex Wyverns died in the terrible killing grounds of Veritable – the largest, longest and most awful battle that the British Army of Liberation fought inside the Third Reich.

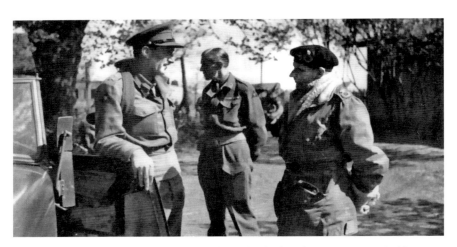

Field Marshal Montgomery, General Horrocks and Whistler after Operation Veritable. (*Imperial War Museum*)

Captured German kampfgruppen troops. (*Imperial War Museum*)

CHAPTER 8

Reaching the Rhine: Operation Blockbuster

General Alfred Schlemm commanded the 1st Parachute Army and by 20 February had repeated the tactics he had used so successfully in Italy at the Anzio beachhead. There he had built up a force from nothing to eight divisions in a few weeks. His force to defend the important Wesel pocket guarding the river Rhine was the remnants of Fiebig's 84th Infantry, Klosterkemper's 180th Infantry, and Hammer's 190th Infantry. He had three armoured formations in place: the Panzer Lehr, reformed after their mauling in Normandy; Maucke's 15th Panzergrenadiers; and von Waldenburg's 116th Panzer Division. But his best troops were the 6th, 7th (Erdmann) and 8th (Wadehn) Parachute Divisions. They had taken a beating in the defence of Goch and the surrounding villages. Milton Shulman described them:

> The resistance of the parachute divisions was as grim and relentless as anything yet seen in the West. In these young, indoctrinated Nazis, fresh from a Luftwaffe that had ceased to exist, the faith in their Führer and in their own cause had not yet died. They had been rushed into the role of infantry troops following the Allied victory in Normandy. Not having personally felt the sickening impact of defeat, they had not yet given way to the despair and hopelessness that by now had gripped most of the Germans fighting in the Siegfried Line.
>
> The parachutists in the Reichswald were that in name only. They had never been taught to jump from an aeroplane. The bulk of them had received no more than three months' infantry training. But they possessed two other compensating virtues – youth and faith. Over 75 percent of them were under 25 years of age, and together with the SS the parachutists contained the best remaining products of young German manhood. And they were nurtured on

Left: German paratroop machine-gunner.

Below: Detail of picture on page 36. (*Imperial War Museum*)

the deeds of their predecessors – the men who had landed at Crete, broken the Maginot Line at Sedan, and held Cassino. They developed an *esprit de corps* which the regular army divisions had long since lost. When they took their places in these new parachute divisions, hastily being formed to take advantage of this spirit, they were given speeches such as this, delivered by Lt Colonel von der Heydte to the men who had just been sent to his regiment: I demand of every soldier the renunciation of all personal wishes. Whoever swears on the Prussian flag has no right to personal possessions! From the moment he enlists in the paratroops and comes to my regiment, every soldier enters the new order of humanity and gives up everything he possessed before and which is outside the new order. There is only one law henceforth for him – the law of our unit. He must abjure every weaker facet of his own character, all personal ambition, every personal desire. From the renunciation of the individual, the true personality of the soldier arises. Every member of the regiment must know what he is fighting for.

He must be quite convinced that this struggle is a struggle for the existence of the whole German nation and that no other ending of this battle is possible than that of the victory of German arms … He must learn to believe in victory even when at certain moments logical thinking scarcely makes a German victory seem possible … Only the soldier who is schooled in philosophy and believes in his political faith implicitly can fight as this war demands that he shall fight. This is the secret of the success of the Waffen SS and of the Red Army – and lack of this faith is the reason why so many German infantry divisions have been destroyed.

Colonel von der Heydte was an outstanding German soldier who had fought in the Cotentin peninsula in Normandy, commanded a kampfgruppe with some success against 30th Corps in Market Garden and was determined to keep on fighting until the bitter end. His boss, General Schlemm, not only faced grave dangers from in front as he defended the Wesel pocket, but also from behind! His orders were simple – to hold. 'Once the battle was joined,' said the general, 'it was obvious that I no longer had a free hand in the conduct of the defence. My orders were that under no circumstances was any land between the Maas and the Rhine to be given up without the permission of the Commander-in-Chief West, von Rundstedt, who in turn first had to ask Hitler. For every withdrawal that I was forced to make due to an Allied attack, I had to send back a detailed explanation.'

Hitler Jugend leave their mark!

Hitler was on von Rundstedt's back, desperate to keep the shipping traffic going along the Rhine for passage of coal from the Ruhr mines, which was shipped along the river to the Lippe Canal, south of Wesel, and from there up the Dortmund-Ems Canal to the northern ports of Hamburg, Bremen and Wilhelmshaven. It was the lifeline for the German Navy, to keep its large U-boat fleet supplied.

Hitler also ordered Schlemm not in any circumstances to blow up any of the nine bridges over the Rhine in his command sector without the Führer's permission. Schlemm moved his HQ from Emmerich to Rheinberg, where he had direct radio communication with each bridge commander. Moreover Hitler threatened Schlemm that if a bridge were captured intact he would answer with his head. No excuses or explanations of any kind would be accepted.

The German 1st Parachute Army had available 717 minnenwerfer mortars, 1,054 guns including 50 dual purpose 88mm guns and a considerable number of SP assault guns. Field Marshal Montgomery wrote, 'the volume of fire from enemy weapons was the heaviest which had been met so far by British troops in the campaign'.

Operation Blockbuster, February 1945.

Operation Grenade had been delayed by the four-foot rise in the water level of the Rhine, caused by deliberate flooding. The original attack by General Simpson's 9th US Army was scheduled for 10 February but was delayed until the 23rd. The German 15th Army, with four weak infantry divisions, was soon in trouble and Schlemm was forced to send two armoured divisions – Panzer Lehr and 15th Panzer – plus 406th Wehrmacht Infantry Division south to help. Nevertheless, by the 23rd, Schlemm had stabilised his front, holding a 20-mile line from the Maas to the Rhine, which forced General Horrocks and the Canadians to engage in Blockbuster 1, what General Eisenhower described as 'some of the fiercest fighting of the war'.

Three British formations now joined Horrocks' huge 30th Corps, Guards Armoured, 11th Armoured and 3rd British. For three days 53rd Welsh had some rest out of the line around Nijmegen, 43rd Wessex Wyverns rested in and around shattered Cleve, 51st Highland around Goch, and 15th Scottish went back to the Tilburg area.

To get to Wesel, the key town of Xanten seven miles to the west had to be captured. The three towns of Weeze, Kevelaer and Geldern, all due

135

west of Xanten, were heavily fortified and the densely wooded Hochwald running laterally north-south for three miles was a formidable barrier. The escarpment that stretched from Calcar to Udem was strongly defended by Kampfgruppe Hauser, 116th Panzer Division and 8th Parachute Division.

53rd Welsh, emerging after their week in the icy jungle of the Reichswald, led the advance in Blockbuster, from Goch following the river Niers towards Geldern via Weeze. During their few days of rest in Holland, over 2,000 reinforcements had to be integrated – an immense task. 4th RWF needed 365 men; 7th RWF 359; 6th RWF 276; 4th Welch 281; 1st HLI 239; 2nd Mons 243; East Lancs 148; 1/5th Welch 137 and the Ox and Bucks 203. In a way these young men from HAA, LAA, anti-tank regiments and conscripts were fortunate. What lay ahead of them, apart from surviving Blockbuster, were eight or nine weeks of 'interesting' fighting, a whole series of small town, small village actions with a casualty rate perhaps a tenth of the Normandy bloodbath. But the PBI, the 'grunts', are always at risk in the very front line. Integration was always very difficult for the rookies and for the old sweats.

Operation Leek was the plan to capture Weeze, then Hees and Wemb five miles south-east of Goch, defended by 15th Panzergrenadier and 7th Parachute Divisions with six battered but still ferocious enemy battalions. 71st Brigade would lead, backed by 8th Armoured Brigade (Red Fox's Mask), a squadron of Crocodile flame-throwers and another of flail tanks. Under a massive bombardment of twelve field regiments and seventy medium and heavy guns, 2nd Mons and 6th RWF led and for two days it was a bloody stalemate with heavy casualties on both sides. Corporal Bert Isherwood of 13th Field Dressing Station noted in his diary: 'Sunday 25th. The battle rages forward. 53 Div is having a hard time, large numbers of casualties are coming back, the FA and the FDSs are busy. The way forward and the way back is littered with dead and the debris of war. A shambles of destruction, the near distance thick with smoke and shot through with the flashes of the guns and the blasts of incessant explosions. An infantry supply NCO tells me that the Div has about fought itself to a standstill before Weeze.' It was St David's Day with leeks being bravely worn on every helmet. One of many enemy counter-attacks was led by three Royal Tiger tanks, which were almost impregnable.

During the night of 1–2 March, the enemy survivors pulled out in the dark, leaving a ghost town of mines, boobytraps, utter destruction and desolation.

Above: The 53rd Welsh Division on objective on the east side of the Reichswald, February 1945.

Right: A mortar team from 2nd Battalion Middlesex Regiment fires its 4.2 inch (107mm) mortar in support of British 3rd Division during the attack on Kervenheim. The 4.2 inch (107mm) mortar was one of the heavy infantry weapons provided by a machine-gun battalion to each infantry division. The Middlesex Regiment supplied heavy machine-guns and mortars via the four of its battalions who were attached to the 3rd, 15th, 43rd and 51st Infantry Divisions throughout the war in north-west Europe. (*Imperial War Museum*)

137

A few miles east, Major General 'Bolo' Whistler's 3rd British 'Ironside' Division was a reinforcement division for Horrocks. Operation Heather was the plan parallel to 53rd Welsh to capture Kervenheim and Winnekendonk, south of Udem, south-east of Weeze. Having relieved 15th Scottish, 3rd British concentrated north of Goch. Captain Marcus Cunliffe, adjutant of 2nd Warwicks wrote: 'Still more enemy units were brought in to fight the northern battle. The effect was comparable to that of the Normandy campaign where British and Canadian formations attracted to themselves the main weight of enemy opposition, thus simplifying the subsequent American advance.' Operation Heather was aptly named. The two divisional centre lines were soft, saturated sandy tracks through woods, heaths of heather and no metalled roads. A nightmare for the heavy Churchill tanks of 6th Guards Tank Brigade and Hobart's flails and Crocodiles. Their first objective was securing the Udem-Weeze road and the vital Muhlen-Fleuth Bridge. When that was taken the 53rd Welsh could attack Weeze from a different flank on the 28th. In the woods, the South Lancs and East Yorks of 8th Brigade had a torrid time in Operation Donald. The German 7th Parachute Division and part of 190th Wehrmacht fought like devils in and around the hamlets of Geurtzhof, Kampshof and Bussenhof. The Corps artillery was firing stonks and barrages against counter-attacks by 1st Battalion 24th Parachute Regiment and 3rd Battalion 22nd Parachute Regiment with support from a few Tiger tanks. Lt Colonel Bill Renison, CO East Yorks wrote: 'It had been what I think Wellington would have described as a "close run thing" but we had won. At a cost of 33 KIA, 123 wounded and 4 missing. We took 150 German prisoners and counted 85 dead of Para Group Hubner in the battle area.' Major General 'Bolo' Whistler, GOC 3rd British, ordered the sappers to place a name board on the bridge with the East Yorkshire's crest and name – 'Yorkshire Bridge'. More or less the same thing happened a mile east where 1st KOSB, 2nd Royal Ulster Rifles and 2nd Lincolns were taking on 1st Paratroop Regiment in Operation Daffodil. They cut the Udem-Weeze road, but tried and failed to get a bridgehead over the Muhlen-Fleuth. The third brigade, 185th, was tasked with the capture of Kervenheim and then Winnekdonk, fortified villages on the minor road south from Udem. 2nd KSLI, 2nd Warwicks and 1st Royal Norfolks took it in turns through woods, waterlogged clay fields, scattered houses under shelling, through minefields and often drenching rain. The young Pte Joseph Stokes of 2nd

Men from the 1st Battalion Herefordshire Regiment cross the anti-tank ditch that surrounds Udem. The ditches were a common type of temporary defence which were thrown up throughout the whole of the Siegfried Line. They caused little difficulty to the infantry and could be bridged in seconds with specialised armoured bridging equipment. Covering fire, smoke and a determined attack meant that troops and tanks could be over the ditch in a very short space of time. The secret was in trying to keep the enemy occupied while the breach was made. (*Imperial War Museum*)

KSLI won the Victoria Cross in the attack on Kervenheim. He personally captured twenty-one prisoners, was wounded eight times, refused to go back to the RAP and eventually fell leading a charge 20 yards from the enemy.

Later, Terence Cuneo painted a fine scene of Stokes' dramatic action, which is now owned by the trustees of the King's Shropshire Light Infantry. The Royal Norfolks suffered 161 casualties capturing Muserhof, Murmannshof and around Kervenheim. Jack Harrod in his book *History 2nd Battalion Lincolnshires* described the final attack on Winnekendonk:

The Bn surged forward under pitiless fire. Many fell including Major Clarke wounded by a grenade. The road junction near the village was reached. Still the enemy parachutists fought back grimly. Snipers fired from first floor windows and Spandaus shot through loopholes in the walls at ground level. Now the light was going fast and the infantry and the 3rd Scots Guards tanks went into the village in billows of smoke, punctuated by the orange flashes of the enemy 88s and criss-crossed by lines of tracer. It was a great and terrible spectacle. The Bn had really got its teeth in and was not to be denied.

Savage fighting continued until the parachutists had had enough. Thirty were killed, fifty were wounded and eighty surrendered. When the village was finally cleared in the morning seventy more gave themselves up. The Lincolns had 107 casualties. Major General Whistler's diary recorded:

We had had our most successful battle. Damn difficult country – centre line non-existent or on a mud track – yet we had done everything asked. We have captured 1,200 prisoners, nearly all paratroopers. We must have killed and wounded many more. The scenes of devastation in Germany are quite remarkable. There is nothing that has not been damaged or destroyed. We have captured Kervenheim, Winnekendonk and Kapellen of the larger places. I would say the 9 Brigade under Rennie have done best, 185 next under Mark Matthews. 8 Brigade have not had so much luck though East Yorks had a terrific night holding a bridgehead against repeated counter attacks ... Am getting on very well with Jorrocks [Lt General Horrocks]. He is a fine leader and well liked, quite ruthless but one has to be ... The Boche are beaten pretty badly here. We are through the Siegfried Line and very near the Rhine. I would not have missed this battle for anything – unpleasant and frightening though it has been. To fight on German soil after all this time is more than I ever expected. Now for the Rhine.

Further north it took the Canadians five days to break through the Hochwald, Balburgerwald and also capture Udem against General Schlemm's Battlegroup Hauser, von Waldenburg's 116th Panzer and Waden's 8th Parachute Regiment. On their left and northern flank Major General Thomas and the Wessex Wyverns, using the main Cleve-Xanten road as their axis, relentlessly advanced south-east of Calcar, capturing Kehrum, Marienbaum, Vynen and Wardt and reached Luttingen, almost in the suburbs of Xanten.

The advance to Wesel.

Blockbuster 2 was the name of the operation to capture Xanten and Wesel. In his excellent book, *The Victory Campaign*, Colonel C. P. Stacey wrote: 'The series of extraordinary orders from Berlin ... as a result the diminishing bridgehead became cluttered with damaged tanks, transport, artillery without ammunition and all the debris of an army fighting a heavy losing action.'

In the Canadian northern sector between Marienbaum and Udem, in fierce fighting, Major F. A. Tilston, the Essex Scottish, won the VC on 1 March, despite wounds which cost him both legs.

General Schlemm's troops were fighting tooth and nail to hold the key lateral road west and in front of Wesel. The line was Xanten, Veen and Alpen. Colonel Stacey pointed out: 'Xanten in history a Roman town, was in German legend the home of Siegfried with a population usually of 5,000, but now crammed full of retreating Huns.'

Because of the limited space, Blockbuster 2 relied on the 2nd Canadian Infantry Division and the 43rd Wessex Wyverns to remove the cork from the bottle. On the afternoon of 3 March, the British 4/7th Royal Dragoon Guards ahead of the Welsh, met the American 17th Cavalry Recce cars in Berendonk, three miles north-east of Geldern. And 52nd Lowland on the western flank passed Wemb south of Weeze and concentrated between Geldern and the river Maas.

On 4 March, Prime Minister Winston Churchill and Field Marshals Alan Brooke, the CIGS, and Montgomery visited General Crerar, the Canadian GOC, and together they drove to the Reichswald and the Siegfried Line. They lunched with General Simonds and visited British 30th Corps afterwards.

To the south of the Balbergerwald, 11th Armoured joined in the fight to push through the Schlieffen Line's Hochwald Layback defences, which ran from Xanten south-west to Sonsbeck and the Winkelsher Busch.

General Thomas had the doubtful honour of mopping up the west bank of the Rhine. 4th Somerset Light Infantry were ordered to capture Xanten and 5th Wiltshires to capture Luttingen. Generals Crerar and Horrocks had several days to get the 'chessmen' in position – hundreds of guns and Hobart's ferocious 'funnies', including Crocodiles, Crabs and AVREs. The 2nd Canadian Division would seize the western sector of

Night attack on Weeze: 82nd Assault Squadron bridge A/TK ditch, supporting the 53rd Welsh Division, 28 February 1945. (*Birkin Haward*)

Monty's moonlight RE assault bridges and fascines support the 51st Highland Division near Goch, 28 February 1945. (*Birkin Haward*)

Skid Bailey bridge launched in night attack on Weeze by 82nd Assault Squadron RE, 28 February – 1 March 1945. (*Birkin Haward*)

Xanten and the high ground to the south. All the attacks for Blockbuster 2 started at 0500hrs on 8 March. Milton Shulman described the scene:

> Schlemm was forced to contract his bridgehead under the mounting pressure of the British, Canadian (and to the south the American) forces surrounding him. By 8 March the bridgehead at Wesel quivered rather uncomfortably in an area about 15 square miles in size. In this postage-stamp sector, because of Hitler's mad refusal to permit the withdrawal of any fit men, there were jammed no less than nine divisions, three corps headquarters and an army headquarters. So crowded were these staffs that one sugar refinery alone housed the headquarters of three divisions. Here these troops who had fought an exhausting battle for a full month without a rest, were pounded relentlessly from the air and from the massed guns of the tireless Allied artillery.

On 6 March, the German High Command grudgingly gave permission for their bridgehead to be evacuated by the 10th and General Schlemm controlled the final operation at 2nd Parachute Corps HQ. General Meindl commanded the rearguard of the remnants of 6th, 7th and 8th Parachute Divisions, 116th Panzer, and 346th Infantry Division. Their only conduits to relative safety were the road and rail bridges at Wesel and numerous ferries.

Schlemm ensured that Xanten was well defended and by the time that the Wyverns and Canadians had captured the town, Wesel itself was practically denuded. The end came on 10 March when both bridges over the Rhine at Wesel crashed into the river, leaving just a small rearguard behind. Many of the houses were inscribed *SIEG ODER SIBERIEN* (VICTORY OR SIBERIA) or *LIEBER TODT WIE TYRANNEI* (BETTER DEATH THAN TYRANNY). The gallant German survivors crossed the Rhine to fight another day.

Operations Blockbuster 1 and 2 finished on 10 March. In Veritable and Blockbuster 1 and 2, the 1st Canadian Army, with its eight British divisions, had a total casualty list of 1,049 officers and 14,585 other ranks. The Canadians suffered 8,942 casualties and the British 6,694. General Schlemm at one point had command of 84th, 180th and 190th Infantry Divisions, 15th Panzergrenadier Division, 116th Panzer, Panzer Lehr Division and 2nd, 6th, 7th and 8th Parachute Divisions – a substantial army of ten divisions. They lost 22,239 prisoners and had estimated casualties of 22,000. The US 9th Army suffered 7,300 casualties in seventeen days of Operation Grenade.

23rd Hussars passing through Wesel in their brand new Comet tanks.

Men of the 1st Battalion Cheshire Regiment landing from Buffalo craft near Wesel, 24 March.

Field Marshal Sir Alan Brooke, Monty, Churchill and General Simpson on the Siegfried Line.

The 21st Army Group, after a month of continuous fighting – and the Parachute Army was the best on Hitler's western Front – were lined up along the western banks of the river Rhine. Hitler sacked von Rundstedt and appointed Field Marshal Albert Kesselring, who had achieved defensive miracles in Italy, to defend the Third Reich.

General Horrocks has the last word:

> This was the grimmest battle in which I took part during the war. No one in their senses would choose to fight a winter campaign in the flooded plains and dense pinewoods of Northern Europe, but there was no alternative. We had to clear the western bank of the Rhine if we were to enter Germany in strength and finish off the war. Although our losses seemed very high, I kept on reminding myself that there had been 50,000 casualties during the first morning of the Battle of the Somme in the First World War. Eisenhower summed up the situation when he wrote in a letter to Crerar, 'Probably no assault in this war has been conducted in more appalling conditions than was this one'.

CHAPTER 9

Capturing Arnhem: Operations Destroyer and Anger

The British Army had suffered a defeat in September 1944, in the Witches Cauldron of Arnhem and Oosterbeek, and revenge was always on the agenda. However, to achieve this, the capture of the desolate, watery No Man's Land of the Betuwe, the so-called 'Island' between Nijmegen and Arnhem, was required. For over six months the British Army took it in turns to garrison the half-dozen or so wartorn villages and hamlets in the south sector while the Germans did the same with the northern sector. Frequently the Germans sent ground, air, water or underwater attacks to try to destroy the Nijmegen road and rail bridges. The 49th West Riding (Polar Bear) Division, commanded in early 1945 by Major General S. B. Rawlins, was nicknamed 'The Nijmegen Home Guard', as they spent more time on the Island than any other formation. The Canadian generals Crerar and Simmonds in the long, bitter clearance of the river Scheldt, which led to the reopening of Antwerp harbour, had jointly recommended to SHAEF that the capture of the high ground between Arnhem and Apeldoorn, 20 miles north, would be most helpful in the planned operations Veritable, Blockbuster, Plunder and Varsity. Christened Operation Anger, the plan was given to Lt General Charles Foulkes of the 1st Canadian Corps, which had just arrived from the Italian campaign. But hostile flooding possibilities of the Island area in March and April were deemed too dangerous. Since the classic capture of Le Havre in September, the Polar Bears had frequently come under the Canadian command.

There were three phases: Operation Destroyer was the overall plan to advance to Apeldoorn. The initial clearance of the south-east sector of 'the Island' was Operation Anger and then 5th Canadian Division

147

Betuwe – the 'Island' between Nijmegen and Arnhem.

Regional emblem of Arnhem. (*Market Garden Veterans Association*)

would clear the remainder of 'the Island' and cross the Lower Rhine at Oosterbeek by a 'scramble' attack, and then push on to capture Arnhem itself in Operation Quick Anger.

The residents of Arnhem and Oosterbeek (over 450 of whom had been killed in the September battle) had been evicted from their homes, which were then systematically looted of anything of value to aid refugees in Germany. The shattered towns were then turned into strong defensive positions to resist future Allied advances. Arnhem had been extensively shelled over the winter and the Arnhem road bridge that the British had fought so hard for had been bombed by the Allies in October 1944 to deny its use to the Germans. In retaliation for a Dutch railway workers strike supposed to aid the Allies' September advance, the Germans banned all inland freight movement. This prevented food being grown in the north from reaching the south and west of the country and caused thousands of deaths among the Dutch population, in what became known as the *Hongerwinter*.

German forces in the Netherlands had been redesignated as Festung Holland and approximately 10,000 troops of the German 30th Corps under General Philipp Kleffel were holding the region Arnhem-Apeldoorn. The 361st Volksgrenadier Division was west of Arnhem and the 1,000-strong garrison of the heavily fortified Arnhem/Oosterbeek objective included elements of 346th Wehrmacht Infantry Division, 858th Grenadier Regiment, paratroops and Dutch SS troops, the Landstorm Nederland, 83rd (Dutch) 55th Regiment and 34th SS Volunteer Grenadier Division. On the day of the start of Operation Anger, Heinrich Himmler decreed that all cities occupied by German troops should be defended at any price, failure to do so being punishable by death.

Operation Destroyer started at 0600hrs on 2 April. Brigadier H. Wood, CO 147th Infantry Brigade, sent the 1/7th Duke of Wellington's Regiment to clear Haalderen and Doornenburg under a huge barrage from five field regiments, four medium, two heavy, two HAA and a mattress of 240 rockets plus a deadly assortment of 'Funnies' and a call on a RAF cab rank. Bemmel church tower was used as an OP and Haalderen, Gent and Doornenburg were bombarded with 125 rounds of H/E per gun. The Royal Scots Fusiliers and the 1st Leicesters secured the right flank, reaching the Lower Rhine later in the day. Brigadier D. S. Gordon's 146th Brigade and 1/4th KOYLI effected a bridgehead over the

A 2nd Kensington carrier on the Island. (*Michael Bayley*)

1st Leicesters on the Rhine en route to Arnhem. (*Charles Pell*)

Wettering canal and cleared Zand. A mile or so to the east, 4th Lincolns seized Angeren and pushed a further three miles to Huissen, where they were rudely attacked by the RAF, who caused casualties. By nightfall, Huissen was captured and the river Rhine reached. At first light on 3 April, the Hallamshire Battalion (York and Lancaster) took Rijkers Waard and fought their way up the autobahn as far as Kranenburg. The 1st Lothian and Border Yeomanry flails led the Polar Bears from Zand to Rikerswaard, but three 'crabs' blew up on mines.

The Hallams occupied Elden and sent a patrol across the Lower Rhine and 4th Lincolns crossed the river Rhine near Loovier. Another patrol penetrated to the river Ijssel and had a good view of Arnhem from Westervoort on the railway line. By 5 April, Operation Destroyer's first phase was completed. At long last the polder battleground of the Island was in British hands. The new GOC, Major General Rawlins, was very pleased.

Operation Quick Anger

Although patrols had probed the outer defences of Arnhem across the river on 3 and 4 April, the next major operation planned with the 1st Canadian Division was to take place on the eastern flank. The west was overlooked by commanding heights and the crossing would have been difficult and expensive in lives. The tower of the Saxen Weimar barracks had a particularly good view. On 8 April, it was decided that the attack would take place east of Arnhem near Westervoort. Twenty-four hours after the landing of the Canadians near Velp, C Squadron of the Recce Regiment nipped across the river Rhine at Emmerich to look at the west bank of the Lower Rhine and the river Ijssel. The logistical problems were immense. Troops were on the move everywhere, and tanks, trucks, carriers and jeeps congested the centre lines. The Polar Bears moved over a period of several days to the Westervoort area, via the Lower Rhine or via Emmerich. The KOYLI moved on the 10th to Zevenaar. The 56th Brigade were to make the night crossing on the 12th with the Glosters leading to form a bridgehead over the river Ijssel with the 2nd South Wales Borderers and the 2nd Essex following up and advancing into Arnhem.

During the day, Typhoons flew violent raids on all of the German positions. The artillery barrage started at 2040hrs with a two-hour

2nd Battalion, the Essex Regiment, Arnhem, April 1945. (*Harry Conn*)

Pepperpot programme. The 11th RTR's Buffaloes would ferry the attack across the river Ijssel from Westervoort. The Royal Navy's Force U would provide several LCMs (Landing Craft Mechanised) and Canadian engineers had built a pre-fab Bailey bridge upstream at Doornenburg, which would be floated down river to Westervoort just before the attack. The sappers would also build and operate a ferry and the RASC run DUKWs across the river. It was a huge task to get over a thousand troops over a wide river at night under fire.

At 2040hrs on a cold, clear night, aided by searchlights, all four Gloster rifle companies set off. Unfortunately Sod's Law was working overtime. The sapper charges that were set to explode the 'bund' riverbank in front of A and C Companies did not detonate. B Company had trouble with their assault craft engines. D Company went ahead into violent opposition but took the 'Spit', which was their objective. In the centre, A Company and C Company manhandled three of their craft over the bund, crowded into them and sailed across to capture an old Dutch fort and a silk factory that the Germans had fortified. B Company got over a bit late, but took their brickworks objective. Captain R. V. Cartwright of A Company captured sixty fully armed Germans cowering in the inner cells of Scheisprong Fort, almost single-handedly. The Glosters suffered thirty-two casualties, but by 0300hrs the 2nd Glosters, the

South Wales Borderers and the 2nd Essex had passed through according to plan, having been ferried across the river all through the night by Buffaloes and DUKWs – a total of 260 loads to get 56th Brigade across. Lt A. A. Vince of 2nd Essex recalled:

> We raced westwards through the heart of the town, but on the high ground surrounding Arnhem, the Boche had masses of artillery and mortars, so had little difficulty dropping his shells in the correct places. Captain Peter Butler died of his wounds, one of a number of casualties. We took 145 prisoners, the remainder fled westwards leaving incendiaries to fire the town. We saw the evidence of the tragedy of Sept '44, the broken guns and equipment, the little shallow slits the Airborne had dug in a few seconds and from which they had fought for days. We saw the little white crosses in corners of Dutch gardens, often with an inscription such as '31 Unknown British Soldiers'. On top of the cross would be a weather-stained Red Beret placed there by the Germans as a tribute to the cream of fighting men.

Pte H. Fensome of the 13th Platoon 2nd Essex, a nineteen-year-old reinforcement, went into his first major attack well briefed by Sgt Conn, his platoon sergeant, a veteran of D-Day. He remembered:

> We crossed in Buffalo assault boats, landed in the factory area and came under heavy shelling from 88s, rockets and mortar fire. Some of our section got caught in the open. When the barrage stopped Sgt Conn and Corporal Frank Hudspeth went on a recce and found Hoppy Hopton, Olly Oliver and Paddy McCulloch – all unharmed. We then moved into Arnhem clearing the area around the railway station and up a street near the museum. We took eight prisoners in one building. Amongst them was a blonde woman who we thought was 'Mary of Arnhem', the radio broadcaster. They were taken away to the POW cage. During one advance Lt Willis banged on the turret of a Sherman tank with his Sten gun, asking for covering fire. I observed Billy Bebber towing a toy brass cannon taken from the museum, for a souvenir.

By nightfall the 2nd South Wales Borderers were firmly into the centre of the town, most of it badly shattered, and they claimed to be the first battalion into Arnhem. The following morning the sappers bridged the river with prefab Bailey pontoons and the 146th Brigade passed through into Arnhem. Lt Colonel Hart Dyke wrote: 'Friday 13th was a most satisfactory day for the Hallams, with three objectives captured. Next morning the advance continued with A Company and tanks overcoming all opposition. In it Lt Davies was killed and 12 ORs wounded. This brought our total losses up to 158 killed and 689 all ranks wounded or a little more than the total strength of the Bn when it arrived in Normandy 11 months before.' Major Godfrey Harland of the KOYLI recalled:

> At first light with the aid of some Canadian tanks we attacked some German positions in the grounds of Sonsbeek hospital. It was to be our last company attack in NW Europe. The company was digging in, having taken the objective, when the customary German counter-attack by shell and mortar fire arrived, landing on a section of the right hand platoon. Three were killed and two were wounded. Sad to lose those three splendid young soldiers, Geordie Alcock, M. Durham and E. Lees who had fought so many battles with the company only to lose their lives so late in the war.

Detail of picture on page 72. (*Imperial War Museum*)

Detail of picture
on page 152.
(*Harry Conn*)

The 4th Lincolns had an all-day battle to clear the huge ENKA BV
factory occupied by the 346th Engineers Battalion and the 46th Festungs
Machine-gun Battalion. Tanks, armoured bulldozers, AVREs and flame-
throwers were needed. The place was so vast that more Germans kept
appearing from all sides to replace those already killed. Eventually, 234
prisoners were rounded up and as many were killed in the fierce fighting.
The Fife and Forfars' Crocodiles, the AVRE bombards of 617th Assault
Squadron and the Lothians' Crabs crossed after 56th Brigade and were
invaluable in helping clear Arnhem in the next two days. The Lincolns
suffered fifty-three casualties. The 147th Brigade moved from the Island
to join the rest of the division on the night of 13 April. The 7th Dukes
passed through the South Wales Borderers towards the railway station.
Lt Colonel Hamilton, their colonel, wrote:

Hugh Le Mesurier appeared leading my 'rear' B Company and A Company's
route had been blocked by the detonation of the enemy MG Bn. Soon my
party were lost in a maze of streets. The company commanders treated every
new horror as a great joke. By dawn the bottleneck of roads, Arnhem station
and the first high ground was ours. The next day – the 14th – the Dukes joined
in a brigade movement to secure all the high ground. The Boche reaction
was confusing. He plastered our area unmercifully for half an hour, killing
brave CSM Fellows of A Company. At dusk a company of [German] infantry

155

supported by three French Renault tanks tried to re-occupy the crossroads. Prisoners said they had no idea we were there. D Company made short work of the complete outfit. The following day – the 15th – Gerald Fancourt's C Company occupied Arnhem Zoo. Fancourt was soon on the air offering the brigadier a live polar bear to replace the wooden one on his caravan!

The Leicesters had come down the river all the way from Nijmegen to Arnhem using the 36th LCAs of the 552nd Flotilla, got to the top of the Westervoortedijt near the harbour and dug in near the Elisabeth Hospital in the western suburbs. The civilian population of Arnhem had been evacuated in late September with the exception of policemen, firemen and the Landstorm Nederland of the 83rd Dutch 55th Regiment. The latter were dug in around the Schelmseweg-Kempenbergerweg crossroads and gave the Dukes some trouble. The Canadians and General Rawlins were keeping up maximum pressure. To the east, Bronbeck and then Velp were soon taken. On the night of 15/16 April, helped by Fife and Forfar flails, the 56th Brigade led again. The 2nd Essex attacked on the north side of Velp, taking 100 prisoners. The 2nd South Wales Borderers forced their way into the residential area. The Glosters captured the Meteor factory on the Ijssel and took fifty prisoners. The Lincolns passed through towards De Steeg, and Rheden was reached by midday on the 16th. The leading tanks and companies of the South Wales Borderers were amazed to be greeted in Velp by a delirious and overwhelming crowd of civilians, with swarms of excited children, all waving flags, throwing flowers and shouting 'Good boy, Tommy'. It was truly an amazing and exhilarating experience, so great was the relief of the Dutch to be freed from their oppressors.

The left flank of 146th Brigade was protected by the Recce Regiment. Major Gooch wrote in their history: 'We had a field day comparable with our best in France (operating from Terlet) taking 143 prisoners, killing many others and clearing the whole flank of the division.' The Hallams and the KOYLI had advanced on Rozendaal, captured it with the Ontario Regiment Shermans, and thundered on via Beekbergen, Zijpenberg and Postbank to De Steeg. The Hallams' B Company, on tanks, moved on to Dieren and Laag Soeren, where they linked up with other Canadian troops. By the end of 16 April, Operation Quick Anger was over, and Arnhem had been taken at a cost of sixty-two killed and 134 wounded. More than 1,600 Germans had been made prisoner and double that number had been put out of action.

1/4th KOYLI officers at De Steeg, north of Arnhem. Left to right: Major Harland (OC A Company), Major Singleton (C Company), Major Barlow Poole (Bn 2i/c), Major Whitworth (D Company), Major Carter (FOO 69 Field Regt RA), Lt Firth (Intelligence Officer). (*Lt Colonel G. Barker Harland MC*)

Matthew Halton, Canadian Broadcasting Company (CBC), reported:

16 April 1945: Arnhem. Today I drove into the smoking shell of that town, once one of the most beautiful in Holland. There was nothing there now but ruin, and a memory.

It was fitting that it should be a British formation, the 49th West Riding Division, that should take Arnhem at long last and write the words 'Paid in full' across another page of British history. Last September the world stopped breathing to watch this town. If the British Army had been able to link hands with the British 1st Airborne Division, which had landed round Arnhem, the Rhine would have been turned while the German armies were disorganised, and the armoured divisions would have poured into the plains of Hanover and Westphalia. But the effort was a bit too much for us, the weather was against us, and in fact we didn't have enough strength at the decisive place.

I drove in from the south today, past powerful German forts and redoubts which had been shelled and bombed and burnt out by thousands of our rockets firing hundreds at a time. The town was a deserted, burning shell. I visited a British regiment, and saw about 200 German prisoners. Fires were blazing. Machine-guns chattered from the high ground north of Arnhem, and two or three German shells whistled into the town. An airplane engine, that had fallen from some British bomber, disintegrating high above, lay in a little park beside a canal. The whole thing was a dreary, disheartening sight – another of the destroyed towns of a beautiful continent.

There were craters everywhere. White tapes through the minefields. A British soldier who'd lost a foot on a Schu mine. Two other soldiers being buried. Engineers making demolitions. Bulldozers, backing up a few feet, shaking their heads in roaring anger, and then tearing into the side of a broken house. A Martian ant hill – a bedlam of men at war. Motor cycles bouncing back and forth. Tanks and Bren-carriers dusting through to the next battle. Convoy leaders going crazy to get their convoys through. All the noisy, clanking machines and paraphernalia of war. A lone Dutchman, the first civilian we had encountered, came slowly down a long street. He shook hands. 'You have come back', he said quietly. Just that. The British had come back, as they always do. Operation Quick Anger was over.

Operation Dutch Cleanser

The 147th Brigade now received orders to launch an attack on Ede, ten miles north-west of Arnhem. The 146th Brigade, together with the South Wales Borderers and the 2nd Essex, had concentrated around Arnhem and the KOYLI remained in Rozendaal. Rex Flower recalled: 'Billeted with local schoolmaster and family. Four days clearing up jobs. Found a sanatorium, many of the patients had been killed or wounded. Found a mass grave, miserable and brooding. We did not dally. We moved to Wolfeze woods, scores and scores of Airborne gliders, some wrecked, most undamaged.'

Ede was held by 300 Dutch SS troops of the 83rd SS Grenadier Regiment, part of the 34th SS Division. They were a motley unit of renegades, but their fighting spirit and fanaticism had already been proven. On the afternoon of 16 April, the Royal Scots Fusiliers led, together with tanks of the Canadian Calgary Regiment. Progress was slow due to defended German roadblocks with anti-tank guns. The following morning, under a thick smokescreen, the advance continued until halted by the Simon Stevin barracks defences. A heavy artillery bombardment of the barracks at midday also unfortunately caused damage to Ede town centre. Now Wasp flame-throwers of the Royal

Scots Fusiliers set the barracks alight. B and C Companies advanced on the railway station where they quenched their thirst, among an elated crowd in the Stationsweg. Fusilier Ken West remembered: 'We were in the beautiful Veluwe district north of Arnhem. Thick woods of silver birch, oak and beech, a haven for wild life.' He had watched his leading platoon run shouting and screaming up the road and out of sight. On top of a very small hill the fusiliers were dancing around and singing 'I'm the king of the castle' until Major Weir, Webley pistol in hand, appeared. 'It's not a damned Sunday School outing – bloody fools,' he said. Pte Bob Day of the 1st Leicesters recalled:

> In woods outside the town of Arnhem which the retreating Germans shelled heavily as we marched in single file through the street, our company was mistaken by other British troops for the enemy. There followed a rocket barrage, the ferocity of which defies description. When the shrieking and blasts of those devilish weapons came to a merciful end, a young officer's arm was left hanging from the shoulder by a shred. I gave the Bren gunner a gentle nudge (I was his No. 2). He fell to one side limply. He was dead. A piece of shrapnel had penetrated his spine killing him instantly. When darkness came we buried him in the dell with a makeshift wooden cross.

On the 17th, the 2nd Essex returned to Arnhem, embarked on LCAs and LCMs and sailed down the river to Renkum. Lt A. A. Vince recalled:

> We disembarked in this completely razed village and marched into Wageningen again without opposition. Here Lt Colonel Butler DSO left us to return to command a Bn of his own regiment. Lt Colonel E. S. Scott MBE took command. Between our own positions and those of the enemy ran the floodable valley of the river Grebbe and once more the battle became static with extensive patrolling by both sides in which the enemy suffered far more heavily than we did.

Fusilier Ken West watched rocket-firing 'Tiffies' screaming down on the Ede barracks, and C Squadron of the Recce Regiment pushed ahead in front of the 11th Royal Scots Fusiliers to Lunteren. West noted: 'Newspaper reporters and Canadian news-reel men were out in force to record the scenes for posterity. It was rather nice to be the centre of attention. Teenage girls ran to place garlands of laurel around our necks as we marched along singing the old Boer's trekking song which had become a favourite of ours.' The Burgomaster assumed the fusiliers were Canadians. West continued: 'We had to inform him that we were indeed British. "If you were English you would be singing 'Tipperary'." So we sang 'Tipperary' again and again and again.'

The Leicesters had advanced to Ede-South, following the railway line much of the way. On the large Ginkel Heath near Ede the 7th Dukes found much airborne equipment and parachutes from the September landings. Lt Colonel Hamilton recalled:

> There was no respite. At 5 o'clock we followed the RSF out of Arnhem along the great autobahn leading west to Rotterdam. By mid-day Ede was captured and, mounted on tanks, C Company pushed south six miles to the Rhine, thus taking 56th Brigade's objective! Their brigadier gave me a cool reception at Wageningen that night! The Boche had gone back five miles to the Grebbe line and our startling advance was halted while negotiations opened for the passage of food convoys through the Boche line for the starving people of NW Holland.

Operation Dutch Cleanser was a full-scale offensive by the Canadian Army to force a wedge from the Arnhem area to the Zeider Zee to cut off 120,000 German forces. On the evening of the 17 April a halt was called. It was now decided that the 1st Canadian Corps would advance no further into north-west Holland in an effort to prevent the enemy flooding the whole countryside west of Utrecht. However, aspects of war continued. Rex Flower of the 1/4th KOYLI wrote on 21 April:

> Assault pioneer platoon lifting German Teller mines, hundreds of them – but their own Pioneer officer Lt J. C. Crabtree, driver Private J. W. Dean were both killed when their vehicle struck a mine. The last casualties of the war. A truce arranged. Seyss-Inquart, the Nazi CO, threatened if the advance continued he would open the sea dykes and flood the countryside. This threat was taken seriously by our Army Commander. No movement whatsoever during the day on pain of court-martial. But A Company killed, wounded and captured part of a German patrol as they tried to get into the company position. The Germans broke the truce, we didn't. They had no chance.

On the 22 April, the South Wales Borderers left to join the 53rd Welsh Division for the last fortnight of fighting in north-west Germany. It was a

A 2nd Middlesex mortar position near Velp. (*Michael Bayley*)

pleasant surprise for the 4th Lincolns at Wolfheze when their regimental band unexpectedly arrived from Lincoln and played at concerts and church parades. On the 26th the battalion marched to Lunteren, played in by the band as Brigadier Gordon took the salute. Three days earlier the 1st Leicesters had their last bitter little battle at Renswoude against German-Dutch SS troops. Eversley Belfield, General Horrocks' co-author, wrote in his diary:

> ... the vast smoke-screens, a feature of all the river crossings made observation often very difficult. The unhappy town of Arnhem was burning hard with smoke towering up to several thousand feet ... To the right was the smaller town of Velp where I saw people running as smoke shells burst above it starting fires. I wondered whether they were civilians ... The process of liberation is often a most unpleasant one: if we were conquering the Germans I should not care so much, but the unfortunate Holland had suffered enough already. [Later by jeep] I passed into the area where the Airborne Division made their final stand. It is a terrifying sight with wrecked houses, damaged trees, torn and slivered by the mortaring and shelling ... piles of equipment lie around, burnt and abandoned ... The whole area devoid of civilians breathes an air of tragedy.

CHAPTER 10

Weapons of Revenge

Adolf Hitler, that dangerous little corporal, was obsessed with secret weapons of mass destruction. In 1939 his friend and architect Albert Speer took charge of the Peenemünde site for the development of rockets. From 1937 to 1940, the German Wehrmacht spent 550 million German marks on the development of a large rocket, hampered by Hitler's 'divide and rule' policy, which involved not only the three branches of the armed forces but also the SS; even the postal system came in on research facilities! General von Brauchitsch had presented plans to Hitler in 1939 for a *long-range* rocket but this had been rejected.

On Christmas Eve 1944 an experimental V-1 was successfully launched from Peenemünde. The Polish underground movement learned enough for the War Cabinet in London to be mildly alarmed. In May 1943, an RAF reconnaissance plane located the Peenemünde research station and air photographs revealed that pilotless jet-propelled aircraft were being developed.

Two months later a V-1 test made a flight of 243 kilometres without deviating more than one kilometre from its course. On 10 July, Hitler ordered Speer to devote special attention to the production of *vergeltunswaffen* (weapons of revenge). Ninety-six sites along the Channel coast were to be ready by 15 December, with production of 5,000 V-1s a month, and a stock of 5,000 to start the offensive; but in August the RAF inflicted serious damage at Peenemunde and the first batches were faulty and useless.

By the end of November, sixty-three sites had been discovered by Allied flight reconnaissance, and on 5 December Allied bombers began attacking the sites. By February 1944, seventy-three out of the ninety-six

A V-2 for Antwerp seen rising from north Holland over the Nijmegen Bridge.

sites had been severely damaged and the Germans decided to abandon the whole project.

A special unit, Flak Regiment 155, was set up to carry out future launching operations and to comb out all non-German elements from the site construction gangs. Because of the bombing of the production sites, sufficient stocks would not be available until mid-1944.

In parallel, from 1941 Professor Ernst Heinkel was developing the world's first jet-engined planes at the Heinkel plant in Rostock. In September 1943, the Me-262 jet fighter plane production – under the overall control of Field Marshal Erhard Milch, State Secretary in the Luftwaffe and armaments chief – was arbitrarily halted by Hitler.

Albert Speer wrote in his memoirs *Inside the Third Reich*:

The jet plane was not the only effective new weapon that could have been mass produced in 1944. We possessed a remote-controlled flying bomb, a rocket plane even faster than the jet plane, a rocket missile that homed on an enemy plane by tracking the heat rays from its motors, and a torpedo that reacted to sound and could thus pursue and hit a ship fleeing in a zig-zag course. Development of a ground-to-air missile had been completed. The designer Lippisch had jet planes on the drawing board that were far in advance

163

of anything so far known ... We were literally suffering from an excess of projects in development. Had we concentrated on only a few types we would surely have completed some of them sooner.

Hitler wanted the Me-262 converted into a light *bomber*.

In the summer of 1944, 8,000 V-1s exploded over London killing 5,000 civilians, wounding 40,000 and damaging 75,000 houses. The 'buzz-bomb' was a truly noisy weapon of casual destruction. This horrible campaign was carried out despite the SS arresting the Peenemünde scientists, including Werner von Braun, their chief designer. In spite of this the V-2, a more formidable weapon, was brought into action in September 1944. With a warhead of 1 tonne, it reached a height of 60 miles and plunged down on its target at a speed of over 3,500 mph. Its range was a little over 200 miles. Altogether about 6,000 were built with 1,265 launched against the port of Antwerp and 1,050 on London. The V-2 was 46 feet long and weighed more than 13 metric tonnes. Hitler wanted more than 900 produced monthly. Speer wrote: 'The whole notion was absurd. The fleets of enemy bombers in 1944 dropped an average of 2,000 tons of bombs *a day* over a span of several months. And Hitler wanted to retaliate with 30 rockets with 24 tons of explosives to England daily. That was equivalent to the bomb load of only 12 Flying Fortresses.' Speer admitted that he was at fault in supporting Hitler's decision:

That was probably one of my most serious mistakes. We would have done much better to focus our efforts on manufacturing a ground-to-air defensive rocket. Developed in 1942, code name Waterfall [translated], to such a point mass production would soon have been possible. The Waterfall was 25 feet long, carrying 660 pounds of explosives along a directional beam up to an altitude of 50,000 feet and hit the enemy bombers with great accuracy. It was not affected by day or night, by clouds or fog ... We could surely have produced several thousand of these smaller and less expensive rockets per month. To this day [1970] I think this rocket in conjunction with the jet fighters would have beaten back the western Allies' air offensive against our industry from the Spring of 1944 on.

As late as 1 January 1945, 2,210 scientists and engineers were working on the *long-range* rockets A-4 and A-9; only 220 were assigned to Waterfall, and 135 to another anti-aircraft rocket project, code name Typhoon.

The Mittelwerke facility, where the vengeance rockets were assembled underground with the use of slave labour.

In June 1944, the Germans unleashed their new V-1 (*Vergeltungswaffe* or vengeance weapon) pilotless flying bombs against targets in the south-east of England and Belgium. They were known popularly as 'buzz bombs' or 'doodlebugs' because of the charateristic noise made by their simple pulse jet engines.

Left: A captured V-2 rocket site, Leese, April 1945.
Right: A V-2 rocket being prepared for launch.

The A-4 had been trial-tested on 7 July 1943 and the film shown to Hitler. Speer wrote:

Hitler bade the Peenemünde men [Colonel Walter Dornberger and the 37-year-old von Braun] an exceedingly cordial goodbye. He was greatly impressed and his imagination had been kindled. Back in his bunker he became quite ecstatic about the possibilities of this project. 'The A-4 is a measure that can decide the war. And what encouragement to the home front when we attack the English with it! This is the decisive weapon of the war and what is more it can be produced with relatively small resources. Speer you must push the A-4 as hard as you can. Whatever labour and materials they need must be supplied instantly ... put the A-4 on a par with tank production. But in this project we can use only Germans. God help us if the enemy finds out about the business.'

From January 1945 Speer was confident that 210 Me-262s could be produced each month. A few were in action against the RAF and USAAF from 18 September 1944. In February 1945 production was 283. They needed exceptionally long runways, which were bombed heavily. They needed very experienced pilots and although the Luftwaffe were extremely proud of them, their overall effect was limited

There were two other forms of horror and vengeance weapons. Both Hitler and Churchill in 1939 decided to build limited stocks, but not to use them first. Corporal Hitler had been gassed in the First World War and knew what an unreliable weapon gas was, dependent entirely on the vagaries of the winds. The nuclear option is shown in an appendix.

So the elimination of the V-1, V-2 and other aerial deadly weapons was an important priority, even though the majority of sites had been captured or bombed. Large areas of northern Holland and north-west Germany could harbour all kinds of dangerous surprises.

Messerschmitt Me-262, Germany's jet fighter-bomber.

CHAPTER 11

Rhine Crossing Battle: Operation Plunder

On 18 March General M. C. Dempsey, Commander of the 2nd British Army, briefed the key Allied journalists including Alan Moorehead at his camp near Venlo beside the river Maas: 'We will cross the Rhine on the night of the 23rd. Four corps are under my command. 30th Corps will cross in the north near Rees and continue northward for the capture of Emmerich. 12th Corps will cross in the centre at Xanten while the Commandos turn south to capture Wesel. On the following morning 18th US Airborne Corps with the 6th British Airborne Division under command will drop near the Ijssel River on the opposite bank of the Rhine and secure the bridges there. Finally the 8th Corps will follow through and I cannot yet tell you how far they will go. The 9th American Army will also attack on my right flank and proceed eastward along the Ruhr.' Alan Moorehead wrote:

> Dempsey was an exact and energetic technician. Ever since the landing in Normandy, whenever we met him one was astonished at the precision with which he elucidated a plan and brought a map to life. Above and below him were two entirely different commanders; Montgomery with his flair, his processes of instinctive divination, his legendary influence with the generals and the soldiers. Then Horrocks of 30th Corps, a man with an ascetic, almost an ecclesiastical face and underneath that more volatility and fire and dash than one could have thought possible in a single man, an ideal break-through general. Both Montgomery (objectively) and Horrocks (subjectively) dealt often in terms of emotion. Between them stood Dempsey, the technician, a lean and nervous figure, a manipulator of facts, not so much a popular leader as a remarkable co-ordinator and a planner ... You must list him among the half-dozen really able field commanders thrown up by England in the war.

The battlegrounds of operations Veritable, Blockbuster and Plunder.

Operation Plunder was the code name for the assault crossing of the great river Rhine and for a deep thrust into the northern half of the Third Reich. Operation Varsity was the code name for the airborne drop by 6th Airborne and the US 17th Airborne Divisions, north and northwest of Wesel.

The RAF and USAAF had severely interdicted the German communications network in a line from Bremen southward to the Rhine and Coblenz. Most of the eighteen vital railroad bridges and viaducts were destroyed. In four weeks from 21 February, forty major bombing raids were carried out, including by the RAF dropping 22,000 lb monster bombs. On 11 and 12 March, over 1,000 bombers each night dropped

169

over 5,000 tons on Essen and Dortmund. The new jet aircraft being introduced by the Luftwaffe had special attention and their jet airfields made unusable.

The Royal Navy carried out some strange manoeuvres. Large LCM and LCV(P) craft were transported overland and by waterway on special trailers up to 45 feet in length and 14 feet wide. Their ferry service would prove invaluable. An LCM could take a Sherman tank or sixty men, and a LCV (P) a bulldozer or thirty-five men. The width of the Rhine for Operation Plunder was between 400 and 500 yards, but at high water it could increase to between 700 and 1,200 yards. The current was usually about 3.5 knots (4 mph). The river bed was sand and gravel and amphibious Dual-Duplex tanks and trestles would have a good 'bearing surface'.

Supplies of equipment, guns, ammunition and smoke shells to shield the crossing poured into the west bank of the Rhine. Sappers had built three Class 70 and nine Class 4 bridges, together with railway bridges at Ravenstein and Mook, to allow the convoys of material to deploy. A railhead and store depot was opened near Goch. In all, 118,000 tons were needed, including 30,000 tons of engineering stores and bridging, which included 25,000 wooden pontoons, very vulnerable to shell-fire and ice, 2,000 assault boats, 650 storm boats and 120 river tugs, together with 80 miles of balloon cable and 260 miles of steel wire rope. Although this was primarily a Royal Engineers affair, it developed into a combined operation. For instance, the ferries and rafts had to be winched across by cable and there were not sufficient Royal Engineers for this purpose, as they were all required for other technical jobs, so 159th Wing of the RAF were asked whether they could spare some of the men who operated their balloons. They produced fifty specialists in 12 hours from a distance of 150 miles, and said that another 300 volunteers were available if required. This was typical of the assistance from the RAF. The Navy were equally helpful and produced a Royal Naval team which established anti-mine booms upstream to prevent the Germans floating down demolitions and destroying the bridges when they were constructed.

No fewer than 60,000 Royal Engineers and men of the Royal Navy were deployed. On the ground there were 400,000 vehicles of every possible description: tanks, SPs, AVREs, carriers, half-tracks, Crocodiles, Wasps, DUKWs, Crabs, DDs (swimming tanks), field ambulances, signals trucks, REME vehicles and more. An unusual group was the military

A smokescreen near the Rhine.

government detachments to administer occupied territory gained in Operation Plunder.

For ten days a smokescreen shrouded the Allied bank of the river opposite Wesel to conceal troop and vehicle movements from German artillery observers. 52nd Lowland Scottish Division was responsible for holding the western bank of the river with fourteen section posts between Buderich and Vynen, and their gunners knocked down the German OPs in the handsome churches in Wesel and Bislich. The ten-mile stretch ran in two wide loops and in the fields were many forlorn cattle, that needed milking, and poultry that laid eggs. In Xanten could be seen fleets of Buffaloes, DUKWs and DD tanks waiting for the off. So too were three eminent figures to be seen on the river banks 'consulting': a bulldog (W. Churchill), a bird (Montgomery) and a grave scholar in uniform (the CIGS, Alanbrooke)!

General Horrocks wrote:

The 8th Parachute Division was in and around the town of Rees, with part of the 6th and 7th Parachute Divisions on their flanks, and supported by approximately 150 guns. Behind them, in reserve, were the 15th and 116th Panzer Divisions, all of whom we knew only too well from previous battles. Although they had

171

Above: Assault crossing of the Rhine.

Left: The Rhine at Rees.

Before dawn Scottish troops embark to cross the river Rhine. (*Imperial War Museum*)

suffered heavy casualties, these had been made up from within Germany. The bulk of their reinforcements of course were callow youths, since by this time the Germans really were scraping the bottom of the barrel to make up losses. But many of these youngsters were dedicated Nazis, and under the guidance of the extremely tough and experienced parachute and panzer officers and NCOs they had been soon moulded into a formidable fighting force. It was bad luck that once more we should be faced by these diehard Nazis; after the crossing we heard stories, from the US and our flanking corps, of German soldiers surrendering in their thousands, and of villages with white sheets hanging from every window, but this did not happen on our front. We had still to fight, and fight hard, right up to the end. I could not resist a feeling of admiration for the sterling qualities displayed by these German paratroopers and panzers, when the bulk of them must have known that the war was irretrievably lost.

Aerial photography had identified 357 German flak (anti-aircraft) positions with a total of about 1,000 guns, which would unfortunately prove extremely lethal.

Generals Dempsey and Horrocks' plan in Operation Widgeon was for the 1st Commando Brigade to cross the river at night to attack the town of Wesel. Twenty-six Buffaloes of 77th RE Assault Squadron would run a non-stop ferry service across. Each could hold twenty men with equipment for the attack and thirty men for the follow-up. Field Marshal Montgomery had specified two Scottish divisions to make the initial break-in. 15th Scottish, in Operation Torchlight, were directed to attack Bislich and Mehr, four miles west of Wesel. The two airborne divisions would land in front around Hamminkeln and Diersfordter Wald, three miles inland from Mehr and Bislich. One lesson had been learned from the Arnhem battle: three miles probably okay, eight miles, disaster! The 51st Highland Division, part of 12th Corps under Lt General Neil Ritchie, would cross on a two-brigade front, one near Honnopel and the other downstream at Rees. Captain Angus Stewart, adjutant of the 7th Battalion Argyll and Sutherland Highlanders, 51st Highland Division, described being carried across the Rhine by the 1st Northants Yeomanry:

> At 0800 we got into our Buffaloes, ponderous great clumsy creatures looking very much like the original tanks of 1916. They stand about eight feet high on dry land and are driven both on land and water by great tracks which travel round the whole perimeter of the vehicle, instead of on bogies as on a modern

Operation Plunder, Rhine crossing, 24 March 1945. AVRE with fascine being ferried across on a scissors bridge, supporting 15th Scottish Division. (*Birkin Haward*)

tank. These machines can carry a platoon of men or a small vehicle like a jeep or a carrier.

At 0815 we started up, and there was a great din of engines revving and guns firing. The 25-pdrs make a sharp crack, while the big heavy guns made a resonant dong! Like the G string of a cello being plucked. What an orchestra! I thought back to Medenine, Mareth, Enfidaville, Sicily and remembered all those other times I had experienced this same experience. This time it was rather different, though, more complicated, more hazardous, and just as vital. This time our division assaulted alone; the next division on our flank didn't cross till three in the morning, others not till ten, while the airborne divs were also landing about ten. We were playing the good old game of trying to draw his reserves onto us again, like Akele out hunting with pack.

At 0900 the first Buffaloes entered the water and chugged across to the other side, none failed, none sank, all landed our men where we wanted them. They were good, those crews. I followed about half an hour later with the 2 i/c and a carrier with a wireless set. Without difficulty we climbed out onto the west bank of the Rhine after a fine crossing. I hardly knew when we were in the water. We tilted our noses right up as we climbed over a bund and then see-sawed on top with our noses right down. There was the water beneath us, and we waddled unceremoniously into it. We looked quite graceful in the water, low and manoeuvrable, though not at all fast. We had about six inches freeboard and shipped nothing. When we came out on the far bank we found a slight fire burning, so we put it out, let down our back and spewed out the carrier. The companies by now were all on their objectives, the track was being swept for mines and we started our job of fielding the vehicles as they came in and disposing of them. So far, no enemy reply, and not a vehicle had been lost; a remarkable feat.

The river crossing took about four minutes and on average it took about 55 minutes to carry a battalion across the Rhine. The four Buffalo regiments made 3,842 craft trips. Of the 425 Buffaloes operating only nine were destroyed and fifty-five damaged, with casualties of only forty.

There were soon efficient Class 50/60 rafting operations for light vehicles, Weasels and anti-tank guns at crossings called Tilbury, Gravesend, Ardath and Abdullah under an intense smokescreen and an artillery barrage of 1,300 guns [the author's 13th RHA fired non-stop for ten hours on selected fire programmes], with H-Hour at 2200hrs.

On the night of 23/24 March, Operation Plunder started under a clear full moon. The Commandos, then the Highland Division, and on the following morning 15th Scottish, crossed in Operation Torchlight, as described by Stewart Macpherson:

> I watched the Commandos take off for Wesel, long a thorn in our side, and their attitude simply defied description. You would have thought that they were embarking on a Union picnic: they just couldn't care less. A few minutes after they were due to arrive on the far side, Bomber Command were to deliver a crushing blow on the enemy in Wesel, while the Commandos lay doggo over there, a bare thousand yards from the RAF target, and waited. Bang on time Arthur Harris and Company [Air Chief Marshal Sir Arthur Harris was C-in-C Bomber Command] arrived and delivered a nerve shaking blow on the Wesel stronghold.

In pitch darkness with white tape guidelines, the Commandos, like thieves in the night, stole into the smashed up town and captured it quickly with the minimum of casualties. On the northern flank the 227th Brigade of the 15th Scottish, Gordons and Argyles leading, were tasked with making a bridgehead in the area Haffen-Mehr, which was held by the German 7th Parachute Division. Further south, 44th Brigade would cross from Xanten, led by the RSF and KOSB with the objective of Bislich, held by the battered 84th Wehrmacht Division. The assault crossing started at 0200hrs on 24 March under a 700-gun barrage and the divisional Pepperpot. This was a curious habit of the British Liberation Army on the doorstep of Germany. It needed careful co-ordination and was fired by supporting tanks, SPs, anti-tank guns, heavy mortars, LAA guns and medium machine-guns plus the Canadian Mattress rocket salvoes.

The whole operation went smoothly. The 1062nd Grenadier Regiment was overwhelmed; Bislich was captured, as were the villages of Vissel and Jockern. In mid-afternoon the KOSB and RSF met up with 17th US Airborne and the Royal Scots linked up with 6th Airborne. The only pitched battle was between a German parachute battalion and the HLI in the villages of Wolffskath, Bettenhof and Overkamp. The Scotsmen had 100 casualties in confused and bitter fighting. For the next few days the German 7th Parachute Division put up one hell of a fight defending vital bridges.

Assault infantry lands on the east side of the Rhine.

The 51st Highland's assault crossing had gone to plan except for the 5/7th Gordons when their Buffaloes were beaten off by the Upper Rhine defences, just east of Rees. 1st Gordons and 5th Black Watch suffered badly in the five-day battle to capture Rees. Their splendid GOC, Major General Thomas Rennie, was killed in a mortar stonk. General Horrocks wrote: 'I have always felt that Rennie had some foreboding about this battle. Like so many Highlanders, I believe he was "fey" ... All three brigades were involved in heavy fighting so I crossed the Rhine in a Buffalo and summoned the three brigadiers to a conference. They were very upset ... no wonder because Rennie was a great leader.' The new GOC was Major General 'Babe' Macmillan, commander of 49th Polar Bears, who led 51st throughout Plunder and Eclipse to the end of the war. General Horrocks wrote:

In the darkness of that warm spring evening, I could imagine the leading Buffaloes carrying infantry of 153rd and 154th Infantry Brigades lumbering along their routes, which had been taped out and lit beforehand, and then lurching down into the dark waters of the Rhine.

Upstream at Wesel I could hear the aircraft of Bomber Command preparing the way for 12th Corps which was to assault later that night. Then at four minutes past nine precisely I received the message for which I had been waiting – in its way a historical message because it was from the British troops to cross

177

A party of VIPs in front of the Citadel of Jülich, just after they had taken lunch in the ruined fortress. From left to right: Major General McLain (US 19th Corps), Field Marshal Montgomery (British 21st Army Group), Winston Churchill (British Prime Minister), Major General Gillem (US 13th Corps), Field Marshal Allan Brooke (British Chief Imperial General Staff) and Lt General Simpson (US 9th Army). (*Imperial War Museum*)

the Rhine – 'The Black Watch has landed safely on the far bank.' The initial crossings went very smoothly, opposition was not as heavy as might have been expected and our casualties were comparatively light.

But the enemy was quick to recover and very soon reports came in that Rees was proving troublesome. As the night wore on enemy resistance stiffened and some very bitter fighting took place. Within 24 hours of the assault the 15th Panzergrenadier Division hit back at us with a vicious counter-attack ...

Reports were coming in of Germans surrendering in large numbers to the British and American forces on our flanks but there was no sign of any collapse on our front. In fact the 51st Highland Division reported that the enemy was fighting harder than at any time since Normandy. It says a lot for the morale of those German parachute and panzer troops that with chaos, disorganisation and disillusionment all round them they should still be resisting so stubbornly. Their casualties during the last nine months had been very heavy, and the reinforcements arriving from Germany had not been of the old calibre at

178

all, yet somehow the rough experienced officers and NCOs who were such a feature of these parachute and panzer formations managed to turn the callow youths into good soldiers.

It was a slow business widening the bridgehead and Rees proved a particularly hard nut to crack. It took the 1st Battalion, the Gordons, 48 hours of dour fighting before the whole place was in their hands.

Robert Barr, 52nd Lowland, noted that the 'bulldog' and his companions had come to see his warriors on the Third Reich battlefields:

25 March 1945. In warm, brilliant sunshine this afternoon the Prime Minister, Mr Churchill, basked on his balcony overlooking the Rhine and discussed casually with General Eisenhower and Field Marshal Montgomery just how the 9th Army bridgehead had been established. Downstream he could see the town of Wesel which the British Commandos had just completely cleared. Through his binoculars the Prime Minister was inspecting the bridgehead just across the slow-flowing Rhine, when quite suddenly he decided to cross. Our planes were still pounding the German positions across the river when Mr

Churchill in a jeep with Monty and Dempsey on the banks of the Rhine.

Churchill aboard a Daimler armoured car Xanten/Calcar, before the Rhine crossing, 25 March 1945.

Churchill walked down to the river's edge and got into a landing-craft. With him went Sir Alan Brooke, Chief of the Imperial General Staff, Field Marshal Montgomery, General Omar Bradley, and General Simpson, Commander of the 9th US Army which had forced the river at this point. We cruised across the Rhine in the tracks of the infantry, and the Prime Minister scrambled up the gravel bank on the other side along the same narrow wired path that the infantry had used, and scaled a high earth dike to get a good view. He studied the bridgehead and discussed the morning's battle with the American generals and then he decided to have a short cruise on the Rhine. It was his first cruise on the Rhine since he sailed it in a motor torpedo boat at the end of the last war. After the short cruise, the landing-craft turned back to shore. The Prime Minister went to Wesel along the river road. At the approach to the great steel and concrete Wesel bridge (the one the Germans destroyed when they retreated across the river) the cavalcade of staff cars halted and the Prime Minister got out. Leaving the party, he found a path through the debris, and climbed up on to the first span of the wrecked bridge. The ruins of Wesel were just across the water, and the sound of machine-gun and rifle fire was still coming up spasmodically from the town. Through binoculars the Prime Minister watched

180

Churchill crossing the Rhine.

the crouching infantry moving through the streets, while Field Marshal Montgomery explained how the British assault had been made.

Alan Moorehead noted:

... naval launches flying the ensign were plying to and fro. Already the bridge builders were at work. The Buffaloes lay about in the fields in the sunshine like prehistoric monsters, their exhausted crews spreadeagled out on the grass asleep after the night's work ... Long lines of prisoners go by carrying and supporting their wounded. An enterprising Military Government officer was distributing General Eisenhower's proclamation in English and German in the [captured] villages. Nazi emblems must be destroyed. All Nazi organisations and courts of law are abolished. Householders must place lists of names of the inmates on the front doors of their houses.

CHAPTER 12

Airborne Attack: Operation Varsity

This was the last great airborne operation of the Second World War. Much thought had gone into the planning for the 1st Allied Airborne Army, so that the painful experience of Market Garden would not be repeated. First of all the whole assault would be made in one lift, not scattered over three days, secondly the whole force would land, not near, but on top of its objective. There would be no long approach march. To ensure this, the operation would take place in broad daylight – a great but necessary risk. Finally the airborne troops would land *after* the large-scale land operations had crossed the Rhine. Only when the key German town of Wesel had been captured by the Commando Brigade (with total casualties of thirty-six!) would the airborne armada arrive.

The 17th US Airborne Division had not been in action before and 6th Airborne not since their heroic battles in Normandy and the Ardennes.

The objectives were for 3rd and 5th Parachute Brigades and the Airlanding Brigade to occupy the high ground east of Bergen in the wooded area of the Diers-Ijssel fordter Wald, the village of Hamminkeln and certain bridges over the river Ijssel.

After Market Garden, Lt General Browning had been 'posted away' and the experienced Major General R. N. 'Windy' Gale took his place as Deputy Commander of 1st AAA. Major General E. Bols had commanded 6th Airborne in the Ardennes and did so for the rest of the war.

The 6th Airborne flew from bases in East Anglia in 669 planes and 429 gliders of the RAF 38th and 46th Groups, while the 17th US Airborne flew from the Paris area in 903 planes and 897 gliders.

The British landed 7,220 officers and men between 1000 and 1300hrs on 24 March. Fighter escorts of 213 RAF and 676/9th USAF

Horsa gliders soar over the Rhine despite smoke and haze. (*Imperial War Museum*)

6th Airlanding Brigade land near Hamminkeln, 27 March 1945.

protected the two armadas. General Eisenhower noted: '46 planes destroyed (3.98% of those employed) was remarkably low ... since no evasive action was taken.' Nevertheless British casualties were 1,400 (347 killed in action) and Americans 1,500. 60 per cent of the British gliders and 50 per cent of the American gliders suffered flak damage. Twenty-two of the seventy-two C46 transports were lost and General Ridgeway was so dismayed by the ease with which they had caught fire, he forbade their use for carrying paratroops in the future.

6th Airborne gliders lifted 4,844 men, 342 jeeps, 348 trailers, 7 Locust tanks, 14 lorries, 2 bulldozers, 11 Bren-carriers, 19 Scout cars, 215 motorcycles, 68 assorted guns, mainly anti-tank, and 10 mortars.

The journalist Richard Dimbleby flew with 6th Airborne and reported what he saw:

24 March 1945. The Rhine lies left and right across our path below us, shining in the sunlight – wide and with sweeping curves; and the whole of this mighty airborne army is now crossing and filling the whole sky. We haven't come as far as this without some loss; on our right-hand side a Dakota has just gone down in flames. We watched it go to the ground, and I've just seen the parachutes of it blossoming and floating down towards the river. Above us and below us, collecting close round us now, are the tugs as they take their gliders in. Down there is the smoke of battle. There is the smoke-screen laid by the army lying right across the far bank of the river; dense clouds of brown and grey smoke coming up. And now our skipper's talking to the glider pilot and warning him that we're nearly there, preparing to cast him off. Ahead of us, another pillar of black smoke marks the spot where an aircraft has gone down, and – yet another one; it's a Stirling – a British Stirling; it's going down with flames coming out from under its belly – four parachutes have come out of the Stirling; it goes on its way to the ground. We haven't got time to watch it further because we're coming up now to the exact chosen landing-ground where our airborne forces have to be put down; and no matter what the opposition may be, we have got to keep straight on, dead on the exact position. There's only a minute or two to go, we cross the Rhine – we're on the east bank of the river. We're passing now over the army smoke-cloud. 'Stand by and I'll tell you when to jump off.' The pilot is calling – warning us – in just one moment we shall have let go. All over the sky ahead of us – here comes the voice – *Now!* – The glider has gone: we've cast off our glider.

6th Airborne troops
after capturing Wesel.

We've let her go. There she goes down behind us. We've turned hard away, hard away in a tight circle to port to get out of this area. I'm sorry if I'm shouting – this is a very tremendous sight.

The ground fighting went according to plan; most of the casualties were during the drops and around the dropping zones. Corporal F. G. Topham, a medical orderly with 1st Canadian Parachute Battalion, over a six-hour period aided many wounded men, though wounded himself, and was awarded the Victoria Cross. Stanley Maxted was there and reported:

Down toward the river beyond the trees a company of men were deployed. The glider-borne troops involved in this part of the action wear the badges of three very famous old county regiments – the Royal Ulster Rifles, the Oxfordshire and Buckinghamshire Light Infantry, and the Devons. In some other setting their actions might have reminded you of some nursery game. One section would rise up and go forward like Indian bush fighters. They'd be covered by fire from the rest. Then another section went forward in the same way until all the platoons had worked their way in a converging movement on to the bridge that was one of their objectives.

It really is an occasion, to watch these airborne troops fight. When they first come out of their gliders, with magazines blazing, to fight for their landing

Detail of picture on page 121.

zone it's more or less or a scramble, but from then on their operations are cold
– deadly methodical.

On 24 March Churchill stood on Xanten hilltop and looked down across
the morning battle mist at the place where the troops were still crossing
on boats and rafts. 'I should have liked to have deployed my men in
red coats on the plain down there and ordered them to charge.' And
he added with vim, 'But now my armies are too vast.' Alan Moorehead
watched Plunder and Varsity:

> The first airborne troops ... a wonderful sight. They passed over only two or
> three hundreds of feet above our heads, the tow planes drawing sometimes one
> and sometimes two gliders and flying in tight formation. Then single planes with
> the parachutists waiting intensely inside for the moment to plunge through the
> open hatches. Here and there among all these hundreds of aircraft one would
> be hit by ack-ack fire and it was an agonising thing to see it break formation
> and start questing vainly back and forth in search of any sort of landing field

186

and then at last plunge headlong to the ground. Within a few minutes nothing would be left but the black pillar of petrol smoke and the unidentifiable scraps of wings and propellers and human beings ... The Germans were waiting for the landing mainly because there was only one obvious place to drop in the vicinity and this was it. A heavy mist, possibly created by the enemy, covered the dropping zone. Unable to see through it at the last moment, in the face of flying shrapnel many pilots judged the ground to be either higher or lower than it was. And so many crashed into farmhouses and ditches. Others broke up in the air and others again dropped sheer to the earth from 30 or 40 feet. At the same time the falling parachutists were picked off in the air during that vital few minutes. In the end the British Airborne Division had nearly 40 percent casualties. But this was to be no second Arnhem ...

Wynford Vaughan-Thomas witnessed the linkup between 6th Airborne and the Scotsmen:

... once on the other bank you do get a feeling of being well over this last barrier before the heart of Germany. For this bridgehead isn't a mere toe-hold on the other bank; you can now drive well inland, past the riverside farms, most of them pretty smashed up by our artillery fire and all with white flags

German prisoners captured on the east bank of the Rhine.

BLA armour link up with Airborne troops. Gliders and German POWs can be seen in the background. (*Imperial War Museum*)

hanging out of the few remaining windows. And then up into the belt of woodland, where we first contacted the parachute division. The wood was full of our parachutists, digging in, and beyond the wood that fantastic coloured landscape you always get after a big airborne landing, with parachutes dangling from the trees, green parachutes, yellow parachutes, and containers scattered over the fields, gliders flung broadcast over the ploughed land. It looked as if a gigantic litter basket had been emptied over the whole countryside. And, in the middle of the litter, small groups of cowed and completely bewildered civilians were gathered at nearly every farmhouse. They were listening patiently while they were lectured by a paratrooper on how they were to behave in future. They were giving no trouble, there were no desperate guerrilla fighters in this lot, they were only too eager to obey. And they didn't even look up as the long lines of tanks and guns came through the woods to join the paratroops. For in this section our link-up with the airborne landing is no narrow corridor, it's complete and the front is united. And all the way in from the river-bank the roads are full of new troops coming up, and infantry marching through the dust, and the farmhouses being taken over as headquarters, ration dumps being set up in the fields. All the signs of the army moving in, in a big way.

Chester Wilmot wrote about the amazing 'Red Berets' at the end of Operation Varsity:

The Airborne paratroops, lacking transport, 'scrounged' everything on wheels – from prams to steam engines!

29 March 1945. They're trained for this kind of footloose fighting on a fluid front, and they thrive on it. At one point yesterday afternoon they struck quite a strong German position blocking the road, and three tanks of the Airborne Reconnaissance Regiment were soon knocked out. Undismayed, the paratroops worked round through the woods, waited for dusk, and then stormed the guns that had held them up. They captured two 75s and four light ack-ack guns and their crews.

Yesterday and last night, as they beat through the woods, they came upon half a dozen self-propelled guns. They ambushed two of them and knocked them out with anti-tank bombs. They captured four others intact, two of these with the crews still sleeping inside.

I saw some of their captured armour on the road today. They had pressed it into service and had found scratch crews from among their own paratroops. The SP guns had joined the strange convoy of airborne forces on the road eastwards today. The airborne troops are always short of transport. They can't bring much with them, and they rely on capturing vehicles from the enemy. And now the 6th Airborne has a fine assortment. As I drove along, I passed men on German bicycles, in Volkswagens, in farm-carts drawn by draught horses. One man had a smart jinker, and another was driving a German bulldozer towing a German trailer. Some of the troops were carrying their ammunition and packs in little handcarts they had found on farms, and some were even pushing their equipment in perambulators.

CHAPTER 13

Affairs of State

At the Yalta Conference, 4–10 February 1945, Stalin and Roosevelt had marginalised Churchill, as they had done previously at Tehran. One key subject was how the conquering Allies should treat the Third Reich post-war. Stalin and Roosevelt exchanged 'brutalities', wanting a very severe settlement for the post-war Germany. Churchill remembered that the Versailles Treaty at the end of the First World War had totally humiliated Germany and thus produced a political climate in which Hitler quickly and shrewdly took great advantage. This was the official statement released to the press:

> It is our inflexible purpose to destroy German militarism and Nazism and to ensure that Germany will never again be able to disturb the peace of the world. We are determined to disarm and disband all German armed forces; break up for all time the German General Staff that has repeatedly contrived the resurgence of German militarism; remove or destroy all German military equipment; eliminate or control all German industry that could be used for military production; bring all war criminals to just and swift punishment and exact reparation in kind for the destruction wrought by the Germans; wipe out the Nazi party, Nazi laws, organizations and institutions, remove all Nazi and militarist influences from public office and from the cultural and economic life of the German people; and take in harmony such other measures in Germany as may be necessary to the future peace and safety of the world. It is not our purpose to destroy the people of Germany, but only when Nazism and Militarism have been extirpated will there be hope for a decent life for Germans, and a place for them in the comity of nations.

On 1 April 1945 it was possible to feel sorry for Prime Minister Winston Churchill. At the Yalta Conference in the Crimea with Stalin, Molotov, Gromyko, President Roosevelt and assorted military and political grandees (twenty-three altogether) from the three great powers, the future of the Western world was, more or less, agreed. There were three interpreters at this historic meeting; one of them was Pavlov, which may explain what eventually happened! Churchill's speech at the Yusupov Palace included: 'We regard Marshal Stalin's life as most precious to the hopes and hearts of all of us. There have been many conquerors in history, but few of them have been statesmen and most of them threw away the fruits of victory in the troubles which followed their wars. I earnestly hope that the Marshal may be spared to the people of the Soviet Union ... I walk through this world with greater courage and hope when I find myself in a relation of friendship and intimacy with this great man whose fame has gone out not only over all Russia but the world.'

Operation Argonaut was the code name of this historic meeting, or as Churchill dubbed it, 'the Riviera of Hades'. The future of Europe, including Poland, was discussed and agreed – except that when Stalin agreed to anything it meant: 'I hear what you say and have no intention of implementing these promises.' Quite soon there were indications that 'Uncle Joe' did not mean to honour any Yalta agreements at all.

President Roosevelt was sick and ailing and died on 12 April, aged sixty-two. Churchill wrote: 'When I received these tidings ... I felt as if I had been struck a physical blow. My relations with this shining personality had played so large a part in the long terrible years we had worked together. Now they had come to an end and I was overpowered by a sense of deep and irreparable loss.' Hitler of course was delighted and hoped that Roosevelt's successor would concentrate on the war with Japan.

Then suddenly, out of the blue, General Eisenhower, without a word to the combined Chiefs of Staff, to his deputy, Air Chief Marshal Tedder, or indeed to Churchill, on 28 March sent a telegram to Marshal Stalin, which tacitly meant that the western Allies would not attempt to capture Berlin. Churchill had always advocated capture. Now Stalin readily agreed, saying that the proposal 'entirely coincides with the plan of the Soviet High Command. Berlin has lost its former strategic importance.' Stalin, of course, was lying through his teeth. It was vital to the prestige

Field Marshal Montgomery and General Eisenhower confer.

and honour of Russia to capture and probably destroy the arch enemy who had launched Barbarossa against it, had probed the defences of Moscow and inflicted millions of casualties – Berlin had to be taken. Revenge is sweet.

Churchill was irked that Eisenhower had acted so arbitrarily and unilaterally, but Ike had taken soundings from his top-ranking generals and the consensus was that the rendition of Berlin would cost at least 100,000 American casualties plus other Allied forces. Politically this would be totally unacceptable. There were no votes back at home for capturing the capital of the Third Reich. He wrote:

> Berlin, I was now certain, no longer represented a military objective of major importance. The Russian advance and the Allied bombing had largely destroyed its usefulness ... military factors when the enemy was on the brink of final defeat was more important in my eyes than the political considerations involved in an Allied capture of the capital. The function of our forces must be to crush the German armies rather than to dissipate our own strength in the occupation of empty and ruined cities.

Above and below: Montgomery's and Eisenhower's plans differ!

Churchill and Montgomery were totally wrong even to contemplate the siege and capture of Berlin. Montgomery's forces were dwindling each day; 5th Infantry Division was summoned from Italy; the Canadians imported massive reinforcements, also from Italy. It would have been lunacy for the battered British Liberation Army to lay siege to Berlin. Marshal Zhukov's huge armies had immense losses in their seizure of Berlin.

The balance of power between the Allies had been swinging powerfully away from Churchill and his British armed forces almost since D-Day. Eisenhower now had under his command an overwhelming majority of forces: over two-thirds of the fighting men on the Western Front. Churchill's influence was waning, week by week, and after five years at the helm that was a difficult situation to accept.

Churchill soon realised that Stalin did not mean to keep to the policies agreed at Yalta. Poland had had a tragic history during the war, over-run in a few weeks by Hitler's panzers in 1939/40, ten thousand Polish officers murdered at Katyn (known to Churchill through intelligence from Ultra) and now it was obvious that Stalin's Red Army would occupy the country as the Germans were driven out. It was obvious too that Stalin was in effect conquering the Balkans and almost certainly had designs on the Baltic States, including Denmark.

With President Roosevelt at death's door, April 1945 was indeed a very difficult month for Churchill, even as his legions battled their way across the Rhine.

CHAPTER 14

Over the Rhine

Max Hastings wrote in his book *Armageddon*: 'Montgomery's Rhine operation was plodding and over-insured, but those [including this author] who crossed the water would be grateful that their objectives were gained at small price. But the casualties incurred by the airborne assault were out of all proportion to its contribution. Gliders were never again employed in war. Operation Varsity was a folly for which more than a thousand men paid with their lives – almost as many as 1st Airborne lost killed at Arnhem. Once again, a baleful reality had been permitted to steer events.'

Certainly most of the American generals mocked Montgomery's ultra-careful methodical build-up for Operation Plunder. After all, Lt Karl Timmerman, with the US 27th Armoured Infantry, had brilliantly and bravely captured the bridge at Remagen and helped set up a bridgehead over the Rhine – all in a matter of hours with few casualties.

In Max Hastings' view, Varsity was a 'spectacular shambles', but he is not correct. Montgomery was a careful commander, apart from the dash towards Arnhem. All his operations had been the same: a set-piece plan involving RAF saturation bombing, a massive artillery bombardment, and then the unleashing of his infantry and armour. In many cases this was successful, in many cases it was an attritional 'draw'. The attempt at Arnhem to capture a lodgement over the Rhine was unsuccessful, with sadly heavy losses. Operation Plunder was 100 per cent successful: the Rhine was crossed easily and quite soon his 'dogs of war', 11th Armoured, Desert Rats, the Guards and Polish armour were 'swanning' through Germany.

In operations Veritable and Blockbuster, in the dreadful mire of the Reichwald and Hochwald, the German defenders were, unfortunately,

6 KOSB over the Rhine, near Bislich.

magnificent. Lt Edwin Bramall (well before he became a field marshal) wrote from the perspective of a KRRC platoon commander at the 'sharp end':

> The Reichswald was the nastiest battle we had fought since Normandy. The Germans had constructed five successive lines of defence, manned chiefly by paratroopers. Flooded ground on both flanks forced the British and Canadians to advance on a narrow front. The thick woodland was almost impenetrable to tanks. Foliage jammed [tank] turret traverses. The Shermans were unable to use their armament effectively – it was too dangerous to fire high-explosive shells lest they hit trees above their own infantry. The tanks were also highly vulnerable to 'faust' ambushes in the dense cover.

General Schlemm had fought a masterly retreat with his paratroop divisions, the *crème de la crème*, fighting every inch of the way back to Xanten and Wesel. Undoubtedly the German formations facing the British and Canadians in the north of the Siegfried Line defences were more resolute and experienced than those in the south. All the combined

A Squadron 3 RTR in Operation Plunder. (*Tank Museum*)

intelligence sources at SHAEF had been totally wrong in the autumn of 1944 in predicting the end of the war 'by Christmas' with their schoolboy cries of 'On to Berlin'. Field Marshal Montgomery could not be sure that his troops would not encounter the same expert and determined defences across the Rhine. He was taking out an insurance policy that the British Liberation Army would get across the Rhine, this time, with the minimum of casualties. His foot soldiers were now a shadow of the fine vigorous 'virgin' divisions which had landed on D-Day nine or ten months back.

The month in the Reichswald had caused considerable casualties. It had proved that the anti-tank regiment and the light anti-aircraft regiment in *every* British division, eleven of them in all, were probably not needed in Operation Eclipse. German panzers were now few and far between and the Luftwaffe was rarely seen. In the armoured divisions the anti-tank regiment was transformed into an extra armoured infantry unit and was greatly appreciated as such.

Edgar Palamountain, staff officer of 11th Armoured Division, in his history *Taurus Pursuant*, wrote a description of the aftermath of Operation Plunder:

The word 'irruption' conveys a force invading a region [the Third Reich] with speed and violence and making a deep penetration into it. Neither 'invasion' nor 'penetration' would sufficiently indicate the pace at which this process was carried out. 'Breakthrough' supplies this deficiency; but 'breakthrough' has come to mean a violent penetration of a defensive position followed by a period of plain sailing which is, strictly speaking, the exploitation of the breakthrough, and this interpretation had been strengthened by certain well-remembered aspects of the campaign in France. In this sense the advance inside Germany was certainly not a breakthrough, for its momentum was interrupted not merely by obstacles and demolitions, but by enemy forces ready to fight hard battles in defence of the positions which they occupied. If there is any other phase of the total campaign which the advance in Germany may be said to resemble, this is probably the offensive through the bocage from Caumont to Laigle [Operation Bluecoat]. There are, however, certain obvious differences, the chief of which is that the Germans were now operating so far inside their own country that the execution of planned withdrawals must have seemed to them somewhat of a mockery. When you are fighting on your own soil you must sooner or later reach a stage where every retreat is a defeat.

Royal Scots Fusiliers move through woods over the Rhine under shellfire.

To describe the condition to which the German armies and the German State were now being reduced by the various invasions, the word 'disruption' could be used. But its employment would remove the spotlight from the division whose story this is and focus it rather on the enemy in his disintegration. Or, alternatively, it might suggest that that disintegration was a direct result of the activities of 11th Armoured; and this would be presumption indeed. Germany lay pierced by many wounds; only one of these was a cornada, a gash inflicted by the horn of the bull. [The black bull was the 11th Armoured insignia]

Montgomery and Dempsey carefully planned the continuation of Operation Plunder into the heart of Germany. The US 9th Army, under Monty's command, on the right, southern flank, then 8th, 12th, 30th Corps, and in the north the 2nd Canadian Corps. All would be led by an armoured division plus the British 4th (Black Rat), 8th (Red Fox's mask) and 6th Guards independent armoured brigades. The river Ems and the Dortmund-Ems Canal were the next hurdles to be encountered.

Lt General Horrocks wrote about his 'Corps de Chasse', armoured divisions available to him in 30th Corps:

The two operated quite differently. The 11th Armoured was the more flexible of the two. Pip Roberts, one of the most experienced tank commanders in the Army would switch his troops rapidly, attacking with tanks only, tanks and infantry, or infantry supported by tanks according to the situation. The Guards on the other hand always worked in regimental groups, Coldstream tanks and Coldstream infantry, Grenadier infantry and Grenadier tanks, etc. The system was not calculated to get the full value from the mobility of an armoured division, but it ensured the closest possible co-operation between the two arms, as the infantry and tank crews all came from the same regiment and had more or less grown up together. Nevertheless I preferred the standard armoured divisional practice of the 11th Armoured Division. Fortunately by now I had gained sufficient battle experience not to interfere with the way a divisional commander handled his command.

In Market Garden the Guards were ponderous, took their time and were not flexible enough, which contributed to the lack of success of the operation. Now in the wide open spaces of Westphalia the Guards did well against their old enemies, 15th Panzergrenadier Division and the 1st Parachute Army. Operation Plunder set off the extraordinary armoured plunge into the very guts of the Third Reich, which was dying and doomed. Everybody in the world knew it: Russians, Americans, British, Canadians, French and Polish formations knew it – everybody except the Austrian corporal in his Berlin bunker. Many of his legions, certainly the SS, the skilled parachute divisions and the renegade SS [Dutch, Vikings from Scandinavia and the East/Ost] were prepared to fight until the last possible moment. The horrors of death came suddenly to the advancing Allies in Operation Eclipse, in many ways. The Hitler Jugend and indeed the young schoolboys equipped with panzerfaust could and did destroy gleaming new British Comet tanks. The unemployed marine divisions buried immense 500-pound sea mines around Bremen and Bremenhaven, which disintegrated lead formations. What lay ahead of the British Liberation Army in their corridor – about 100 miles wide and 250 miles in length on the way to the Baltic – was of course not known. But the astonishing fight back by the Führer's forces in Market Garden, the Ardennes, and operations Blackcock, Veritable and Blockbuster surely could not continue – or could it? Five more river barriers and the two great cities of Bremen and Hamburg lay ahead.

Were there more secret weapons ahead – maybe vengeance weapons, perhaps gas, or chemical, even atomic (although that concept was not known outside the 'Tube Alloys' cognoscenti at the time)? 'Over the Rhine' was an extraordinary, daunting prospect. 'Bomber' Harris had destroyed every major city and town in Germany, but in Normandy, Holland and in the western Rhineland, demolished towns were defended tooth and nail by German kampfgruppen. Would that continue inside the Third Reich?

Street fighting was hated and smashed towns and villages favoured the defenders. Among houses, tactical radios, usually unreliable 19- and 21-sets, all ceased to function. Tanks were vulnerable to petrol bombs, grenades, and especially to the cheap one-shot panzerfausts. 'Clearing a town is an arduous process which cannot be hurried,' was a British briefing dogma.

So the leading reconnaissance units – the Cherry Pickers, the Inns of Court, the Household Cavalry and others – would encounter a small village, perhaps with obstacles and felled trees blocking the road. The roadside verges might be mined. The lead vehicle and its crew were always at risk and with the war inevitably, slowly, coming to an end, the easiest military tactic was to put an artillery stonk into that hapless village, just in case. And that happened frequently.

On 30 March, Stadtlohn, north-east of Wesel had been heavily bombed by the RAF. The Royal Engineers built this Bailey bridge over the river.

Another alternative was to introduce a Crocodile troop if the village was known to be held by the enemy. Lt Andrew Wilson commanded one of these terrible Churchill flame-thrower troops of the Buffs and wrote in his book *Flamethrower*:

He looked for places where the enemy might still be hiding. There was a wooden shed. As the flame hit it, the wood blew away in a burning mass, and there in the wreckage was the body of a Spandau [highly effective machine gun] ... The [tank] gunner gripped his trigger. Swinging the turret down the front of the burning village, he began firing off the 75 [tank gun] at point-blank range. Where, oh where was the [supporting] infantry? As always in action he lost count of time. Wherever he swung the cupola, he saw fire and smoke and the track of destruction. Then all at once it was over. By the barn a little group of grey-clad Germans appeared without helmets or weapons, waving a sheet or a pole. He gave the order to stop firing and opened the hatches. The air was full of smuts and the sickly-sweet smell of fuel. Eventually there were 30 or 40. They moved slowly. In the hush of the moment, he felt a great elation; if ordered he could have driven through the smoking village right on to the enemy's divisional HQ. Nothing could have stopped him. He couldn't be harmed. Then the infantry came swarming into the village, dodging the mortar shells which the enemy had started dropping down. In the confusion the Germans began to bring out their wounded, blinded and burned, roughly bandaged beneath their charred uniforms. Some of them looked at the Crocodile. What were they thinking? He went back to refuel.

CHAPTER 15

Battle for the Teutoburger Wald

Hitler had decided to replace the veteran Field Marshal von Rundstedt, and selected Field Marshal Albert Kesselring to defend the right bank of the river Rhine against Eisenhower's huge armies of nearly four million men. Kesselring had performed defensive miracles on the Italian front behind the Hitler and Gothic Lines. He was a stubborn and resolute man with a blunt jaw and stocky figure and Hitler expected miracles from him. General Günther Blumentritt took over command of the 1st Parachute Army on 27 March as General Schlemm had been wounded during Operation Blockbuster. Blumentritt wrote:

> I reported to Colonel General Blaskowitz at Army Group H and he and his Chief-of-Staff both agreed that once the Rhine had been crossed the situation, with the forces at our disposal, was past repair. But since orders from above were to continue resisting I was to do the best that I could. When I took over my new command on 28 March I found that there were great gaps in my front, that I had no reserves, that my artillery was weak, that I had no air support whatever and hardly any tanks. My communication and signal facilities were entirely inadequate and there was one corps under my command that I was never able to contact. The reinforcements that still came to me were hastily trained and badly equipped, and I never used them so that I could save needless casualties.
>
> Nevertheless orders from the Supreme Command were still couched in the most rigorous terms, enjoining us to 'hold' and 'fight' under threats of court-martial. But I no longer insisted on these orders being carried out. It was a nerve-racking time we experienced – outwardly putting a bold face on the matter in order to do one's duty as one had sworn to do – while we secretly

allowed things to go their own way. On my own responsibility I gave orders for lines to be prepared in the rear ready for a retreat. By 1 April I had decided to direct the fighting in such a way that the army could be withdrawn in a more or less orderly manner and without suffering any great casualties, first on both sides of Munster and then behind the Ems Canal and finally to the Teutoburger Forest.

Blumentritt had nine or ten divisions lining the river north of the Ruhr, which in the first week of Operation Plunder had suffered over 30,000 casualties, mostly men taken prisoner.

Surging out of the Wesel-Rees bridgehead, Montgomery's Army Group, including Canadians and Americans, was tasked with striking north-east towards Bremen, Hamburg and the river Elbe, a distance of about 200 miles. On arrival, Kiel was a prime target 100 miles north of Hamburg, and the Danish frontier, 50 miles north of Kiel. Initially Horrocks' 30th Corps and Ritchie's 12th Corps would link up with 6th Airborne and expand and widen the bridgehead for General Barker's 8th Corps.

By the end of March the British Liberation Army was almost in a line abreast. In the far north 49th Polar Bears, with the Canadians, were battling into Holland east of the Grebbe defence line. Two Canadian divisions would form the northern flank of Operation Plunder, then 3rd British, 51st Highland and 43rd Wessex Wyverns, led by the Guards Armoured. Further south the 7th Desert Rats armoured would lead 52nd Lowland, 15th Scottish and 53rd Welsh. The *schwerpunkt* striking force south would be 11th Armoured, occasionally 15th Scottish, with 1st Commando Brigade, who had done so well in Blackcock, with 45th Marine Commando and, of course, 6th Airborne, who had 6th Guards Independent Brigade of Churchill tanks under command.

The whole British Army, apart from the Polar Bears, was involved in Operation Plunder.

After the Rhine crossing the commando units were seasoned water-barrier crossers. In front of 8th Corps were the river Ems, the Dortmund-Ems Canal, river Weser, river Leine, river Aller and finally, the great river Elbe. All of these were ideal defensive barriers.

The 11th Armoured Division soon realised that one of the main weapons of destruction for their new and shiny Comet tanks was the cheap little throw-away, hollow-charge panzerfaust. In bazooka country

Convoy of 'soft' vehicles move into Germany behind the armoured division..

The Teutoburger Wald. Since the time that Caesar's Legions were defeated here, this has proved a superb 30-mile wooded defensive position. 11th Armoured made the first attack on 1 April. The Author's halftrack .50MG was used to shoot down a Focke-Wulf plane!

it was necessary always to carry infantry with the leading squadron of tanks. Unfortunately the shiny new Comets all needed modifications to their driving sprockets and the necessary parts were *eventually* flown out from England a few hours before the tanks were loaded on transporters. By the morning of the 29th, the 'Black Bull' formation was assembled in Wesel and was directed initially on Holtwick, 17 miles north-east, which was captured by 3rd RTR, then Horstmar. All the minor roads were diabolical and continued to be so for the next four weeks; twenty tanks were bogged down in thick mud. On the left, northern flank, the roads were so bad that 7th Armoured were unable to move for two days. The small town of Burgsteinfurt was captured by 4th KSLI on the night of 30 March, the first of many successful night actions by the division. The bridge at Emsdetten, predictably, had been destroyed, but 3rd RTR found a good bridging site at Mesum, 5 miles north.

Between villages, the armour 'brassed' up every wood and bit of cover with Besa machine-gun fire. In Schoppingen, Holtwich and Gessen bazooka parties damaged half a dozen tanks. Fortunately the Comet armour was far tougher than that of a Sherman.

Some 12 miles west of the large town of Osnabruck runs a long strip of denser woodland, two to three miles in width, some 30 miles long,

Ibbenbüren. The Teutoburger Wald ridge was stubbornly defended.

an escarpment with three key villages – Ibbenbüren, Holthausen and Tecklenberg. At its north end it is less than a mile from the canal, and at its south end 10 or 12 miles away.

The journalist and author, Chester Wilmot, described the initial battle:

2 April 1945. Last Saturday evening, just at dusk, tanks of the 3rd Royal Tank Regiment reached the Dortmund-Ems canal, the line on which the Germans were expected to make their next stand. Our tanks had orders to seize a bridge, but as they got within striking range of the canal half a dozen white Verylights shot up into the sky. On this signal German engineers somewhere on the far bank pressed the switches that led to the high explosive charges in half a dozen bridges; and up the bridges went. But our orders were that if the tanks couldn't get a bridge, the infantry of the King's Shropshire Light Infantry (KSLI), who were following close behind, were to get across the canal as best they could and hold a bridgehead on the far side.

They had no storm boats and the canal at high water is 40 yards wide. But when they reached it well after dark they found that the RAF had prepared the way for them; because our bombing had breached the banks farther up, the water-level was only three feet instead of the 20 they'd expected. At one point they found a huge barge was aground, and what's more had swung round so that it lay across the canal forming almost a ready-made footbridge.

Along this barge the KSLI scrambled across. But they hadn't gone far beyond the bank when they ran into some difficult customers – some young Germans who'd just been sent up from an NCOs' training school in Hanover, where they'd been training to become sergeant-majors and warrant officers. Our troops soon found that these young Germans were as tough as sergeant-majors in any army are usually reputed to be.

The Germans moreover had an ideal defensive position. The canal here runs under the lee of a thickly wooded ridge that rises sharply and dominated the whole area. This ridge is part of the famous Teutoburger Wald where the Germans in the past have stopped so many invaders, including Charlemagne. Our infantry soon found they couldn't get on and might even be in danger of being forced back if they couldn't get some heavy weapons across the bridgeless canal that night. The Engineers came to the rescue. Near the barge, where the water was shallow, the canal runs between two high embankments. With an armoured bulldozer, the Engineers pushed these embankments into the bed of the canal, and within a few hours that night they had the tanks across.

Teutoburger Wald – April 2nd, 1945. 2 FF Yeo supporting 3 Mons 11th Armoured Division.

The tanks also towed over some guns, and with this double support the KSLI were able to hold the enemy off all yesterday, while Engineers built a bridge over the canal behind them. This was no easy task, for the bridgehead was under fire and it even drew on itself an attack from the Luftwaffe. The bridge was nearly finished when some German fighter-bombers came over, and they put one bomb less than 20 yards from the bridge where the Engineers were still working; but the bomb stuck in the mud.

With this bridge in action we soon had more troops and tanks across, but the German NCOs on the timbered ridge couldn't be shifted easily. Last night and today infantry of the 11th Armoured Division have been beating through these woods, having almost to drive the Germans from tree to tree; and while the NCOs held out here, some of our reconnaissance tanks [15/19th Hussars] got through along the main road. There they forced a passage up a narrow defile that was defended by a second-rate reinforcement battalion. By getting round this way, they reached the top of the ridge, swung round behind the German NCO battalion, and when I left the front this afternoon its defence was cracking under this sandwich attack.

Meantime, having opened up the road up the escarpment, the 11th Armoured Division was pushing on, rolling up the defence of the bridge by attacks on the flank. At one town they reported they were having some trouble with civilians. Presumably the SS police had been sent into this town also to make the people fight. But now, having broken out on to the plateau behind the Teutoburger Wald, the 11th Armoured is barely 12 miles from Osnabrück. Today's battle yielded them even more than that. Hidden on that wooded ridge they found one of Germany's great secret oil refineries. The loss of this refinery at this stage of the war is probably almost as serious for the Germans as the loss of the Dortmund-Ems Canal.

Chester Wilmot was an optimist. The gallant 3rd Monmouths who had done so well in Normandy were torn apart in the woods, although they acquitted themselves well and in the hand-to-hand fighting Corporal E. T. Chapman won the Victoria Cross. They captured 100 cadets and inflicted many other casualties, but by mid-morning on 4 April they had had forty-one killed and eighty wounded; three consecutive commanding officers had been killed in action. Their C Company had had six consecutive commanding officers killed in action since D-Day, and they had lost 242 killed in action, including twenty-five out of sixty-seven officers; their overall casualties were over a thousand. General Pip Roberts had to withdraw them and the survivors went back to Wesel to guard the bridges.

Desert Rats tanks in Ahaus, probably 1 RTR Shermans. (*Imperial War Museum*)

The north-west sector of the Teutoburger Wald was officially within the 7th Armoured Division sector. The Desert Rats had crossed the Rhine on 27 March, led by the Cherry Pickers, the most experienced of the armoured car reconnaissance regiments in the British Army. They met the 6th Airborne at Hamminkeln. The enemy ahead had been identified as two battalions of 857th Grenadier Regiment and 33rd Panzergrenadier Ersatz Battalion, with infantry, dozens of Czech-made SP assault guns, 88mm anti-tank guns and many panzerfaust teams. The Desert Rats' line of advance was to be towards Bremen via Borken, Stadtlohn, Ahaus and Rheine. They followed the 'Yellow' route to Raesfeld, took Heiden, and encountered bazooka teams in Ramsdorf. Night attacks followed to clear Ahaus, Heek and Nienburg. Major Tom Craig, 1st RTR, wrote: 'We had infantry in APCs and 5th RHA in close support, "artificial moonlight" to light our way, and covered ten miles before dawn. It wasn't plain sailing with opposition from SPs and the inevitable hand-held panzerfaust anti-tank weapons. We sadly lost two tanks.' Major Freddy Pile, 1st RTR, noted:

As the advance started we normally moved down roads or tracks for speed. One troop (a different one each day as it was demanding and dangerous) would be ordered to lead the squadron. Squadron HQ came next and the four

Close support tanks of 15/19th KRH giving infantry support with their 95mm Howitzers, in the Teutoburgerwald battle, April 1945.

A Challenger, slave carrier and Cromwell of 15/19th KRH on the Teutoburger Wald,
April 1945.

other (reserve) troops behind. Nearly always we made some contact, perhaps
some infantry in personnel carriers with a few motor cycles, possibly two or
three tanks or SP guns. With their superior guns they could inflict enormous
damage on our Cromwell tanks if these were caught in the open ... We were
required to keep going at all costs and enemy resistance had to be overcome
without much delay or there would be sharp criticism on the radio from our
Brigade HQ, even with heavy losses the instruction from above was always
'Sorry, you must press on regardless'. The phrase 'pocket of resistance' is
rather a misnomer: it was usually a small but very well-armed mixed group
of tanks, guns and infantry, usually sited on a main approach road, or in a
wood or village, difficult for us to circumvent. Because we often ran into them
without much warning we had casualties quite out of proportion to the size or
importance of many of these actions. As we approached towns or villages we
often used incendiary machine-gun ammunition to set fire to the houses in the
path of our intended advance. This, of course, did cause much damage.

During the night of 30 March Ahaus was entered – a dangerous wrecked
town with many bomb craters, mines and booby traps. On 1 April,
Rheine was reached after 20 miles of a real 'swan'. However, the Desert
Rats encountered Panzerjagd Kommandos, groups of selected officers
and men who stayed behind to act and behave as dangerous 'werewolves'.
On the 2nd the Desert Rats crossed the river Ems at Rheine and joined
in the attritional battle of the Teutoburger Wald. By then 7th Armoured
had advanced 120 miles, almost continuously opposed. 11th Armoured

had left behind a battlegroup to hold the bridgehead over the canal. On the 3rd the Desert Rats infantry, 9th DLI and 2nd Devons supported by 5th 'Skins' Dragoon Guards began a grim battle against the fanatical officer cadets defending Ibbenbüren. It failed. On the 4th again it failed. The 1945 official divisional report says: 'The battle continued until dusk with deadly enemy sniping and fanatical resistance from well-concealed positions. Tanks who spotted the enemy in houses burnt them down immediately – but the enemy remained in the blazing ruins firing to the last, before themselves being burnt in the holocaust.' The Desert Rats were ordered to resume their advance.

Some of the SS cadets escaped from Ibbenbüren and specialised in ambushing HQ and B echelon vehicles. They killed Captain Cordy-Simpson, 1st RTR, in the forest of Langeloh. A few days later his friend and commanding officer, Major Tom Craig, wrote: 'We had a lucky stroke of revenge shortly after John was killed. North of Soltau near the village of Jarlingen, I was right behind my leading troop, was astonished to see marching across a T-junction about 300 yards away, a group of about 40 SS cadets marching towards the village towing eight carts laden (we discovered later) with panzerfausts and ammunition.' Major Craig sent a troop of his Cromwells to the left to stop the cadets escaping back to the village, brought up his HQ squadron troop into line. They all opened fire with HE and BESA. 'It was quickly over. There were no SS survivors.'

The 52nd Lowland Scots Division, the Mountain and Flood Division – blooded in Walcheren, matured in Blackcock and Veritable – had moved steadily out of the Wesel bridgehead and headed for the town of Rheine, 25 miles due west of Osnabruck. It is a most unlikely story! Their RAOC unit had a bath unit: a monstrously heavy truck with portable water tanks, furnaces and perforated pipes, which rapidly assembled would give the battle-weary PBI a hot spray/shower/bath. The sergeant in charge managed, by driving down devious side roads – lost perhaps – to enter Rheine without opposition. They found a railway bridge spanning a main street, stopped, set up shop, got the water hot, even boiling, and the fires were burning nicely, ready to provide hot showers. Rheine, of course, had not been captured. An astonished platoon of Lowlanders advanced ready for street fighting and were invited to have a hot shower before finishing their attack and capturing the town! A substantial battle followed, helped by 4th Armoured Brigade and the town was taken by midnight on 2 April.

On 1 April the Lowland recce found the bridges blown along the river Ems, and identified their German opponents as the 60th Panzergrenadiers, the 1st Battalion Grossdeutschland Regiment, plus NCO candidates from the Hanover training establishment. Major General Hakewell-Smith now had to force a crossing of the Dortmund-Ems Canal, where all three bridges were down. The canal had high steep banks. It was an area of poorish farmland, ditches, wire fences, winding streams, hedges, farm tracks, thick copses and spinneys, small farm houses, crofts and, above all, a sodden countryside difficult for tanks and carriers. On 4 April 7th Cameronians forced a canal crossing and 5th Highland Light Infantry widened and extended it. Their objective was Dreirwalde, three miles east. Hungarian SS troops lost 400 men in its defence, mainly to the Glasgow Highlanders.

The next objective was a night attack by the RSF and 6th Cameronians on Hopstein. George Blake, the divisional historian, who was there, described:

> ... the eerie journey of exquisitely cautious movement, of likely surprises from the many streams, crawling in the darkness. At dawn a good old-fashioned infantry charge with fixed bayonets, 'the blood of the Covenanters was up' as they killed or wounded all the defenders. Eight miles south of Hopstein was the Teutoburger Wald ... the finest defensive position, two long heavily wooded ridges – the most notable feature of the expanse of the flat lands of North Germany. Local quarries provide a fine yellow sandstone. Solid houses built of this material please the eye, with relief from the monotonous red brick of a thousand red brick hamlets. Between is the rather dull Westphalian Plain. Ibbenbüren lies cosily between the two spurs of the main ridge, a comic, contorted little place in the Walt Disney tradition ... looking amiably towards the fields that slope down from the western spur.

Brigadier McLaren's 155th Brigade was left to deal with the town, which has a tortuous defile a mile to the west similar to a Bournemouth or Sandown chine. 7/9th Royal Scots and 6th Highland Infantry attacked on 4 April from a cement factory and quarry. By nightfall the wooded ridge was secured. One 6th HLI platoon commander said: 'This is one hell of a place. We have been driven off here [like the 3rd Monmouths two days earlier] once already. We've been counter-attacked all night. Good luck and goodbye.' Indeed 7/9th Royal Scots, 6th HLI and finally

212

'Flying Dustbin' Spigot mortar bomb fired by an AVRE to demolish a road block in Bocholt, 29 March 1945. (*Brian Haward*)

4th KOSB all took casualties before the town was cleared for 53rd Welsh Division to pass through and mop up.

The 53rd Welsh Division had had a very bad week in Blockbuster trying to capture Weeze in their local operations Leek and Daffodil. They crossed the Rhine on 26 March opposite Vynen, then crossed the river Ijssel just west of Ringenberg, Dingden and had a battle to capture Bocholt, an important road centre with many narrow streets, road blocks and minefields. They were helped by 4th Black Rat Armoured Brigade and by the AVRE bombards on the Churchill tanks of 82nd Assault Squadron RE. The 4th RWF mounted in Kangaroos fought four successful actions on the Hohe Heide overlooking the town. Eventually 1st HLI cleared the final opposition in the northern factory area during the night of 30/31 March. It was a curious route for the Welshmen along the German-Dutch border; in Winterswijk and Bredevoort in Holland there was a great patriotic welcome with flags, bunting, cheers, smiles and happiness. In Vreden, Rhede, Stadtlohn and Alstatte, the inhabitants were sullen and dispirited in their smashed German villages. Next came Gronau with the first of many large hospitals containing 700 German wounded soldiers. Then the Rheine aerodrome was cleared by 2nd

Monmouths. By 5 April the division was established on the line Gronau – Ochtrup – Saltzbergen and their new role was to put two brigades to mop up the Ibbenburen area. In the four weeks up to 7 March the 53rd Welsh had 3,700 casualties, of whom 20 per cent had 'battle stress'. Supported by 7th RTR Crocodiles, 71st and 158th Brigades mopped up the town and area. The RAF had bombed and medium and heavy artillery bombarded the cadet companies and still they hung on defiantly.

Desmond Milligan's Oxfordshire and Bucks carrier group helped clear Ibbenbüren town for the final time:

> We made a house-to-house search through this now battered little town, constantly dodging the shells lobbed into the area by artillery supporting the cadets. About eight enormous very tall trees had blocked the road and stopped the tanks the previous night. An armoured bulldozer came up to move them and our carriers were given the job of protection. Two German officers carrying a white flag appeared. Lt Hawley led two of us to take possession of a hospital full of Allied wounded [11th Armoured, 7th Armoured and 52nd Lowland]. A ragged cheer went up – the wounded lay and sat everywhere so heavily bandaged you could hardly see them.

On 7 April Lt Colonel Burden, CO the East Lancs, wrote: 'Only 21 PW taken. The Nazi cadets seemed to prefer death to capture, exposing themselves to the full blast of MGs or flame jets from the crocodiles, as they chanted Nazi slogans to the last, obstinately determined to die for Adolf Hitler. The party propaganda worked on impressionable young minds.'

The battle of Ibbenbüren and the Teutoburger Wald had taken a week of incessant close-quarter fighting. Four of Montgomery's finest divisions had taken it in turns and had suffered in the process. The armour of course were tasked to get *through* the Teutoburger Wald and to continue to smash their way to Bremen and Hamburg.

CHAPTER 16

T-Force: 'Thieving Magpies'

The British Army is usually composed of regular regiments with soldiers making a military career. In the First and Second World Wars the vast majority of formations were intended to be active only for the duration of the war. But there were also a number of 'irregulars'. The classic was 'Popski's Private Army', but also there were Phantom, the secret radio sections, and 30th Assault Regiment, which specialised in retrieving secret naval information and technology from captured enemy ports and harbours – and then there was British Target Force.

The western Allied leaders knew that the Third Reich was developing many forms of technical warfare – particularly in rocketry, jet aircraft, deadly new gases, highspeed submarines, infra-red gun sights, radar systems and possibly nuclear weapons, and other, totally new deadly concepts. In July 1944, General Eisenhower issued a secret order from SHAEF to raise a 'Target-Force'. Lt General W. B. Smith, on 27 July, ordered senior commanders to raise a secret force to secure vital intelligence and scientific targets, not only the weaponry but if possible to capture their designers too. So T-Forces, American, British and Canadian, came into being, that would operate *independently* from the regular armed forces. Serious planning started in August. In the National Archives at PRO Kew, document WO/219/818 has the original brief: 'T-Force = Target Force, to guard and secure documents, persons, equipment with combat and intelligence personnel, after capture of large towns, ports in liberated and enemy territory.'

Commander Ian Fleming RN, later to be famous as the author of the James Bond books, had developed an Intelligence Assault Unit (IAU) that was described in ADM 223/500 as 'a force of armed and expert authorised looters', and was renamed 30th Assault Unit. It served in North Africa, Sicily and Italy with impressive results including uncovering German Enigma code machines. 30th AU also did yeoman work in France and in Belgium, discovering 12,000 important intelligence documents.

Germany would be the target area designated for T-Force activities, and Brigadier G. H. C. Pennycock, head of the Chemical Warfare Group whose staff was seriously underemployed, had the resources to be the nucleus for the new T-Force. His second in command was Lt Colonel R. Bloomfield, and FO 1031/49 contains their secret tasks. The first troops allocated were six companies of Pioneers, whose main task in operations Veritable and Plunder was to create smokescreens. They had forty-nine trucks and trailers. The first infantry formation to join was 5th Kings Regiment, a D-Day 'Beach Group' unit under Lt Colonel B. D. Wreford-Brown. It was deployed to Antwerp in February 1945 as a mobile reserve, and in March took part in the Dunkirk 'blocking' operation. The next unit to join was 1st Buckinghamshire Battalion of the Ox and Bucks Light Infantry, and then came No. 19 Bomb Disposal Section RE, plus many interpreters speaking English, Dutch, German and some Russian. T-Force then mustered itself in Venlo, a large Dutch town on the river Maas. Finally in March the 400-strong 30th AU joined and the combined unit moved to a huge steelworks in Krefeld, east a few miles into Germany. Scientists joined this curious group. Sean Longden, in his evocative book *T-Force* noted the composition of the 'authorised looters': 'A strange mixture of D-Day veterans, teen-age "virgin" soldiers, ex-Royal Marines, former gunners, soldiers returned straight from hospital and shell-shock cases, but they were to embark on a journey that would have enormous repercussions for the postwar future of the whole western world.'

An immense amount of work had been done by a recently formed intelligence section of the Buckinghamshires. Map boards pinpointed which targets would be acquired and checked once across the Rhine. There were three key categories: factories and plants manufacturing military equipment; government and military HQ buildings and staff; military R & D buildings. The capture of key personnel was paramount and of course the preservation of the enemy facilities, and the latter possibility of sabotage or booby traps.

At long last T-Force, plus 150 target investigators, followed the armoured columns swarming over the Rhine and in two days, led by the

Officers of 5th Battalion the Kings Regiment (T-Force) May 1945. Lt Colonel Guy Wreford-Brown, the CO, is fifth from right on the front row.

Kings troops, were on their way into the Third Reich. Splintered into small groups, they were controlled by GSO2 at Army HQ. Targets were made from town plans and maps and aerial photographs. In Osnabrück, the Kupfer und Drahtwerke factory yielded new metallurgical processes for submarine parts. In Hengelo, Holland, they found new types of anti-aircraft predictors. In Rheine they found a vital main telephone exchange and the Takke Fabrichen plant, making U-boat gearboxes, and a huge stockpile of ball-bearings. In Cologne in the US zone, a factory was captured, which produced equipment for guided rocket systems and jet- and rocket-propelled aircraft.

Field Marshal Montgomery's Chief of Staff, Major General de Guingand, issued an official pass or *laisser passer* to ensure that T-Force personnel were not only allowed free, unimpeded access to these targets, but also were permitted to secure and defend the targets. In the event, one of the key problems was the tens of thousands of displaced persons of all races who, once freed from captivity, wrecked and looted anything that took their fancy. Unfortunately, in the American sector, T-Force were often treated with deep suspicion, as an illegal private army seeking profitable 'loot'.

The military area of Wehrkreis in Hannover, and the huge Hanomag truck factory producing radar equipment using sintered iron instead of copper, was inspected. The Maschinen Fabrik disgorged infra-red technology and Professor Hase, a distinguished physicist. Doctor Max Kramer produced secret X4 and X7 rocketry of great interest. The Continental Gummiwerke specialised in synthetic rubber. Often the T-Force investigators were the first

Above: A jeep of B troop, 30 AU, Royal Marines at Minden, Germany, May 1945.

Left: T-Force Royal Navy investigator John Bradley (left) with Commander Dunstan Curtis of 30 AU. Bradley was a metallurgist.

T-Force evacuating equipment from a factory in Köln (Cologne), March 1945.

to enter towns such as Delmenhorst and Bomlitz before the regulars turned up. In Bomlitz, a Focke-Wulf aircraft factory and a helicopter factory were captured. So it went on: diesel submarine engines in Twistringen; radar assemblies in Nienburg; a natural gas field in Bentheim; marine mines to be fired by U-boats in Starkshorn; a Krupps test area in Meppen; a Blohm and Voss aircraft factory in Wensendorf; a huge underground factory with two miles of Focke-Wulf aircraft parts in Celle near Belsen.

Major Brian Urquhart, the discredited Intelligence Officer in Market Garden, had joined T-Force. He was responsible in late April for capturing professors Groth, Suhr and Faltings, distinguished scientists working on the isolation of isotopes of uranium for nuclear purposes. They and their crated-up laboratory were flown back to the UK under guard. And almost by mistake Professor Otto Hahn, the distinguished physicist at the Technische Hochschule in Hannover, and the chief scientist for atomic research in Germany, joined the others in a benevolent captivity. Rather unpleasant chemical weapons were discovered at Hunstadt, Frankenberg, Rehden and Espelkamp. These unknown gases and filled shells were sent, very carefully, to Porton Down research facility. Their staff flew out to Munsterlager, the major gas munitions centre in Germany, for chemical warfare. At Bassum near Bremen, naval fire-control apparatus and torpedo predictors were discovered dispersed in barns, farms and houses.

'The Thieving Magpies', as they were rudely but accurately described, will turn up again in this book.

CHAPTER 17

Bergen-Belsen
Concentration Camp

Major General Pip Roberts, GOC 11th Armoured, after leaving the terrible Ibbenbüren battlefields to be cleared by the follow-up infantry divisions, wrote:

> Our next obstacle was the Osnabrück canal and the bridge over it at Eversheide, north of Osnabrück. The clearing of Osnabrück [a significant town] was the task of 6th Airborne Division who were keeping abreast of us, almost impudently as it seemed to us, for apart from their own recce regiment they had only a Churchill tank regiment from 6th Guards Tank Brigade, excellent machines but far outpaced by our [brilliant, shiny, new] Comets. Yet every day they inched up on our right and even now as we were moving to cut off Osnabrück from the north, their leading troops were within a few miles of its southern perimeter. Obviously we must do another night 'march' as we had done at Amiens with 3rd Royal Tanks in the lead. But the way was not easy. The Germans resisted by night as they had by day and several defended road blocks had to be cleared before the canal could be reached.

Actually 6th Airborne had had a two-day head start in Operations Plunder and Varsity and they had not received a bloody nose by the Hannover cadets in the Teutoburger Wald. The two bridges at Eversheide were seized intact and the race was on!

Wynford Vaughan-Thomas reported on the right flank advance:

> 7 April 1945. Our 11th Armoured Division, with the 6th Airborne on its southern flank, has raced down the main roads from Osnabrück towards the river Weser. As they went they threw out little parties to form roadblocks on

Crusader Comet tank at Neustadt on the way to Bergen-Belsen. (*Tank Museum*)

the side roads to the north and south of them, just in case any stray Germans should come in on the flank. And the airborne boys travel in the most varied collection of transport I've yet seen, in fact they can't call themselves airborne any longer, they're either lorry-borne or tank-borne, motor-bike-borne, even cart-borne infantry. The Germans have little before us now to stop our racing columns. They rushed some units up, but their trouble is that they're at least 24 hours behind in their information. One of our columns bumped into a regiment that had come down from Denmark. Apparently these Germans were on their way to defend Osnabrück, oblivious of the fact that it had already fallen days before. We caught one battalion of it just as it was moving into billets in a small village. Well, those Germans are now billeted in our prison cages.

But speed brings with it its own problems. Apart from that ever-present nightmare of supply, how to get the petrol and the food up to our leading tanks, there are one or two other headaches for our Army. There's the problem of the prisoners, for example. What on earth are you to do with these thousands upon thousands of shabbily uniformed, middle-aged, and undersized warriors that are all the High Command has got left with which to try and stop our armies. For now we really are coming to the bottom of the bag. The German manpower is exhausted. But here are the survivors of warfare, cluttering up the roads and offering to give themselves up to the first person who will have

221

them. It's difficult for an armoured division to begin to cope with them. Our tanks have got to get on and our lorries are wanted to bring up supplies. The only thing to do with the prisoners is to disarm them and send them off to the rear. And with an advance as fast as ours the rear may be 60 miles away. These are just the ordinary spectacles – miles behind the line, long columns of prisoners, sometimes led by their officers, quietly tramping along in the middle of our back areas. And with nobody paying the slightest attention to them. And with none of them making the slightest effort to escape.

Most divisions had increased their mobility and manpower by making alternative use of their surplus artillery formations. 11th Armoured called theirs 'Todforce' as the CO of their anti-tank regiment, Lt Colonel A. F. Tod, redeployed his unit as two squadrons of 17-pdr 'tanks' and two companies of mobile infantry, whose towed anti-tank guns were put into store.

The next difficult river barrier was the Weser. On the way Stolzenau and Schlusselburg were captured, but both bridges, predictably, were blown. The bridging operations were rudely interrupted by a rare Luftwaffe air attack by Junkers 88s and Messerschmitt 109s. They were seen off by Tempests and Typhoons, but the Training (Ersatz) Battalion of 12th SS Panzer Division and 100th Pioneer Brigade put up strong resistance. A sergeant of the 12th SS described the battle for Stolzenau:

I was a sergeant instructor in the battalion. My own service had been with the Leibstandarte in Russia. Usual decorations, Iron Cross, Infantry Assault, Close Combat, wound badge in silver. I lined my platoon along the railway embankment. This stands about 20 feet above the ground between the river Weser and the village of Leese. The first British probes were easily repulsed – our field of fire was excellent. We could see every movement that the Tommies made. I had my mortars behind the railway embankment with the Reserve sections and three, tripod-mounted MG 42s firing on fixed lines. The battalion had ammunition enough. We had been ordered to hold to the last. We did not know it then but there was a V-2 assembly plant about two kilometres behind the railway line, just north of Leese, and it was our task to hold until the civilian scientists had got away.

1st Commando Brigade arrived and a triple attack was made: the commandos against Leese, and battle groups of 15/19th Hussars and

1st Cheshires over the bridge at Petershagen (lent to 11th Armoured by the 6th Airborne) and by 23rd Hussars bombardment from the west bank. An enormous quantity of good German hock was discovered in Stolzenau, to everyone's delight! Once over the Weser, Todforce was tasked with guarding explosives factories, some V-2 sites, and large dumps of gas shells in the many woods. 11th Armoured's battle groups pushed hard to the next line of defence held by 12th SS, the river Aller.

The town of Winsen was well defended but over 12–13 April, it and the villages of Walle, Bonstorf, Bergen and Hetendorf were taken with several hundred prisoners captured and a dozen anti-tank guns destroyed. The 11th Armoured's battle groups of tanks and infantry were working well.

During the night of 11 April, 4th KSLI crossed the river Aller to help widen the commando bridgehead. The author was FOO with 4th KSLI and crossed the wide river in one of several black rubber boats. He called up defensive fire that night as young German marines launched attacks in thick woodlands. His Sherman tank was the first to be ferried across on sapper rafts the next morning. His OP was attacked on the morning of the 12th by a Tiger tank and supporting cast of marines, which was distinctly unpleasant. 13 April was 'Black Friday'. 3rd RTR had many encounters with Tiger tanks, which they rarely won. Many Comets were bogged down in streams and marshes – sitting targets. All four of the 13th RHA FOOs were in trouble on the way to Winsen, which was defended by an anti-tank officers' training unit equipped with 88mm, 75mm SP guns and many panzerfaust teams. All day long the slow, tedious and painful battle to clear woods continued. Typhoons in 'Limejuice' targets helped, but 11th Armoured casualties mounted.

Knowledge about the appalling concentration camp of Bergen-Belsen only slowly came to light. On 12 April at Buchholz, preliminary negotiations started when the commander of the German garrison troops approached 159th Infantry Brigade HQ. The Germans were blindfolded and sent back to 8th Corps HQ. In exchange for an exclusion zone for medical reasons, the German garrison would give 11th Armoured free passage, including access over the bridge on the river Aller at Winsen. Negotiations went on back and forth until a local agreement was concluded, fixing a limited typhus zone around the camp itself. The enemy then blew the Winsen bridges. Alerted to the danger of typhus, every member of the division was doused by the RAMC with white

SS camp guards amid hundreds of
dead prisoners – Bergen-Belsen.

DDT powder from head to food; it was sprayed inside shirts, trousers
and boots. Very early on the morning of the 15th, a Commando jeep
sped through the camp, then some Inns of Court armoured cars, and the
23rd Hussar Comets and 3rd RTR with 29th Armoured Brigade HQ
under Brigadier Roscoe Harvey. The author, as an FOO with 3rd RTR,
was in a Sherman tank and as chance would have it, his part of the long
armoured column halted for about two hours in the centre of the camp.
The minor metalled road divided the men's camp from the women's.

No one had come across such appalling evil before. The smell and
stench of decomposing bodies hit one. Behind the high wire fences the
grounds were covered in tattered grey rags and bundles of the dead or
dying. It was difficult to detect any movement. Immediately on the
right, most of the forty-four German/Hungarian staff were lined up,
quite casually looking at the overwhelming forces in their midst. The
infamous scar-faced Colonel Josef Kramer, a professional SS gaoler from
Auschwitz, was the male camp commander. Irma Grese, a tough, tall
blonde SS woman aged twenty, his assistant and reputedly his lover, was
the manager of the women's camp. Originally the joint camps were meant
to hold 10,000 inmates. On 15 April 1945, they held 60,000 (35,000
men and 25,000 women). What this author and the armoured column

224

saw was 13,000 unburied corpses. One looked at Kramer and Grese and they looked back with mild curiosity, certainly not fear or sorrow. They knew the British would keep their word. They had 24 hours' grace to scarper. About eight tanks behind the author's Sherman was his CO, Lt Colonel Robert Daniel, a professional soldier who had commanded 1st RHA in North Africa, earning him the DSO. He came from a distinguished Jewish family. After a short time there was the sound of shots. The colonel had climbed down from his Sherman, walked into the camp and shot four of the camp guards. He came back and said to the brigadier: 'It's not much, but it is a token of my disgust and horror.' Bergen-Belsen was not an official extermination camp like Auchswitz. From the beginning of 1945, tens of thousands of Jews had been brought from the slave labour camps of Silesia and Eastern Europe. The Germans did not want them to fall into the hands of the Russians, but at Belsen there was no work for them to do, unlike at the vast slave labour camp 100 miles further south, at Nordhausen. Once at Belsen, prisoners who had already survived three, four, or even five years of the rigours of camp life elsewhere, were left, with almost no food or medical help, to starve and to rot.

Bergen-Belsen was originally a detention camp holding prominent Jews who, in theory, were to be exchanged for German nationals abroad. It was also classified as a *krankenlager*, a reception camp for sick prisoners. From November 1944 conditions deteriorated rapidly. There was evidence that Kramer was selling food rations meant for the prisoners. An outbreak of spotted fever caused Kramer to ask for closure of the camp. The newsreel cameras showed the 'Beast of Belsen': stocky and well-fed among the dying and the dead, his cheek scarred beneath the dark stubble.

Every camp in Germany had a *totenbuch* (a death book) giving records of inmates and their deaths. In Belsen, 7,000 died in February, 18,000 in March and 9,000 in the first two weeks of April. There were no facilities for burial; most of the corpses were piled up randomly around the camp. There was no water and no sanitation. Dysentery and typhus were rampant. And despite the very best efforts of the British Army Medical Corps, which included Lt Colonel J. A. D. Johnson, captains Derek Sington, R. Barber and Dr Rosensaft, and Brigadier Llewelyn Glyn Hughes, in the next eight weeks 13,944 prisoners died.

Poor little Anne Frank, the intelligent fifteen-year-old Dutch girl, and her sister Margot, aged eighteen, both died in Belsen in March a few weeks before the British arrived.

Anne Frank.

Appendix O to Chapter VII of 2nd Army History deals extensively with the Belsen camp, and the following extracts are taken from it:

Disease of all kinds was rife and in a vast number of cases it was difficult to tell which condition predominated – whether it was typhus, starvation, tubercle or a combination of all three, which was responsible for the shattered wrecks of human beings who formed the majority of the inmates ...

It was impossible to gauge the daily rate of new cases (of illness) as so many, if too weak to call for help, received neither food nor treatment ... Conditions in the huts were indescribable. Rooms and passages were crowded with both living and dead; only by entering the huts could the real horrors be appreciated ... the appalling sanitary conditions in which excreta from those too weak to move or help themselves fouled the rooms or trickled through from upper bunks to those below ... Latrines were practically non-existent and what there were consisted simply of a bare pole over a deep trench without any screening ...

There had been no water for about a week owing to damage by shell fire to the electrical pumping equipment on which the system depended. Food was of poor quality and the number of meals varied from one to three per day. During the last days (of German control) the entire rations issued were one bowl of soup per person on each of four days and once only a loaf of black bread, divided between several people ... There was no shortage of food stocks from which supplies could have been drawn ... Red Cross boxes were found containing tinned milk, soups, meats, etc, which had been sent by Jewish societies for Jews; these had been stolen by the guards and ... nothing had been distributed.

As a first step the British Army sealed the camp using men from one of the batteries of 63rd Anti-Tank Regiment. A Field Hygiene Section was sent in by 11th Armoured Division and twenty-seven water carts supplied fresh water in place of the camp's infected supplies. So bad had been the mismanagement of the prisoners that during the first few days of British control, 548 of the inmates died in a single day. But within a short time the British Army had the situation in hand. The typhus-ridden were isolated; diets were provided to ensure that the camp inmates did not die from over-eating, the dead were buried and the area was disinfected.

Josef Kramer's staff of forty-four included Dr Klein, who headed the camp administration and also invented tortures, one being injecting creosote and petrol into the prisoners' veins. The staff included sixteen SS men, sixteen female SS guards, and twelve KAPOs including six Poles. Camp 1 (men) was 2 km distant from Camp 2 (women).

The conditions that the British soldiers encountered as they entered Belsen on 15 April were carefully and meticulously documented by the British medical personnel who arrived in the camp in late April. An investigation carried out by Lt Colonel F. M. Lipscombe of the Royal Army Medical Corps reported that camp inmates had been subsisting since January on a daily diet of 300 grams of rye bread, watery soup, and a root vegetable called mangold wurzel, a cousin of the beet and normally used as cattle feed. As in all concentration camps, 'what each individual actually received depended mainly on his ability to obtain it' – that is the weak and feeble went without. 'The great majority of the internees had received no food or water for some five days before the camp was uncovered.' The inmates suffered from scabies, dysentery, sepsis of sores and wounds, typhus, tuberculosis, and the debilitating effects of prolonged malnourishment. The psychiatric scars were also visible. According to Lipscombe, 'the loss of moral standards and sense of responsibility for the welfare of others was widespread.' The normal human 'fear of death and cruelty was blunted by repeated exposure – this especially noticeable in children'.

The concentration camp at Bergen-Belsen, liberated by the British on 15 April 1945. The photograph shows a soup kitchen operated by British soldiers.

An exhausted and emaciated prisoner near death in liberated Belsen. (*Imperial War Museum*)

SS Colonel Josef Kramer, styled the 'Beast of Belsen' in the British press, shown in a mug shot while awaiting trial. He was hanged in December 1945. (*Imperial War Museum*)

7 RTR Crocodile, belching flame, clearing fouled ground, Belsen Concentration Camp, 16 April 1945.

There are many true and totally appalling accounts of the horrors of that evil place. This is Richard Dimbleby's account for the BBC:

19 April 1945. I picked my way over corpse after corpse in the gloom, until I heard one voice raised above the gentle undulating moaning. I found a girl, she was a living skeleton, impossible to gauge her age for she had practically no hair left, and her face was only a yellow parchment sheet with two holes in it for eyes. She was stretching out her stick of an arm and gasping something, it was 'English, English, medicine, medicine', and she was trying to cry but she hadn't enough strength. And beyond her down the passage and in the hut there were the convulsive movements of dying people too weak to raise themselves from the floor.

In the shade of some trees lay a great collection of bodies. I walked about them trying to count, there were perhaps 150 of them flung down on each other, all naked, all so thin that their yellow skin glistened like stretched rubber on their bones. Some of the poor starved creatures whose bodies were there looked so utterly unreal and inhuman that I could have imagined that they had never lived at all. They were like polished skeletons, the skeletons that medical students like to play practical jokes with.

At one end of the pile a cluster of men and women were gathered round a fire; they were using rags and old shoes taken from the bodies to keep it alight, and they were heating soup over it. And close by was the enclosure where 500 children between the ages of five and 12 had been kept. They were not so hungry as the rest, for the women had sacrificed themselves to keep them alive. Babies were born at Belsen, some of them shrunken, wizened little things that could not live, because their mothers could not feed them.

One woman, distraught to the point of madness, flung herself at a British soldier who was on guard at the camp on the night that it was reached by the 11th Armoured Division; she begged him to give her some milk for the tiny baby she held in her arms. She laid the mite on the ground and threw herself at the sentry's feet and kissed his boots. And when, in his distress, he asked her to get up, she put the baby in his arms and ran off crying that she would find milk for it because there was no milk in her breast. And when the soldier opened the bundle of rags to look at the child, he found that it had been dead for days.

There had been no privacy of any kind. Women stood naked at the side of the track, washing in cupfuls of water taken from British Army water trucks. Others squatted while they searched themselves for lice, and examined each other's hair. Sufferers from dysentery leaned against the huts, straining

Burning the last hut at Belsen, 21 May 1945.

A sign erected at Belsen.

helplessly, and all around and about them was this awful drifting tide of exhausted people, neither caring nor watching. Just a few held out their withered hands to us as we passed by, and blessed the doctor whom they knew had become the camp commander in place of the brutal Kramer.

I have never seen British soldiers so moved to cold fury as the men who opened the Belsen camp this week, and those of the police and the RAMC who are now on duty there, trying to save the prisoners who are not too far gone in starvation.

It is an evil story and soon the whole world knew about Belsen, certainly the whole of the English-speaking world.

There are various endings to the story. In the 24 hours after the truce ended, the camp guards and also Kramer and Grese were captured. They were tried appropriately and justly at a war crimes tribunal and were hanged.

Later in this book there is a chapter on war crimes tribunals. The author served as the junior member of those in Hamburg and Oldenburg; the first aged twenty-one and the second aged twenty-two. He was one of the official British Army of the Rhine observers when Mr Alfred Pierrepoint hanged thirteen camp guards at Hameln on Friday 13 December – before lunch.

On 21 May 1945 flame-throwers burned down the last of the hundreds of wooden barracks at Belsen.

CHAPTER 18

Operation Forrard On to Bremen

Lt General Brian Horrocks' 30th Corps was given the task of heading for Bremen, on the northern flank of Montgomery's great surge towards the Baltic; it consisted of 43rd Wessex Wyverns, 3rd British and 51st Highland divisions. Behind the infantry in the early stage would be Guards Armoured and, initially leading the way, 8th Red Fox's Mask Armoured Brigade.

Once across the Rhine at Rees and Haldern, the 51st Highland would take the right, southern flank, the Wyverns in the centre and 3rd Canadians on the left, northern flank. The 3rd British Division under Major General 'Bolo' Whistler would follow up behind the Guards on a route following the Dutch-German border via Aaltern Groenlo, Haaksbergen, Enschede to Oldenzaal.

Captain Guy Radcliffe, adjutant of 2nd KSLI, wrote:

The area on the east bank of the Rhine had been utterly pulverised by the bombing and the artillery fire. Dead cattle surrounded every derelict farm, the debris of war lined the roads with the torn-off boughs of the trees. The Germans moved about in a dazed state ... we had very little trouble with them ... of repentance there seemed to be none, only a grovelling self-pity. On 1st April the Bn arrived at Lichtenvoorde in Holland. We were overjoyed to be back in friendly country. One could feel the 'freedom' in the air, every house had put out the flags which had long been concealed. We reached Enschede the next day and experienced for the first and last time in the campaign what a large town did when it was liberated.

43rd Division Wessex Wyverns on the march. (*Stan Procter*)

On 30 March Operation Forrard On started with the 43rd Wessex Wyverns and 8th Red Fox's Mask Armoured Brigade on the 250-mile advance towards Bremen. The Staffordshire Yeomanry DD Sherman tanks 'swanned' across the Rhine, almost three-quarters of a mile, and pushed through the 51st Highland Division towards Speld Dorp and Bienen against the old enemy, 15th Panzergrenadier Division. The Sherwood Rangers Yeomanry crossed the river by raft on the new RE bridge to help the Black Watch and Seaforth Highlanders capture Ijsselburg.

Captain John Stirling, 4/7th Royal Dragoon Guards, wrote: 'It took the best part of a week and the names of Rees, Bienen, Millingen, Megchelen, Ijsselburg all represented a stiff tussle before they became ours. We were still battering our heads against the paratroops and they fought with a grim hopeless bravery that no man could fail to admire. To defeat them was to kill the majority and then a few might surrender. In Megchelen, they even continued to fight from houses that we had set on fire with Crocodiles. Fanatical and misguided yes, but brave and well disciplined, also yes.'

Lingen, a sizeable garrison town about 15 miles east of the Dortmund-Ems Canal, was the next task. It was defended by 111th Battalion

German prisoners *en route* to the POW cages.

Grossdeutscher Brandenburger Training Regiment backed up by 700 paratroops. Guards Armoured had progressed well from Groenlo, Borculo, Enschede and Hengelo (all in Holland) and back into Germany to Gildehaus and Bentheim, and had made a daring 12-mile assault through the night to try to seize the bridges over the river Ems at Lingen. Despite capturing three bridges in Nordhorn they were foiled at Lingen. However, a mile or so north, Captain I. O. Liddell won the Victoria Cross by climbing a roadblock and cutting the wires connecting the demolition charges at Altenlingen.

3rd British Division had been trailing Guards Armoured and were tasked with the capture of Lingen, so 2nd KSLI arrived and in total silence at 0230hrs on 4 April crossed both river and canal with rafts and boats and formed a bridgehead. Captain Marcus Cunliffe wrote in the history of 2nd Royal Warwicks:

> The attack [from the north side at 1015hrs] was pressed with admirable speed and success. Field Marshal Montgomery's men fought like veterans. Many of them actually were reinforcements, youngsters who had just recently joined. At mid-day the 1st Norfolks came through us [against several hundred paratroops] and fought through the streets, house by house and block by block

2nd Gordon Highlanders
cross a temporary
bridge north of Celle,
12 April 1945.

until evening. Then in turn the Lincolns who cleared some houses in the dark. Street fighting is a laborious business and nerve-racking. Lingen was a large town.

It was defended by paratroops, SS, Wehrmacht and the Volksturm (Home Guard). Help soon arrived; the Buffs sent a squadron of Crocodiles who helped the Lincolns clear many streets. A squadron of Staffs Yeomanry Shermans and a number of assault gun SPs led several counter-attacks, and twenty Luftwaffe Messerschmitts suddenly swooped down out of the blue. Fighting went on until 6 April when Lingen was finally cleared. Charles Graves, 2nd Royal Ulster Rifles, notes: 'This final phase of Lingen produced bitter, lethal fighting. The fanatical Germans [of 7th Parachute Division] asked no quarter and received none. Hand-to-hand fighting took place and the bodies of the Germans lying within a few yards of our wounded and dead testified to the fierceness and severity of the fighting.'

The Wessex Wyverns were given the task of keeping open 'Club Route' north from Anholt into Holland to the Twente Canal at Lochem, east to Hengelo, and back into Germany at Nordhorn and Lingen. The tough, irascible Major General Ivo Thomas created his own Armoured Thrust

Royal Norfolks take prisoners in Lingen. Left to right: Pte Wilby, Pte Phillipson, L/Cpl Gould.

Group, led by 8th Armoured Brigade, followed by mobile groups from 129th, 214th and 130th Infantry Brigades. Lt Sydney Jary, 4th Somerset Light Infantry, an intrepid young infantry leader who wrote *18 Platoon*, recalled: 'It was Bank Holiday spirit until the leading Sherwood Rangers tank encountered the first enemy roadblock covered by 88mm guns or SPs or two or three Spandau teams. We had three nasty little battles at Sinderen, Lochem and Osterlinden. In Sinderen the leading Sherman was brewed up by a Mk IV SP hidden in a haystack. Its passengers were killed by Brens, but 20 Germans charged us with bayonets shouting. Brave lads, they didn't stand a chance. My only order was "cease fire".'

Captain Hancock, an FOO with 4th SLI noted:

As the leading tanks were entering Ruurlo, 6 miles short of Lochem, they were fired upon by Panzerfaust and Spandaus and two of them were hit and burst into flames. The only building nearby bore a large red cross. It was immediately treated to concentrated fire from BESAS (tank MG) and 17-pdrs. Out of it came one German officer and 56 soldiers. It was the Flak HQ of the area containing much transport and six 20mm guns. We reached Lochem by 1000hrs on 1 April. The road between was littered with shot-up trucks, dead horses and waggons, assorted staff cars, some with their bullet-riddled

237

occupants still sitting as they were when the RAF [Typhoons] caught them fleeing to the rear.

The Guards captured Enschede and the Wyverns followed the line of the Twente Canal. The 5th Dorsets and 1st Hampshires captured Hengelo on 3 April, where they found a factory which made the latest type of AA predictor. The Canloan officer, Lt W. I. Smith with 4th Wiltshires, tried to get his platoon to sleep in the loft of a barn:

> It was impossible. The Dutch [farming] family were overjoyed at being liberated. There were two or three nuns in the house. When I returned from Company HQ I found the Dutch – boys, girls, even old men and women as well as the nuns with British troops of all ranks hand in hand dancing in a ring and singing Dutch and English songs. I have rarely seen such pure delight as was shown by these Dutch people.

From Winterswijk to Lochem near the Berkel River and canal, the Wyverns met strong resistance from the 23rd SS Freiwilligen Panzergrenadier Division (Nederland). Unfortunately there were well over 20,000 young Dutch SS troops who, when captured, faced an uncertain future. In Borne, 3 miles ahead of Lochem, the Dorsets were so popular that the main square was renamed Dorset Square!

In Bawinkel, AVRE petards had to be fired to destroy roadblocks and Captain J. A. H. Clark, 7th Somerset Light Infantry, remembered the battle of Buckelte-Hamm: 'on a very hot fine day. Off we went, Kangaroos, tanks, TCVs [troop-carrying vehicles], appendages of every sort ... so we motored into Buckelte, a charming village in the sunshine – daffodils, forsythia, tulips, jonquils, fat farms and blossom. All the young Nazi troops were sunbathing and captured; dozens were caught hastily changing into civvies [civilian clothes].' In Haselunne two gin distilleries were captured and Colonel Alabaster, the 30th Corps Welfare Officer, rushed up to take over the stocks for the NAAFI to sell! Another centre line towards Cloppenburg was christened 'Heart Route'. Holte and Herzlake were taken and by dawn on 11 April, 4th Dorsets in Loningen outfought a battalion of the Grossdeutschland Brigade of young cadets. Herssom and Vinner fell to 4th Wiltshires but at Wachtum mines and a huge road block held them up. Pte R. Gladman, 4th Wiltshires, noted: 'We carried on through Germany, sometimes walking, marching, sometimes

Royal Norfolks with 'Big friends', on way to Bremen.

in a TCV. If the road was blocked by fallen trees, vehicles would have to go round through the grass. To avoid landmines, we crawled in line probing with bayonets but a problem with anti-personnel mines. Our officer said to step on one would mean the loss of your wedding tackle, a cause of problems on your honeymoon.' Cloppenburg took two days for 7th Hampshires 5th DCLI to capture, which resulted in 300 cadets being killed, wounded or captured. Inevitably, in street fighting at night, the Wyverns suffered badly. On 14 April, the river Leithe was reached near the Ahlhorn crossroads. In the dense, dark and gloomy spruce and pine forest of Cloppenburg, Major Peter Hall of the 1st Worcesters noted:

> The vanguard company's job was frustrating and hazardous hard work. Along this single axis they had to contend with mines, road blocks, booby traps and periodic mortaring and occasional sniping for good measure. They reached the river Leithe, 20 yards wide, with steep banks and the bridge was blown. On the 15th about 0545hrs there was a tremendous artillery thunder on my forward platoon, followed by a massive enemy infantry and tank assault. From my Company HQ I saw the forward platoon soldiers running back hastily. I organised the new forward positions. My two signallers were killed.

The wireless was destroyed. The only link was through the regimental wireless network of 15/18th Hussars. We were on our own. For the next two hours the battle raged through the woods. This was one of the last serious counter-attacks of the war. We took numerous prisoners, between 400 and 600 enemy dead and one Royal Tiger tank out of action. The Germans included Luftwaffe, panzer units, Waffen SS and Wehrmacht troops.

Both the Sherwood Rangers Yeomanry and 13/18th Hussar Sherman tanks gave invaluable support to the Wyverns in the capture of Cloppenburg and in the counter-attack in the forest.

Most historians have glossed over the number of quite extraordinary, bitter and determined defences made, usually by the Hitler Jugend, by cadets of all ages, and always by the Waffen SS. It has been seen how the Teutoburger Wald battle sucked in some of Montgomery's troops. There are some more examples.

It took the 15th Scottish Division five days – all of the division with massive supporting arms – to take the towns of Uelzen and Stadensen. The first was a key communications centre as part of the German defences west of the river Elbe. Fresh troops had just arrived from Denmark, including reserves of panzergrenadiers, and a Flak regiment with 20mm cannon mounted on trucks. They were fresh, well-fed, truculent, undefeated and longing for a fight. There were also youngsters

Seaforth Highlanders clearing houses under fire in Uelzen, 18 April 1945.

240

Tac HQ 22
Armoured Brigade,
Brigadier Wingfield
and his staff.

from the GAF, the Luftwaffe ground troops. At dawn on 14 April the Highland Light Infantry were devastated around Holdenstedt two miles south-west of Uelzen, which has the little river Ilmenau flowing through it. Panzer Division Clausewitz overwhelmed the 15th Scottish Division Recce Regiment at midnight on 14/15th, causing sixty casualties and capturing thirty-nine prisoners. Some of the attack force were very drunk French SS troops, who howled, screamed and took outrageous risks in the village of Nettelkamp. In Stadensen, the Glasgow Highlanders were attacked at four in the morning. Most of the houses were set on fire. Scottish ammunition trucks blew up and the dreadful ordeal went on until dawn. The Scots had fifty-four casualties including twenty-two taken prisoner. Scores of German civilians were also killed during the night. On 15 April the hapless HLI were attacked by a Light AA group from Denmark with SP guns, bazooka squads and plenty of Spandaus and they, and the Gordons, were pinned down by fire all day. By the 19th, Uelzen was in ruins, bloodstained ruins.

The Guards Armoured encountered 2nd Marine Division and their GOC, Major General Adair, wrote: 'They were nearly all ex-sailors, lately submarine crew with little time for military training, lacked the fighting skill of the paratroops but their discipline and bravery were exemplary.

PBI on their 'Big Friends'. Better than walking. (*Imperial War Museum*)

They were well equipped with bazookas, used in daring fashion. Their tactics often involved them in annihilation, but their aggressive spirit certainly delayed our progress most effectively.'

The Scots-Welsh battle group attacked Visselhovede from the south and the Coldstreams attacked from the north-east. 'A furious battle arose suddenly without any warning. Our mortar carriers were destroyed by bazookas; a bombardment of the houses where the battalion HQs were sited. Fighting spread along both sides of the main street. For two hours the situation was hopelessly confused.' Fighting went on into the evening. Eventually the German Colonel Jordan and 400 marines were captured from 5th and 7th Marine Regiments. The Guards Armoured Division then took Tewel, Deepen, Sohlingen, Scheesel (a hospital town with 2,000 German wounded), Rotenburg (another important hospital centre), Heidenau and Sittensen. Most of these villages were briefly defended but in Wistedt and Elsdorf there was serious trouble. Lieutenant von Buelow, of 15th Panzergrenadier Regiment destroyed the Irish guardsmen and recaptured Wistedt. Guardsman Eddie Charlton, the only survivor, manned his Bren gun valiantly, but was hit many times and was killed. His heroism earned him a posthumous Victoria Cross. Elsdorf's Irish defenders were badly mauled by the 15th Panzergrenadiers.

In their last battle of the war on 'Black Friday', 13 April, the 1st Hampshires of the Wessex Wyverns had a bitter battle for Cloppenburg against the officer-cadets of the Grossdeutschland.

The 53rd Welsh Division found Battlegroup Hornemann and the 5th Marine Regiment defending Rethem and its bridge over the river Aller. The German 2nd Marine Division had obviously taken Himmler's death penalty threat rather seriously. The three grenadier regiments were backed by an artillery regiment, an anti-tank (88mm) regiment, engineers and fusiliers. They were all naval personnel aged 17–23 and their GOC, General Hartmann, an ex-U-boat commander put up a ferocious defence, unfortunately for the Welsh. There were also experienced SS in Rethem, so it took the Welshmen nearly three days to succeed.

The highly experienced Brigadier H. Essame, OC 214th Brigade, noted: 'It must be admitted that Lt General Erdmann conducted the withdrawal of the German armour to Bremen with great professional skill. Travelling in a captured jeep he raked together the remnants of many formations into battle groups which still fought on.'

The savage battle for Rethem.

CHAPTER 19

Capture of Bremen:
Operation Clipper

'Bremen lies astride the river Weser, the greater part of the town is on the north of the river. To the south the town is only some two thousand yards before the fields begin. But outside this there are a series of villages or small towns which form a suburban ring. On the west there is Delmenhorst [a significant smallish town], Brinkum, Leeste, Arsten and Dreye which was only 300 yards from the river Weser. The fields between these villages were very low and had been extensively flooded by the enemy. North of Brinkum was flooded to a depth of four feet. Between Sudweyhe and Dreye there was little flooding but the ground was so soft that tanks could only move on roads. A wide stream flowed across the front from the floods north of Brinkum between Sudweyhe and Dreye to the Weser.' This was Major Guy Radcliffe's, 2 i/c of 2nd KSLI, description of the battlefields of the six-day Operation Bremen.

Bremen was the tenth largest city-port in Germany, with a population of well over half a million. Although it is 37 miles upriver from the North Sea, it is bisected by the great river Weser, due south of the main port of Bremerhaven. It was also very important to the Allies. Antwerp was the major port supplying the British and Canadian forces, and Bremen and Bremerhaven had been 'reserved' for General Eisenhower's armies, who were still being supplied from the Mediterranean and Normandy, mainly Cherbourg because Brest was still being repaired.

'Bomber' Harris had been blasting Bremen with saturation bomb attacks since 1942. The main targets were the Focke-Wulf aircraft factory, Atlaswerke shipbuilding works, Bremen Vulkan shipyard, Deschlwag (AG Weser) shipyard, Korff oil refinery, Norddeutsche Hutte steel works, Valentin submarine pens, Borgward motor transport plants and Bremen

One of the heavy AA guns knocked out by five 5 RTR tanks at Rethem.

Osleghausen railway station. There was an airfield just south-west of the town and two concentration camps (obviously not targets) at Bremen-Farge and Bremen-Vegesack. Nor of course was Becks' famous brewery be a target. Both Adolf Hitler by radio, and Himmler by paying a visit, had ensured that Bremen was designated a *festung*, a fortress, and in theory to be defended to the last man.

The remains of the 1st Parachute Army, which had been battered during operations Veritable, Blockbuster, Plunder and many small, nasty actions east of the Rhine, had now reinforced the Bremen garrison.

Lt General Fritz Becker was in overall command of the 40,000 defenders of Bremen and its ring of suburban defences. Major General Sibert, a big fat man with a broad, unintelligent sour-looking face, and Colonel Mueller had the powerful 8th Flak Division under command. Its dual purpose 88mm AA guns had been trying to ward off Bomber Harris's RAF bombardments. The 280th Wehrmacht 'Stomach' Regiment, 6,000 Volksturm 'veterans', and a 2,000-strong mixed bag of Ost, coastguards, police, and including 500 first-class soldiers from 18th SS Horstwessel Training Regiment, were all part of Becker's command. There were also over 2,000 Kriesgmarines, either unemployed U-boat crews, marine cadets, or other ship-less naval bodies commanded by a vice-admiral. This immense flotsam and jetsam, of paratroops, SS Flak troops, Ost, Wehrmacht, Volksturm, police and fire brigade would fight hard against overwhelming odds in the last major battle fought by Montgomery's British Liberation Army in the Second World War. It was going to be a six-day battle. Operation Cricket, against the cream of the infantry divisions, included: Whistler's 3rd British, Thomas's 43rd Wessex Wyverns, Hakewell-Smith's 52nd Lowland and MacMillan's 51st Highland. In support were Brigadier Carver's 4th Black Rat Armoured Brigade and a vast array of 'Funny' flame-throwers, Crocodiles, AVRE bombards, some Flails and the *schwim-panzers*, which would cause consternation.

Lt General Brian Horrocks consulted Montgomery about the complicated plans for the much-increased 30th Corps to capture such a large city surrounded by flooded fields, astride a major river.

Intelligence had shown that the powerful 15th Panzergrenadier Division, a first-class formation, had moved from the west of Bremen to the east, to deny the road and rail links between Bremen and Hamburg to the British. The implication was that Bremen would be strongly defended. Nevertheless Horrocks tried for a peaceful move. Nearing the end of the war he certainly wanted more than ever to minimise casualties. By 20 April 3rd British and 51st Highland, two key 'chess pieces', were in position, south-west and east respectively, of Bremen. So propaganda leaflets, in German naturally, were fired by 33rd Field Regiment RA in 500 special non-lethal shells over Bremen: 'The choice is yours! The British Army is lying outside Bremen, supported by the RAF and is about to capture the city. There are two ways this can take place. Either by the employment of all means at the disposal of the Army and the RAF or by the occupation of the town after unconditional surrender … You have 24 hours to decide.'

However, General Becker was never going to surrender tamely. Bomber Harris unleashed 500 Lancasters and Halifaxes flying at 4,000 feet on the afternoon of Sunday 22 April, and continued to send them in day after day until the ground forces in the smoking ruins were satisfied. The ubiquitous Chester Wilmot was there:

23 April 1945. The telephone they used was found in the station at Achim, ten miles east of Bremen, when the 52nd Lowland Division took Achim this morning. This afternoon I was there when the ultimatum was phoned through. The stationmaster at Achim was asked to call up the stationmaster

Infantry of 156th Brigade 52nd Lowland division and Sherman tanks of the 4th Armoured Brigade entering Bremen.

REs support the 52nd Lowland Division clearing roadblocks, Bremen, 26 April 1945. (*Birkin Haward*)

52nd Division clearing the ruins of Bremen.

at Bremen, and then he handed over the phone to our intelligence officer. He spoke to a German lieutenant, who then went off to convey the message to the Bremen garrison commander, and to bring back a senior officer to discuss the ultimatum. We waited for over an hour. Then the phone from Bremen rang again. Not to tell us the reply, but to give us the friendly warning that the RAF was bombing Bremen, and to say that no senior German officer would come to the phone. Then the line went dead. The bombs had evidently cut it.

We couldn't see much of the bombing because of the low cloud, but hundreds of Lancasters attacked the ack-ack defences and installations in and around the city. We've warned Bremen that yesterday's heavy raid is only a small foretaste of what is to come if they try to hold out, and already our heavy and medium guns are pounding away at the defences. Occasionally we're putting over a few more propaganda shells, filled with 'free-passage' leaflets, for those who've had enough. And these appeals are being reinforced by loudspeaker vans blaring out across no-man's land on the fringe of the city; but so far the Germans have shown no signs of cracking.

No doubt, when Himmler visited Bremen in his special armoured train last week he tightened up the Nazi grip on this port. A Nazi chief has been installed

Glasgow Highlanders fighting in the Focke Wulf Factory at Bremen.

to organise control of the SS, the Gestapo, and the local police, and to make sure that the garrison commander, General Becker, doesn't weaken. Civilians who've escaped say that already the local führer has sacked the burgomaster, who wished to surrender. Nevertheless the plight of the city is now serious; it's three-quarters encircled and the Germans control only two good roads leading out of it, and these only lead north into the peninsula which we've already sealed off between Bremen and Hamburg. Refugees say that inside Bremen there are about 300,000 German civilians; some 50,000 foreign workers and more than 20,000 troops are around the city. Civilians also say that they've been short of food in recent weeks, but their greatest problem now is going to be shortage of water. The city's local supply has been put out of action by bombing; and their main outside source, a pipeline from the Harz Mountains, was cut off today by us just before the RAF bombing began.

Today they also lost their main source of fuel, an oil refinery at Achim which the 52nd Division captured this morning. The refinery and its storage tanks are hidden underground in a wood near Achim, and it was working until yesterday. In fact petrol and oil from this refinery moved the 15th Panzergrenadier Division when it transferred from the south to the north of Bremen last week to counter the Guards' outflanking movement. There are, no doubt, other storage tanks in Bremen, but the loss of this refinery at this stage must be a considerable embarrassment.

The Germans are now being driven steadily back into Bremen and the garrison of 20,000 may well be increased to 30,000 by the time all the units fighting outside the perimeter have withdrawn inside. There they'll have a very strong defensive position, for Bremen is very difficult to attack. It stands almost on an island in the flood plain of the Weser. On the south it's protected by a belt two miles wide which the Germans have flooded, and on the north-east and north the low-lying ground is laced with dikes and canals.

Borstel, two miles north-east of Achim, cost 5th HLI fifty-one casualties but yielded 242 prisoners and thirty-nine guns from 88mm to 20mm. 5th KOSB pressed on to Embsen, a mile ahead.

The ring of strongpoints around the city had to be laboriously overcome. 3rd British were tasked with capturing Brinkum, which was defended by four companies of young SS fanatics of the Horstwessel Battalion. Supported by Crocodiles from 7th RTR, Shermans of 4/7th Dragoon Guards, and a troop of Valentine SP 17-pdrs, it took the Suffolks, Norfolks and Warwicks almost two days to succeed. Field Marshal Montgomery visited the division on the 20th and Major General 'Bolo' Whistler wrote in his diary: '20 April. Monty keeps a very close eye on everything. He has certainly done me jolly well and made my battle both possible and profitable. We have captured five officers and 1,259 men on April 15th and another 1,800 between 15–19th. We have killed about 200–300 more. Not much shelling from the Boche for which I

German soldiers, some only young boys, surrender to the British in Bremen, 26 April 1945.

One of the young German soldiers surrendering to the British, 26 April 1945.

Blasted, ruined Bremen, 26 April 1945. (*Birkin Haward*)

am thankful. Lovely weather! Had a close look at Bremen yesterday. It appears rather undamaged in spite of 'Bomber' Harris and his efforts.'

The 51st Highland Division had captured Rees in Operation Plunder and had moved north via Empel to Isselburg and Anholt. Every infantry unit in the British Army desperately needed reinforcements after ten months of intensive fighting. The 1st Black Watch stayed in Isselburg until 5 April and received reinforcement officers from LAA, the Suffolks,

Argylls, Duke of Wellingtons, West Yorkshires, Durham Light Infantry and redoubtable Canloans. 'They all proved excellent Black Watch officers as if to the manner born,' wrote Lt Colonel John McGregor in *The Spirit of Angus.*

Two unusual features appeared now in every advance east towards Bremen, Hamburg and the Baltic. In addition to the inevitable panzerfaust teams, which caused many tank casualties, every road was 'seeded' with huge sea-mines – the large black ball filled with HE and with little pressure-spikes. Buried to a depth of three feet they blew everything that set them off to kingdom come. Comets, Shermans, half-tracks and carriers were simply blown to pieces. It was Hitler's unemployed naval Kriegsmarines who were responsible. The other strange feature was the plethora of German hospitals crammed full of wounded. The Highland Division found one in Vechta with 2,500 patients, one in Lohne with 250 and three more around Quakenburg. When the Highland Division reached Delmenhorst, which was a large, undefended town that had been reached by the Derbyshire Yeomanry recce armoured cars on 20 April, the burgomeister of the town informed them that there were no fewer than fifteen hospitals in the town crammed full with German wounded.

Major Martin Lindsay, second in command and often in charge of the 1st Gordons, calculated that up to 27 March, 102 officers had served with his battalion. The usual strength was thirty. The average service of the fifty-five officers commanding the twelve rifle platoons was thirty-eight days or five and a half weeks. Just over half had been wounded, a quarter killed, 15 per cent invalided home and 5 per cent had survived. These terrible figures were duplicated in most of the infantry divisions. 'Everybody had a prejudice against being killed in the last month of a six-year war, so people were playing for safety ...'

The Highland divisional 'cage' harboured nearly 200 men on charges of desertion. Many were veterans of North Africa, Sicily, Italy or Normandy who, poor devils, had exhausted their store of courage. Many others were eighteen-year-old reinforcements, poorly trained and disciplined, who were just completely out of their depth. A third group were from rear lines of communication that had been hauled out of comfortable safe jobs and thrown into the cauldron of the 'sharp end'. It seemed to be lunacy that the SS, the Hitler Jugend, the officer cadets, the paratroopers and the young marines were all prepared to fight, fight and die.

German prisoners in Bremen.

George Blake's history of the 52nd Lowland Division notes:

On April 12 the troops knew that their next objective was Bremen, the glittering prize of victory, some 30 miles ahead. Now they were to enjoy the pleasures and triumphs of 'swanning' ... to go 'swanning' is to ride in or on a vehicle through strange country with little interference from the enemy. For an *infantry* division in particular to go swanning encouraged the gala mood, so that the troops, true to the British code of humour, rode on tanks [Scots Greys to Etelsen, 44 RTR to Volkersen, with 2 KRRC protecting the right flank from Langwedel to Bassen and Baden on the Bremen-Hamburg autobahn], in strange headgear, waved to the native children, chirruped facetiously at the womenfolk of the countryside and generally took Germany for their own.

It was the 6th Cameronians who took Etelsen and Baden, and 4/5th Royal Scots Fusiliers who finished off Baden, but 5th Highland Light Infantry were counter-attacked during the night of 21/22 April. Achim was an important road junction captured by 7/9th Royal Scots and 4th KOSB. In three villages the unfortunate ersatz 'ear and stomach' defenders and Flak troops had 750 put 'in the bag'.

Just before the move on Bremen, the fiery GOC of the 43rd Wessex Wyverns was not a happy man. 130th Brigade was loaned to 52nd

In Bremen the fire brigade was captured, and is here seen lining up for checking.

Lowland to provide fire support, 129th Brigade was lent to 51st Highland and 214th Brigade was left behind to mop up German pockets of resistance around Ahlhorn, so for a short time Thomas was a general without a division.

The 30th Corps' plan was for 51st Highland to make a feint attack on Delmenhorst on the west side of Bremen, which in the event was surrendered by the burgomeister for humanitarian reasons. The 3rd British in Buffaloes would put in a surprise attack across flooded countryside from the south-west, while 52nd and 43rd attacked the main part of the city from the south-east.

The Crocodile flame-throwers of 7th RTR were much in demand and were involved in actions in Uphusen, Mahndorf and Hastedt. B Squadron helped 52nd Lowland to capture 800 defenders on 25 and 26 April, and A Squadron flamed 3rd British into Dreye, Arsten and Harlenhausen. The AVRE petards of 16th, 82nd and 22nd Assault Squadrons blasted their way into Bremen clearing road blocks, laying a skid Bailey bridge and dropping fascines into the many huge craters caused by the sea-mine explosives. Wynford Vaughan-Thomas wrote for his BBC programme:

157th Infantry Brigade 52 Lowland division clearing Bremen docks.

26 April 1945. I am in the centre of the city of Bremen, if you can call this chaotic rubbish-heap in which our bulldozers are working as I speak, their men with handkerchiefs round their throats to avoid the flying dust, if you can call this rubbish-heap a city any more. There are walls standing, there are factory chimneys here and there, but there's no shape and no order and certainly no hope for this shell of a city that was once called Bremen. It's the sheer size of the smashed area that overwhelms you. These endless vistas down small streets to the houses leaning at drunken angles and this inhuman landscape of great blocks of flats with their sides ripped open, and the intimate household goods just blown out into the bomb craters. Bremen was a city of many thousand inhabitants, but once you are past the outer suburbs there is hardly a house intact in which these people could live, because they haven't even tried to live in them. Everybody has gone into those giant air-raid shelters, these great blocks of almost solid concrete that are dotted all over the ruins of Bremen. They stood up to the bombings well, and now, from the one opposite us, the people are coming out, to stare at the tanks and the bulldozers, and at the guns now rolling past us into the heart of the city. Some of these people are already starting to potter about in that seemingly aimless way that bombed-out people do among the dusty rubble.

Some of the fifty submarines captured by 52nd Division on the stocks at Bremen.

Burgher Park, a junction of six roads, also housed fourteen underground bunkers. On the way there, Captain C. N. B. Hancock, 94th Field Regiment RA, wrote: 'I was FOO with the Somersets. Darkness had fallen and the Crocodiles were put to work on a couple of large houses which were giving a lot of trouble. It was a grand sight to watch them belching great tongues of flame, 70 or 80 yards long and in a short time both houses were burning furiously. The Boche inside had an unpleasant choice, the flames within or the waiting machine guns of our infantry and tanks outside. The battle was now well under control with the tanks, Crocodiles and infantry providing mutual covering fire as together they assaulted house after house.'

The 3rd British meanwhile had to capture the bridge over the Kattenturm Canal intact in order to clear the aerodrome and Focke Wulf aircraft works south of the river. Two journalists, one from *Reuters*, the other from Associated Press, watched the extraordinary 'marine' attack as a fleet of forty-seven Buffaloes of 4th RTR under Captain Harris made 115 trips across three feet of flood water to carry 2nd Royal Ulster Rifles over 2,000 yards of flooded fields to capture Arsten. Across

General Horrocks talking to a group of soldiers after the capture of Bremen, April 1945.

the bund they went and captured the vital bridge before it could be blown. The sappers made safe all the huge bombs around the bridge. Later 1st KOSB and 2nd Lincolns occupied the aerodrome and factory, capturing 350 prisoners. The German general later said: 'It was not fair using 'schwim-panzers' like that!' The 3rd British pushed steadily into the Neuenlander suburbs and into the barracks. Iain Wilson, 1st KOSB wrote: 'In the chilly morning light of the 25th, as the guns continued to pour shells into Bremen, one could feel that the great port was in its death-throes and that its doom was approaching. The approaches to the city were flooded and in the ruins we knew the SS were waiting to fight it out. Life became more precious and desirable as the chances of death or wounds became less.'

Bomber Command kept up their relentless attack on Bremen for 5 hours continuously on the 24th, by which time 'Von Thoma', as Thomas was nicknamed, had regained control of his lost sheep. Brigadier J. O. E. Vandeleur (he of Guards Armoured fame during Market Garden) had been promoted in rank and joined the Wyverns. He wrote:

The attack upon Bremen was the last big battle in which we were engaged. My 129th Brigade was to capture the Burgher Park, a stronghold on the eastern side of the city. 52nd Lowland were to capture the U-boat yards. We approached Bremen cautiously two up: right 4th Wilts, left 5th Wilts. I kept the Somerset LI in reserve. Our opponents were German marines who were lusty fighters. I had been instructed not only to capture the Burgher Park but also the army, naval and Luftwaffe commanders. When darkness fell I decided to launch 4th Somersets under Colonel Lipscomb and smash our way into the big bunkers where the German HQ and core of their defences were situated.

From Rockwinkel the two Wiltshire battalions advanced steadily, leap-frogging, platoon by platoon, company by company. A huge seven-storey-high Flak tower was taken, and its garrison of 160 surrendered without a shot fired. AVREs petarded each roadblock and Crocodiles flamed difficult targets and the Sherwood Ranger Shermans did their stuff.

Brigadier Walter Kempster, OC 9th Brigade 3rd British, noted on the 26 April: 'At first light I passed 2 RUR through 1 KOSB to capture the gasworks and docks on the south bank of the river. By then the Hun was utterly demoralised. 2 RUR just walked on to their objectives and by 0930 I reported to Division that we'd done our job – nearly 30 hours in advance of the estimate.' Some interesting spectacles were seen – the bag of prisoners included, besides many SS, some weary old men and young boys, a sadistic displaced person camp commandant and a large portion of the Bremen police force. Kempster's men also took prisoner 800 from the 18th SS Regiment and Hitler Jugend, whose average age was sixteen–seventeen, the Chief ARP Warden of Bremen, a city fire engine crew and many Volksturm, elderly chaps complete with well-packed suitcases. At daybreak on the 27th, the 4th Wiltshires of the Wessex Wyverns battered their way into the main bunkers. Major Pope captured there Lt General Fritz Becker, a vice-admiral, the Nazi Bishop of Bremen, Major General Siber, and thirty other senior officers. Within 36 hours the Wiltshires had taken two generals and over 600 other prisoners. And a considerable amount of Zeiss binoculars! Brigadier Essame wrote: 'All day on the 27th prisoners streamed into the Divisional cage. By nightfall 2,771 including 94 officers and 831 hospital cases. The people were broken spirited and lifeless, docile, bewildered and hopeless. Fighting, rape and open murder broke out among the thousands of released slave labourers. We handed over this charnel house, once a civilised city to 52nd Lowland Division and moved out into the clean air of the Cuxhaven peninsula on the 28th.'

The Lowlanders had done well. The Glasgow Highlanders took their two factory objectives. The 6th Cameronians seized the whole suburb of Hemelingen and 4/5th Royal Scots Fusiliers found themselves in the

The battle of Bremen.

heart of Bremen. 186th Field Regiment RA shrewdly took over the great sports stadium on the south side of the city for its gun positions. And the 7th Cameronians and 54th Anti-tank Regiment, in its recent new role of an assault SP unit, came into the dock area to check on one-man submarines. A German full admiral in charge of the dock area insisted on a formal ceremony of surrender of his motley marines to 5th KOSB. They included four Helferin (German WRENs). The burgomeister of Bremen, not to be outdone, had a parade of a thousand very mixed soldiers, and insisted on a series of barrack square drill movements before surrendering to a slightly bemused 4th KOSB. The Lowland historian, George Blake, who was present, wrote: 'The control of this bear-garden was a heavy responsibility on the cool and terribly tired Scottish soldiers who had taken the city after such a long and gruelling battle. It was immensely complicated by the litter of smashed and fallen masonry left by the bombers. A central area of the city, some four miles by one, had ceased to exist.'

The 'Thieving Magpies' T-Force and 30th Assault Unit sent separate foraging units ahead into Bremen. For T-Force, 5th Kings and the

Buckinghams seized the city's main police station as their HQ, from which they could conduct a week's detailed search of the city. There was an American interest as well, and 125 targets had been previously identified. Lt Commander Dalzel-Job sent his engineers out to work. They blew ninety-five safes, which contained useful documents and literally billions of reichsmarks. The huge bunker-shipyard at Bremen-Farge – a concrete monster – housed thirteen pens for 150 of the ultra new high-speed U-boats. At the Descimag U-boat assembly plant a Narvik class destroyer and sixteen U-boats nearing completion were found. T-Force put a guard over the Focke-Wulf aircraft engine factory. these were all key places and records for the incoming American HQ when it was set up.

Major Raymond Burt, 22nd Dragoons, whose Shermans (without Flails) had been supporting 2nd RUR, 2nd Lincolns and 1st KOSB for the six days of fighting, described the last days of Bremen:

> So this was how the city was falling – without fight, in rain and betrayed by those who had brought it to its present squalor. For all their boasts and threats, the Nazi leaders had gone and the city was abandoned to a few thousand AA gunners and marines and the old men and women and children who waited our arrival in the air raid shelters. The advances into the suburbs were something of a formality. But they were carried out, block by block, with care and precision – companies and supporting tanks leapfrogging through one another along the silent and mined streets. It looked formidable enough. The road blocks were defensible. Slit-trenches and anti tank ditches had been dug across street intersections. Enormous land-mines had been laid and wired ready for explosion by the roadsides. The windows of the ruined houses provided the 'heroic twilight' of the Nazis of the city of Bremen. But no shot was fired. Hitler's war was running down – it had collapsed into a dreary mopping up operation which went on because no one in authority had the desire to cry 'stop'.

CHAPTER 20

Alpenfestung: Göbbels' Hoax

In the autumn of 1944 stories began to circulate in Switzerland that the Nazis had set up a vast military complex in the mountains of southern Germany and Austria. They probably derived from Dr Josef Göbbels, that master of spin. Agents of the SD (SS Intelligence Department) forwarded this 'information' to Gauleiter Hofer of the Tyrol. In November, Hofer sent a report to Martin Bormann, the deputy Führer, to the effect that US experts had forecast unacceptably high casualty rates for the campaign by the Americans to overcome this final bastion. Moreover Hofer noted that 'East-West tension will become visible if the war drags on too long'. This situation could be exploited by the Nazis who should open negotiations with the West at the expense of the Soviet Union. Hofer urged that a defence redoubt *festung* be set up in mountainous areas, such as his own Gau (shire) in the Tyrol. In fact, Hofer had strengthened areas already, which he modestly called 'The Hofer Line'. He recommended that Allied POW camps be moved there to deter Allied air interdiction. The garrison would need élite military units backed by 30,000 men of the Standschutzen (local defence unit's equivalent to the Volkssturm). General Ritter von Hengl was ordered by Berlin to command the redoubt garrison, but his mountain troops' corps, between 1–5 April 1945, consisted of only 30,000 men. He produced a thoroughly damning report and dismissed the Hofer plan as a slogan: 'The Alpine Redoubt existed merely on paper.'

Göbbels wrote about Hofer's recommendations as though they were operational: food stocks were already stockpiled; underground factories were in full production; the élite units garrisoning the *Alpenfestung* were in action; and German scientists were working hard to produce another super vengeance weapon, which would ensure a German victory!

On 11 March 1945 SHAEF produced this intelligence summary: 'Accumulated information and photographic evidence made possible a more definite estimate of the progress of plans for the "Last Ditch Stand". German defence policy is to safeguard the Alpine Zone. Defences continue to be constructed in depth in the south through the Black Forest to Lake Constance and from the Hungarian frontier to the west of Graz ... In Italy defence lines are built up in the foothills of the Italian Alps. The results of air reconnaissance show at least 20 sites of recent underground activity as well as numerous natural caves mainly in the region Golling, Feldkirch, Kufstein and Berchtesgaden [Hitler's personal chalet-retreat atop a mountain] ... accommodation for stores and personnel. The existence of several underground factories has also been confirmed ... As regards actual numbers of troops, stores and weapons ... evidence indicates considerable numbers of SS and specially chosen units are engaged on some type of defence activity at the most vital strategic points ... The most important ministries are established within the Redoubt area ... while Hitler, Göring, Himmler and other notables are said to be in the process of withdrawing to the mountain stronghold.'

At SHAEF a large map was on display headed 'Unconfirmed Installations in Reported Redoubt Area' covering 20,000 square miles, the Alpine meeting point of southern Germany, northern Italy and western Austria with Hitler's Berghof near Berchtesgaden in their midst. Moreover symbols were printed on the base of the map indicating ammunition and fuel dumps, HQs and barracks, food depots, radio installations, factories, troop locations and a chemical warfare site.

Adolf Hitler received Hofer's November 1944 memorandum during April 1945 and ordered that the gauleiter's plans be put into immediate effect. At that late stage it was an impossible pipedream.

Nevertheless Eisenhower, Bradley and Lt General Walter Bedell Smith, in particular, felt strongly that: 'After the Ruhr was taken we were convinced there would be no surrender at all so long as Hitler lived. Our feeling then was that we should be forced to destroy the remnants of the German Army piece by piece, with the final possibility of a prolonged campaign in the rugged Alpine area of Western Austria and Southern Bavaria known as the National Redoubt.'

The SHAEF summary continued: 'This area is by the nature of the terrain practically impenetrable. The evidence suggests that considerable numbers of SS ... are being systematically withdrawn to Austria ...

American paratroops
reached the Berghof,
Hitler's retreat in
the Bavarian Alps,
in May 1945. This is
Hitler's own residence,
with an RAF bomb crater
in the foreground.

The Berghof, April 1945.
An American GI looks at
Hitler's home. The Nazis'
'last stand' in a non-
existent Alpine redoubt.

Here defended both by nature and by the most efficient secret weapons yet invented the powers that have hitherto guided Germany will survive to reorganise her resurrection. Here armaments will be manufactured in bomb-proof factories, food and equipment will be stored in vast underground caverns and a specially selected corps of young men will be trained in guerilla warfare [Werewolves] so that a whole underground army can be fitted and directed to liberate Germany from the occupying forces.'

General Eisenhower's report 'D-Day to VE Day' published in 1946 devotes several pages to the Redoubt. There is no doubt that Eisenhower concluded that the National Redoubt was now of greater significance than Berlin: 'Military factors when the enemy was on the brink of final defeat were more important in my eyes than the political considerations involved in an Allied capture of the capital since this no longer represented a military objective of major importance.' By taking a unilateral decision (but backed by General Marshal in Washington) his new plans involved his right wing of armies driving south-east to meet the Russians in the Danube valley, west of Vienna, and *seizing the Redoubt before the Nazis could organise it for defence.*

Churchill was furious. Montgomery was furious. They had always wanted the Allies to get to Berlin come what may. On 28 March Eisenhower sent his plan direct to Marshal Stalin, who was undoubtedly delighted. Ike wrote: 'The Prime Minister was greatly disappointed and disturbed because my plan did not first throw Montgomery forward with all the strength I could give him *from American forces* in a desperate attempt to capture Berlin before the Russians.'

Alpenfestung was of course a brilliant Göbbels hoax! What actually happened was that by mid-April most of the key ministries from Berlin had been moved to the Berchtesgaden area, and had taken their documents and administrators with them. Most of the OKW staff (Supreme Command) had also been transferred to the Redoubt area. However, on 20 April, Hitler decided to stay in Berlin – and die there – defending the city to the last. SHAEF had probably noted the movement of staff to the area – and assumed that the Wagnerian Götterdammerung would follow. A new German Army, the 11th, under General Walter Wenck, had five modest divisions which, in theory, guarded the Redoubt as part of their command area. On 18 April Wenck's 10,000 men were trapped by the US 1st Army around Dessau near the Harz Mountains. That was the end of *Alpenfestung.*

CHAPTER 21

Capture of Hamburg

7th Armoured Division had been tasked with the capture of the great city of Hamburg, which lies 60 miles north-east of Bremen. The Desert Rats' 'swan' from the Rhine had taken them through Hoya and Verden, both defended small towns astride the river Weser, then east through Barven, Wagenfeld, Diepholz, Bassum and Twistringen. They encountered the flank guards of 15th Panzergrenadier Division, whose assault SP guns and several Tigers caused grief. Indeed the panzergrenadiers counter-attacked rather vigorously around Syke, Wildeshausen and Harpstedt. By the time the division had arrived, 3 miles south of Bremen, the Desert Rats in four days had taken 1,700 prisoners from 18th Ersatz Battalion and 15th Panzergrenadiers. Bypassing Bremen they were ordered to make tracks for Hamburg via Walsrode, and Fallingbostel of course, and Soltau, where in close country amid beech woods and thick pine trees, assault SPs, Panthers, Spandau and bazooka teams caused casualties to 8th and 11th Hussars. The tracks through the woods resembled appalling peat bogs. On 18 April around Todtglusingen, the enemy, with 88mm anti-tank guns and SPs, were so strong that 'Limejuice' calls for Typhoon support were frequent. North of Soltau were the far-ranging moors and forest of Luneburg Heath, full of scratch kampfgruppen from the resident training centres. The last remnants of General Student's 1st Parachute Army were escaping from Bremen to get to Bremervorde and the river Elbe crossings and ferries.

For two weeks the division was occupied in clearing up a vast salient pointing towards Hamburg. It had a frontage of some 60 miles, and was 25 miles wide. Two entirely unrelated battles were being fought: in the north to mop up the area around the great autobahn from Bremen to Hamburg, and to the south to defeat a large pocket of enemy resistance east of Soltau.

265

Desert Rats
captured Soltau
near Lüneburg
Heath.

Postcard of Hamburg before 'Bomber' Harris had fire-bombed the city.

Several infantry divisions post-Bremen were involved in the two weeks of mopping up, including the 53rd Welsh and 15th Scottish. The 43rd Wessex Wyverns and Guards Division were tasked with clearing the Cuxhaven peninsula, a large square area bounded on three sides by the river Elbe, Bremerhaven, 40 miles north-west, and Cuxhaven, some 60 miles due north. There were many sea mines and many carriers and armoured cars were blown to pieces with their crews. WASP flame-throwers were used frequently. There were often vile, cold days with drenching rain, and the rearguards of 15th Panzergrenadiers were certainly dying hard. Unbelievably, every village and hamlet was still bitterly defended and all the contestants knew that the war would finish – soon. The German Naval HQ for the North Sea was an enormous institution in Buxtehede, a series of modern barracks planted in the green countryside. It harboured among the kriegsmarines 500 female 'WRENs' in 'grey mouse' uniforms, who stood up during their lunch of hot potatoes and glared at their British captors. At the end of the barracks was a Nazi chapel with no religious emblems, or paintings, or altar. On the walls were ethereal paintings of Hitler and other Nazi leaders, surrounded by the swastika and the Nazi invocations to faith and war where one could worship the Führer – quietly and with deep conviction.

The German Commandment arriving at Cuxhaven at the mouth of the Elbe, in order to surrender the town.

Air Marshal 'Bomber' Harris organised Operation Gomorrah, the mass bombing of Hamburg. It was planned on 27 May 1943. On 24 July 2,300 tons of high explosive were dropped and in the Blitz week that followed the USAAF made 1,672 daylight sorties and 1,500 civilians were killed. The RAF used 'window' bales of ten-inch strips of aluminium foil to confuse German radar. On 28 July, a 43-minute firestorm was created when 2,326 tons of bombs were dropped on a warm night with low humidity and by dawn 42,000 civilians had been killed and 48,000 buildings destroyed. One-third of the damage was in the central districts of Hamburg, a flourishing Hanseatic commercial and cultural centre with a population of about one and a half million, including the suburbs. In the dock area were acres and acres of rubble, which had once been houses. Whole streets were buried. The majority of buildings still standing were gutted by fire or badly damaged and uninhabitable. The ruined buildings had comprised 275,000 apartments or 61 per cent of Hamburg's total living accommodation. A further 109,000 homes were damaged. No trams ran, there was no running water, no electricity, no gas, no radio, no postal service and no telephone.

A million people had fled the city and were homeless. The targets for the bombing raids were eighty military installations, twelve bridges, 112 Nazi party offices and 3,785 industrial plants, all of which were destroyed or badly damaged.

In his book *Inside the Third Reich*, Albert Speer recorded the bombing of the magnificent city of Hamburg: 'On July 25 [1943] shortly after midnight, 791 British planes attacked Hamburg and on the 25th and 26th daylight raids by 235 American bombers followed on 27th by the second night raid, staged by 787 British planes, and a third by 777 British planes on July 29. This succession of heavy attacks ended on August 2 with a mission flown by 750 British bombers.' Speer often gave his Führer advice. He advocated a pinpoint bombing strategy on a limited number of carefully selected strategic targets, i.e. not mass bombing:

While I was trying to convert Hitler and the General Staff of the airforce to this policy, our Western enemies launched five major attacks on a single big city – Hamburg – within a week. Rash as this operation was, it had catastrophic consequences for us. The first attacks put the water supply pipes out of action, so that in the subsequent bombings the fire department had no way of fighting the fires. Huge conflagrations created cyclone-like firestorms: the asphalt of the streets began to blaze; people were suffocated in their cellars or burned to death in the streets. The devastation of this series of air raids could only be compared with the effects of a major earthquake. Gauleiter Kaufman teletyped Hitler repeatedly begging him to visit the stricken city. When these pleas proved fruitless, he asked Hitler at least to receive a delegation of some of the heroic rescue crews. But Hitler refused even that. Hamburg had suffered the fate Göring and Hitler had conceived for London in 1940.

Hamburg had put the fear of God in me. At the meeting of Central Planning on July 29 I pointed out, 'If the air raids continue on the present scale within three months we shall be relieved of a number of questions we are at present discussing. We shall simply be coasting downhill smoothly and relatively quickly.'

On 19 March 1945 the Führer issued an appalling order to every gauleiter in the remains of the Third Reich. In effect it was for Götterdammerung, the self-inflicted destruction of 'all military, transportation, communications, industrial and food-supply facilities. All resources within the Reich that the enemy might use immediately or in the foreseeable future for continuing the war, are to be destroyed by dynamiting, fire or demolition.' Albert Speer very bravely issued his own directive countermanding much of Hitler's 'Wagnerian' edict. Speer then *forbade* the destruction of locks, sluices, dams, drawbridges and harbour installations.

Gauleiter Kaufman asked Speer to visit Hamburg urgently as the navy was preparing to demolish all the port installations and shipyards. Speer and Kaufman prevailed diplomatically.

On 1 May a conference between Admiral Dönitz, the new Commander in Chief of the German armed forces, and Field Marshal Ernst Busch took place concerning the fate of Hamburg. Busch wanted to attack the superior British forces advancing on the city, while Dönitz was against offensive plans. Moreover Himmler then brought the news that Gauleiter Kaufman intended to surrender Hamburg *without* a fight. Kaufman told Speer that if necessary he would mobilise the masses to active resistance against the defenders of the city. Speer then phoned Dönitz: 'I told him of the threat of open rebellion in Hamburg.' An hour later Dönitz agreed to the surrender without a fight.

On 1 May the 2nd Argyll and Sutherland Highlanders of 15th Scottish Division and supporting Coldstream Guards tanks were patrolling

The opening of surrender negotiations for Hamburg, by officers of the 2nd Argyll & Sutherland Highlanders. From left to right: Major Vyvyan Cornwell (with flag), Major McElwee, Lt Colonel Russell Morgan and the Recce troop leader with the German colonel.

Major General Barber, GOC 15th Scottish, and intelligence officer interview the German Chief of Staff, Marshal Busch, prelude to the surrender of Hamburg, 2 May 1945.

vigorously from Bergendorf towards Hamburg. In the midst of an action to subdue Spandau posts, two German officers walked towards the battle group. Waving their white flag they were the forerunners of a surrender delegation. By stages it went to Majors Cornwell and McElwen, to Lt Colonel Morgan and eventually to Major General 'Tiny' Barber, GOC 15th Scottish Division. The German chief of staff to Marshal Busch started the surrender talks.

Admiral Dönitz and what was left of the German navy were trying to rescue seven million Germans – civilian and military – in the east, who were hoping to be shipped to the west. The rescue convoy was bringing back some of the refugees freezing on the open beaches and docks, and it was vital that the ports and harbours of Schleswig-Holstein be kept open. Hence the Hitler order to Major General Alwin Woltz, who had become the Town Commander of Hamburg on 15 April, to keep on fighting hard to delay the Allied advance towards the Baltic ports. Woltz's garrison included the Training (Ersatz) Battalion of the SS Hitler Jugend Division, a number of Volksturm battalions, a garrison regiment, many Flak battery gunners and Lt Commander Cremer's tank-distribution unit of U-boat crews.

So Woltz wanted war and Gauleiter Kaufman wanted peace. Major General L. O. Lyne, GOC 7th Armoured, sent a polite but threatening letter to Woltz on 29 April mentioning that famous German generals Josef Harpe, GOC 5th Panzer Army, Fritz Bayerlein, GOC 53rd Corps, and many others had already surrendered – and above all that Reichsführer SS Himmler had already made an offer of unconditional surrender to the Western Powers. Lyne was only 'economical with the truth' when he mentioned that Bremen fell in 24 hours, instead of six days! Woltz sent back a polite answer on 1 May, suggesting a rendezvous 'for discussion'. However, on the same day Woltz received an order from General Keitel initiated by Dönitz that Hamburg could be surrendered on the afternoon of 3 May. General Lyne sent Woltz and his delegation to General Dempsey of 2nd Army at the Lüneburg HQ.

The gallant Cherry Pickers under Lt Colonel Bill Wainman arrived in the Rathausplatz and 1/5th Queens Infantry rolled over the two great iron bridges in stately Kangaroos of 49th APC and their adjutant raised the regimental flag over the city's Rathaus. And Colonel Wainman was busy in the Rathausplatz feeding the pigeons!

In spite of the awful damage, the streets were full of Germans walking about with purpose. The children looked at the Tommies with great

Hamburg, May 1945.

curiosity but were kept well back by their mothers in case they might be kicked. Most of the women – and who can blame them – looked at the khaki-clad invaders with hate in their faces, but the men looked more cowed and ashamed. There were still 600,000 civilians living in the ruins.

Wynford Vaughan-Thomas, the BBC correspondent, was at Lauenburg on the river Elbe, 12 miles south-east, where this author, FOO with the 3rd RTR/4th KSLI battlegroup, had just been blown up. This is what Wynford Vaughan-Thomas saw:

3 May 1945. Since two o'clock this morning this endless stream of transport has been pouring through this town, under the white flags hung over the shattered houses by the inhabitants who are standing in the streets looking dumbfounded at this wreckage of the Wehrmacht that's going past us. For, make no mistake about it, this army we see going by us is the most curious collection of wreckage you ever saw – improvised cars with people riding on the bumpers, half-track vehicles, thousands of them going through in a steady stream, and to make matters even more fantastic they've got their own traffic

policemen directing them, under British orders, standing on the corner waving
listlessly on, as the thing goes steadily by us.

These people are defeated soldiers – you can see it in their eyes. In the middle
of them there comes a much more joyous note. We see a charabanc full of RAF
released prisoners, cheering as they go by, and the Germans on the half-tracks
looking glumly on.

The next day the correspondent was in Hamburg where he broadcast
from the station of the infamous, but unwittingly very funny 'Lord Haw-
Haw', William Joyce:

I wonder what Lord Haw-Haw's views on the news are now? For Hamburg,
the city he made notorious, is this evening under the control of the British
Forces, and we found a completely and utterly bomb-ruined city.

We thought Bremen was bad, but Hamburg is devastated. Whole quarters
have disintegrated under air attacks. There are miles upon miles of blackened
walls and utterly burnt-out streets, and in the ruins there are still nearly a
million people and 50,000 foreign workers living in the cellars and air-raid
shelters. Today you don't see a single civilian on the streets; as soon as we came
in we imposed a 48-hour curfew, and there's a Sunday quiet over the whole
city; all that stirs in the streets is a British jeep or an armoured car, or a patrol
of British Tommies watching that the curfew is strictly enforced.

The docks are even more devastated than the town, the great shipyards of
Bloem and Voss are a wilderness of tangled girders, and in the middle of this
chaos 14 unfinished U-boats still stand rusting on the slipways. Work on them
finally stopped two months ago; after that date Hamburg was a dead city.

Rummaging through Lord Haw-Haw's desk we found a revealing timetable
he drew up for his work, for 10 April 1945, and at the end of it is the glorious
item: "1450–1510 hrs a pause to collect my wits." Well – he and the citizens
of Hamburg have now got plenty of time to collect their wits, for tonight the
sturdy soldiers of the Devons, the famous Desert Rats, are on guard over Haw-
Haw's studios, the Allied military authorities are now running his programme,
and instead of "Germany Calling" the colonel in charge gives you now the new
call-sign of "Station Hamburg". This is Radio Hamburg, a station of the Allied
Military Government.

The 'Thieving Magpies' had identified 100 targets in the Hamburg area
for inspection and possible seizure. The first target was of course the city's

Above and below, left and right: Ruins of Hamburg, May 1945.

1/5 Queens enter Hamburg greeted by cheerful German troops. (*Imperial War Museum*)

radio station, which was handed over to military government and named British journalists. The Phoenix Rubber Works in Harburg, a suburb in the south, making rubber protectors for U-boats, with technicians working on a 'stealth' or 'invisible' submarine, was a prime target. Other factories inspected were Electroacoustic and Germaniawerke. Scientists and specialists detained included Dr Karl Badstein (super-gun project); Johannes Engeike (guided aircraft-to-aircraft missiles); and Dr Dohler (spark plug pulse generator). 30th Assault Unit spent much time in the U-boat pens and Blohm and Voss shipyards examining submarine prototypes.

Major General 'Bobby' Ross, 53rd Welsh Division, entered Hamburg on 4 May to assume responsibility and garrison the city. The general sent his two key administration officers, Joe Grimond and Jim Cooper, into Hamburg the day *before* the surrender. Divisional HQ and the officers' mess was in the Hotel Atlantic. The 2,000-seat Schouspielhaus Opera was taken over for showbusiness, and a cabaret had to be arranged for the general's splendid victory dinner in the Atlantic Hotel. A large German naval marine warehouse contained hundreds of cases of Angus Mackay Scotch whisky, which Divisional HQ collared by quickly sending

Desert Rats tanks in the centre of Hamburg.

The shattered centre of Hamburg.

Hamburg after its fall. Here submarines litter the dockyard at the great Blohm and Voss works.

twenty-four troop carrying vehicles (TCVs) to collect and distribute them – probably fairly!

Fairly soon after VE Day, the author got to know Hamburg city rather well. The top-class Atlantic Hotel was quickly repainted and re-civilised and became a very smart officers' restaurant and hotel. It overlooks the charming Alster lake, where he sailed. In the evening Herr Schmidt-Isserstedt, the conductor of the well-known Norddeutsche Rundfunk radio orchestra, emerged from the ruins and played scintillating opera and concert *musik* to the well-behaved troops of the British Army of the Rhine, as the British Liberation Army became known. The author had some serious business in Hamburg too as the junior officer on a war crimes tribunal. His division held a German *Gau* with a very large chunk of Schleswig Holstein, mainly agricultural, which was reasonably undamaged. There he became Intelligence Officer of 3rd Regiment Royal Horse Artillery in the Desert Rats Division.

CHAPTER 22

Racing the Russians to the Baltic

It had taken Lt General 'Bubbles' Barker's 8th Corps a month to advance from the Rhine in Operation Plunder to reach the river Elbe. It had covered more than 200 miles and on the way captured 700 German officers and over 30,000 men. 11th Armoured Division had led for most of the way, although the 6th Airborne, having recovered from their mauling in Operation Varsity, kept up at an astonishing rate. The author's battle group, 3rd RTR/4th KSLI, were the first to see the great river on the morning of 19 April. The long metallic railway bridge across into the town of Lauenburg was within 200 yards of the leading 3rd RTR Comets when it was blown up in their faces.

In the meantime, Prime Minister Churchill was having a heated exchange with Marshal Stalin over the fate of fifteen Polish diplomats sent to Moscow to try to negotiate future boundaries with the Russians. Eventually, true to form, a show trial on 18 June meant that the leadership of the Polish Underground Movement was liquidated. President Roosevelt, ailing for months, died on 12 April, which of course inspired Hitler in his Berlin bunker and depressed Churchill. Anthony Eden, British Foreign Secretary, was in Washington to meet President Harry Truman, newly elected. Churchill sent Eden a telegraph message on 19 April:

> This is for your eyes alone. It would seem that the Western Allies are not immediately in a position to force their way into Berlin [despite Eisenhower's unilateral message to Stalin on 28 March]. The Russians have two and a half million troops on the sector of the front opposite that city. The Americans have only their spearheads, say 25 divisions, which are covering an immense front and are at many points engaged with the Germans … It is thought most

11th Armoured Division drive to reach the Elbe opposite Lauenburg.

important that Montgomery should take Lubeck [key port half way between Hamburg and Wismar], as soon as possible, and he has an additional American Army Corps to strengthen his movements if he requires it. Our arrival at Lübeck before our Russian friends from Stettin would save a lot of argument later on.

There is no reason why the Russians should occupy Denmark, which is a country to be liberated and to have its sovereignty restored. Our position at Lubeck, if we get it, would be decisive in this matter.

Churchill also wanted the Americans to check the region south of Stuttgart: 'In this region are the main German installations connected with their atomic research and we had better get hold of these in the interests of the special secrecy attached to this topic [known as Tube Alloys]'.

Detail of picture on page 130. (*Imperial War Museum*)

The last remnants of the German Army move on to Luneburg to surrender.

The Allied dash to the Baltic, reaching Wismar before the Russians was vital.

Appendix B, 'Hitler's Nuclear Option', relates how the 'Thieving Magpies' flew into action with some success.

Montgomery now had to choose how to get the British Liberation Army across the Elbe and corral the two million Germans, many of whom were wounded in hospitals, and end the war. He still hoped that Eisenhower and SHAEF would allow him to advance on Berlin despite the latter's embargo. He thought, on 19 April, that Bremen and Hamburg would need serious attacks and he genuinely believed that he could not launch Operation Enterprise – the forced crossing of the Elbe – quickly. Then Eisenhower recalled the US 9th Army, which was still nominally under Monty's control!

In his official account published in the *London Gazette* on 4 September 1946, Montgomery wrote: 'The main drive to the Elbe continued towards Lüneburg, which was reached on the 18th [April] and our forces began to line up on the southern bank of the river masking the city of Hamburg. The Elbe was crossed on 29 April and spearheads made straight for Lübeck in order to seal off Schleswig-Holstein peninsula.' There is no mention of what his great army did for the days 19–29 April. No mention of the urgency that Churchill in particular wanted to get to the Baltic *before* the Russians.

Right: Captain Graham Scott, A Squadron 3 RTR, marking up his map. (*Les Slater*)

Below: A Squadron 3 RTR Comets on the move north towards the river Elbe. (*Les Slater*)

General Eisenhower's report, written on 13 July 1945, 'D-Day to VE Day', spelt out his and SHAEF's policy:

In the north a route lay across the North German Plain towards the Baltic and Berlin. Berlin was the symbol of victory before the eyes of every Allied soldier from the day we set foot in Normandy, but other gains would spring from an advance to the northern sector, gains which were at least as important as those to be derived from capture of the German capital. By a thrust to the Baltic we should cut off from the main enemy armies those elements which were located in Denmark, Norway, northwest Germany and Holland, at once depriving them of supplies and preventing their *coming to the assistance of the forces in the center of Germany.*

Furthermore we should gain the north German ports [Bremen for the Americans] and thus deny the enemy use of his naval bases and ship-building yards, bringing to an end the activities of the submarines and other craft which had for so long preyed upon our supply routes. Finally we should link hands with the Russian forces sweeping across Pomerania to the north of Berlin.

The American 9th Army, under Montgomery's command for Operation Plunder, reverted to General Bradley. When Montgomery complained that the British Liberation Army was not strong enough to force a crossing over the Elbe (see Chester Wilmot's report below), he was allocated the US 18th Airborne Corps to help:

30 April 1945. Here in the north, there's still an army to be reckoned with; an army whose fighting power Himmler [he had been appointed C-in-C Home Army, after the 20 July plot] may still regard as a bargaining weapon. We have smashed the German Army as a whole and its Air Force; but we haven't yet broken the power or the spirit of the German Navy. And it's now fighting hard in defence of its great ports and naval bases in the north. Even though the navy has never been thoroughly pro-Nazi, it has been unquestionably loyal to the German High Command. In Kiel, Wilhelmshaven and the northern ports there are more than 100,000 German naval personnel – most of them with some training in the use of weapons, and they're being put into the land battle. We're meeting marines, sailors, and even submarine crews, and they're fighting well.

Moreover, when Field Marshal Busch became Commander-in-Chief North-West, he took over an area where the organisation and discipline behind the lines was still good, because the navy still had the situation firmly in hand.

Busch also found that in addition to the troops fighting south of the Elbe he had four other divisions that he could bring from Denmark. He thus had the core of a force to protect the naval bases, and the navy was determined that he should use it to do so. This combination of circumstances has provided the 2nd Army with the immediate task of isolating and smashing this force, and of seizing the naval bases behind it. We can't afford at this stage of the war to pause in the task. So long as there are any pockets of resistance as well organised as this one, the Nazis may be encouraged to fight on elsewhere. And so here in the north the 2nd Army is striking at what amounts to Himmler's last hope.

Eisenhower's report continued:

Although it was not conceivable that resistance could long be maintained in the north German plain, it was possible that some withdrawal might be attempted into Denmark and Norway with a view to make a last stand in those countries while 'Fortress Holland' would also continue to hold out behind the water barriers. The prevention of such a withdrawal by means of a *rapid* [author's emphasis] Allied advance to the Baltic, thus became the primary objective of our operations in the northern sector. For the subsequent reduction of Norway, in the event that the German garrison there [nearly 400,000] continued to hold out, a task force was assembled in Scotland under the command of Lt General Sir Andrew Thorne.

Eisenhower and SHAEF certainly made sure that Montgomery's 'orders' were to be a very rapid drive, come what may, to the Baltic, including Kiel, the whole of Denmark and the remainder of Holland.

Operation Enterprise was a slow, thorough, methodical assault plan to gain two bridgeheads over the river Elbe, in the Alamein and Rhine crossing style, for the assault. Montgomery chose 15th Scottish Division to make the main attack; they were christened 'The Crossing Sweepers' after the Seine, the Escaut, the Rhine and now the Elbe. The Commando Brigade would be tasked to capture the town of Lauenburg, and 11th Armoured and 6th Airborne would set off north to thwart Marshal Konstantin Rokossovsky's 2nd Belorussian Army, which was making rapid progress through Mecklenburg and heading west.

For a week, very complicated plans were being drawn up for the assault crossing of the river Elbe. 8th Corps was given the honour of establishing a bridgehead, initially 1,500 yards deep and 2,500 yards wide. This would be the responsibility of 15th Scottish with 1st

Above: Prisoners being interrogated after the capture of Zeven, among them youths, only fourteen years old, from the Volksturm.

Right: The final battlegrounds beyond the Elbe, Operation Enterprise.

285

Operation Enterprise: 10 HLI troops have crossed the river Elbe, 19 April 1945.

Commando Brigade under command. And 11th Armoured would then pass through and thrust north for Lübeck, Kiel and the Danish frontier.

The complications arose because the northern bank of the river Elbe is a substantial steep escarpment, which would make Buffalo or DUKW landings difficult. Moreover, enemy observation points had clear observation of the southern bank activities for several miles. No vehicle movements were allowed in the forward positions during daylight. The Elbe in April is about 300 yards in width in the Artlenburg-Lauenburg stretch and flows at about two knots. There was only one road into Artlenburg, a small town with narrow side streets with gardens and woods, and another from Scharnesbeck to Lauenburg. Enemy strength was estimated at about nine battalions of very mixed provenance with about 100 guns, and rather surprisingly supported by daring Luftwaffe jet plane attacks.

The final plan for Operation Enterprise was for a two-brigade attack at 0200 hrs on 29 April, under 'Monty's Searchlights', supported by a substantial barrage from seventeen artillery regiments.

1st Commando Brigade was tasked with a crossing west of Hohnstorf, to capture Lauenburg from the rear. 44th Brigade, led by the Royal Scots and RSF on board the LVTs of 11th RTR, would attack through the Grünhof forests to capture Schnakenbeck, starting from just west and east of Artlenburg.

Colonel R. Foster, Commander of 11th Army Group Royal Engineers, who had masterminded the complex Rhine crossing so successfully, was in charge of the plan for the Elbe crossing. This included suitable DD tank and LVT approaches; river entries and exits; a DUKW crossing; two 12-person assault boat ferries, at the Lauenburg crossing a Class 9 raft ferry and a Class 9 bridge of folding-bridge equipment; for the Artlenburg crossing a Class 40 raft ferry and a Class 40 Bailey pontoon-bridge. Colonel Foster also had to provide boom protection above and below the crossing places.

The follow-up plan was for 46th Brigade to go through the Commando bridgehead, and for 227th Brigade through 44th Brigade. The Recce Regiment would land its armoured cars and carriers in the van of the assault and push out patrols to the north, west and east. The bridgehead was a country of field and farm, deer forests and lakes, lonely castles, villages and little country towns, and west, along the Elbe, the outskirts of the sprawling mangled port of Hamburg.

Operation Enterprise went well. The courage of the sappers who built the pontoon bridges regardless of damage or casualties was beyond all praise. The immense fire plan fell on the German 245th Wehrmacht Division strongpoints. At exactly 0218hrs the huge black Buffaloes of 11th RTR, with the 77th Assault Squadron RE AVRE bombards, carried the 8th Royal Scots and 6th RSF across from two crossing points: Hohnstorf opposite Lauenburg and Artlenburg on the left. At 0330hrs the Argylls and KOSB crossed, as did the Seaforths on the Commando front. Altogether Hobart's 'Funnies' made 1,139 lifts during Enterprise, of infantry carriers, jeeps, scout cars, Weasels, anti-tank guns and trailers.

15th Scottish took a different centre line over the Elbe at Lutau, where the Glasgow Highlanders had a fight, Royal Scots met enemy SPs in Kollow. KOSB sent patrols into Gülzower Holz wood, took many prisoners and found two long-range 12-inch guns, which had shelled the Enterprise bridgehead, then Grünhof and Tesperhude. The HLI reached Wiershop, the Argylls Krummel and the Gordons Hamwarde. On 1 May Geesthach and its garrison surrendered over the phone to Brigadier Colville. In the town was a store of V-1 rocket fuel and ammunition and a dangerous stock of poison gas containers. 15th Scottish were joined by 53rd Welsh and also 5th British Division (arriving from Italy) to clear the huge forest to the west of Sachsenwald. The KOSB captured the Prince and Princess von Bismarck in the schloss of Friedrichsruh. The sixteen-eighteen-year-old cadets from the Flak school in Hamburg had a bitter last battle with the HLI in Hohenhern and Neu Bornsen. In deep hillside gulleys, east of Bornsen, they used their 20mm light A/A guns to good effect until artillery and tanks dealt with them.

The Recce Regiment in Elmenhorst noted: 'We were checking the amazing procession of the defeated German forces along the Hamburg road. They were coming from the east and the north. There were men on foot, men on bicycles and men in carts. There were wheezing, massive dilapidated lorries dragging three or four or five trailers, all piled high with passengers and baggage. When stopped, some of the lorries managed to start again. Many did not. Looking at this motley collection, one wondered how the German Army had managed to resist so long.'

The endless stream of uniformed jetsam poured along every road: Luftwaffe, Flak units, marines, panzergrenadiers, U-boat crews, town police, Volksturm, a few Hitler Jugend, a few SS (some were still fighting in the Forst Segeberg). However, their fierce discipline and allegiance to their now-dead Führer kept them going indomitably. The Allied air forces ruled the skies. The Allied tanks and AFVs and artillery forces

6th Airborne paratroops meet Russians at Wismar. (*Imperial War Museum*)

outnumbered the Wehrmacht by ten to one, and the writing was on the wall during Overlord and the irresistible Russian advances. However, it was not until all the German towns were crammed with dead and wounded, with red crosses painted on the hospital roofs and the survivors penned into Schleswig-Holstein that there was a final surrender. And that was mainly due to the death of Hitler in a sordid Berlin bunker.

The Commandos rapidly cleared Lauenburg and captured the road bridge over the Elbe-Trave Canal. On the same day the Scots Greys Sherman tanks of 4th Black Rat Armoured Brigade teamed up with two brigades of 6th Airborne Division, and crossed over and reached Boizenburg in the evening. Early on 2 May the Scots Greys and Airborne troops covered the 70 miles to Wismar in about 8 hours. Lt Edmiston's troop were followed by Lt Colonel D. N. Stewart, the Greys' CO in a scout car, followed by the CO of 3rd Parachute Brigade riding pillion on a despatch rider's motorcycle! Wittenburg was passed, despite meeting towed 88mm guns. They went through Lutzon and Gladebusch with minor actions on the way. Eight miles short of Wismar, B Squadron destroyed five trains laden with German soldiery and equipment. At 1300hrs the Greys' recce troop reached Wismar and their eleven Honeys

The British 6th Airborne Division's first contact with Russian troops at Wismar.

(small fast tanks) discovered an aerodrome north-east of the town on the seashore. Some shooting took place and 200 Luftwaffe troops marching in threes in perfect step came out of the hangers and surrendered. During the evening Russian troops, male and female, drunk and sober, appeared in 'White' scout cars, fraternised for half an hour shaking hands and drinking vodka, then withdrew eastwards and erected a monster road block, the first instalment of the Iron Curtain! By late evening the whole of 3rd Parachute Brigade had taken control of Wismar.

The 11th Armoured Division in two mixed brigade battle groups crossed the Elbe in the early evening of 30 April and by the evening of 1 May had reached Sandesneben and Gronwold. On the next day they had occupied Bad Oldesloe and Reinfeld and liberated a POW Luft camp containing RAF personnel, near Kastorf. At 1530hrs the 2nd Fife and Forfars' Comets with 1st Cheshires' infantry entered Lübeck while 23rd Hussars and 8th Rifle Brigade headed towards Travemünde and Neustadt. By evening the naval installations and airfields were taken and reported to be in good condition. Between 2 and 4 May the division captured 70,000 prisoners and no fewer than twenty-five generals and admirals, and freed hundreds of Allied POWs. Major General Pip Roberts, the dashing GOC of the Black Bull Division, had one final task. He took a Comet tank squadron and infantry to Flensburg on the Danish border to tell Grand Admiral Dönitz, Hitler's reluctant successor, and Field Marshal Keitel, head of OKW (German Armed Forces) with the Supreme HQ of OKW, that pending the arrival of a special mission from SHAEF, they were under 11th Armoured orders.

A day or so before the Fife and Forfars entered Lübeck a terrible disaster had taken place. The German SS concentration bosses at Neuengamme KZ had decided to liquidate the remaining 10,000 prisoners before the British arrived. The camp was just outside Hamburg and over the last seven years 40,000 mainly Jewish men, women and children had been murdered there. The SS guards numbered 800 and Rothenburgsort, a Hamburg suburb, was a killing centre. An uprising by Russian prisoners was savagely put down. As the BLA approached Hamburg over 7,000 prisoners were marched or were sent by train to Lübeck and herded into two large passenger liners, 2,000 into the *Deutschland* and 5,000 into the *Cap Acona*, both used as prison hulks. Nine Typhoon fighter bombers of the RAF 198th Squadron, led by Squadron Leader Martin Rumbold, saw the tempting target of four ships in Lübeck harbour. In their attack

The route to Lübeck and the end
of Operation Enterprise.

Lübeck harbour: 11th Armoured
Division Cromwell tank.
(*Imperial War Museum*)

291

British soldiers interrogating members of the staff of the German State Railway HQ, captured near Lübeck while they were trying to leave the country.

over 3,000 POWs were burned to death on the *Cap Acona*, and many others, including Poles, Czechs, Norwegians and many Russians died.

Major Anthony Hibbert was Brigade Major of 1st Parachute Brigade and was taken prisoner at Arnhem, but he escaped. Having broken his leg in a car accident he was unable to rejoin the Paras in an active role, so in March 1945 he was appointed the co-ordinating officer for an airborne operation to seize the vital port of Kiel. He reported to Lt General Browning's AA HQ. Apparently Eisenhower had requested plans in December 1944 for an operation to seize Kiel. However, T-Force personnel had to be included, with a Royal Naval officer as second in command. As the British Liberation Army advanced so swiftly into the heart of Germany, the airborne drop was not needed. Hibbert then joined his friend Brian Urquhart, the intelligence officer in Market Garden whose advice went unheeded. Both were therefore key members of T-Force and tasked with investigating 150 targets in Kiel (compared to 75 in Hamburg). With a T-Force of 500 strong, they had to confront the Kiel garrison of 40,000 kriegsmarines with their slave army of 420,000 foreign labourers.

One key problem was that General Dempsey's order from Montgomery's HQ 10 minutes after the 4 May surrender said: 'No advance beyond

The Hamburg-American Line's 27,000 ton *New York* after being bombed during an air attack on Kiel.

this line to take place without orders from me.' All four Corps were to stand fast on the line Dömitz, Ludwigslust, Schwerin, Wismar, Neustadt, Bad Segeberg, Wedel, Stade, Bremervorde and Bremen. So Kiel was in *verboten* territory. Another problem was that T-Force, although a law unto themselves, had no written authority to advance to Kiel.

Urquhart told Hibbert that it was possible that the Russians contained at Wismar could launch an amphibious commando operation to seize the port of Kiel, which was an ice-free port with easy access to the North Sea. The prime target for T-Force was the Walterwerke factory and its chief designer, Dr Hellmuth Walter, whose new developments for U-boat design were important. Brigadier G. H. C. Pennycock, the OC T-Force and Lt Colonel Ray Bloomfield, the senior staff officer, concurred: '... advance to Kiel and investigate the specified targets'.

Besides the 5th King's battalion of infantry, there were detachments of the Special Boat Squadron (SBS), the Special Air Service (SAS) and Royal Marine Commandos in this T-Force battle group. D Squadron 1st SAS Regiment led in jeeps from Bad Segeberg at 0800hrs on VE Day [Ref. WO 285/12]. In Neumünster the jeeps of 30th Assault Unit Royal Marines with their White Ensigns fluttering surged into the lead. Later there was controversy about the first unit to enter Kiel: SAS/SBS/30th Assault? Over 80 per cent of the city was in ruins, the cathedral in pieces, the railway station shattered and 40 per cent of T-Force targets had been obliterated. Hibbert headed for the Naval Academy under Kapitan Wilhelm Möhr, who was sceptical that 200 assorted British had authority to ask for surrender [Ref. WO 205/1049]. A phone call to Admiral Dönitz in Flensburg achieved his agreement to the surrender. Among the vessels in the port were the *Prinz Eugen* and *Admiral Hipper*, two powerful heavy cruisers. The King's men secured most of the port, quays, wharfs and docks. The three intrepid majors, Hibbert, Gaskell and Lambert, issued orders from the city's police HQ at 2.30 p.m. German troops for the time being could keep their weapons, while the freed slave labourers were forbidden to carry arms. The latter were told in French, English and German that they would be returned to their homes as soon as possible. 30th Assault unit soon 'captured' Dr Walter, a heavy, flabby, black-haired Nazi. He was an important find and soon a posse of high-powered Royal Navy scientists under Commander Aylen arrived to supervise investigation of Dr Walter's microfilms, machinery and plant. T-Force targets included ELAC, whose Dr Fisher was an outstanding

German POWs in Lübeck. (*Imperial War Museum*)

torpedo designer, Krupp Germania, where a complete Type XXIII submarine was discovered, and Deutsche Werke, where small U-boats were being built. Eventually, two days later, a Guards unit of 8th Corps arrived to organise a Victory Parade. Hibbert was officially in disgrace. Lt General Barker arrived in Kiel and told him that Admiral Baillie-Grohman, whose powerful naval squadron had 'liberated' Copenhagen, now intended to 'liberate' Kiel. Nevertheless, Hibbert and Urquhart had shown splendid initiative. After the war the grateful citizens of Kiel awarded Hibbert the 'Great Seal of Kiel' for his role, along with 500 commandos and paratroops, in capturing the port-city, which prevented the Russians from invading Denmark.

Guards Armoured were tasked with clearing up the rectangle west of Hamburg and the Elbe, which included Bremervörde, Stade, Himmelpforten, Hechthausen and most importantly, the naval port of Cuxhaven. After liberating the camps of Westertimke and Sandbostel, they found eleven enormous craters, 60 feet across and 40 feet deep caused by sea mine explosions around Bremervörde. Every army bulldozer for miles around was co-opted and within 24 hours eight of the craters were filled up.

A whole battalion of 351st Marine Division was guarding the Hamme-Oste canal bridge and 51st Highland Division was asked to take them on. The Guards moved east to tackle Stade, also protected by giant craters. A Coldstream battle group managed to find a way round cross-country. Stade, with five hospitals containing over a thousand German wounded, surrendered without a fight. The Irish battle group then took Elm and Oldendorf after the news of the deaths of Hitler and Göbbels was heard on the radio. It must have demoralised many local listeners. Bremervörde then capitulated unexpectedly.

Major General Allan Adair, in his history of the Guards Armoured details the complicated negotiations of the days just after the Armistice was signed. The German General Goltzsch, commander of Corps Ems in the Cuxhaven peninsula, General Erdmann, GOC 17th Parachute Division, and two well-known kampfgruppen COs, Colonels Grassmel and Hardegg, were all involved in surrender negotiations. The Royal Navy sent a detachment under Captain Lawford RN, as Cuxhaven was a great port. The 101 ships in the harbour included a destroyer, nine submarines and eleven minesweepers. In the middle of the night five more destroyers arrived from Norway, anxious to surrender. The 7th

Tank dozer pushes an enemy tank off the Bremervorde road, 1 May 1945. (*Birkin Haward*)

Assault bridge laid by 82 Assault Squadron RE in final action at Bremevorde, 2 May 1945. (*Birkin Haward*)

Field Marshal Montgomery meets General Rokossovsk at Wismar.

Parachute Division under Colonel Menzel was paraded on the captured airfield and surrendered with great dignity. They ranked among the very finest troops in the German Army and refused to surrender to any unit except the Guards Armoured.

On 11 May the Guards provided a company of Scots Guards plus sappers from 615th Field Squadron to accompany and guard Rear Admiral Muirhead-Gould RN on an expedition in four minesweepers to accept the surrender of Heligoland, an island 50 miles north-west of Cuxhaven in the North Sea. The admiral's flotilla rendezvous was off the island of Neuwerk at the end of the Elbe estuary. There were 7,000 kriegsmarines on Heligoland, plus 2,000 TODT workers kept busy repairing the continual damage done by the RAF over the years. The artificial manmade harbour had space for two large 'basins', a huge submarine pen, barracks and other military buildings. But cut deep in the rock was a naval town, offices, power stations, torpedo rooms, food and wine stores, hospitals. The whole garrison could live there in complete safety. It was the German Rock of Gibraltar.

Montgomery signalled the War Office in London on 3 May as soon as he knew that 6th Airborne had made contact at Bunz, 7 miles east

The Baltic round-up by the British Liberation Army.

The author (right) in Kiel, early May 1945. Detail of picture on page 8.

of Wismar: 'There is no doubt that the very rapid movement from the Elbe bridgeheads north to the Baltic was a very fine performance on the part of the troops concerned. There is no doubt also that we only just beat the Russians by about 12 hours. All's well that ends well and the whole of the Schleswig peninsula and Denmark is now effectively sealed off and we shall keep it so … the flood of German troops and civilians fleeing from the approaching Russians is a spectacle that can seldom have been seen before.'

It was indeed a close-run thing. The Russians vigorously attacked and held the Danish island of Bornholm, 57 miles from the mainland. It was a German naval base occupied by the kriegsmarines since 1940, commanded by Commander Kamptz. Prime Minister Churchill signalled Anthony Eden, then in San Francisco: 'The British Naval Attaché in Stockholm reported that the Russians may have dropped parachutists a few miles south of Copenhagen and that Communist activities have appeared there.'

Field Marshal
Montgomery
decorates Marshal
Zhukov.

CHAPTER 23

Admiral Dönitz's 'Fourth Reich'

By the middle of April there were three main groups of power remaining in the Third Reich. Firstly, the Berlin garrison headed by Hitler, Göbbels, Bormann (deputy Führer) and General Krebs. Secondly, the Oberkommando der Wehrmacht (OKW) comprised Keitel, Jodl, Friedeburg and Dönitz. They abandoned Hitler in the capital and moved or were pushed steadily north-west until the little cluster arrived at the port of Flensburg on the Danish frontier. Hamburg was the last remaining big city under their control. Thirdly, part of the OKW was operating with the armies in the south. Hitler had sacked Göring on the 15 April and only Himmler was capable of liaising with the OKW. He had visited Bremen to threaten and bluster, trying to force General Becker to keep on resisting. For a week until 24 April, Himmler had been in touch with the Swedish Count Bernadotte, trying to elicit an answer to the question, 'Will America and Britain accept our unconditional surrender *now*, and allow us to concentrate all our remaining forces fending off the Red Army?' Just outside Hamburg was Bismarck's ancient castle, the Friedrichsruh, the HQ of the International Red Cross where Himmler carried out his hopeless talks.

Grand Admiral Karl Dönitz was commander of the German navy from 1943 and was Führer of Nazi Germany for seven days in May 1945. His U-boat warfare in the Battle of the Atlantic had nearly brought Britain to its knees. The Royal Navy and RAF, helped by Bletchley Park's Ultra detection, eventually got the upper hand. Since the declaration of war in 1939, 863 U-boats had gone out on operational patrols and eventually 754 had been sunk or damaged beyond repair. The losses of U-boat crews, officers and men killed in action, totalled 27,491, but they had sunk 2,800

Sketch of Dönitz's HQ, Schloss Glücksberg.

Allied merchant ships and 148 Allied warships. Dönitz continued to be one of Hitler's favourites, particularly since exciting new stealth techniques and fast mini-subs promised future miracles. He was described as having a cold, expressionless face with a piercing gaze, and had the nickname 'The Big Lion'. Even when the British troops were on the river Elbe, 50 miles from his HQ at Ploen, he declared: 'Europe will realise that Adolf Hitler is the only statesman of any stature in Europe.' When Hitler committed suicide in the Berlin bunker on the afternoon of 30 April, by default Dönitz was destined to succeed him. Göring had decided to leave the bunker, claiming urgent tasks in southern Germany. When he telegraphed Hitler offering to take command of the surviving German forces, Martin Bormann, Hitler's poisonous shadow, interpreted this to his master as a treasonable act. Göring was ordered to be arrested and stripped of all offices and honours. Hitler's last will expelled him from the Nazi Party. Hitler had got wind of Himmler's secret peace negotiations, so he was blacklisted. Bormann was not acceptable as the next Führer, so that left Dönitz, who remained the logical candidate. On 1 May, he became Führer and appointed his first cabinet. Göbbels was dead, Bormann was missing believed killed, Göring banished, Ribbentrop and Thierach (Minister of Justice) were ignored. So Schwerin-Krosigk became Foreign Minister and State Secretary Stuckardt became Minister of the Interior. Himmler turned up and tried hard to join but was rejected immediately. At his first conference in Flensburg Schoener, Army Group Czechoslovakia, Frank, Reich Protector of Bohemia, Seyss-Inquart, the Overlord of Holland, Lindemann, Governor of Denmark, and Terboren, political leader in Norway, were either present or communicated their views. Their main object was to save their people and troops in the east from capture by the Red Army, which would be followed by imprisonment and gulags in Russia. This was clear in Dönitz's mind. German newspapers appeared on 2 May with black borders. One of these newspapers, soon to fall into the hands of the advancing British, bore the three-word headline: 'Unser Führer gefallen'. By implication, 'our Leader' had fallen *in battle*, presumably during the Russian onslaught on Berlin.

Admiral Karl Dönitz and Albert Speer, Hitler's architect and Minister of Armaments, Buildings and War Production, had long worked closely together on naval issues, building of U-boat pens, and U-boat production. They had a healthy respect for each other. Speer wrote *Inside the Third Reich,* a fascinating and more or less warts-and-all book. When Dönitz became the new Chief of State, Speer wrote: 'For 12 years we had served the ideas of the National Socialist regime ... But the death of Hitler broke that mental bind which had for so long warped our thinking. For Dönitz this meant that the objectivity of the trained military officer came to the fore. From the moment he took over, Dönitz held that we should end the war as quickly as possible and that once the task was done, our work was over.' On 1 May, the first military conference between Dönitz as the new Commander in Chief of the armed forces and Field Marshal Ernst Busch took place. Busch, in effect, wanted Götterdämmerung attacks on the superior forces advancing on Hamburg. Dönitz did not agree. He said: 'All that should be done was to keep the way to the West open as long as possible for the refugees from the East.' Columns of them were blocked near Lübeck. A delaying action by the German troops in the West should be continued only to allow the flow to continue. Busch made a great to-do about the Grand Admiral no longer acting in Hitler's spirit, but Dönitz was no longer moved by such exhortations.

At thirty-seven minutes past ten o'clock on the night of 1 May, Dönitz broke the news to the German nation by the following announcement over Radio Hamburg:

German Wehrmacht! My comrades! The Führer has fallen. Faithful to the great idea of preserving the peoples of Europe from Bolshevism he had consecrated his life, and died a hero's death. One of the greatest heroes in German history has passed away. We lower our flags in proud reverence and sorrow. The Führer had appointed me to succeed him as Head of the State and Supreme Commander of the Wehrmacht. I take over the command of all branches of the German Wehrmacht in the determination to continue the struggle against Bolshevism until the fighting troops and the hundreds of thousands of families in Eastern Germany have been preserved from enslavement or destruction. I must continue to wage war on the British and Americans in so far and for so long as they hinder me in the prosecution of the fight against Bolshevism. The situation demands of you, who have already accomplished such great historical feats and now long for the end of the war, further unconditional service. I demand discipline and obedience. Only by the unquestioning execution of my orders can chaos and the downfall of Germany be avoided. He who now shirks his duty, thus bringing death and enslavement upon German women and children, is a coward and a traitor. The oath pledged by you to the Führer now applies for each one of you to me as the successor appointed by the Führer.

German soldiers! Do your duty! The life of our nation is at stake!

Intense negotiations followed between Dönitz, his various emissaries, and Field Marshal Montgomery and SHAEF. On 5 May all German forces in Holland, north-west Germany and Denmark surrendered to Monty. At 1427hrs that afternoon, the newly appointed German Foreign Minister, Count Schwerin von Korsigk, broadcasting from Flensburg, the headquarters of the German government, announced that Germany's fighting troops had surrendered and that the war was over. His words, although couched in the rhetoric of untarnished pride, were unambiguous:

German men and women, the High Command of the German armed forces, on orders of Grand Admiral Dönitz, has today declared unconditional surrender of all German fighting troops. As the leading minister of the Reich government, which the Admiral of the Fleet has appointed for dealing with war tasks, I turn at this tragic moment of our history to the German nation.

After a heroic fight of almost six years of incomparable hardness, Germany has succumbed to the overwhelming power of her enemies. To continue the war would only mean senseless bloodshed and futile disintegration. The government, which has a feeling of responsibility for the future of the nation, was compelled to act on the collapse of all physical and material forces and to demand of the enemy cessation of hostilities. It was the noblest task of the Admiral of the Fleet and of the government supporting him, after the terrible sacrifices which the war has caused.

Chester Wilmot reported on the BBC:

8 May 1945. I don't think you can realise the completeness of the German defeat until you've been to Flensburg, the present seat of the Dönitz government and of Keitel's High Command.

In the streets civilians were going about their normal business with expressionless faces, but the crowds outside the food shops were much larger than those gathered to read Dönitz's proclamation about the end of the war in the northwest. Neither the civilians nor the ordinary troops any longer care.

All this wasn't surprising, but I did expect that somehow the atmosphere at the High Command Headquarters would be different; but this was the scene. A rather dirty Marine barracks housed the headquarters and the government; outside it, 18 scruffy sentries, as dirty and dishevelled as the troops in the town. In the car park beyond the gate there were a dozen big staff cars, replicas of those great sleek black Mercedes in which the Nazi leaders have swaggered through the capitals of Europe. And now, here they were in the last bolt-hole, their shining black surfaces hastily camouflaged with paint that had just been slashed on, and with branches of trees tied on so that they looked like Macduff's men who carried Birnam wood to Dunsinane.

Here in these cars was the end of Nazi glory. The only evidence that this was the High Command's Headquarters was a small sign painted in black on the torn-off bottom of a camouflaged boot-box. It bore the letters 'OKW' [Oberkommando der Wehrmacht – High Command of the Armed Forces].

British officers who had been inside told me that the interior is just as dirty and decrepit. It has the same atmosphere of defeat and despair. Yesterday a British officer tried to deliver a message to Field Marshal Keitel. He found him in a poky room at the end of a long passage, no sentries outside the door – three Germans lounging at the window at the end might have been sentries. He went in through an outer office, pushing his way past typists and clerks, through a small door and into Keitel's office, a room 20 feet by 15. Keitel sat at a small table in full uniform with his Field Marshal's baton beside him. Behind his chair was a photograph of Hitler. On the wall in front was a large school map of Europe, which Hitler conquered but couldn't hold down. Here in this miserable little room, a far cry from the great chancelleries of Europe where he so often laid down terms, sat Keitel himself. Here and in Dönitz's office, the German Führer and Chief of the High Command had come to the fateful decisions of the past few days. The power and glory of the greater Reich, the pomp and pageantry of Hitler's empire, had been reduced to this. Only the glittering uniforms remained. During yesterday afternoon Keitel was handed the text of the surrender terms which Jodl had signed at SHAEF, a document which meant not even peace with honour but defeat with humiliation.

When Dönitz himself broadcast from Flensburg on 8 May, his reference to the Soviet occupation of the eastern half of Germany was oblique: 'The German people should walk in defeat "dignified and courageous",' he said, 'in the hope that our children may one day have a free, secure existence.' He was able to announce one change that the Allies considered essential in any future Germany. All connection between the German state and the Nazi party had been severed. 'The Nazi party has left the scene of its activity,' he said. A few hours later Flensburg radio announced that the Nazi salute 'Heil Hitler!' was abolished. That same day the German navy, which the new ruler of Germany had commanded at the height of its powers, suffered its final humiliation, as all U-boats, which had caused such enormous losses to Allied and neutral shipping and to the lives of sailors and merchant seamen, were ordered to surface and to report for instructions to the nearest Allied commanders.

The German Operation Rainbow in the final week of May ordered submarine commanders in port or harbour to scuttle their craft, so fifty-six did in Flensburg, thirty-one in Travemünde, twenty-six in Kiel, fifteen in Wilhelmshaven and ten in Hamburg. Finally the British Royal Navy in Operation Deadlight ordered all U-boat commanders at sea to surface and fly a black flag or pennant. More than 100 were then taken out into the Atlantic and sunk in deep water west of Ireland. Presumably their crews were taken off first!

Winston Churchill sent a memo to the Foreign Office on 14 May:

It is of high importance that the surrender of the German people should be completed through agencies which have authority over them. I neither know nor care about Dönitz. He may be a war criminal. He used submarines to sink ships … the question is has he any power to get the Germans to lay down their arms and hand them over quickly without any more loss of life? We cannot go round into every German slum and argue with every German that it is his duty to surrender or we will shoot him. There must be some kind of force which will give orders which they will obey. Once they obey we can do what we like to carry through unconditional surrender.

At Flensburg, Grand Admiral Dönitz had continued to act as if he were the head of the German government. Every morning since VE Day, wearing his admiral's uniform, he had been driven in the armoured Mercedes, which Hitler had given him, from his living quarters to the nearby naval school in which his government was housed. Each day he had held a meeting of his cabinet. On 21 May, as this masquerade continued, a British naval mission reached Flensburg by air. This mission was accommodated on board the Hamburg-Amerika liner *Caribia* in Flensburg harbour. Berthed on the opposite side of the pier was the liner *Patria*, in which was accommodated the Allied Control Commission, established by Eisenhower, under the command of an American, General Rooks. A Russian military mission was also present, with Eisenhower's authority to interrogate members of the German government.

'As might be expected,' the head of the British Naval Mission, Commodore G. R. G. Allen, wrote in his official report, 'the political atmosphere was somewhat confused; on the one hand the German naval authorities were ready to co-operate under the terms of the capitulation, and to discuss matters of naval policy and technical matters quite freely. The German armed forces, both naval and military, appeared to be in good shape with good morale and well disciplined. The naval ratings were smart and well turned out, and there was no visible sign of demoralisation. The civil population were evidently well fed and appeared reasonably contented, self-confident and relatively indifferent to events happening around them. On the other hand, General Rooks told me that Admiral Dönitz himself had recently stated that the conditions were likely to deteriorate sharply in the near future if the Western Allies insisted upon maintaining their present policy of non-co-operation with the Germans in the occupied areas.'

On the afternoon of 22 May Dönitz's adjutant received a telephone call summoning Grand Admiral Dönitz, General Jodl and Admiral von Friedeburg to meet the head of the Allied Control Commission, General Rooks, on board the liner *Patria* at 0945 hrs. the next morning. When he was told this, Dönitz said curtly, 'Pack the bags.'

Jodl, Speer and Dönitz are arrested at Flensburg by troops of 11th Armoured Division during Operation Blackout.

Commodore Allen was on board the *Patria* on the morning of 23 May when the arrest of Dönitz and his government took place. Allen reported to London:

> General Rooks had confined all officers to the ships during this event to prevent any untoward incident, and a British brigade with tanks was deployed in the town to maintain order. Admiral Dönitz conducted himself with much dignity; the other two appeared nervous. Rooks told them, 'Gentlemen, I am in receipt of instructions from Supreme Headquarters, European Theatre of Operations, from the Supreme Commander, General Eisenhower, to call you before me this morning to tell you that he has decided, in concert with the Soviet High Command, that today the acting German government and the German High Command, with several of its members, shall be taken into custody as prisoners of war. Thereby the acting German government is dissolved.'

After General Rooks had announced what was in effect the final end of the Third Reich, Dönitz commented that 'words at this moment would be superfluous'. All German naval officers at Flensburg were confined to their quarters. A detachment of British troops surrounded the police buildings in Mütvik where Dönitz and the members of his

Speer (in the raincoat), Dönitz and Jodl under arrest at Flensburg, the final seat of the government of the Third Reich, May 1945.

administration were brought under guard, each of them permitted one suitcase of personal belongings.

Operation Blackout took place on 23 May. At 1000hrs the 1st Cheshires and 1st Herefords with 15/19th Hussar Comets of 11th Armoured Division swooped on the barracks, the government buildings in Flensburg and the Hamburg-Amerika liner *Patria*. A naval patrol of two destroyers cruised along Flensburg Fjord to ensure there was no escape by sea for the Dönitz government and the town garrison. A very well-planned attack on the massive Schloss Glücksburg on the lake took place, although no shots were fired. By 1130hrs, 5,000 prisoners had been taken, including Grand Admiral Dönitz, General Jodl, Generals Reinbecke, Dethleffsen and Reich Minister Alfred Speer (Admiral von Friedeburg committed suicide). The VIPs were escorted to 159th Brigade HQ, thence to Flensburg aerodrome and into captivity. Nuremberg loomed for the VIPs and prison camps for the rest.

The day ended with the Hussar Comets thundering noisily through the narrow cobbled streets of Flensburg.

Dönitz's 'Fourth' Reich had come and gone. Ahead lay death for Jodl, 20 years in Spandau Prison for Speer and 10 years for Dönitz.

CHAPTER 24

Final Surrender: Operation Eclipse

The situation in Germany at the very end of April 1945 was frankly chaotic. It was beyond comprehension that this proud, dominant country known as the Third Reich, destined as its leaders thought to last for a thousand years, had not just crumbled but completely collapsed. Fifty great cities, including Berlin, Hamburg, Bremen and those in the Ruhr, were in ruins. Some of the photographs in this book, such as those taken by the author in shattered Hamburg, bear witness to this. Many cities had no electricity, gas or clean running water. The national government had disintegrated and Dönitz's Fourth Reich in Flensburg was just a comic opera. Alan Moorehead wrote:

> Like ants in an ant-heap the people scurried over the ruins, diving furtively into cellars and doorways in search of loot. Like ants you would see women scuttling down a side-track with their bundles only to be blocked by débris and then turn irresolutely back, shoving and bumping against one another. Everyone was on the move, and there was a frantic ant-like quality about their activity. Life was sordid, aimless, stacked to the roof with city refugees living on soup and potatoes. From the Ruhr across Germany an occasional factory chimney smokes, but 90 percent of the country's industry was at a standstill. No trains ran. Every family was bereaved or broken up. The housing situation was impossible and likely to get worse. A very large part of the population was simply wandering on the roads with the millions of foreigners. And to these was now added the German army itself. A mass flight from the Russians towards the Elbe and the Anglo-American lines began. Officers stripped off their uniforms and begged or stole civilian clothes from the nearby houses. Mass fear had gripped them so greatly that when aircraft appeared in the sky

The Third Reich – completely collapsed.

the shout went up: 'The Russians! The Russians!' and the mob would break
out in panic across the countryside.

Negotiations for surrender started on the Italian front. In the last week
of April Bologna fell and the Allies reached the river Po; on the 26th
Milan was taken by partisans. Colonel General Heinrich von Vietinghoff,
the commander in chief of all German forces in Italy – after Hitler had
recalled Field Marshal Kesselring to try to stem the Allied advances in
the west – had lost 150,000 men as prisoners, taken in less than three
weeks. Waffen SS General Karl Wolff's efforts to make peace with Allen
Dulles, the American head of the OSS in Switzerland, on behalf of all the
German troops in the Mediterranean, had come to naught. The Allies
would only accept unconditional surrender, so no progress was made.
But on 29 April, the day before Hitler committed suicide, von Vietinghoff
and Wolff *unilaterally* agreed to the unconditional surrender of the one
million Germans in Italy. Cessation of hostilities took place on 2 May.
This started the rot!

General Patton's armoured cohorts had sealed the fate of the 'last
redoubt' in Bavaria, no doubt much to Eisenhower's relief. Göring and
many OKW officers were captured. The Third Reich was now effectively
split in two.

Mass surrender of the Wehrmacht north of Hamburg.

The end of the Third Reich, May 1945.

21st Army Group Front situation on 5 May 1945.

Chester Wilmot reported the situation:

3 May 1945. The general surrender of the German forces opposing the 2nd British Army may now come at any hour; except in the pocket west of Bremen there is no longer any real opposition on General Dempsey's front, and pilots today reported that there are white flags flying from the houses 50 miles behind the nominal enemy line.

It's been a day of surrender and negotiation for surrender by German officers ranging from commanders of regiments to commanders of armies. Last night two German divisions surrendered intact. Early this morning the commander of the Hamburg garrison, General Wolz, agreed not only to hand over unconditionally Germany's greatest port, but also personally to lead the 7th British Armoured Division into the city this evening. During the morning the 11th Armoured Division received word that the garrison of Neumünster, 35 miles north of Hamburg and only 30 miles from the great naval base of Kiel, was ready to give in. The Neumünster garrison also said that other troops on the Kiel canal itself were anxious to surrender.

But the biggest news of the day was the complete break up and the attempted surrender of two of the German armies in Army Groups Vistula, the group which has been opposing Rokossovsky and was defending the area north of Berlin. These armies had retreated about 150 miles since the Russian breakthrough on the Oder last month, and yesterday our columns cut right through the area where they were vainly trying to reorganise. Their fighting spirit was already broken, and they disintegrated at once.

Today, their commanders, General Manteuffel of the 3rd Panzer Army and General Tippelskirch of the 1st Panzer Army, offered to surrender their complete forces to Field Marshal Montgomery. This was refused, though we have accepted the personal capitulation of the two generals and many senior officers of Army Group Vistula.

The official British attitude is that as these two armies are still engaged in fighting the Russians, we can't accept their surrender, and in any case their commanders are in no position to hand over the armies to us. And so tonight in the woods and villages between the Baltic and the Elbe there are tens of thousands of Germans from Army Group Vistula vainly trying to find someone who will accept them as prisoners. Their commanders have surrendered, their staffs have disintegrated; only those units still in direct contact with the Russians continue fighting – fighting rather than yield to the Red Army.

The fact is that at all costs the Germans want to avoid surrendering to the Soviet troops. They know how great are Germany's crimes against Russia, and they know that the Russians won't forget.

Field Marshal Busch, commanding the Schleswig-Holstein area, and General Lindemann, the commander in Denmark, sent an emissary to Stockholm to say that when the British Army reached the Baltic *before* the Russians they would surrender. On 3 May therefore, they asked to surrender the 3rd Panzer, 12th and 21st Armies. The delegation appeared at Field Marshal Montgomery's HQ, under Admiral von Friedeburg, who had replaced Grand Admiral Dönitz as head of the German army.

The 2nd Army Report of Operations describes in very sober words the events of those exciting days:

Meanwhile conversations were held at the Headquarters of 21st Army Group with the delegation headed by General Admiral von Friedeburg. He stated that he had arrived from Keitel to negotiate surrender of the German forces (in the North) to Field Marshal Montgomery. He stated that they were extremely worried about their soldiers and the valuable people being savaged by the Russians. He further requested the passage of civilian refugees moving back from the Russian sectors to safety through our lines, stating that he had been trying to get the population fleeing from the Russians back into Schleswig Holstein. He added that a considerable number had already been moved into that province, that conditions were fairly chaotic and that food would last for only 14 days.

The General Admiral suggested that, to allow the occupation to keep pace with the enormous administrative tasks, 2nd Army should agree to advance bound by bound. This would give the Germans time to organise their administration and to hand over something workable.

The commander of 21st Army Group stated that under no circumstances would he agree and that first of all von Friedeburg must surrender. After that it would be the duty of the staffs to work out the most suitable ways and means of enforcing the act.

The German high command knew that if they could drag out the negotiations, probably more civilians and military fleeing from the Red Army would be able to surrender to the more benevolent Allies.

On 4 May von Friedeburg had received permission from Dönitz and Field Marshal Keitel, the chief of the German high command, that unconditional surrender of all German armed forces, land, sea and air in north-west Germany, Holland, Schleswig Holstein and Denmark could be signed and agreed. General Eisenhower wrote in his report, 'D-Day to VE Day': 'I had instructed Field Marshal Montgomery that a capitulation covering these areas *might be regarded as a tactical matter* and, as such, be dealt with by him. It was arranged that a Russian officer should be present to accept the German submission on behalf of his government. The instrument of surrender was accordingly signed on 4 May and it became effective at 0800hrs on 5 May.' On 4 May, Chester Wilmot reported:

Hallo BBC, this is Chester Wilmot speaking from Field Marshal Montgomery's tactical headquarters on a high windswept hill on the wild Lüneburger Heath near the river Elbe.

It's ten minutes past six on Friday 4 May: the hour and the day for which British fighting men and women and British peoples throughout the world have been fighting and working and waiting for five years and eight months. The commanders of the German forces opposing Field Marshal Montgomery's 21st Army Group have come to this headquarters today to surrender. To make unconditional surrender. The plenipotentaries are General Admiral von Friedeburg, Commander-in-Chief of the German Navy, who succeeded Admiral Dönitz in that post when Dönitz became the new Führer. With him are

Above: Field Marshal Montgomery signing the Instrument of Surrender. (*Imperial War Museum*)

Right: The front page of the *Sunday Graphic* showing General Kinsel signing unconditional surrender.

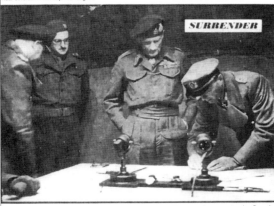

Instrument of Surrender
signed by Field Marshal
Montgomery. (*Imperial War
Museum*)

28. The 'instrument of surrender', signed by Field Marshal Montgomery and the German command – Friedeberg, Kinsel, Wagner, Polleck and Friedel – on 4 May 1945. (*Supplied by John Frost*)

General Kinzel, Chief of Staff to Field Marshal Busch, Rear Admiral Wagner who is Chief of Staff to von Friedeburg; and another staff officer.

They came here yesterday hoping to parley – to talk terms. But they were told to go back and return today with power to make unconditional surrender. They have come back through the lines again today, to make that surrender. And now we're waiting for them to come through the trees that surround Field Marshal Montgomery's headquarters. And here they are now. General Admiral von Friedeburg is leading with Colonel Ewart, of Field Marshal Montgomery's Staff; with him is the General of Infantry Kinzel … Rear Admiral Wagner, and they're now walking up to the caravan which the Field Marshal uses for his HQ in the field …

However, on 5 May Admiral Friedeburg arrived at Eisenhower's HQ 'wishing to clarify a number of points'. He was sent packing but he and Field Marshal Alfred Jodl, on behalf of Admiral Dönitz's 'Reich', turned up again on 6 May procrastinating and asking for more time. Eisenhower remained very firm and at 0241hrs on the morning of 7 May the Act of Surrender was signed by Jodl, by Eisenhower's Chief of Staff, Bedell Smith, and by Major General Ivan Suslaparov for the Soviet High Command.

It was all over – at long last.

But in fact it wasn't!

Hugh Lunghi, in Moscow with the British Military Mission, later recalled:

> On Monday May 7 we received the news that Eisenhower at his Reims headquarters had in the early hours of that morning accepted General Jodl's total capitulation of all German armed forces with a cease-fire at midnight on May 8. A General Susloparov had signed the surrender document on behalf of the Soviet Command. Again the Soviet media ignored the historic event.
>
> Instead of congratulations, we received a curt communication addressed to the then Head of our Military Mission, Admiral Archer, copied to the United States Head of Mission General Deane, from the Soviet Chief of Staff, General Antonov. He demanded that what he called the 'temporary protocol' signed in Reims should be replaced by 'an act of general unconditional surrender' which would be drawn up and signed in Marshal Zhukov's headquarters in Berlin on the following day, May 8.
>
> Stalin, it was obvious, intended that the only 'real' surrender should be to a Soviet commander. Years later we learned from Soviet generals' memoirs that Stalin had been furious that a Soviet representative had added his signature to the Reims surrender: 'Who the hell is Susloparov? He is to be punished severely for daring to sign such a document without the Soviet government's permission.'

Marshal Josef Stalin was not at all happy that the surrender would take place at Reims with just one relatively unimportant Russian general present. It gave the impression to the outside world that the Western Allies had won the war, whereas Russia had made the most spectacular victories in driving the German hordes out of his country, and as from 2 May the capital, Berlin, had been conquered and captured by his Red

THE MOMENT OF DEFEAT General Jodl signs, above, the unconditional surrender of German forces at Reims on May 7. "With this signature, the German people and the German Army fall, for better or for worse, beneath the victors," said Jodl. On his left is Admiral von Friedeburg, and on his right the Luftwaffe representative, General Oxenius. General Jodl was later sentenced to be hanged

THE MOMENT OF VICTORY General Eisenhower's headquarters, Reims. The Russian, American and British, above, celebrate Jodl's capitulation. From left: Generals Susloparoff, Morgan, Smith and Eisenhower. On the right, Air Chief Marshal Sir Arthur Tedder. Eisenhower holds the pens used for the signatures.

Newspaper cuttings from the time of the surrender.

Army. He had a point! He demanded a final formal ratification in Berlin, under Russian arrangements, in the early hours of 9 May. Marshal Zhukov signed for the Russians; Air Chief Marshal Tedder for SHAEF; Field Marshal Keitel for Germany; and General de Lattre de Tassigny witnessed on behalf of France.

And that was that.

At the end of the First World War in 1918 the German army claimed correctly that it had not been beaten. It was political problems behind their lines that led to the Armistice. In the Second World War, the Germans could not make the same claim. The vast majority of their armed forces had been smashed, encircled and made prisoner. However, there were seven outposts of the Third Reich, which still had not been beaten: in Norway 360,000 troops; Denmark almost 250,000; north-west Holland 120,000; Dunkirk 40,000: the Channel Islands 40,000; and Lorient 30,000. The British Liberation Army, with the Royal Navy and RAF, had to tackle Norway, Denmark and north-west Holland (with the Canadians). There was a distinct possibility that the Führer's die-hard gauleiters might wish to stage their own Götterdämerung and fight to the end.

Map showing the four zones of occupation – Russian, American, French and British. There were 23 million demoralised Germans in the British zone re-named 'British Army of the Rhine'.

Once the Allied armies entered the Third Reich as the British Liberation Army early in 1945, Operation Eclipse came into force. It was designed to embrace the complete destruction of the German war potential. The initial stage consisted of herding the troops into compounds where they were disarmed. The sheep were separated from the goats! The SS and every unit considered to be violently Nazified were sent at once to prisoner of war camps such as Westertimke. There they would be closely identified and potential war criminals would be set aside for possible trials. The majority were concentrated under titular command of their own officers before being released to work on the farms or to other vital but peaceful work essential to keeping the German community alive. The most efficient were, of course, members of the Nazi party, and this made for difficult judgements.

Major General Francis de Guingand was Chief of Staff to the 21st Army Group, soon to be renamed the British Army of the Rhine (BAOR). He was given the responsibility to enforce the terms of surrender, i.e. to implement Operation Eclipse. The first very large conference took place on 8 May with representatives from Army Group HQ, the new military government, the chiefs of staff of the 2nd and Canadian Armies, the naval liaison officer, and Air Vice Marshal Groom of 2nd Tactical Air Force. Once they had agreed upon a firm plan to carry out the first stage of Eclipse, they herded and shepherded the huge German armies into captivity. General Kinzel, Chief of Staff to Field Marshal Busch who commanded the German Army group opposing 21st Army Group, was a brilliant conduit. He was an efficient staff officer, who sported an eyeglass and wore a magnificent field grey greatcoat with scarlet lapels, in every respect the typical Prussian General Staff Officer. He would carry out all of de Guingand's orders.

This was the prisoner state at the middle of May:

In the Wilhelmshaven-Emden Peninsula
Already in the area 60,000
To be moved from West Holland 120,000
Total 180,000

In the Cuxhaven Peninsula
Already in the area 160,000
From the area north of the Elbe 100,000

Map of the Concentration Plan for the captured forces of the Reich.

Total 260,000
In south-west Schleswig Holstein
From Denmark 160,000
From north Schleswig Holstein 250,000
Total 410,000

In south-east Schleswig Holstein
From south Schleswig Holstein 134,000
From East Prussia 75,000
From Wismar Pocket 360,000
Total 569,000

TOTAL 1,419,000
Not including the Magdeburg Pocket (from USA) 300,000

In the British zone of occupied Germany there were about 23 million people. In addition there were 200,000 German prisoners of war behind the Allied lines already in camps. All the sinister SS troops would be isolated on Nordstrand Island for security reasons.

There were reputed to be 130,000 Allied prisoners of war: British, Belgians, French, Yugoslavs, Poles, Italians and others, plus two million desperate Russians.

Finally there were 925,000 displaced persons either west- or east-bound – the former slaves of German industry and agriculture. And there were hundreds of thousands of sick and wounded German military and civil casualties in hospitals in the area.

General Templer was head of the Allied military government organisation and he was in charge of this extremely complex situation.

Once the million and a half soldiers of the Third Reich were safely behind barbed wire, each was carefully investigated.

Lt General Horrocks, GOC 30th Corps, found that he was responsible for the Hanover corps district. He wrote:

> Monty laid down the priorities as (1) food and (2) housing; he then, as always, gave us a free hand to look after our own districts until such time as proper military government could take over from us. It was a fascinating task. I found myself to all intents and purposes the benevolent (I hope) dictator of an area about the size of Wales. At my morning conference, instead of considering fire plans and laying down military objectives, we discussed such problems as food, coal, communications, press and so on. I soon discovered the merits of a dictatorship. I could really get things done quickly. One day in the late autumn a staff officer reported that the output of coal was dropping every week in our corps district. This was very serious with winter approaching. The reason, I was informed, was that the miners lacked clothes. I immediately ordered a levy to be carried out in certain nearby towns to provide adequate clothing for the miners, and sure enough a few weeks later the graph showing coal production began to rise.

Montgomery produced a series of operational 'civilian' orders to help keep the traumatic situation in Germany under reasonable control. Operation Barleycorn would demobilise German soldiers who volunteered to work on the land and bring the Westphalian harvests in. Operation Coal Scuttle was a scheme for German soldiers to gather fuel or work in the mines. Montgomery had many sensible, practical ideas for the future of his huge bailiwick. He ordered that the workers of Wolfsburg should be encouraged to produce the first post-war Volkswagens, the people's very cheap and reliable car.

To the victors, the spoils! Despite the barely concealed hostility of Stalin's obvious ownership of Berlin, a public relations operation ensured that Winston Churchill and the new US president, Harry Truman, should arrive together on 16 July 1945 to participate in a series of post-war meetings and rather grand victory parades. Churchill visited the Chancellery and the Russian guides took his entourage to Hitler's air raid shelter. Churchill was convinced that his late opponent's death 'was much more convenient than the one I had feared. He could have flown to England and surrendered himself saying, "Do what you will with me, but spare my misguided people!" I have no doubt that he would have shared the fate of the Nuremberg criminals.' On 18 July he lunched alone with President Truman: 'We had now emerged from the war with a great external debt of three thousand million pounds.' Truman, to his great credit, answered: 'If you had gone down like France we might be fighting the Germans on the American coast at the present time.' That night the indomitable Churchill dined with Stalin, and Majors Birse and Pavlov, the interpreters. Stalin told Churchill that the Russians had mobilised 12 million men, and 5 million of those were lost, killed or missing. The Germans had mobilised 18 million! During his stay in Berlin, Churchill learnt that the atomic bomb tests had been positive.

This is a description of the unique Victory Parade in Berlin: 'The first parade took place on 6 July. The Union Jack was hoisted in the Grosse Stern at the foot of the Franco-Prussian War memorial and Lt General Sir Ronald Weekes inspected the 1st Battalion Grenadier Guards (borrowed for the occasion), 1/5th Queens, 2nd Devons and the Canadian Composite Battalion (also borrowed). 5th RHA arrived on 10 July and moved into Kladow barracks and Divisional HQ on the 18th. Field Marshal Montgomery arrived on the 12th to invest the three Russian commanders, Marshals Zhukov, Rokossovsky and General Sokolovski. They all gave each other colourful and appropriate medals! This time the Grenadiers and 8th and 11th Hussars lined the route as Guard of Honour.'

Captain Bill Bellamy, 8th Hussars, recalled: 'We travelled the length of the Charlottenburger Chaussée as far as the Brandenberger Tur, the great triumphal Gate, marking the divide between British and Russian zones. Then the Tiergarten (zoo) and the Siegessaule. The trees in the parks on both sides of the avenue were stripped of their leaves – the aftermath of a First World War battle. The fighting must have been horrific.'

On 13 July the first full-scale Divisional Parade, a rehearsal for the Victory Parade, took place. Two days later the delegates for the Potsdam Conference started to arrive, including Prime Minister Winston Churchill, Anthony Eden and Clement Attlee. This was followed by

Watched by thousands of German civilians, Major General L. O. Lyne takes the salute as the Desert Rats enter Berlin on July 4, 1945.

Field Marshal Montgomery and Russian Marshal Zhukov inspect the Grenadier's Guard of Honour in Berlin.

All that was left of Josef Göbbels' Propaganda Ministry. 310 bombing raids reduced Berlin to what Roosevelt called 'a second Carthage'.

Ruins of Anhallen Station, Berlin, destroyed by the RAF and the US 8th Air Force.

Left: Bitburg – devastated.

Below: Comet tanks approaching the saluting base at the Victory Parade.

7th Armoured Division enters Berlin. Major General Lyne taking the salute.

another frenetic week of last-minute rehearsals and flag poles and stands being erected for the great day – Saturday 21 July. The bands were provided by the Royal Marines, 11th Hussars and 2nd Devons, and the troops on parade were found from 3rd RHA, 5th RHA, 8th Hussars, 11th Hussars, 1st Battalion Grenadier Guards, 1/5th Queens, 2nd Devons and representatives from the Navy, RAF and RAF Regiment.

3rd RHA fired a nineteen-gun salute in honour of the Prime Minister and Field Marshals Montgomery, Alan Brooke and Alexander. Tom Ritson recalled: 'A few days later Mr Churchill was dismissed by the electorate and Mr Atlee returned to Potsdam in his place.' Vernon Besley, 1/5th Queens, wrote: 'We were all ready, the Queens right in front of Churchill waiting to start when there was a cascade of motor bikes escorting President Truman, with their sirens sounding, and the parade started.'

Captain Bill Bellamy observed:

The Russians outnumbered the British. They were quite smart in their loosely cut service dress, flat hats, gold or silver epaulettes, and polished jack-boots and they all had so many medals! As we approached the saluting base, being

327

leader of the 8th Hussars column I had a very clear view. Mr Churchill stood slightly to the fore wearing a light coloured service dress and a peaked dress hat. He was standing, looking directly up the Chaussée and saluted us in answer to the colonel's salute. Standing next to him was Mr Atlee in civilian clothes and bareheaded. Then Field Marshals Alan Brooke and Montgomery with the tall bare-headed figure of Mr Anthony Eden to the left. General Lyne was standing to the PM's left, together with a senior naval officer. I also spotted Mr Morrison. Then it was all over and we were past.

The new Winston Club for 7th Armoured Division Other Ranks was later opened formally by Winston Churchill, where he made the famous speech that included:

Now I have only a word more to say about the Desert Rats. They were the first to begin. The 11th Hussars were in action in the desert in 1939 and ever since you have kept marching steadily forward on the long road to victory. Through so many countries and changing scenes you have fought your way. It is not without emotion that I can express to you what I feel about the Desert Rats.

Dear Desert Rats! May your glory ever shine! May your laurels never fade! May the memory of this glorious pilgrimage of war which you have made from Alamein, via the Baltic, never die!

It is a march unsurpassed through all the story of war so far as my reading of history leads me to believe. May the fathers long tell the children about this tale. May you all feel that in following your great ancestors you have accomplished something which has done good to the whole world; which has raised the honour of your own country and which every man has a right to be proud of.

When Field Marshal Montgomery eventually signed the Articles of Surrender by the various officers at the end of the Third Reich, he and the splendid British Army had, in just over the four months of early 1945, rescued and liberated from captivity nearly 20 million souls: the populations of Holland, eleven million; Denmark, four million; Norway, three million; two million displaced persons; and many hundreds of thousands of prisoners of war. And at least two or three million German citizens would be happier now their years of misery were over.

Nevertheless, by May 1945, the British forces in north-west Europe were the junior partners to the Russians and Americans in the great 'end game'.

On 13 May 1945 five years almost to the day since he became the King's First Minister, Winston Churchill spoke of the task ahead:

> On the continent of Europe we have yet to make sure that the simple and honourable purposes for which we entered the war are not brushed aside or overlooked in the months following our success and that the words 'freedom', 'democracy' and 'liberation' are not distorted from their true meaning as we have understood them. There would be little use in punishing the Hitlerites for their crimes, if law and justice did not rule and if totalitarian or police governments were to take the place of the German invaders ... It is the victors who must search their hearts in their glowing hours, and be worthy by their nobility of the immense forces that they wield.

Architect of victory: Field Marshal Sir Bernard Montgomery

CHAPTER 25

Liberation of *Festung* Holland

After his panzers and Luftwaffe had devastated Poland in late autumn 1939, Hitler planned his next, even more audacious move. His intentions were more or less described in *Mein Kampf.* The destruction of his old First World War enemy, France, and its huge army was irresistible. The only two ways of bypassing the redoubtable Maginot Line were either south through the Belgian Ardennes, or north through neutral Holland and Belgium. Hitler sent his main *schwerpunkt* through the former and his airborne army into the latter. Holland was a peaceful country with a population of about 11 million, prosperous with a well-established monarchy. Hitler could see many advantages to the capture of Holland: an excellent agricultural system; a Luftwaffe base; a kriegsmarine base for E-boats and U-boats to harass the Royal Navy and Allied convoys in the North Sea and English Channel.

Early on 10 May General Kurt Student unleashed 4,000 of his 4,500-strong parachute army to drop and secure the key bridges at Rotterdam, Dordrecht and Moerdijk before the Dutch could blow them up. His light infantry division of 12,000 men was landed on captured airfields in transport aircraft. The Dutch army put up a strong resistance in Rotterdam and Dordrecht and captured 1,000 German paratroopers, who were promptly shipped by sea to England for safe keeping. The German 9th Panzer Division raced through a gap in the southern flank and on the third day linked up with the paratroops.

The French 7th Army intended to move into Holland to help, but were too late. After Rotterdam was heavily bombed on the 14th killing 900 civilians, Göring threatened to bomb and destroy Utrecht, so inevitably the Dutch army surrendered. German casualties were 11,000, and 3,000

Aspects of war in Holland. (*Michael Bayley*)

civilian deaths were incurred in the Luftwaffe deluge of bombs. The Dutch army had 9,300 casualties. Queen Wilhelmina, her family and parliament reached London safely; she then appointed Pieter Gerbandy as her new prime minister. He was a more aggressive man than Dirk Jan de Geer.

Hitler then promoted a fellow Austrian Nazi, Arthur Seyss-Inquart (1892–1946) to head the country as civilian governor (Reichskommissariat Niederlande). Two other key appointments were the Dutch renegade Anton Mussert (1894–1946), who founded the National Socialist Movement in the Netherlands, and Hanns Albin Rauter, another Austrian, who became the SS commander and police chief in the country. Between them this terrible triumvirate brought the proud, peaceful country to the edge of destruction. All key aspects of life fell under Nazi control. There was food rationing and ration cards, and the press, radio, labour unions and political parties were controlled by selected Quisling-style collaborationists. Complete factories were dismantled and shipped into Germany to be reassembled there. Cattle, food, metals, machinery and textiles were sent over the border to reinforce

Hitler's war efforts. Almost half a million Dutch people, mostly men of eighteen to forty-five years of age, were sent as slave labourers into the Third Reich factories. Many thousands were conscripted (*Arbeitseinatz*) to build parts of the gigantic Atlantic wall along the Dutch coastline. Some towns including Scheveningen were evacuated: 20,000 homes were abandoned and 65,000 people were forced to move.

In 1941, the persecution of the Jewish race started and the first batch of Jews was sent to a concentration camp at Mauthausen. In May 1942, all Jews were forced to wear the Star of David, and Dutch concentration camps were built at Vught and Amersfoort. The Dutch resistance groups – the Order Service of ex-army officers, the Council of Resistance, and the LKP – tried their best, but the German Gestapo and the OKW (Oberkommando der Wehrmacht) headed by Wilhelm Canaris, Herman Giskes of the Abwehr, and Josef Schrieder of the Sicherheits Polizei, aided by informers, kept a stranglehold over any efforts to resist Hitler's henchmen. Nearly 50,000 young Dutchmen were recruited to form two renegade SS units: the 34th Grenadier Brigade Landstorm, which fought vigorously against the British and Canadians in 1944/45, and 4th Panzergrenadier Brigade Nederland, which was sent to fight alongside the Wehrmacht on the Eastern front.

Martin Bormann, the Führer's devoted Head of Secretariat recorded Hitler's table talk for several years. The book, *Hitler's Table Talk*, edited by Hugh Trevor-Roper, contained three curious extracts:

27 February 1942. I need a man for Belgium. The difficulty is to choose the man. No question of sending there a North German, somebody brutal, a martinet. I need an extraordinarily clever man as supple as an eel, amiable – and at the same time thick-skinned and tough. For Holland I have in Seyss-Inquart a man who has these qualities … Seyss has succeeded in encouraging in Holland a movement that is numbering more and more adherents and is waging war against Wilhelmina without our having to put a shoulder to the wheel. The idea of German solidarity is making more and more impression on the minds of the Dutch.

5 April 1942. [the Reichsführer SS Himmler talked to Hitler.] What struck me is that Anton Mussert is trying to get back his Dutch legion which at present is fighting on the Eastern front. For territorial defence he has no need of a Federal Dutch Army.

6 September 1942. What a fine race the Dutch are! The girls are splendid and very much to my taste.

Hitler regarded the Dutch people as part of his Aryan Herrenvolk who were forced to take part in his *Gleichschaltung* (enforced conformity). This meant that gradually all political parties were *verboten* except for the NSB.

German brutality was everywhere. In February 1943 General Lt Hendrik Seyffard, a Dutch renegade charged with the recruitment of Dutch volunteers to the Waffen SS, was assassinated in The Hague. SS General Rauter ordered the killing of fifty Dutch hostages as a reprisal. Further war crimes followed in 1944 after the German garrison of the village of Putten was attacked. The entire male population of 552 was deported to the camps, and only forty-eight survived. Each time the trade unions carried out a strike about conditions, the SS would execute the leaders and associates. In February 1941, 17 Dutch were killed in Amsterdam. In April 1943, a national strike ended with 150 civilians executed. A total of 2,800 were murdered by the Nazi regime.

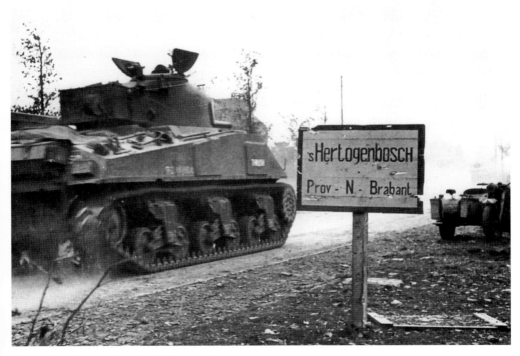

A battle-scarred road to 's-Hertogenbosch.

Anxious civilians in Eindhoven, scared that the 'Moffen' might counter-attack and return. (*Imperial War Museum*)

After the sad failure of Operation Market Garden in September 1944, the entire population of Arnhem was forced to abandon their homes and leave the town because they might have helped the British paratroops. In March 1945, after a minor skirmish at De Woeste Hoeve, General Rauter ordered the execution of 250 hostages. By the time of liberation in May 1945, after systematic hunting and purging, no fewer than 105,000 out of the original 140,000 Jewish population of Holland were murdered in the camps. This was the highest percentage of any Western European country. Only 20,000 Dutch Jews survived the war.

Market Garden and 'Dolle Dinsdag' ('Mad Tuesday') on 5 September 1944 had encouraged high hopes of a complete Allied victory. By the autumn of 1944, much of North Brabant, Nijmegen and Eindhoven had been liberated. Zeeland and Walcheren were painfully captured by the Canadians, the Scottish 52nd Lowland Division, many squadrons of Hobart's Funnies, a Royal Marine commando, and a powerful Royal Navy squadron. In early winter, in Operation Aintree, the British army captured all the Peel countryside around Venlo and Overloon. But sadly, the more densely populated cities in the north had to endure the *Hongerwinter* of 1944/45. To make things worse, the RAF bombed many towns, seeking V-weapon sites, submarine and E-boat depots and

A Coy 4 Lincolns
pass a wrecked
German A/TK gun
in Willemstad.

2nd Troop A Squadron 15/19th Hussars in Geldrop.

335

'Dolle Dinstag' or
'Mad Tuesday', and
news of possible
freedom.

Gestapo HQ. In the process, unfortunately, many Dutch civilians were killed. Nijmegen alone lost 500 of its citizens who were killed in air raids. The Netherlands Red Cross begged the British to reconsider air attacks on Dutch cities, but not to much avail.

For his bravado attack in the Ardennes in December 1944, Hitler had created no fewer than twenty-five Volksgrenadier divisions, recruited mainly from reluctant industrial workers, convalescents, 'difficult' veterans and distinctly middle-aged conscripts. Their discipline and zeal for fighting was third class, compared to the élite SS and Waffen units. Major General Gerhard Franz commanded 256th Volksgrenadier Division in Holland and issued this order to his troops:

256 Volksgrenadier Division Commander Headquarters
11 October 1944

Certain events among units have impelled me to point out that discipline and *esprit de corps* among the troops must be raised in the shortest possible time. For this, all formation commanders, in particular company commanders, will be held personally responsible to me ...

It cannot be tolerated that a formation commander should get drunk, then wander about the woods at night shouting and firing his pistol at the sentry …

It shows little discipline in a company when members of the company call each other 'cheats' during a discussion about captured loot …

A unit shows little *esprit de corps* if a soldier can declare that owing to difficulty in walking he can no longer serve with the artillery since he could not escape quickly enough if the Tommy arrived. Such a statement is a basis for defeatism and this case should be dealt with by courts-martial.

It shows lamentable carelessness if one soldier while cleaning his arms injured four comrades by sheer negligence and in such a way that they will be unable to do any duty. Before cleaning weapons, in particular new weapons, sufficient instruction must be given in stripping and assembling so that everyone who may have to use these weapons is fully conversant with their use …

During the last eight days no less than 11 desertions have been reported, seven of whom went over into enemy lines … Reports about desertions are lamentable and generally arrive too late. In one particular case a soldier deserted his unit on 29 September 1944, and the official report was not made until 10 October 1944 …

FRANZ

On 5 March 1945, Colonel General Blaskowitz of Army Group H doled out death for stragglers:

General Johannes Albrecht Blaskowitz (1883–1948)

337

As from midday 10 March, all soldiers in all branches of the Wehrmacht who may be encountered away from their units on roads or in villages, in supply columns or among groups of civilian refugees, or in dressing stations when not wounded, and who announce that they are stragglers looking for their units, will be summarily tried and shot ...
BLASKOWITZ
Colonel General

In early April 1945 Hitler designated the Netherlands as *Festung* Holland, to be defended at *all* costs.

In *Defeat in the West*, Milton Shulman wrote:

... the Nazi chiefs resorted to harsher and more terrifying methods as the end loomed nearer and nearer. Fear was still the weapon that was most effective in cowing the masses, and Göbbels wielded it with abandon. The bogy of Bolshevism was raised everywhere to frighten the nation into submission. On 16 March 1945 the following directive was issued to the National Socialist indoctrination officers of 15th Army in Holland. These officers performed a similar function in German units to the role carried out by Communist commissars in Russian units, but with far less success. This document

Infantry with Churchill tanks in Holland.

illustrated the propaganda line to be adopted in talks to the men and consisted of a series of warnings of catastrophes that would befall the German people 'in the event of capitulation'.

'As a natural consequence of the reparations demanded by the Reparations Commission in Moscow,' it reads, 'the whole German agricultural potential is to be at the disposal of Moscow, and hunger, calculatingly produced, will be applied as a means of oppression, at any time.

'German labour will be used as "reparations production"; as a natural consequence Moscow will deport German slave labour to Siberia by the million. German industry will then profit only Germany's enemies.

'Moscow will tear asunder all families by deportation, slave labour, etc. forever, with the full intention of destroying the family as the basis of the life of the race ...

'The German women will be raped by beasts in human guise, dishonoured and murdered ...

'German children will be torn from their parents by force, deported and brought up as Bolsheviks.

'The German people as an organic community will be literally murdered. Germany will become a vast graveyard. Whoever survives has nothing more to hope for in this life ...

'The want and suffering of the present war situation are nothing compared to the aims of extermination by our enemies. These will be carried out in the event of capitulation. The entire German people has risen against this fate and fights as a single armed Nazi army.'

Sporadic negotiations for surrender were taking place all along the various fronts, usually at a divisional or even lower level. But as long as Hitler still lived and dominated his Third Reich surrender was impossible. Except for those who had been forced to surrender in the Ruhr, no officer commanding an army or an army group was yet prepared to follow von Vietinghoff's example in Italy. Typical of this stubborn, unthinking, automatic adherence to a code was the behaviour of Colonel General Blaskowitz in Holland. A man of sixty-two years with a flattened, frog-like jaw, broad nostrils and thinning hair, Blaskowitz was a sterling product of the German General Staff. His forces in Holland had been pushed back to the Grebbe Line by the Canadians and British and were obviously incapable of resisting much longer. However, Blaskowitz and his superior civilian authority, Arthur von Seyss-Inquart, still held one trump card in their hands. They controlled the dykes protecting the Netherlands from the waters of the North Sea and the Zuider Zee.

On 14 April 1945, the Canadians reached the North Sea and took Leeuwarden and captured the last of the many V-1 and V-2 sites. Alan Moorehead reported:

> The last rocket and flying bomb had fallen on England. All around on the line of march we came on stranded trains filled with the V-weapons; V-2s packed with rounded wooden struts and wickerwork but so large that each projectile overlapped by half its length into the truck ahead. And in the railway yards there were many great drums of explosives and strange steel cranes and scaffoldings were latticed over with the branches of trees and there was evidence that they travelled only at night. But it made no difference. They lay there either broken by the RAF or sabotaged by the retreating Germans themselves, or simply abandoned in the cuttings by the wayside stations, a series of weird tossing shapes among the spring wheat, a brutal warning of what might have happened had the war continued another year.

Hobart's Funnies had been integrated into the Canadian Army for many months. At Leeuwarden, in Friesland, Crocodile flame-throwers of the Fife and Forfars helped 8th Canadian Infantry Brigade while 7th RTR Crocodiles assisted the Canadians to capture Deventer on 19 April. The Buffaloes of 11th RTR and 49th APC carried 2nd and 3rd Canadian Infantry divisions into the Zutphen and Appeldoorn areas.

William Hitchcock's book *Bitter Road to Freedom* details most of the grim suffering that the four million Dutch people in the main cities endured in the *Hongerwinter* of 1944/45: 'Starvation kills slowly. Thousands of Dutch people during the early spring of 1945 knew this only too well. While the Allied powers dithered thousands of people in western Holland simply wasted away. The average diet fell to about a thousand calories per day [the Allied troops enjoyed about 4,000 calories per day] and for the poor and elderly it often slipped below that.' One resident of Amsterdam wrote: 'The city is Oriental. Garbage heaps piled against tree stumps. Starved dogs, warped with hunger, tails between their legs, pawing at the heaps. Barefooted people, grey-haired people, sitting or lying in doorways and begging children with hunched up shoulders and gunny sacks under their arms.' People went very slowly on hunger walks into the countryside trying to barter goods for dairy products and vegetables.

The pressure applied by Queen Wilhelmina's court and government, Prime Minister Gerbrandy, and the Red Cross on Eisenhower, Churchill and Montgomery was intense. Unless the Allies invaded and drove out Seyss-Inquart and the 25th German Army garrisoning Holland, the Dutch population would suffer irrevocably. Over 3.6 million inhabitants were starving. But, and there were two great 'buts', Seyss-Inquart could destroy Holland by deliberately flooding 70 or 80 per cent of the country by destroying dams, dykes and all the polder-bunds. He made sure the Allies knew that. Also every week that delayed Operations Eclipse and Plunder meant that the German defenders could strengthen the many barriers in front of the Allies. Time was vital for Hitler and his generals. The alternative rendition of north and north-west Holland would take time and cause very heavy Allied and civilian casualties. The British Liberation Army had taken a bloody nose in Market Garden and subsequent operations: Aintree, the Battle of the Bulge, Blackcock, Veritable and Blockbuster had met fanatical and skilled defensive actions by Hitler's generals.

And one more 'but', which was not necessarily known at the time: all of Hitler's twelve or fifteen extermination (not necessarily concentration) camps were slaughtering the inmates in the gas chambers and other means, including starvation (vide Bergen-Belsen). Of the two million or more Russian prisoners of war in Germany, a very high percentage were dying of deliberate starvation.

Eisenhower pressed on with his strong attacks over the Rhine, across the river barriers, as fast as the deliberate Montgomery and the more rapid American generals could manage. However, the intense Dutch pressure on the Allies for succour caused Operation Manna to take place, after considerable negotiations with Seyss-Inquart. Eventually, four months later, on 25 April, 3,000 British RAF bombers parachuted 6,000 tons of supplies to the Dutch behind German lines, mainly around Rotterdam and The Hague. In late January, a small Swedish-inspired relief operation sent two ships, the *Noreg* and *Dagmar Bratt,* with 3,000 tons of flour, margarine and cod-liver oil to Delfzyl in northern Holland. By April they had sent 20,000 tons of provisions to help feed the starving millions.

Eisenhower had ordered 109,000 tons of various foodstuffs and medicines to be made available for Holland, and the great depot at Oss used by Germans and British (not necessarily at the same time) at

Operation Manna. (*Ken Dillon*)

Three Dutch children in battered Arnhem clutch Red Cross parcels after months of privation.

one stage had 30,000 tons available. The Germans deliberately put up excuses for delay week after week, but by mid-April even the die-hard Seyss-Inquart realised that some co-operation on humanitarian grounds was possible, so a local truce brought some more relief.

On 29 April Lancaster bombers flew over The Hague and other districts, dropping supplies to cope with the threat of starvation among Dutch civilians until land transport could be got through to them. The editor of the Netherlands News Agency flew in one of the Lancasters and described the mission:

> The grocer called on the people of The Hague today – for the first time for years. True, it was Sunday, but this was definitely a case of 'the better the day, the better the deed'. He called at Rotterdam and Leyden as well. It was closing day too – not only because it was Sunday but also because the shops have had no food to sell for a long time.
>
> I was with the RAF delivery men on their rounds. We travelled in a Lancaster bomber, and as a result of the day's activities rations were provided for thousands of starving Dutch people, many of whom had not had a square meal for months. Our squadron, for example, carried sufficient food – 42 tons of it – to feed one-fifth of the population of The Hague for one day. But there were other squadrons as well.
>
> Each of our aerial delivery vans carried food with which first-class meals can be produced. There were flour and yeast for bread-making, tins of meat and bacon, with pepper and salt and mustard to taste. The Dutch love for vegetables was met by tins of dehydrated potato, as well as bags of peas and beans. Sugar, margarine, dried milk, cheese, dried eggs and chocolate completed the order. Weeks of preparation and experiment had gone into the scheme, including the devising of special slings to ensure that in place of huge 12,000-pounders, each aircraft could drop 355 20-pound food bombs.
>
> We crossed the North Sea on our mercy mission shortly after midday and approached The Hague at a very low level. Our target area, the Ypenburg civil airfield south-east of the town, was clearly visible. It had been marked out by Pathfinders with green flares, and in the centre was a white cross surmounted by a red light.
>
> From the moment we crossed the Dutch coast, people in the fields and roads, and in the gardens of the sad little houses, waved frantically. But it was not until we were actually flying over The Hague that we saw what this manna from heaven really meant for the Dutch. Every road seemed full of

Above and left: The famous Delft ceramics celebrated the relief of Holland.

The river Grebbe was the unofficial boundary between occupied and free Holland.

people waving flags, sheets, or anything they could grab. The roofs of tall buildings were black with Dutch citizens welcoming us. On a barge we saw the Dutch tricolour bravely hoisted; across a large flat roof an Orange flag was colourfully stretched.

The people were certainly overjoyed to see these huge bombers emptying their bomb bays one after another on the target area, as thousands of food bombs fluttered out like confetti from a giant hand. And along the roads

345

leading into The Hague were carts, perambulators and bicycles as the populace seemed to race to join in the great share-out. Unfortunately, owing to the recent spell of bad weather, we were just too late to give them their Sunday dinner, but with amazing enthusiasm the RAF aerial grocers today certainly delivered the goods.

'These were the best bombs we have dropped for years,' said Flight Officer Ellis, the bomb-aimer of our aircraft.

By 18 April the Canadians, British and the Polish Armoured Division had battered their way to the shores of the Zuider Zee. As a result the bulk of the German 25th Army was cut off from its home base and penned into the Grebbe and Eem lines enclave in the west and north-west. Eisenhower's staff received messages indicating that a truce, perhaps a surrender might be negotiated, so he and Bedell Smith instructed Major General Francis de Guingand, Chief of Staff 21st Army Group, to have preliminary talks. These took place on 28 April with Ernst Schwebel, commander of Zuid-Holland on behalf of Seyss-Inquart and Blaskowitz. De Guingand described the talks: 'My opposite number across the table – Schwebel – was one of the most revolting men I have ever seen. A plump sweating German who possessed the largest red nose I have ever seen, the end of which was like several ripe strawberries sewn together. With him he had Naval, Air and Army representatives as well as a food expert.' De Guingand had Lt General A. Galloway, who was head of the organisation to feed Holland, plus senior Canadian and SHAEF officers. Meeting No. 1 was an exchange of views. Meeting No. 2 on the 30th at the Hotel de Wereld in Wageningen was larger and included Prince Bernhard of the Netherlands, C-in-C of the Dutch troops in 21st Army Group. Bedell Smith came, as did Seyss-Inquart. The arrangements for food relief had been agreed but it was Admiral Dönitz in Flensburg who had to make the final decision about surrender, which took place at 0241hrs on 7 May.

One curious feature of the German surrender was the appearance of a group of Russian officers led by General Ivan Susloparov. They were of course interested in repatriating all Russian prisoners of war released by the Allies.

Since January 1945, SHAEF had been working with the Netherlands military administration – the provisional Dutch military power in the liberated part of Holland – to prepare fifty-one medical feeding teams to be rushed into the west and north-west of the country. Each team included a doctor, six nurses, five social workers and other staff. All had received Red Cross training and were supplied with special emergency rations. Overall they treated 279,000 patients in the early summer of 1945. SHAEF separately delivered 189,000 tons of supplies. On 5 May ships arrived in Rotterdam and the bulk came in by truck, then barge, to the target area. Within two weeks the Allies were able to offer the Dutch people a daily ration of 2,000 calories. For a week, food convoys poured through the Polar Bear lines and through the still heavily armed German troops on the river Grebbe truce lines. Lt Brian Lott of the 55th Anti-tank Regiment returned from leave to rejoin his unit at Ede. He recalled:

> We were involved in a humane role helping to feed the Dutch who in the towns and particularly Amsterdam, were starving. I was given a platoon of trucks and we moved to Bilthoven. The trucks travelled to Utrecht each day where food was being flown in by the RAF. We distributed the food from Bilthoven. The people were very grateful. Once I took a motor cycle and rode into Amsterdam. It was incredibly quiet and a terrible smell of death hung over the city. I did not see any Germans. I think I may have liberated Amsterdam on my own!

On 3 May much activity was noticed in the small shattered town of Wageningen. The Kensingtons saw many staff cars in the square outside a small hotel and an imposing array of red tabs. There was a BBC mobile recording van there as well. General von Blaskowitz, GOC of the German army in Holland, his face a grey mask of defeat, had just signed the unconditional surrender. The Lincolns noticed Lt General Bedell Smith of SHAEF, Prince Bernhard of Holland, the GOC of the 1st Canadian Corps and also, for the opposition, Seyss-Inquart.

Just two days later, Major S. Jacobson MC, second in command of the Recce Regiment, was sent to the HQ of an SS battalion beyond Utrecht to negotiate their surrender. He recalled:

> I went off in my jeep with Private Hall my driver, a Dutch Resistance interpreter (with a Sten) and a German SS officer as guide. It was a queer drive through an area not yet occupied by Allied troops. The villages seemed deserted except for armed German sentries. But as we drove through curtains were drawn aside, windows flung open, flags put out … The SS colonel and adjutant had

A Squadron, 49th Recce Regiment, arriving in Dam Square, Utrecht, 7 May 1945. (*Monty Satchell*)

obviously just bathed, shaved and put on their best uniforms. I was in rather tired battle dress.

[When the capitulation papers were signed, he continued:]

We were faced by an amazing sight. Piled high with flowers, the jeep was hemmed in on every side by men, women and children, all perfectly quiet. But when I came out with the bit of paper in my hand, something snapped. They cheered, laughed and cried. I made a speech. It was funny, exciting, deeply moving. The war was over.

On the evening of the 4th came news that all German troops in north-west Germany, Denmark and western Holland had surrendered unconditionally, to take effect from 0800hrs on the 5th. On 6 May Major General Rawlins, GOC the Polar Bears 49th Division, met the commander of the German 88th Corps to arrange the occupation of north-west Holland and the disarming and concentration of the enemy. All units took part that day in Thanksgiving church parades, and there were double rum issues that night.

Amsterdam in early 1945.

Lt Colonel C. D. Hamilton of the 7th Dukes recalled:

The plan was for the 49th Division to disarm the three divisions holding the Grebbe Line based on Hilversum and Utrecht, while the following day the Canadian 1st Division went on to the Hague and Rotterdam to put the coastal divisions behind the wire of their own defences. Our customers were our old opponents of 4 December, the 6th German Parachute Division, who had found us in the way when they tried to take the Nijmegen bridge.

Somewhere between 150,000 and 200,000 assorted soldiery of the Third Reich were trapped inside the Grebbe and Eems river enclave. Inside were several million half-starved Dutch men, women and children, mainly in the cities of Amsterdam, Rotterdam, The Hague, Haarlem, Delft, Leiden and Amersfoort. The enclave was 60 miles wide at its southern point, narrowing to a triangle between the North Sea and Ijsselmeer.

The Canadians and British were tasked with the swift 'peaceful' entry into the enclave, keeping their fingers crossed that *all* the German forces would accept the terms of *immediate* surrender. General Blaskowitz was ordered to seize and disarm all the renegade Dutch SS soldiers under his command. This was accomplished slightly reluctantly, and soon

8,000 were arrested. Moreover the 120,000 German troops who had surrendered on 5 May were ordered to build their own barbed wire enclosures in lieu of camps, as a prelude to being shipped out east to the camps in Schleswig Holstein. For the time being they were allowed to keep their small arms, but they were forced to clear all the minefields they had set up.

Almost undamaged by war, the great city of Amsterdam had waited for liberation longer than most European cities. On the morning of 7 May, German forces were still present in large numbers in the centre when armoured cars of the Polar Bear Division arrived.

B Squadron of the 49th Recce Regiment achieved fame in the *Daily Express* of 8 May 1945 under the headline NAZIS CLEAR WAY. According to the reporter John Reffern, the first troops into Amsterdam produced: 'the greatest liberation scenes I have know. The hated Grunepolizei, German security police, were made to clear a way for them through the rejoicing crowds.'

Leonard Marsland Gander, a journalist at the *Daily Telegraph*, was also there wearing a British uniform and red beret. He remembered:

> The Dam Square was a wild sea of celebration within a ring of sullen German troops. We clawed our way through with difficulty, dispensing cigarettes, more in demand than food. After we left, the scene erupted. Attempts were made to disarm a German officer. German marines in De Groote Club fired into the crowd and at least 20 civilians were killed. Scattered fighting broke out until the Dutch Resistance leader arranged a truce. Our small troop was reinforced and a column of ten armoured cars returned to the centre of Amsterdam.

On 31 August 1944, SHAEF had set up the Dutch Forces of the Interior (Nederlandsche Binnenlandsche Strijdkraft – the NBS) under Prince Bernhard, who reported direct to General Eisenhower. By April 1945, there were 9,350 armed resistance members of the NBS organised in six zones and fourteen regions under Major General Koot.

On 7 May, the Recce Regiment in Otterloo led the advance into western Holland. A Squadron was directed on Utrecht, B Squadron on Hilversum and Amsterdam and C Squadron on Baarn and Amersfoort. The Germans fulfilled their surrender conditions with correctness. The only impediment was the Dutch civilians. The vehicles could only just get through the enthusiastic crowds. B Squadron was at Otterloo

Tony Van Renterghem, Chief
of Staff, South Amsterdam
Resistance District, April 1945.

and on the morning of the 7th, two troops were detailed to proceed to
Amsterdam: No 1 Troop (two heavy and two light recce cars) under Lt
George Bowman MC and No 4 Troop (six Bren gun carriers) under Lt
John Rafferty. Trooper Percy Habershon was the gunner operator in a
heavy armoured car commanded by Sgt Dai Davis, the driver of which
was Lance Corporal Seagrove. Percy Haberson recalled:

> The route was via Hilversum and once we started moving through the villages
> the reception was tremendous. National flags and Orange banners were hanging
> from all the buildings. At one of the bridges on the outskirts of Amsterdam we
> were met by a Dutch Resistance officer [Lt Tony van Renterghem], the liaison
> officer of the local Resistance group. He led us through the suburbs into Dam
> Square in front of the Old Royal Palace. Several thousand people had turned
> out but eventually two heavy armoured cars managed to get to the main doors
> of the palace where Lt G Bowman posted a notice regarding the surrender. The
> situation was becoming very volatile. There were fully armed German soldiers
> on the streets and Resistance fighters brandishing Sten guns were appearing.
> We then moved to a building some distance away at the side of a canal, the HQ
> of the German occupational forces. Lt Bowman and Lt van Renterghem went

351

Rotterdam port in early 1945.

inside. We were near a local hospital and a large crowd of nurses descended on us. Being 20 years old I lost interest in military matters until we were rescued from a fate worse than death by Lt Bowman who told us we were to move to a RV outside the city. What a shame!

Utrecht, a large prosperous city, was entered by the 4th Lincolns on the 7 May. They arrived in style, debussed on the outskirts and, led by their regimental band, marched in to scenes of indescribable enthusiasm. The battalion HQ was in the Hotel Terminus. Armed German troops looked on apathetically and were completely ignored by both Dutch and British. The Polar Bear vehicles were swamped by the numbers of people who clambered all over them. In the evening a band concert, the Dutch and the Lincolns, played all the nostalgic tunes, including of course the Dutch National Anthem 'Wilhelmus', followed by 'God Save the King'. Peter Stursberg, a journalist on the *Daily Herald* wrote an article on 8 May. The headline was DUTCH BEAT ALL FOR CHEERS:

The Dutch, whom we have always thought a stolid people, have outdone the Belgians and the French in their wild welcome to our troops during their victory march into Holland. The sound of cheering is still ringing in my ears as I write this in a hotel lobby here. I arrived in this ancient city with the first

British armoured cars. All the way from our starting point on the Grebbe line we drove through lines of people, but it was not till we got to the outskirts of the city that we were almost mobbed.

There had been some shooting in Utrecht between Nazis and Resistance men, and we stopped for a moment on a wide boulevard. A cheering, singing crowd descended on us and took over our vehicles. My coat was almost torn from my back, and I found that there was no room in the jeep for me except on the spare tyre. A girl had her arm round my neck, and a man was sitting on my knee. There were between 40 and 50 persons on the jeep and trailers, and more got on as we entered Utrecht.

This is the greatest liberation and the strangest, too. On our way up Germans drove past us in army cars and Volkswagens, and for a time, as we slowly edged our way through the crowds, two Germans cycled beside us. They had machine pistols slung over their backs, and might have been our escorts. The Dutch just ignored them. The girl who had her arm round my neck stuffed golden tulips into my raincoat. Our jeep and trailer load – by now a full chorus of 60 voices – broke into 'The Orange' as we passed a German headquarters.

The effect of starvation is noticeable in the pinched faces of the people. Some are so weak from hunger that they can hardly wave to us. I talked with the leader of the Resistance Movement here, and he told me that there was so little food that people were going round from house to house begging for a potato.

Other Polar Bear units took part in the official capture of Utrecht. The 1/4th KOYLI left Ede at 1300hrs on the 7th. Rex Flower recorded: 'The whole Bn in troop carriers along the road to Utrecht, as we came to the outskirts, everyone was out. There were thousands lining the streets. The convoy had to slow down. The people were absolutely going mad! They were ecstatic! It was definitely our best welcome of all. First we had children jumping on the vehicles, then a few young ladies. (We were not complaining.) It was fiesta time in the staid city of Utrecht. Poor semi-starving children clustered round the cookhouse. Everyone gave up part of their meals; the cooks gave them all leftovers. Doug, Jim and I were plied with drinks all day.'

The Hallams also 'fought' their way into Utrecht. The column was a splendid sight. Tulips bloomed in every rifle barrel, while hundreds of girls walked arm in arm with the Allied soldiers as they eventually marched in triumph through the town.

Above: Dutch SS troops interned after Holland's surrender.

Left: In Utrecht, Dutchmen shoulder welcome boxes of food and supplies shipped in by Allied forces in the days following the German surrender.

On 8 May, a thanksgiving service was held in Utrecht Cathedral and on Sunday 13th there was a victory parade followed by a service attended by the Burgomeister and Lt General C. Foulkes, GOC the 1st Canadian Corps.

On 9 May, the 4th Leicesters moved to Maarssen, six miles north-west of Utrecht, to disarm German troops. The battalion pioneer officer, Lt Daykin, arranged for the enemy working parties to blow up all dangerous ammunition.

Lt Colonel C. D. Hamilton of the 7th Dukes recalled:

The German paras first passed completely equipped through our 'sausage machine'. They dumped personal small arms, binoculars and watches in one house with A Company, then passed on to the open fields where their larger weapons, steel helmets, anti-gas kit and all the other multitudinous impedimenta of the division was stacked. For two days roads were blocked by hundreds of horse-drawn carts, the platoon trucks of one of the crack German divisions. Afterwards the Germans marched into a large wood where we guarded them for a week as they made themselves fit for their long march back to prison camps in northern Germany. I had one exhausting day inspecting every unit of two enemy brigade groups.

On the same day the Dutch newspaper *Het Parool* published a letter in English from Maurice Western, a journalist: 'We know that a dark nightmare has been lifted from your hearts and minds. While Germans in the end would have been driven from Holland regardless of any decisions which General Blaskowitz could make, most of us feared that the country would have been ravaged by the grimmest kind of war before freedom was secure again. Now as if by a miracle your dreads and ours are banished for ever and you have expressed your joy in rousing demonstrations that literally swept us off our feet and off our jeeps.'

Lt Tony van Renterghem, a key Resistance leader in Amsterdam wrote:

25,000 Dutch civilians had already died of hunger and thousands more were on the point of dying, particularly newborn babies and the very old. We were down to a diet of 330 calories a day, down from 1,200 calories in the summer of 1944. Even the German army in Amsterdam was down to 1,000 calories a day. The SS and Gestapo (unlike the Wehrmacht who were ready to surrender) still executed large numbers of the Resistance, Jews and hostages before the arrival of the Polar Bears. There was no electricity, gas, fuel of any kind. The sewage system had stopped pumping. There was no soap, no hot water. Meanwhile the Resistance was trying to feed 70,000 people who had gone underground such as Jews in hiding, or like myself, people who had been condemned to death, but were hiding. They had to stock up food for some 10,000 Resistance fighters who were called up to fight a guerilla war as soon as the Allies were near enough, and ordered us to attack the Germans from the back. Even more important was the protection of dykes and canal locks which the fanatical

Right: The Polar Bear monument on the Kade, Roosendaal, Holland. (*Bill Hudson*)

Below: 49th Division memorial, Utrecht, Holland. (*Bill Hudson*)

SS wanted to blow up to flood and destroy Holland. I was chief of staff of the South Amsterdam Resistance District. My main task at liberation was to prevent any fighting in my district between the trigger-happy Resistance and die-hard German army or SS, until a large enough Allied force was present. On 3 May the German Command finally allowed the Allied Air Force to drop food near the big cities, but collection and distribution without vehicles would take at least two weeks. Lt Bowman, out of radio contact, was advised by the Resistance CO when the shooting in Dam Square started, to withdraw to the town outskirts. Back at the bridge he called in reinforcements and Major H Taite joined him there with the main force a little later. At City Hall Major Taite met the German CO, Lt Kolonel Schroeder, a 'good' German who had long co-operated with the Resistance. The main Canadian force arrived the next day, 8 May, to take over military control of Amsterdam.

A new brigade of division artillery was formed with most of their guns laagered behind the lines. They concentrated at Doorn to start supervising the notorious 34th Landsturm Nederland SS Division. The Kensingtons formed part of the new brigade and, their historian wrote, rounded up: 'the avowed Nazi SS and all foreign Fascist volunteers, notorious in occupied Holland for their brutality. We received a rapturous welcome by the inhabitants of Doorn when the SS officers were evicted from the best houses.' On 10 May, the Kensingtons disarmed the 84th SS Regiment of 77 officers and 1,415 other ranks. Then two days later, Operation Pied Piper took place, to comb the area for German deserters and Dutch Nazis, as a result of which fifty-three arrests were made. The 1st Leicesters moved to Hilversum, where they also started to disarm the Wehrmacht. There was a certain grim satisfaction in doing so, and a carnival atmosphere in the town every evening. The 2nd Glosters were given the pleasant duty of disarming the 346th Infantry Division at Amersfoort, 12 miles from Utrecht. That division had opposed the 56th Sphinx Brigade in Normandy throughout their advance to Stampersgat and again at Arnhem. The regimental historian ended by saying: 'It was altogether a very satisfactory arrangement!' By 12 May all German divisional troops were disarmed and concentrated. HQ, signals and administrative companies of the German 88th Corps were disarmed by the Recce Regiment on the 13/14th.

The islands north of the Scheldt were captured by the British 4th Commando Brigade and 116th Royal Marine Infantry Brigade and E-boats, U-boats and many kriegsmarines were made prisoner. T-Force, the intrepid

Thieving Magpies had eight Category A and 140 Category B targets to investigate, so 30th Battalion of the Royal Berkshires and two companies of the Buckinghamshires advanced into Holland on 8 May to carry out their invaluable searches. In the Utrecht area T-Force found a torpedo-firing pistol unit for use in *midget* submarines and a number of botanical laboratories specialising in moulds and fungus for a penicillin equivalent. At Haaksbergen the Polar Bears gave T-Force permission to move ahead to identify targets. Capt. Lowe of the Buckinghamshires reached Rotterdam and met the NBS. National Archives WO/71/5161 shows that A Company entered Amsterdam, B Company Utrecht, C Company Rotterdam and D Company The Hague and islands near the Hook of Holland. The Thieving Magpies trawled through Groningen, Deventer, Wageningen, Leeuwarden, Harlingen, Norden, even Borkum island and Delft as well as the major cities for 'secrets' and 'secret men' of all kinds.

Many victory parades were held all over Holland on 21 May. The most important was held in The Hague with the salute taken by HRH Prince Bernhard in the presence of Queen Wilhelmina and General Crerar. Each Polar Bear battalion – twelve of them in all – was present with 200 men each, and sixteen pipe and five brass bands provided appropriate music. Overhead flew No 84 RAF group of fighters and fighter bombers.

There was spit and polish of course for the Polar Bears under their RSMs and they had a heavy infantry drill practice the day before. Lt Colonel D. A. D. Eykin's orders to his 11th Royal Scots Fusiliers included: 'Each company will provide ten men of not less than five feet ten inches in height. Decorated men will be given preference. Medals will be worn. Best battledress will be worn, boots will be highly polished. Brasses will be highly polished. Webbing, belts and gaiters will be blancoed. Caps (tam-o'-shanters) will be worn.'

On 25 May, 117,629 German troops (the Dutch renegade SS were left for local justice) moved from the Netherlands to concentration areas in the Wilhelmshaven/Emden peninsula. General Blaskowitz was responsible for co-ordination and control of evacuation and chose the route and the transit camps for the batches of 10,000 Wehrmacht who covered 15 miles per day into captivity.

During the war 205,900 Dutch men and women had died. The Netherlands had the highest death rate in Western Europe: 2.36 per cent of their population of about nine million. The Jewish suffered the worst with 104,000 deaths; forced labour in Germany another 27,000; in the

Resistance 23,000 died; 20,400 civilians died of starvation or bombing; and 7,850 armed forces were killed. The balance of 27,450 deaths was 'unclassified'.

In the final throes of retribution and justice over 200,000 cases of pro-Nazi activity were investigated. Of the many subsequently tried by democratic courts, forty received the death sentence, but many others were sentenced to between one and five years' imprisonment. Seyss-Inquart was hanged at Nuremberg on 16 October 1946; Anton Mussart was hanged at The Hague on 7 May 1946; General Johannes von Blaskowitz committed suicide in 1946. *Festung* Holland had been conquered and liberated.

On the 40th anniversary of the liberation of Arnhem on 15 April 1945, a Dutch postage stamp was issued that showed an Allied soldier in action. Initially it was supposed to be a Polish soldier, but the photographer, Mr Van-de-Weerd of Ede identified it as Pte Joseph Slatter, C Company, 2nd Essex Regiment (the Pompadours). The photo was taken on the Utrecht Weg, a hill near the Gemeente Museum in Arnhem. The Essex Regiment, part of 56th Brigade of the 49th Polar Bear Division, had fought in Operation Quick Anger west of Ijssel, on their way to Rijnbrug and Eusebuiskert. On 4 May, the Essex Regiment was in the front line at Wageningen when the German High Command surrendered. The postage stamp is reproduced below.

The 1985 Liberation stamp of Private Joseph Slatter, 2nd Essex.

„Poolse" soldaat blijkt Engelsman

(Van één onzer verslaggevers)

ARNHEM-EDE – De „Poolse Soldaat in Arnhem" die een van de bevrijdingspostzegels van de PTT siert, die op 5 mei, worden uitgegeven, blijkt een Engelsman te zijn. Het is Joseph Slatter die deel uitmaakte van de 2nd Battalion van The Essex Regiment, ook wel „The Pompadours" genaamd.

De Edese amateur historicus E. van de Weerd wist de gebruikte afbeelding direct thuis te brengen. Zij staat namelijk in een boekje over The Essex Regiment „,D' Day to 'Ve' Day". „De foto is gemaakt op de Utrechtseweg nabij de helling naar het Gemeentemuseum in Arnhem. Waarschijnlijk op 15 april", aldus Van de Weerd.

Joseph Slatter moet, als hij nog leeft, ongeveer 65 jaar zijn. Na de oorlog is hij teruggekeerd naar Londen waar hij waarschijnlijk in het zuidoostelijke deel heeft gewoond. Op dit moment is Van de Weerd bezig met naspeuringen om uit te vinden of Slatter nog in leven is.

Slatter was „Private" (soldaat) in de C-Compagnie. „The Pompadours" maakten deel uit van de 56ste brigade die bij Normandie landde en later met de Polar Bear Divisie optrok naar Nederland.

In de nacht van 12 op 13 april is The Essex Regiment nabij Westervoort de IJssel over gezet. In de loop van de 13e april heeft men zich een weg gevochten naar de Rijnbrug en de Eusebiuskerk. Een dag later werd de binnenstad gezuiverd en de dag daarna, de 15e april (de dag waarop de foto werd gemaakt) staat bij de kenners bekend als een dag van „consolidatie en reoganisatie". Later heeft de Essex Regiment nog in de frontlijn bij Wageningen gelegen. Vier mei was het ook voor hen voorbij.

* De postzegels van de PTT waarop de Engelsman Slatter voor Pool wordt aangezien.

TRANSLATION OF ATTACHED CUTTING FROM THE DUTCH NEWSPAPERS

1)
   Polish Soldier now proved to be an Englishman.

Arnhem-Ede.
        The Polish soldier in Arnhem, featured in the commemoration, liberation stamps issued by the Post Office, to mark the anniversary of the 5th May, has been found to be English.
        He is Joseph Slatter, of The 2nd, Battalion The Essex Regiment, also known as (The Pompadours). The amateur historian from Ede, Mr. E, Van-de-Weerd, recognised him from a photograph which he had at home. He is currently writing a book on The Essex Regiment, entitled "D" Day to "VE" Day. The photo, was taken on the Utrecht Way, on the hill near the Gemeente Museum, in Arnhem. Probably on the 15th April, said Mr. Van-de-Weerd.
        Joseph Slatter, if he is still alive, must be nearly 65 years old. (actually nearer 70 years old). After the war he returned to London, and was de-mobbed to an address in the South East. At this moment Van-de-Weerd, is researching his where-abouts, and if he is still alive.
        Slatter, was a Private, in "C" Comapny. The Pompadours, formed part of the 56th Brigade, during the Normandy landings, and later with the Polar bear, Divisions, march up through Holland.
2)
   During the night of the 12th/13th of April. The Essex Regiment, advanced to the West of Ijssel, and stayed. In the advance of the 13th of April, they fought their way to Rijnbrug, and Eusebuiskerk. A day later they had taken the old town and the following day (the day the photograph was taken) their leaders agreed it should be a day of consolidation and re-organisation. Later The Essex Regiment, were in the front line at Wageningen. By the 4th of May they were victorious.

Polar Bears reach Amsterdam first.

2nd Essex move into Zetten, Private Slatter's comrades-in-arms. (*R. E. Gough*)

CHAPTER 26

Liberation of Denmark

All the Scandinavian countries emerged from the First World War with their faith in neutrality unshaken; it was a cardinal principle of their foreign policy. In 1939, Germany had a treaty of friendship with Norway and Denmark.

Denmark, a peaceful, democratic monarchy, with a population of over four million, had a special word to define the country – *Hyggelig* – which means cosy, comfortable and agreeable. This later earned the nickname 'Hitler's little canary'. King Christian X was very popular and his public image combined quiet heroism with regal dignity. Denmark's southern border with German Schleswig Holstein meant that many families intermarried and relations remained cordial between the two countries.

Adolf Hitler knew how to suborn the territories that in *Mein Kampf* he indicated he would subjugate. Looking at photographs of the Youth Group leaders from Norway, Denmark and Holland, his *Table Talk* biographer Martin Bormann recorded what he said:

Even in Denmark the opposition of the older generation will not prevent the youth from adopting in ever-increasing numbers the German way of thought for they feel they spring from the same racial origins. By methodically supporting the development of this movement I am cutting the ground from under the feet of the old King of Denmark and drawing his people away from him … I have endowed the Hitler Jugend with the bold motto '*Die Jugend von Jugend gefürt werden soll*' (Youth must be led by Youth). I have set up in their very early years a process of selectivity amongst young people whereby the little group leaders soon select themselves. It is between the ages of ten and

Copenhagen, Amalienborg Palace and harbour in 1945.

17 that youth exhibits both the greatest enthusiasm and the greatest idealism and it is for this period of their lives that we must provide them with the best possible instructors and leaders.

Having digested the capture of Poland, Hitler determined to attack and capture Norway and Denmark before, as he expected, Winston Churchill sent a joint Anglo-French expeditionary force to Norway to seize the vital ports. Lt General Nikolaus von Falkenhorst was appointed by Hitler to plan and execute Operation Weseruebung. The conquest of Denmark appeared to be easy – it was flat, open and ideal for tank warfare. Falkenhorst deployed two Wehrmacht divisions, a motorised rifle brigade with Mark I and II tanks, three motorised SP gun battalions, two batteries of heavy guns and three armoured trains. The Luftwaffe supplied a company of paratroops and some AA mobile guns. The Danish government had received specific information about an attack from friendly military attachés in Berlin, but Capt. Kjolsen, the Danish naval attaché's report was simply not believed. Nor did King Christian believe an attack was imminent.

In April 1940 the Danish army consisted of 15,000 poorly trained troops. In February of that year Winston Churchill had told journalists: 'I could not reproach Denmark if she surrendered to Nazi attack. The

Copenhagen Town Hall and centre, *c.* 1945.

other two Scandinavian countries, Norway and Sweden, have at least a ditch over which they can feed the tiger, but Denmark is so terribly near Germany that it would be impossible to bring help. Personally I would in any case not undertake to guarantee Denmark.'

At dawn on Tuesday 9 April the 170th Wehrmacht Division and 11th Motorised Rifle Brigade smashed across the border into Jutland. Panzer units were unopposed. On the island of Fyn assault troops captured Middelfart and Nyborg without a fight. In Copenhagen, General Kurt Himer, chief of staff of the German battlegroups involved, had personally in civilian clothes made a comprehensive survey of the city's defences. The troopship *Hansestadt Danzig* with a German assault battalion aboard, passed the coast forts without a challenge, tied up at Langelinie Pier, swept ashore and, before 0500hrs captured the city's Citadel. The king conferred with his ministers in the palace at Amalienborg Square. General W. W. Prior, the Danish C-in-C, wanted to fight but Luftwaffe bombers flying en masse low over Copenhagen persuaded the King to surrender at 0620hrs. Danish casualties in the three-hour war were thirteen killed in action and twenty-three wounded (in Jutland). The Germans had twenty casualties.

In his book *The Bitter Years* Richard Petrow wrote: 'Denmark led by its government and [seventy-year-old] king had embarked on a road that would earn for the country the reputation of Germany's model protectorate. Nevertheless fear and anger seethed below the outwardly calm exterior. The invasion sent a hard knife edge of terror through the country's eight thousand Jews and among thousands upon thousands of patriotic Danes the performance of the Danish Army and Navy was cause for shame and humiliation.' To this author it was clear that the very modest army, full of recruits, stood no chance at all against Hitler's stormtroopers and above all, his Luftwaffe, who had terrorised the huge Polish forces in a few weeks earlier in 1940.

For three years Denmark retained a degree of independence, which diminished steadily. The German Foreign Minister in Denmark, Cecil von Renthe-Finke, was sympathetic to the Danes, who supplied huge agricultural exports of meat and butter to the Reich. But in July 1940, severe press censorship was imposed and the King appointed the pro-German Danish politician Erik Scavenius to head the Danish Foreign Ministry. His policy was: 'Denmark should not under any circumstances come into conflict with its great neighbour in the south. The great German victories which have struck the world with astonishment and admiration have begun a new era in Europe which will bring with it a New Order in political and economic spheres under Germany's leadership. It will be Denmark's task to find its place in mutual active co-operation with Greater Germany.' A Danish-German Association was designed to foster better relations between the two countries. Dr Fritz Clausen was the leader of the Danish National Socialist Workers Party (DNSAP), who were in effect Dutch Nazis; and Lt Colonel P. C. Kryssing became the commanding officer of Frikorps Danmark, which became the SS Viking unit and fought for Germany on the eastern front against Russia. The 1,000-strong battalion suffered heavy casualties south of Leningrad. In the book, *Hitler's Table Talk*, it is recorded on 27 February 1942:

As regards the monarchs the worst nuisances are those who've grown old in harness. They become in a sort of way, tabu [sic]. You scarcely touch them and everybody begins to howl ... If the Dane goes about it like the old Swede (who does nothing but gather his strength by playing tennis he'll reach the age of Methuselah) ... It's by dint of doing nothing that these puppets become impudently old. In Denmark, we already have the successor. That's Clausen. When we've reached that point, we'll have three men who'll have sinned so much that they'll be obliged to remain allied to us whatever happens. We can count on Clausen and likewise on Mussert [in Holland].

Hitler kept on stepping up pressure on the Danes as minor resistance, demonstrations, secret newspapers and evidence of SOE activities increased. Dr Werner Best, a leading Gestapo and SD agent was sent by Hitler as German Commissioner to Denmark and was ordered by the Führer to 'rule with an iron hand'. Lt General Hermann Hannekin, a tough Wehrmacht officer, took over the army command. Best produced figures that showed that eighty-five German civilians and an additional 130 employees 'governed' Denmark!

SOE sent Captain Rottboll and a wireless operator on 16 April 1942, and a group called 'Table' was started up; they made contact with the 'Dansk Samling' and 'The Princes', who were linked to the Danish General Staff. By the end of 1942 all the SOE operators were caught and either killed or captured by the Gestapo, except for 'Hammer'. In February 1943 SOE had two successful sorties and landed eight men and two radios. Flemming Bruuin Muus became SOE's chief organiser for the next eighteen months, with Duus Hansen, alias 'Napkin', plus Flemming Junker from Jutland as key agents. In the summer of 1943 no less than 28 sabotage attacks were made by fire and explosive on shipyards and factories working for the Germans, and there were also some attacks on German shipping. The Germans reacted predictably. President Scavenius resigned and on 29 August the Danish Army and Navy were disbanded. Many officers were arrested or fled to Sweden. However, Lt Svend Truelsen, a lawyer and reserve officer, soon worked up a first-class intelligence network. Rather surprisingly, the Swedish government co-operated and formed Danish police battalions. They eventually expanded to become Danforce, with 5,000 men and two British officers for liaison. Sabotage increased rapidly and in the first six months of 1944 there were fifty 'incidents'; from October 1944 to the end of April 1945 there were no fewer than 252 major incidents. On 22 June 1944 eighty saboteurs attacked the Dansk Industri Syndikat in Copenhagen, which was making guns for the Germans. Other attacks were made on the large Burmeister and Wain shipyard in Copenhagen. A general strike in June 1944 was followed by the Germans burning down the Tivoli Gardens.

The Danish Freedom Council was created in the autumn of 1943, and included Professor Mogens Fog with several other communists, and representatives of 'Ringen' and 'Dansk Samling' with Flemming Muus as the SOE representative. Ronald Turnbull was the SOE's London representative for Sweden and Denmark. Major Winkelhorn became Planning Officer of the SOE Danish section, which from 1 May 1944, was integrated into SHAEF Mission for Denmark (September 1944) under Major General Dewing.

On 6 October 1943 the Danish physicist Niels Bohr, who had identified vanadium-235 as being a vital ingredient of what became the nuclear fission atomic bomb, was smuggled out of Denmark to Sweden in a fishing boat. On 6 October he was flown in the bomb bay of a BOAC Mosquito on the first stage of a journey to the United States.

By the end of the war, fifty-seven SOE-trained Danish agents had been sent in, of whom thirteen were captured and six killed. There were 414 aircraft sorties of which 285 were successful, but with the loss of seventeen aircraft. Some 6,670,000 Danish Krone were expended in cash and repaid later by the government of the day.

In August 1943 national strikes and several hundred acts of sabotage by the Resistance groups, often equipped by SOE agents, forced martial law by the German occupying forces. The Danish army had to surrender their arms and the Danish navy scuttled or sank twenty-nine vessels and many more were severely damaged; thirteen escaped to Sweden and only thirteen small ships were captured by the Germans. In September, Heinrich Himmler sent his Gestapo agent K. H. Hoffmann and the horrible Dr Rudolf Mildner, an expert of extermination camps in Katowice (Poland) and Auschwitz, to plan a 'Final Solution' to the 8,000 Danish Jews who had been relatively unscathed since the occupation in 1940. Major Rolf Günther, a deputy of Adolf Eichmann, was to carry out this operation on 1–2 October just after Rosh Hashanah, the Jewish New Year. Two German freighters arrived in Copenhagen harbour to take the intended Jewish captives back to the Reich's extermination camps. Richard Petrow charts their remarkable escape in his book *The Bitter Years*. The vast majority escaped to Sweden by fishing boat and 'only' 284 men, women and children were arrested. Adolf Eichmann, Rolf Günther and their Führer were all furious. However, the fishing boat captains earned fortunes.

The Communist-led underground group BOPA and the Freedom Council (Freihetradet) carried out many spectacular sabotage acts in 1944 and early 1945. So much so that the 9,000-strong Danish police were arrested, disbanded and several thousand deported to Germany. The British RAF sent daring Mosquito fighter-bomber attacks: three squadrons destroyed the Gestapo HQ in Aarhus on 31 October 1944 and on 21 March 1945 the Gestapo Copenhagen HQ in Shellhus building and Odense HQ in April. Despite civilian casualties these three daring and successful raids smashed up the Danish Gestapo teams and records.

Demobilised veterans of the Danish SS Frikorps founded the pro-German Danish Schalburg Corps, known as Hipos or Hilfepolizei and controlled by Nazi officers, began a retaliatory campaign of sabotage and terror against facilities and objects dear to most Danes. This reprisal was known as *Schalburtage* and they set fire to the Royal Danish porcelain factory, put incendiary bombs into the famous Tivoli Gardens, wrecked the Students' Union at Copenhagen University, bombed the main community centre in the city and set fire to the East Asiatic Company HQ. In June 1944 there was a huge national demonstration at the end of which 226 Danes were killed or wounded. The Hipos were extremely dangerous, well-armed fanatics who terrorised most Danish towns and villages.

Scandinavian prisoners, a mixed collection of policemen, teachers, journalists, diplomats, clergymen and underground Resistance workers, were imprisoned in camps in Poland and Germany. After complicated negotiations between Count Folks Bernadotte, Himmler, Ernst Kaltenbrunner – chief of Germany's secret police, and Ribbentropp, the vast majority of the Scandinavians were transferred to Neuengamme concentration camp near Hamburg. By 1 April 1945, 2,200 Danes and Norwegians from Sachsenhausen camp, 600 from Dachau, 1,600 from Buchenwald, and smaller groups from other camps including Natzweiler, were assembled in Neuengamme. The original prisoners there – Russians, Poles, Ukrainians, Dutch, French and others were sent off, mostly to Braunschweig and Belsen. These poor devils, called 'Mussulmen', walking skeletons, almost certainly died of starvation in the next few weeks.

Astonishingly, Himmler agreed that the Jutland Corps' 'White Bus' charitable group could transfer by 21 April 7,100 Scandinavians to Froslev in Denmark; but 2,100 died in captivity in Germany.

As the British Liberation Army swept into Hamburg and Schleswig Holstein, urgent negotiations started between Admiral Dönitz in his

Flensburg HQ and the German gauleiters in Denmark, Norway and Holland. Should they continue the struggle against the Allies even after their Führer's death on 30 April in his Berlin bunker?

General Georg Lindemann was GOC of the German troops in Denmark. They numbered 136,000 Wehrmacht, 19,000 Kriegsmarines and 17,000 Luftwaffe – a total of 172,000. However, Admiral Skagerrak, who was Naval C-in-C Denmark, had 40,200 men under his command on 1 April 1945.

Mr Jens Andersen of the Copenhagen Museumscenter Hanstholm has kindly supplied the map of the German dispositions in Denmark at 4 May 1945. The 233rd Panzer Division, stationed on the frontier, only had twenty-five battle tanks including two Panther Mk IVs. All the units were for training recruits, and equipment was scarce. The Luftwaffe had 1,100 planes on Danish airfields but only 261 tons of petrol to fuel them! In Copenhagen harbour were the heavy cruiser *Prinz Eugen* and light cruiser *Nurnberg* in a combat-ready state but with insufficient fuel. About 10 per cent of Lindemann's troops were non-German: Hungarians,

Concentration of German
forces in Denmark.

Russians and Poles. Many troops were elderly, portly or convalescing from wounds. No élite regiment served in Denmark – Hitler needed them to help defend the Reich.

In 1944 when the end of the war in Europe was approaching, the Russians and the Western Allies realised that, as their armies started to converge, clear rules of engagement would be needed to avoid accidental clashes. The plan for Operation Eclipse laid down the zones of occupation and lines of demarcation, later approved at the Yalta Conference in February 1945. These lines of demarcation, later named 'the Iron Curtain' by Winston Churchill, ran from Wismar in North Germany to Switzerland, with *Denmark and the Danish islands firmly in the Allied Sector.*

The BBC Danish radio at 2035hrs on 4 May broadcast the news that the German High Command had surrendered all their forces in north-west Germany, Denmark, Norway and Holland to Field Marshal Bernard Montgomery.

In Operation Eclipse the British High Command had made intricate and careful military preparations by air, sea and land to occupy *Norway* but, as will be seen, Denmark was another matter! It is a complicated story with many threads and strands. Winston Churchill cabled his deputy, Anthony Eden, who was in Washington, on 5 May: 'sending Monty to Lübeck to cut off any Soviet advance from the Baltic to Denmark: we are sending in a moderate holding force to Copenhagen by air and the rest of Denmark is being rapidly occupied from henceforward by our fast-moving armoured columns. I think therefore having regard to the joyous feeling of the Danes and the abject submission and would-be partisanship of the surrendered Huns, we shall head our Soviet friends off at this point too.'

The American General Bradley wrote of Field Marshal Montgomery about 21–22 April: 'Monty, denied the glory of taking Berlin, had lost all heart for the fight... I believe he viewed his primary mission of sealing off the Danish border as demeaning ... Monty no longer seemed to have a sense of urgency about his mission.' After visiting Churchill in London on 20 April, Eisenhower flew back to meet Montgomery in Diepholz, south-west of Bremen, on the next day. Monty grumbled about his lack of manpower so he was allocated General Ridgway's US 18th Airborne Corps to help him on his drive to the Baltic. Monty wanted time to complete the capture of Bremen, which eventually fell on 27 April. Ike warned Monty that Marshal Konstantin Rokossovsky was making rapid progress through Hecklenburg heading for the Elbe and the Baltic beyond. It was a race alright and at Wismar at 0900hrs on 2 May the 3rd Parachute Brigade mounted on Royal Scots Greys' tanks arrived *within half an hour* of the Russians.

In early April 1945 British and American leaders had learnt, from their most secret Intelligence source, Ultra, the Germans' own coded radio signals, that the Soviet army was preparing to take political advantage of its advance along the Baltic by occupying Denmark. This knowledge altered Allied strategy and was to bring the British troops to the Baltic as the occupying, and for some, the liberating power. A top secret diplomatic despatch from the Japanese Ambassador in Sweden to the Foreign Ministry in Tokyo, which had been intercepted on 7 April, showed that the Russian move and Britain's response had been noted. The despatch began:

> From the Russian declaration that Denmark will shortly be liberated it is plain that Russia intends to bring Denmark into her sphere of influence and thus secure an outlet from the Baltic into the North Sea. Moreover the Russians have recently been making covert inquiries about what the Danish people who have taken refuge in Sweden have been doing. These are probably intended to provide material for their designs on Denmark. It is a fact also that the free Danish minister here recently left for Moscow in company with Kollontay, the Russian Minister here.
>
> While not a word had been said in public in Britain about Soviet intentions the British have since changed the direction of the drive on the Western Front by Montgomery's armies and turned it towards Hamburg. Moreover the recent heavy bombing of Kiel seems not so much to have been directed against the Germans as intended to prevent the Russians from being able to use it.

Viewing Anglo-Soviet disputes in the most optimistic light, from a Japanese perspective, the Japanese Ambassador told his government: 'The problems of the future of Denmark, the Near and Middle East, the Aegean Sea and China are very likely to provide the *motives for a third world war.* (Source: 'British-Soviet relations', Top Secret Ultra, telegram sent at 12.30 p.m., 7 April 1945; circulated to the Prime Minister and others, London 11 April 1945. Reference HW1/3683, Public Record Office, Kew.)

THE ✦ TIMES

BRITISH CRUISERS AT COPENHAGEN

The cruisers Birmingham and Dido soon after their arrival at Copenhagen. Between them is the destroyer Zodiac. The destroyers Zest, Zephyr, and Zealous were moored farther along the quayside. Cheering crowds greeted th[e] arrival of the British warships.

The Times article of the British arrival in Copenhagen, 5 May 1945.

Vice Admiral Tom Baillie-Grohman commanded a considerable fleet of Royal Navy warships. In effect his mission was a Grand Tour encompassing all the Norwegian ports, Copenhagen, and finally Kiel. He despatched a flotilla to clear the enemy minefields and then steam to Copenhagen. So the mine-sweeping flotilla under Captain Palmer DSC cleared the minefields in Kattegat and led cruisers *Birmingham* and *Dido* and four Z-class destroyers, *Zephyr, Zeus, Savage* and *Iroquis* into Copenhagen harbour on 4 May. Captain H. W. Williams, OC of the whole powerful squadron, took the surrender of the German Admiral Skaggerack's fleet: not only the *Prinz Eugen* and *Nürnberg*, but the *Leipzig*, three destroyers, two torpedo boats, ten minesweepers, thirteen Flak ships, nineteen armed trawlers and two armed merchant ships – fifty-one vessels altogether in Copenhagen, Aabenraa and other Danish ports. There were 600,000 tons of merchant shipping lying in the bay off Copenhagen harbour. Admiral Baillie-Grohman visited Kiel harbour on 8 May to take the surrender of the badly damaged *Hipper* and *Emden* cruisers and the battleship *Scheer*, sunk there by the RAF on 9 April.

6th Airborne land in Copenhagen.

The RAF was involved in Operation Eclipse. On 4 May a squadron of Typhoons landed at Kastrup airport outside Copenhagen, followed by another squadron two days later. Quite soon 8304th Air Disarmament Wing landed in Denmark to inspect the 1,100 forlorn Luftwaffe planes and equipment. The RAF also provided thirty Curtis Commando planes for the VE celebration.

On 5 May Danforce, 5,000 soldiers residing in Sweden, crossed over the Kattegat with the SOE liaison officer Major Ray, who became the first British officer to enter liberated Denmark.

Alan Moorehead was nearly always the first of the team of authorised journalists to get to crucial episodes in North Africa and North-west Europe. In his book *Eclipse* he details his Scandinavian adventures. A dozen Dakotas with a considerable fighter escort took off from Luneburg airfield on the morning of 5 May:

A company of airborne troops in their red berets and curious lizard-coloured camouflage jackets, a general [Dewing], an admiral and their staffs ... the general idea was destination Copenhagen and we should take over Denmark from the Germans. A pair of gleaming leather top-boots was passed on board. Young officers ran about ticking off names. The sun came down on the red caps and the red tabs and a Rolls Royce drove up debouching brigadiers ... so this was peace and peace this morning seemed wonderful. A full three months had passed since we had come into Germany; three months of army rations, and no fraternisation; three months of refugees and ruined cities; of shuttered shops and no electric light and no hot baths; of lumpish German women and traffic blocks and artillery and mud and the endless dragging knowledge that the war dragged on. All this time we had been promising ourselves Scandinavia. Out through Germany into the light again. Past Lübeck and Kiel and out over the Baltic. German ships seeing us coming ran up the white flag and turned away apprehensively. Then, one after another the green Danish islands. Every house on that liberation morning flew the national flag on a pole, the white cross on the red background and from the air the effect was as if one was looking down on endless fields strewn with poppies. On arrival there was no fighting. The German General Lindemann surrendered to General Dewing, and all German troops were confined to barracks. The Danish Resistance troops took control.

We passed in a procession of 20 to 30 cars with Dewing at the head, wreathed in chrysanthemums, into the lovely city. We had never seen such pretty girls, such gay dresses, such glistening shops and gardens. Each time the procession stopped the crowd closed in on us touching our sleeves and tunics to make sure we were real.

[Dewing made his HQ in the Hotel Angleterre] The scene in the lobby bordered on hysteria ... recollections of corks coming out of champagne

General Dewing inspecting MILORG resistance troops in Copenhagen.

Enthusiastic welcome for British 6th Airborne troops. (*Imperial War Museum*)

bottles, of tables laden with smoked salmon and caviar, of grilled steaks and strawberries, of singing, of laughing faces, of bright flowers.

Moorehead and the others visited the Royal Palace and listened to the brass band playing in the pleasure gardens of the Tivoli.

Major A. A. McLoughlin, B Company, 13th Battalion 5th Parachute Brigade, was the first to arrive in Copenhagen from Wismar: 'accompanied by more war correspondents than I would have believed possible'. He was the bodyguard keeping Dewing and the VIPs safe.

8th Parachute Battalion of 8th Parachute Brigade landed in thirty Curtiss Commando planes at 1500hrs. on 6 May at Kastrup airport. Pte Raymond Hutchings, a twenty-one-year-old, wrote: 'We collected our gear and piled into a large lorry commandeered by the Danish Resistance. On one side was painted HOLGER DANSKE, the mythical personage who lives in the underworld and whenever Denmark was in trouble he goes into action and everything is all right again.' 8th Para chased the Gestapo General Gunther Pancke, who was later captured.

Lt General 'Bubbles' Barker commanded 8th Corps and sent battle groups into Denmark including 4th (Black Desert Rats) Armoured

375

Brigade with the 2nd Dragoons (Royal Scots Greys) tanks, 1st Royal Dragoons armoured cars and 2nd KRRC motorised infantry. The Greys had 'carried' 6th Airborne troops to Wismar where they met the Russians. Lt Edwin Bramall, who later became a field marshal, had spent 5 May with 2nd KRRC near Hamburg. On VE Day they moved north to Pinneburg. 'The whole area was in chaos. The SS and other potential war criminals were trying to avoid capture. To our relief two or three days later the battalion was given orders to move into Denmark. We crossed the frontier at Flensburg where Dönitz had set up Germany's final supreme HQ and entered a different world of cheering and welcoming crowds and with a countryside free from the ravages of war where food and female company were plentiful.'

Lt J. A. Dimmond was a troop commander with the 1st Royal Dragoons, whose CO was Lt Colonel Anthony Pepys. The regiment spent six months helping to garrison Denmark. He wrote: 'Like Caesar's Gaul, Denmark is in three parts. On the left the tall feature of Jutland extends 250 miles northwards from the German border. In the centre the small island of Fyn (pronounced Foon) included the second city, Odense. On the right the larger island of Sjaeland (pronounced Seeland) contains the capital. There are numerous smaller islands and away towards the Arctic Circle the huge colony of Greenland.' Initially A at Arhus and B Squadrons were stationed in Jutland, C in the citadel in Copenhagen, and D, HQ and RHQ in Odense and Juelsburg. After six months, ninety young Royal Dragoons were engaged to Danish girls.

T-Force was ordered to move into Denmark in the general capacity as troops on the ground in addition to 4th Armoured Brigade and the Paratroop battalions. They also, of course, had many targets to investigate. On 7 May, the 5th Kings detachments crossed the frontier, one group heading for Kolding and the other for Aarhus. Lt Tom Pitt-Pladdy's column had several jeeps, a captured Wehrmacht Opel, three armoured cars of 1st Royal Dragoons, four large Mack trucks with the Pioneer Corps troops, a ration truck and two 'liberated' amphibious DUKWs. In Kolding the Stald-Gaarden Gestapo HQ was a key target. On the island of Fano was a V-2 rocket experimental plant. A batch of German scientists at Horuphav was held for interrogation. At Sæby, one-man torpedos had to be identified and sent back to the UK. In Arhus, twelve midget submarines, torpedos for harbour defence and other items of naval interest were found.

5th Kings Regiment of T-Force in Denmark.

When the 100 men of the 5th Kings arrived in Arhus they found the German garrison was 8,000 strong and was refusing to surrender to the Danes. They had already 'surrendered' to Field Marshal Montgomery! The Danish Resistance all over Denmark was hounding the Gestapo and this caused mini civil wars. The 5th Kings obtained a Danish army liaison officer, which helped calm down the warring tribes. Batches of 200 German prisoners were marched off to the frontier with Schleswig Holstein. One truck of Kings men carried food and blankets for the prisoners of war. Major Brian Urquhart's report on T-Force in Denmark is in the PRO at Kew (WO205/1049). One comment was: 'a tremendous and stupefying welcome was, and still is, being extended to those fortunate detachments.'

The island of Bornholm, 57 miles east of Copenhagen was Danish owned, garrisoned by a German force under Commander Kamptz with the chief Danish administrative officer, Peter Stemann. It was a strong garrison of 20,000 men. Kamptz would surrender to the British and the Royal Navy ships, which were only half a day's sail away. Russian aircraft bombed Nekso and Ronne, settlements on the island. Curiously neither the Danish government nor the British forces were interested in solving the problem. So the Russians sent a 50-bomber force, which dropped 1,500 200-pound bombs on the island. On 9 May, the Russians

Field Marshal Montgomery in a victory parade in Copenhagen, 12 May 1945.

landed without opposition and by the 16th the German garrison had been shipped off into captivity. Rather surprisingly, eleven months later the Russians returned the island to the Danish government.

The 160,000 troops under General Lindemann were marched in large batches, armed, carrying some loot, to the Danish frontier where grateful dragoons and Kings men relieved them of everything before the undefeated Germans entered the nearest camp in Schleswig Holstein.

The main German villains, Werner Best, Major General Herman Hanneken, SS General Gunther Pancke and Otto Bovensiepen, Gestapo Chief, were all tried for war crimes. The death penalty for Pancke and Bovensiepen was later, on appeal, reduced to imprisonment. In the post-war period, 20,000 Danes were arrested; 12,877 men and 631 women received prison sentences. Life sentences were imposed on sixty-six men and foty-six were executed for war crimes.

Jørgen Nissen, a schoolboy aged ten when the Germans invaded in 1940, grew up during their occupation:

We had a great many troops in the area because Europe's biggest fortress was on our doorstep. The Hanstholm fortress was part of the Atlantic Wall

Field Marshal Montgomery inspects 6th Airborne in Copenhagen, 12 May 1945.

and was – together with a fortress in Norway and extensive minefields in the Skagerrak – supposed to seal off the entrance to the Kattegat and the Baltic. It had artillery ranging from 17 cm guns up to four massive 38 cm guns, weighing 110 tonnes each. A bit like *Guns of Navarone*! Even Rommel paid us a visit I'm told. When they did the first trial shoot, windows were shattered all over town. Later fortifications were built all along the North Sea coast to prepare for an 'English' invasion (British was always called English), that never came of course.

By the beginning of 1945 it was clear that the end of the war was near, but we didn't know whether we would become a battlefield for a last stand effort by the Germans and whether the Russians would get to us before the British. But as the Germans started exchanging their good troops with inexperienced troops and a motley mix of troops from the East: Russians (deserters from the Russian army), Poles, etc their focus was clearly on the war in Germany itself.

During 1945 there was intense activity of our resistance movement sabotaging our railways and any facility relevant to the German war effort including supply facilities. An increasing number of soldier and civilian refugees came across the border and many ended up with us, and in February, Count Folke Bernadotte of Sweden brought back 7,000 Danes and Norwegians from

German concentration camps and there were rumours that he was go-between in surrender negotiations.

Our link to the outside world was Danish broadcasts from the BBC World Service and we all remember how it was interrupted at 20.35 on 4 May with the news of the capitulation to Montgomery. We wondered about Norway, but they had to wait for the complete surrender to Eisenhower on the 8th, and Bornholm, our island in the Baltic, was occupied by the Russians who didn't leave until April 1946 – so it was a close run thing!

The German troops started next morning walking back to Germany – not marching or singing as they usually did – throwing their weapons and ammunition by the wayside. We were a well-armed bunch of boys those days!

In Haderslev, the Freedom Council of Denmark noted: 'Montgomery's brave men, we know you have fought and won. We know you have fought and suffered and that you too have men that fell on the field of glory for their beloved country ... Together we have fought the Nazidom which has desecrated the word man, through bloody cruelty. Together you and we will make part of the Allied front in times to come and watch and guard around the peace and freedom we won. Blood and tears were the price of the fight, and happiness and right are to be made safe through the victory.' A bit convoluted but the right spirit!

The Danish resistance troops were immensely active during the liberation period. Much of their time was spent bringing the hundreds of dangerous Hipo terrorists to book. When Field Marshal Montgomery arrived in Copenhagen on 12 May he was given a hero's welcome by resistance and civilians alike. After all he was *the* commander to whom the gauleiters of Denmark, Norway and Holland surrendered.

CHAPTER 27

Liberation of *Festung* Norwegen

The first incident of the Second World War that involved Norway was unfortunate. Richard Petrow in *The Bitter Years* devotes a fascinating chapter to the 'Altmark Affair' of September 1939. The powerful pocket battleship *Admiral Graf Spee* had sunk many British merchant ships in the Atlantic and had transferred 300 British seamen to its supply ship, an 11,000-ton naval auxiliary tanker, the *Altmark*. He recounts the classic naval encounter when three lightly armed British cruisers, *Exeter*, *Ajax* and *Achilles* so chivvied and harassed the mighty 42,000-ton German ship that it took refuge in Montevideo on the river Plate. It was sufficiently damaged by gunfire that Captain Langsdorff scuttled it rather than face ignominious capture by the three 'hounds' waiting for it at sea. The *Altmark* under its wily captain, Heinrich Dau, headed north towards Germany and entered Norwegian waters. Despite being stopped and interrogated three or four times by amateurish Norwegian naval officers the *Altmark* was eventually pounced upon by Captain Philip Vian, with HMS *Cossack*, who boarded and rescued the 300 British merchant seamen imprisoned below decks with the memorable cry 'The Navy's here!'. The Norwegian actions were shameful. The whole of Britain rejoiced and Hitler was absolutely furious.

Norway was the vital conduit for the supply of iron ore from the Kiruna-Gallivare district of northern Sweden, using mainly the Norwegian port of Narvik. Germany needed 750,000 tons of ore *per month*, or it would have risked major industrial breakdown. The renegade Norwegian Nazi, Vidkun Quisling and his Nasjonal Samling Party put up a plan to Hitler's adviser Alfred Rosenberg to mount a coup. At a meeting in Berlin on 14 December 1939 between Hitler and Quisling, the latter stated: 'A British landing is planned in the vicinity of Stavanger and Kristiansand as a possible British base. The present Norwegian government and parliament and the whole foreign policy are controlled by the well-known [Carl] Hambro – a Jew – and President of the Norwegian Parliament.' Hitler promised financial and moral support. He then ordered 'Studie Nord', a preliminary plan for the Scandinavian assault. In February, the plan became 'Weseruebung' under Captain Krancke, the skipper of the cruiser *Scheer*. By the middle of the month the Anglo-French Supreme War Council pursued their Scandinavian venture. Both the German and the Anglo-French war plans would violate the neutrality of Scandinavia.

General Alfred Jodl, chief of OKW (Armed Forces High Command) recommended Lt General Nikolaus von Falkenhorst to command Weseruebung. He wanted a full Wehrmacht division to attack and secure Oslo, Stavanger, Bergen, Trondheim and Narvik harbour. On 1 March, Hitler issued his official directive, with all forces assembled for the 10th and embarked on the 13th. But when Marshal Mannerheim surrendered Finland to Russia, a consequence was that the Allied Operation Wilfred and the German OperationWeseruebung were, by coincidence delayed until 9 April.

Admiral Raeder commanded the kriegsmarine armada of warships and transport ships, and Marshal Herman Göring the Luftwaffe air fleet of 500 transports, 300 bombers and 200 Stuka dive-bombers. Both the Danish and the Norwegian governments received advice of the forthcoming onslaught from friendly embassies in Berlin. They chose to do nothing although the Norwegian High Command had assigned an army division to guard the six most important civilian and military centres.

Hitler's bold all-arms attack and conquest took only eight weeks in the period 7 April–10 June 1940. The Anglo-French army were defeated and King Haakon and his government sailed sadly from Narvik on the British cruiser *Devonshire*. The Royal Navy had performed superbly as one might expect and gave the Führer many anxious moments. The German casualties were 3,692 and the Allies 6,165 (British 4,400, Norwegian 1,335 and French and Poles 530). The Royal Navy lost the aircraft carrier *Glorious*, cruisers *Effingham* and *Curlew*, and nine destroyers and four submarines. The Germans came off worse. The cruisers *Blucher*, *Königsberg* and *Karlsruhe*, ten destroyers, six submarines and sixteen other naval craft were sunk. The pocket battleships – pride of the German

Navy – *Scharnhorst* and *Gneisenau*, and battleships *Luetzow*, *Hipper* and *Emden* were also damaged. The only comfort Winston Churchill could take was that Germany only had one heavy cruiser and two light cruisers fit for action. This was: 'of major importance potentially affecting the whole future of the war'. Weseruebung was however a superb success for German arms as the Luftwaffe played a significant part in the campaign. Hitler was pleased: 'The Norwegian campaign was not only bold but one of the sauciest undertakings in the history of modern warfare.' He had secured his vital supply line for Swedish iron ore and secured excellent Norwegian harbours for his warships, when repaired, and U-boats to try to dominate the North Sea and Atlantic.

For Norway the campaign was a disaster. Soon a crushed and demoralised country of over three million inhabitants would be ruled initially by the renegade Vidkun Quisling, and then by Hitler's Reichskommissar Joseph Terboven, who was a tough loyal Nazi street fighter who ruled Norway until his noisy death in May 1945. Terboven introduced the usual terror actions which were set up in every conquered country. The concentration camp in Grini outside Oslo (later renamed Ilebu) initially harboured hundreds of Norwegian school teachers, then resistance loyalists, Jews (700 were deported) and dissidents. Terboven was 'a short, thin, humourless man with an icily cold manner' according to Richard Petrow's *Bitter Years*.

The German top brass in Norway in March 1945 during a ceremony at the German cemetery near Oslo. In front General der Gebirgstruppen Frantz Böhme, C-in-C of the Wehrmacht in Norway (giving a Nazi salute) and Dr Herr Reichkommisar Josef Terboven. Second from left, Chief of the German Air forces in Norway General Ernst Roth, Böhme's Chief of Staff Major General Hölter, Chief of the German Navy in Norway, Admiral Krancke, and extreme right Lt General Baesler, Commandant of Oslo.

The Gestapo arrived at No. 19 Mollergaten and their HQ was on Victoria Terrasse, Oslo. The SS police general was Wilhelm Rediess who also came to a noisy, sticky end in May 1945, as did Jonas Lie, the Quisling police chief.

Total censorship soon followed and all political parties were forbidden except for the Nasjonal Samling Youth movement, which was modelled on the Hitler Youth movement in Germany. Quisling made membership compulsory for all Norwegian youngsters aged between ten and eighteen. By the end of 1940, membership stood at 26,000 and had doubled by the end of the war. The Norwegian SS Legion of 5,000 misguided young men was sent to fight on the Russian front, where 700 died.

There was one brave resistance movement in Norway, Milorg (military organisation) which soon developed links with the Special Operations Executive (SOE) in England. Often split by warring factions on the thorny problem of either very active resistance, which would bring heavy and brutal retaliation on the Norwegian public, or a steady 'go-slow' pinprick campaign of discreet sabotage. Often betrayed by informers or alert police or Gestapo, the first three years were not happy at all.

There are two interesting vignettes in the book *Hitler's Table Talk*:

On 2 August 1941: 'The exploitation of electricity generated by water power is in Germany only in its infancy ... if water flows it's enough to build a dam to obtain energy ... One day Norway will have to be the electrical centre of Northern Europe. In that way the Norwegians will at last find a European mission to fulfil.'

In May 1942 the Führer to Martin Bormann: 'In Terboven I am pleased to have found a man capable of assuming control of Norway, the most difficult commissarship of the Reich. As he told me this very day, if he relaxes his authority for a single instant, he feels as though he were standing on quicksands. He was compelled to arrest a number of Norwegian teachers who had seen fit to try to sabotage certain measures taken by the German High Command. He is now employing them in building fortifications.'

Early in 1943 a 28-year-old lawyer named Jens Christian Hauge took over command of Milorg. A meeting in Stockholm with representatives of the Norwegian High Command from London proved very helpful. Also an agreement was made with the civilian resistance at home. A policy was agreed to establish an underground army, ready to spring into action when Allied rescue was imminent – and a minimum of sabotage.

Location of German armed forces and Allied POWs in Norway, May 1945.

Winston Churchill had always been interested in plans for further operations in Norway. The first was Wilfrid, to mine the Norwegian ports in 1940, before the ill-fated expedition. Operation Jupiter in the spring of 1942 was a plan to land a British Expeditionary Force (BEF) in northern Norway to wipe out the Luftwaffe airports preying on the Allied shipping convoys. Considerable U-boat fleets did immense damage in the North Atlantic, operating from Namsos, Narvik, Trondheim, Bergen and Stavanger. Hitler was convinced in mid-1942 that the British would once again invade Norway and in 1943 there were eighteen divisions and even early in 1945 no fewer than seventeen, with a total armed manpower of over 300,000 including kriegsmarines and Luftwaffe. In Operation Fortitude in May/June 1944, the 'fake' attack or attacks by the Allies against Hitler's Atlantic Wall, planned radio leakage convinced the Führer that a subsidiary attack would come against Norway.

In the 'Bitter Years' of 1940 to early 1945, the RAF bombed many targets including stranded pocket battleships and the heavy water plant in Vemork, the Norsk hydro-electric installation. The SOE sent dozens of missions. In March 1941, a large-scale raid by Combined Operations and SOE was made against the Danish-owned Lofoten Islands off Narvik. For the Allies it was a total success. Four fish oil factories and six ships were blown up and 314 Lofoteners volunteered to join the Norwegian forces in the UK. The Germans reacted brutally as feared and seventy men were sent to Grini concentration camp; many homes on the islands were burnt as reprisal. Operation Archery was a repeat performance in late December 1941 against the coastal towns of Måløy and Vagsöy and again on the Lofotens (Operation Anklet). Both raids were completely successful and so unfortunately were the inevitable German reprisals. Milorg was not involved in the raids and thought that their fairly peaceful existence was threatened.

The German conquerors and Norsk Hydro technicians had repaired the extensive damage to their plant buildings done by the SOE saboteurs, and the first heavy water was being shipped to Germany in August 1943. The American General Leslie Groves, head of the Manhattan Project (development of an atomic bomb) was so worried at the German development that on 16 November 155 Flying Fortress bombers dropped over 700 bombs on the Vemork plant. It was not successful. The Norwegian civilian casualties upset the Norwegian government in exile but the Germans decided to move all the heavy water equipment to Germany including 14 tons of heavy water. Lt Knut Haukelid, a very brave SOE agent, succeeded in blowing up and destroying the ferry boat carrying the potentially deadly cargo from Norway to Germany. He thoroughly deserved the award of the Distinguished Service Order (DSO).

In late 1944, the success of the Russian army in capturing Finnmark northern province with Finnish support had caused SHAEF to make plans in case the Red Army sought to conquer Norway by capturing Narvik and continuing south. Fortunately Stalin was concentrating his main efforts on the Eastern Front, with modest help from Dutch, Danish and Norwegian renegade SS battalions. Colonel Arne Dahl, the CO of a Norwegian Mountain Company sailed on the British cruiser *Berwick* to Murmansk in late October 1944 and, in early 1945, took part with the Russians in a renewed push from Finnmark using Kirkenes as his base. His force had been built up to 3,000 and it reached Lyngenfjord. To everyone's surprise all Russian troops left northern Norway by May 1945.

In the spring of 1945, Lt General Franz Böhme had taken over the command of the German forces in Norway after General Falkenhorst had returned to Germany. Böhme's HQ was at Lillehammer. Admiral Kranke, based in Oslo, commanded the bulk of Hitler's navy. General Lothar Rendulic commanded the 20th Mountain (Gebirg) Army, which had been defending Finnmark, the most northerly province at the North Cape, against Russian and Finnish attacks. Rendulic's troops had been forced back and had obeyed Hitler's order of scorched-earth policy, laying waste Hammerfest and a dozen large villages. His army, reduced to 140,000 men, guarded a 450-mile coastal strip from Namsos to Lyngenfjord. The German 33rd Korps commanded by General Titel in Oslo had five defence sectors: General von Nissen (Trondheim with 70,000 men); General Vogel (Hamar); General Weckman (Stavanger with 42,000 men); General de Boer (Bergen with 30,000 men); and General Bezeler (Oslo with 82,000 men). The Luftwaffe 14th Division under the two divisional generals Brabener and Remolt had many significant airfields including Gardermoen, Skoganvarre and a dozen or more radar stations along the coast. General Stumpf commanded Luftflotte 5 at Stavanger. For attacks on the convoys to Russia the Luftwaffe often deployed over 200 bombers.

SHAEF had drawn up various plans for the British Army, Navy and Airforce units to take over *Festung* Norwegen. Various operation code words were Amber, Apostle and Doomsday, all part of the overall Operation Eclipse, the final control of the Third Reich.

It was anticipated that General Böhme, the German C-in-C, would obey Admiral Dönitz's order from Flensberg to surrender the huge forces of almost 400,000, despite containing die-hard Nazis such as Josef Terboven, Quisling, Jonas Lie, Henrik Rogstad and many fanatical members of Nasjonal Samling (56,000 strong in May 1945). On 1 May Böhme and Terboven were summoned to Dönitz in Flensberg, where he convinced or perhaps ordered them to surrender unconditionally. However, at 2215hrs on Monday 7 May, Böhme told his troops over Radio Oslo:

> The Foreign Minister Count von Krosigh has announced the unconditional surrender of all fighting forces. This capitulation hits us very hard, because we are unbeaten and in full possession of our strength in Norway, and no enemy has dared to attack us. In spite of all that in the interest of all that is German, we also have to obey the dictates of our enemy. Clench your teeth and keep discipline and order. Obey your superiors. Remain what you have been up to

now – decent German soldiers who love their people and homeland more than anything else in the world.

The *Daily Express* article of 8 May had the headline: 'No one dared attack us' after Böhme's speech.

The Milorg forces came out of the darkness into the open and began – as instructed under the leadership of Jens Christian Hauge – to occupy important plants and military installations. They were organised in twenty-two districts, each divided into two-four sub-districts: East Norway (strength 24,130); South and West (6,240); Central (1,100); and North (750). On VE Day another 10,000 joined, bringing their strength to 40,000. They were, of course, invaluable.

By 10 May 13,000 Norwegian troops trained in Scotland or Sweden had arrived to join the liberation forces. They comprised eight battalions of police reserves and eight state police companies. A further 3,000 Norwegian police returned from refuge in Sweden.

Scottish Command had been harbouring the Norwegians who had escaped by the Shetland Bus (fishing boats which carried cargoes of men or arms from one country to the other), or other means. As early as September 1941 Scottish Command harboured all the practical elements for an eventual rescue of Norway from the Nazi *Festung* Norwegen. Operation Rankin later became Operation Apostle. In August 1944 SHAEF decided that 'Force 134', a *theoretical* invasion force of a British infantry division, initially 52nd Lowland, a US Task Force (reinforced infantry regiment) plus the existing Norwegian brigade (in exile) would be required. Liaison with Milorg in Norway was of course vital. Eventually, as late as 5 May, SHAEF was able to allot 1st Airborne Division (the reinforced survivors of Market Garden) and the key commander, the highly experienced General Sir Andrew Thorne, as C-in-C of the liberation force. One airborne brigade was detached to reinforce the Danish liberation force and the airborne artillery units were co-opted into being their replacement. 38th Group RAF was ready to fly the division into Norway. Rear Admiral Ritchie would command the Royal Navy fleet and Air Vice Marshal Boret commanded the RAF air fleet. At the last moment a Special Air Service brigade (SAS) was also made available.

Since the Allied invasion force at full strength would not exceed 30,000, plus Milorg of course, it would be extremely difficult to control, disarm,

War games with the Scottish Command in the autumn of 1944. The Norwegian C-in-C, Crown Prince Olav, is seated centre with the British General Sir Andrew Thorne, set to become Allied Chief for the liberation of Norway, on his left. Behind Thorne (standing) is Brigadier General Percy Hansen of Scottish Command. To the left are seated Major General Johan Beichmann of the Norwegian Army Command and Major General A. T. Millar of Scottish Command. Major General Strugstad of Norway and Lt General Grasset from Eisenhower's staff at SHAEF to the extreme right.

intern, guard and administer an enemy twelve times as numerous, and heavily armed as well. SHAEF approved the only possible solution: that the Germans should be left as an army in administration and that Allied control should be effected through the German system of command. This would be highly unpopular with the Norwegian population who would expect to see every German safely behind barbed wire as quickly as possible. So control and disarmament parties called 'Heralds' were quickly organised and trained by the brigadier (Disarmament) R. Hilton. He led the SHAEF mission that reached Oslo on the afternoon of 8 May and the band of Heralds made their way to Lillehammer, 80 miles north of Oslo where General Böhme had his HQ.

However, several mildly impetuous sorties 'beat the whistle' and arrived earlier than they should have done. Alan Moorehead, that dashing journalist, had had a wonderful day when General Dewing's posse liberated Copenhagen on Monday 7 May. The following morning, he, Alexander Clifford, another journalist fluent in German, two

RAF air commodores in uniform, two stray Swedes in green, and two photographers flew in a RAF Dakota to find out what was happening in Norway. Flying over Anholt, Laso, Jutland and the Skaggerak: 'The most uplifting scenery passed below us. Mile after mile of inlets, and scattered waterways among the pines, a world of bright lakes, little beaches and gabled hamlets made of timber. Far ahead the eternal snow sat on the great backbone of the country. We swooped down towards Oslo. Considerable crowds were scuttling about the streets and open places like black ants. Two German Messerschmitt fighters, black and evil, shot by and vanished.' A German colonel festooned with medals followed by his officers made for 'our two commodores'. When Clifford explained who the British party were, the colonel replied: 'We had no warning of your coming. We were told to expect an Allied mission to discuss terms, flying in a Catalina and Sunderland painted white. In any event the German capitulation does not take place until midnight tonight.' The RAF commodore, the journalist, the photographers, plus three RAF officers who had broken out of their prison camp that morning, hurtled the five miles into Oslo in three battered brown Wehrmacht cars driven by Germans, to be greeted by ecstatic crowds: 'At first the people did not recognise the airforce blue uniforms but then seeing the khaki [which the three journalists wore] they became lost to all reason. They rushed headlong upon the cars ... This was different from Denmark. Different also from France and Belgium and Holland and the other places. There was a convulsive quality about their welcome, something almost religious, deriving from what could one say? ... The Norse temperament? ... Here in Oslo this afternoon we were seeing all gradations of the human power to feel happiness. The overall expression was clear enough: spontaneous, explosive, full of contagious colour and noise. The people poured themselves into the streets and once there they took fire from one another, from the flags, from one another's excitement ...'

Encrusted with flags, emblems, bunches of flowers, they reached the Grand Hotel and 'were pushed out on to a balcony overlooking the central square. The people flowed out beyond the square, up into the sidestreets, a great pink carpet of upturned faces and waving red flags.' Everyone made speeches. Everyone sang the National Anthem – several times, and *Hallelujah* for some reason. Champagne flowed. At the Bristol Hotel the group met the town governor, the chief of police, and the former British Legation solicitor and were told: 'Quisling has resigned

British paratroops of 1st Airborne Division land near Oslo, 11 May 1945. (*Imperial War Museum* CL 2629)

awaiting arrest by the Allies.' Then quickly back to the airport: 'Far down the fjord a Catalina and a Sunderland, both painted white, were heading past us towards Oslo. Norway was out of the war. Denmark was out of the war ... so many liberations. So much tragedy between them.'

On 6 May Wing Commander Len Ratcliffe with the Norwegian Captain Hysing-Dahl flew in a Hudson plane to Trondheim to take the surrender of the 50,000-strong garrison. On arrival they were greeted by 300 Resistance Milorg fighters.

In the *Daily Telegraph/Morning Post* of Tuesday 8 May, W. E. Mundy reported from Stockholm that Von Krosigk, the Reich Foreign Minister, had unconditionally surrendered all forces: 'An Allied naval force of 48 ships has been sighted at the entrance to Oslo Fjord said Swedish Radio tonight.'

General Sir Andrew Thorne, the Commander-in-Chief Allied Land Forces Norway, mentions the composition of the huge Royal Navy fleet that took part in Operation Eclipse:

Cruisers *Devonshire, Norfolk, Bellona, Diadem, Dido, Berwick, Birmingham, Conrad* (Polish)

Our Sky-Men of Arnhem Take Over in Norway

Press article: 'Our Sky-Men of Arnhem Take Over in Norway.'

1st Airborne arrive in Norway.

SHAEF mission in Norway: General Sir Andrew Thorne in the middle with Air Vice Marshal J. A. Boret to his right and Rear Admiral J. S. M. Ritchie to his left.

Destroyers *Campbell, Iroquois* (US Navy), *Savage, Onslow, Obdurate, Orwell, Offa, Opportune, Onslaught, Obedient, Arendal* (Norwegian), *Stord* (Norwegian), *Piorun* (Polish), *Zambesi, Zebra, Haida* (US Navy), *Huron* (US Navy), *Carysfort, Scourge, Hesperus, Havelock, Mackay, Viceroy, Zest, Zephyr*　　(25)
Minelayers *Apollo, Ariadne*
Anti-Aircraft *Broadway, Venomous*
Frigates *Conn, Stayner, Seymour, Flint Castle, Oakham Castle*
Minesweepers *Bangor, Blackpool* and many others
Motor Torpedoboats *54th* (Norwegian) *Flotilla*

On 13 and 18 May two destroyers were sent to Oslo, Kristiansand, Stavanger, Bergen, Trondheim and Tromso. Commander Bob Welland, commanding the destroyer *Haida* sailed into Trondheim to liberate the area occupied by 84,000 German troops. He sent his unarmed 'Liberty men' ashore to celebrate with the Norwegians but warned them to be on their best behaviour as his crew were outnumbered by 1,000 to one! Each pair of destroyers carried Herald parties to supervise disarmament and detachments for counter intelligence, civil affairs, and coffee, sugar etc as presents to the Norwegian population. In fact, the SHAEF

Preparations for a victory parade in Oslo, General Thorne is in the centre foreground.

mission had arranged that 43,000 tons of food be brought in between 8 May and 13 July and distributed to six distribution points: Oslo, Kristiansand, Stavanger, Bergen, Trondheim and Tromso. The supplies consisted of flour, biscuits, canned meat, canned milk, fats, sugar, coffee, salt, V-chocolate, peanut butter and wheat. And in the same period soap, clothing, footwear, battledress, overcoats, berets, steel helmets and Dodge trucks, destined for the 50,000 Milorg and police units.

From 9 May General Thorne's troops were flown or shipped in daily from 1st Airborne Division under Major General R. E. Urquhart, much under strength after the September 1944 Arnhem disaster. Commanders were Brigadier Bower, 1st Airlanding Brigade (Oslo north area); Brigadier Loder-Symonds, Artillery Brigade (Stavanger); Brigadier Calvert (SAS Brigade). Two new infantry brigades had been formed in the UK from units, mainly AA artillery, which were not needed in the final months of the war. These arrived in June with 303rd Brigade under Brigadier Smith (Trondheim) and 304th Brigade under Brigadier Saunders (Tromso). SHAEF also sent an American task force with 474th US Infantry Regiment under Colonel Edwin Walker.

A considerable RAF presence included 88th Group with twenty-five wing commanders under Air Vice Marshal J. A. Boret. The units were 8,301 (Air Disarmament), 1,318 and 1,336 (RAF Regiment) and 128, 129, 130 and 132 operational wings. RAF units were located at Oslo, Fornebu, Stavanger, Kristiansand, Bergen, Trondheim and Tromso.

The Norwegian brigade arriving from Scotland was soon deployed and measures were taken to expand them into a small national defence force with arrivals from Sweden.

SHAEF were highly organised. General Böhme's staff of 1,200 was reduced to 400 and moved from Lillehammer to a camp at Bogstad; 150 senior generals and staff officers were flown out of Norway to captivity in the UK. And 2,700 members of the sinister SIPO, SD, Gestapo and Abwehr were identified and put under arrest for possible war crimes tribunals to investigate.

One very difficult problem was that 87,000 Allied prisoners of war in over 400 stalags were located all over Norway, even on isolated islands. The majority were Russian, and a mission under General Ratov arrived on 31 May; 72,000 were identified many of them very ill, even starving, and by early June 40,000 had been repatriated by rail to Sweden, thence by sea to Murmansk. There were 15,000 Poles, 14,600 Czechs and 6,500 French. The whole situation was complicated because many had served with the Wehrmacht; 9,000 were displaced persons, who were deemed unacceptable to return home – for instance Sudeten Germans. Altogether there were 37,000 non-German/Austrian personnel belonging to forty nationalities.

On 12 May three British cruisers arrived in Oslo carrying more troops and Norway's Crown Prince Olav who held the title of Chief of the Norwegian Forces. With him were three ministers from the Norwegian government in exile. Their welcome was less warm. Midshipman C. B. Koester served on HMS *Devonshire*. In Operation Kingdom the Crown Prince sailed on HMS *Apollo,* which flew the Norwegian Royal Standard:

We overtook the minesweeping flotilla, reduced speed to remain astern of *Apollo*. We had air cover all the way consisting of Sunderlands, Catalinas, Mosquitoes and Beaufighters. On Sunday 13 May we passed through the Skaggerak into Oslofjord, met by people in small boats, decorated with fir boughs. There were motor boats, canoes, kayaks, fishing boats, row-boats, sail boats, every craft that could float packed full of people waving, cheering, singing, shouting, old men waved their hats, women, handkerchiefs, partisans stood up and presented arms and boy scouts saluted. Our baker had made extra bread that morning and our sailors threw the white loaves down to the people in the boats. The jetties and landing places along the fjord were lined with people. At every flagstaff a Norwegian flag was flying. We were saluted from shore so often that we stationed two signalmen aft to dip our ensign in return ... As we approached Oslo, ferries towing up to 20 boats each joined the throng of small craft. Many of their passengers were shouting 'Kronsprins! Kronsprins!' We pointed aft to *Apollo* and *Ariadne* overtook us to lead the Task Force into harbour. We paraded a Royal Marine Guard and band on the quarter deck to salute as they passed. We heard for the first time that beautiful Norwegian anthem 'Ja Vi Elsker Dette Landet', which we were to know by heart and in Norwegian before we left.

[The crew went ashore]. It was a vast holiday crowd. Women and girls in national costume or summer frocks, blond, freckled boys in shorts, students of all ages wearing their black, tasselled student caps, and sailors from the British, Canadian, American and Norwegian ships of the Task Force all mingled in one happy crowd of holidaymakers. Yet there was a grimmer side as well. The British airborne troops, Norwegian police, some Swedish-trained Norwegian soldiers and partisans all armed with rifles or tommy-guns slung over their shoulders, and the Germans still to be seen on the streets wore pistols in their belts. They were largely ignored by liberators and liberated alike.

Young midshipman Koester and HMS *Devonshire* sailed back to Rosyth, and on 5 June was part of the RN task force to bring King Hakon VII safely back to his kingdom. *Norfolk* was the flagship for the king and *Devonshire* was followed by *Onslow, Obdurate, Orwell* and *Stord*. They passed a flotilla of six U-boats being escorted from Wilhelmshaven to a UK port, chaperoned by two RN frigates. Early on 7 June, the task force reached Oslo and the Crown Prince came out to meet his father the King, and similar rejoicing occurred. On 12 June the task force left for Copenhagen.

Justice and retribution soon followed. Reichskommissar Joseph Terboven and General Riedess of the SS blew themselves up in a bunker. The head of the Norwegian SS, Jonas Lie, shot himself dead. Other Quisling officials took their own lives. By 1 July, 14,000 suspects of the NS Party were in prison. By the end of 1945, 90,000 had been arrested, investigated or interrogated. More than 46,000 were convicted of wartime offences, 18,000 received prison sentences and 28,000 fined or deprived of their civil rights. Thirty Norwegian collaborators and fifteen Germans were sentenced to death for wartime treason or atrocities. Vidkun Quisling's trial started on 20 August in Oslo's main Freemasons' Lodge. Found guilty, he appealed and on 13 October the court upheld the original verdict. In the courtyard of Akershuis castle on 24 October, Norway's most infamous man was shot to pieces by a ten-man military execution squad.

By the end of May, 272,000 Germans were corralled in their resettlement areas, with a further 32,900 due to arrive. Eventually, by the summer of 1946, the last batch of German prisoners of war were expatriated via Sweden to their home country. The vast majority – undefeated in battle – had behaved well. They had obeyed Admiral Dönitz's orders and those of General Böhme. They had clenched their teeth and kept discipline and order.

It was the end of Hitler's *Festung* Norwegen.

CHAPTER 28

Liberation of POW Camps

International rules governing the humane treatment of prisoners had been agreed at The Hague conventions of 1899 and 1907. Only Russia, out of the six major combatants in the European battlegrounds, was the exception. Civilised standards were set and prisoners of war (POW) were to be decently housed, properly fed and allowed privileges of religious worship, medical treatment and correspondence with their families. They were not to be beaten, interrogated, tortured or severely punished even for attempts to escape. The rank and file could be put to work and there were often many *arbeit* outstations located around POW camps in Germany. Officers were to be held in separate quarters. All were to be accessible for inspection by the International Red Cross.

130,000 Allied POWs were held in captivity, including 60,000 British in German oflags and stalags: veterans from Dunkirk, North Africa, and bailed out bomber crews. The 4.5 million German prisoners in Russia and 5.2 million Russian prisoners in Germany fared very badly indeed and comparatively few survived. Under Stalin's Order No. 270, which treated their own prisoners as deserters, those who were returned and repatriated were charged with treason. The officers were shot and the rank and file sent to gulags with little chance of survival.

There were officially twenty-three POW camps in Germany, known as stalags; five of them were Luft camps for captured RAF and USAAF personnel. Some of them like IV-C Colditz Castle were oflags, for officers only. In theory the Germans kept to the Geneva Conventions allowing Red Cross parcels and occasionally visits by the Swiss Red Cross inspectors. Under the Third Geneva Convention the use of POWs to produce explosives and gunpowder was prohibited.

The BLA liberated a number of these camps but the biggest prize was on 16 April when the armoured cars of the indomitable 11th Hussars, the Cherry Pickers, nosed their way into Fallingbostel camp, situated 20 miles north of Hannover. Major P. H. Huth's B Squadron found on their arrival at the great prison camp south-west of Fallingbostel, an extraordinary sight. RSM Lord, a Grenadier guardsman, had taken over. Sentries from the 1st Airborne Division captured at Arnhem, immaculate in scrubbed belts and gaiters and well-creased battledress were guarding the main gate. RSM Lord was in 'his' office giving orders to his Orderly Warrant officers. Soon Lt Colonel H. Moore, chief admin officer of 7th Armoured Division, had provided as requested rations, cigarettes and even newspapers. Chester Wilmot, the intrepid journalist, who always seemed to be in the right place at the right time reported:

16 April 1845. Twenty thousand Allied prisoners of war gained their freedom today when British tanks liberated two large prison camps, Stalag 11b and Stalag 357. More than 10,000 of them were British or American, and the British troops included 600 men of the 1st Airborne Division captured at Arnhem last year, and many more who were taken at Dunkirk.

This morning, when tanks of the 8th Hussars reached these two camps near Fallingbostel, 35 miles southeast of Bremen, they found that our troops (the prisoners) had already taken charge of the camp and interned their German guards. An airborne sergeant major, an ex-Guardsman, was in command, and the British guards were as spick and span as any parade ground troops. Their boots were polished, their trousers pressed, and their belts and gaiters blancoed. The British troops had taken over the German offices, and their liberators found clerks busy typing out nominal rolls on German typewriters.

The prisoners had been running the camp since last Friday, when three-quarters of the German guards departed, leaving a skeleton force of 60 to carry on. For the past four days German and British troops have been on guard together, but this morning the Germans were disarmed.

This afternoon, at Stalag 11b, I saw some of the 20,000 and learned from padres, doctors and NCOs how they'd been treated. They told me that in this camp there were 4,256 British troops and 2,428 Americans. Of these 6,700, more than 1,000 are in hospital suffering from wounds, injuries, or starvation, and I saw several thousand more suffering from starvation who should have been in hospital in any civilised country.

Above: British section of the prison camp at Fallingbostel, Stalag XIB/357.

Right: Over 12,000 released prisoners of war at Fallingbostel.

16 April 1945, British POWs, veterans of Dunkirk and Normandy and others greet their liberators at Stalag 11B, Fallingbostel. (*Imperial War Museum*)

Here in this camp I saw clear evidence of the German neglect and wanton disregard for the lives and health of their prisoners. Of the 4,250 British prisoners, some 2,500 have come into the camp in the last three weeks. The Germans have marched them from Poland, lest they should be set free by the Russian advance. Ten days ago in this camp there were 3,000 other British and American prisoners who had made this terrible trek from Poland; but when the 2nd Army crossed the Weser, the Germans put these 3,000 on the road again, and sent them marching back towards the Russians. They were determined to stop the 3,000 being liberated, because they were airmen and paratroops.

How far they'll be able to march I don't know, for I saw today the pitiable condition of those who have already made the nightmare journey from Poland. They certainly were exhausted at the end of that journey. I saw them in hospital – drawn, haggard, starved – starved beyond description – limbs like matchsticks, bodies shrunken till their bones stood out like knuckles.

The doctor in charge of them said to me, 'Nothing has kept these men alive except Red Cross parcels and their own spirit'. But on that journey from Poland they had very few Red cross parcels, and some got none.

One padre who was captured at Calais in 1940 told me that this party had marched 400 miles in 52 days, and their rations, in the depth of winter, had been nothing but a bowl of watery soup and a couple of slices of army bread per day. He had marched with 800 British and 6,500 American airmen, many thousands of whom had been sent marching back again almost as soon as they'd finished their journey.

I wish those people who think the Germans should be treated lightly had seen what I saw today. But I also saw something that was inspiring and encouraging. All this German oppression and brutality and starvation hadn't been able to kill the spirit and self-respect of these men of Arnhem, men of Crete, of Dunkirk and Calais, men of Bomber Command and the 8th Air Force. They'd managed to rise above their sordid environment and today those of them who were on guard or on duty were as soldierly in their bearing as they were the day they were captured. They were proud that they had their own camp running when our tanks got there. They felt they had almost liberated themselves. And this afternoon they had the supreme pleasure of watching their German guards being marched away to our prison cage; and as they watched, they cheered.

Robert Barr, another journalist, covered part of the American army advances and wrote:

Other Arnhem prisoners were liberated by the US 9th Army and celebrated their freedom by strolling to a nearby village, where they quickly established a typically British atmosphere.

17 April 1945. How can I explain what that village looked like – it had become an English village – there were hundreds of British paratroopers lining its pavements – happy, smiling, giving the 'thumbs-up' sign, some sunning themselves by the village duckpond, some playing around on bicycles. Two of them were trying to get a stubborn motor-cycle to work. Most of them were parading the pavements in twos and threes – they were parading the village streets, just as you saw them walk out of an evening in England; clean-shaven, smart, walking in step, and this village had suddenly become more than just an English village, its pavements held a living cavalcade of our story in this war, because amongst the Red Devils – outnumbered by them but not outshone – were other British soldiers, and New Zealanders and Australians whose stories briefly told were the story of our part in the war. It was an American officer, I think, who summed up that spirit; he said 'Prisoners? Gee, I thought they were troops going into the line.' That was no exaggeration – they looked just like it – if you'd seen them today you would have been proud. But what I don't understand is where some of them got the blanco.

Later in the campaign, near the river Elbe, 11th Armoured Division liberated 1,600 RAF officers on 2 May at Westerau. The Guards Armoured had to negotiate with Lt General Roth, GOC the 15th Panzergrenadier Division, for the relief of Westertimke on 26 April, which contained over 8,000 POW, half of them British Merchant Navy (and forty-two Guardsmen).

Close by was the even larger camp of Sandbostel on the way to Bremenvorde, with 22,000 prisoners, of whom half were civilians, mainly French and Russian but there were also 300 British POW. Lt Colonel T. W. Davidson, the Director of Medical Services of 30th Corps, with Brigadier Gwatkin and Lt Colonel Moore of Guards Armoured toured the camp on 28 April.

Lt General Horrocks wrote in his memoirs:

> Sandbostel, one of those horror camps. When General Adair and I entered we came across the most ghastly picture I have ever seen. The floor of the first hut we visited was covered with emaciated figures, clad in the most horrible striped pyjamas. Many were too weak to walk, but on seeing us they heaved themselves up and gave a pathetic cheer. Most of them had some form of chronic dysentery and the stench was so bad that I disgraced myself by being sick in the corner. I was so angry that I ordered the Burgomeister of every one of the surrounding towns and villages to supply a quota of German women to clean up the camp and look after these unfortunate prisoners who were dying daily at an alarming rate. When the women arrived we expected some indication of horror or remorse when they saw what their fellow countrymen had been doing. Not a bit of it. I never saw a tear or heard one expression of pity from any of them.

Brigadier Prior-Palmer, commanding 8th (Red Fox's Mask) Armoured Brigade, also visited the Sandbostel camp and sent 168th Light Field Ambulance and six lorries of food supplies from each of his seven regiments to help feed the prisoners.

Sandbostel X-B and Westertimke were official prisoner of war camps but with the intense pressure on the German systems squeezed into a sandwich with the Russians in the east and the Allies in the west, tens of thousands of refugees were crammed into camps which simply could not cope with the extra numbers.

The rescue of Colditz Oflag was a far happier event. At Colditz, more than a thousand British, French, Polish, Czech, American and other

On 27 April 1945, Westertimke POW Camp was freed by the British. Russian ex-POWs were loaded on to lorries in Stittensen, to go to a camp run by the British Army.

About 80 per cent of five million Soviet POWs died in German captivity. Most of the survivors were killed by the NKVD on return to the USSR.

More than 7,000 former Allied prisoners of war, liberated by the Americans at VII-A
Moosburg on 29 April 1945.

Allied prisoners of war, all of them officers who had earlier escaped from
other camps and been caught before reaching freedom, were confined
within a formidable fortress. An eyewitness reported the scene:

> On 15 April a single GI arrived. An Allied officer standing near the gate
> advanced with outstretched hand and shook the hand extended by the
> American, who grinned at him and said cheerfully: 'Any doughboys here?' The
> spell was broken.
>
> Suddenly a mob was rushing towards him, shouting and cheering and struggling
> madly to reach him, to make sure that he was alive, to touch him, and from the
> touch to know again the miracle of living, to be men in their own right, freed
> from bondage, outcast no more, liberated by their Allies and their friends, their
> faith in God's mercy justified, their patience rewarded, the nobility of mankind
> vindicated, justice at last accomplished and tyranny once more overcome.
>
> Men wept, unable to restrain themselves. It was not enough that the body
> was free once more to roam the earth. Feelings, pent up and dammed behind

Westerau – 2 May 1945. Liberated RAF officers and German POWs.

the mounting walls of five successive torturing, introverted years, had to erupt.

They welled up like gushing springs, they overflowed, they burst their banks, they tumbled unhindered and uncontrolled. Frenchmen with tears streaming down their faces kissed each other on both cheeks – the salute of brothers. They kissed the GI, they kissed everyone within range. The storm of emotion burst. The merciful rain descended. The grey clouds drifted from the horizon of the mind, borne on fresh salt and moisture-laden breezes across the unchained oceans of memory from the far-off shores of love. Home and country beckoned; loved ones were waiting. Wives and sweethearts, mothers, fathers, and children never seen, were calling across the gulf of the absent years.

POW Camps in Germany

Stalags	
IX-C	Bad Sulza
XI-B	Fallingbostel
79	Brunswick
VII-B	Eichstatt
XIII-D	Nurnberg
VII-A	Moosburg
XIII-C	Hammelburg
IV-C	Colditz Castle
XI-A	Alten Grabow
III-A	Luckenwalde
IV-B	Mühlberg
VIII-A	Gorlitz
XX-B	Marienburg
XX-A	Thorn
344	Lamsdorf
VIII-B	Teschen
Luft-1	Barth
Luft-4	Gross Tychow
Luft-7	Bankau
Luft-6	Heydekrug
X-B	Sandbostel
Marlag und Milag Nord	Westertimke
Luft-3	Sagan

CHAPTER 29

Freedom for Hitler's Slaves

Primo Levi wrote in his book *The Re-Awakening*, when on 27 January 1945 he was liberated from Auschwitz extermination camp: 'There were men, but a good number of women and children. There were Catholics, Jews, Orthodox Christians and Muslims, people with white or yellow skins and Negroes in American uniforms … In Germany they had found bread, barbed wire, hard work, German order, servitude and shame. They were often herded into open cattle trucks, frightened, their closed bitter faces, their evasive eyes displayed a disturbing animal-like humiliation and resignation.' They became the displaced persons when they were freed.

Fritz Saukel, the Third Reich Director of Labour (1942–45) ordered five million people from occupied Europe to work as slaves in Germany. In March 1942 Hitler decreed the mobilisation of labour, both German and foreign to meet the demands of Albert Speer's armaments and munitions production. In 1942, the Third Reich dominated 400 million subjects so this seemed to be a reasonable task. Saukel (1894–1946) was Hitler's Plenipotentiary for Employment and he extracted 5.8 million workers from the occupied territories.

Forced labour in the Reich was directed mainly at farming, mining, metallurgy, chemicals, building and transport. This is where Sauckel brought his slaves from:

USSR	2,406,895	Czechoslovakia	177,679
Poland	1,440,254	Belgium	177,451
France	954,966	Holland	174,358
Italy	486,326	TOTAL	5,817,929

German labour camp workers.

Of these 75 per cent were civilians, 4,375,882, and the rest were various prisoners of war.

On 20 April 1942 Sauckel stated his policy:

> The aim of the new gigantic labour mobilisation is to use all the rich and tremendous sources conquered and secured for us by our fighting armed forces under the leadership of Adolf Hitler for the armament of the armed forces and also for the nutrition of the Homeland. The raw materials as well as the fertility of the conquered territories and their human labour power are to be used completely and conscientiously to the profit of Germany and her Allies ... All prisoners of war from the territories of the West, as well as the East, actually in Germany must be completely incorporated into the German armament and nutrition industries ... consequently it is an immediate necessity to use the human reserves of the conquered Soviet territory to the fullest extent. Should we not succeed in obtaining the necessary amount of labour on a voluntary basis we must immediately institute conscription or forced labour. The complete employment of all prisoners of war as well as the use of a gigantic number of new foreign civilian workers, men and women, has become an indisputable necessity for the solution of the mobilisation of the labour programme in the war.

At the Nuremberg trial Sauckel admitted: 'Out of the five million workers who arrived in Germany not even 200,000 came voluntarily.' His instructions in April 1942 were: 'All men must be fed, sheltered and treated in such a way as *to exploit them to the highest possible extent*, at the lowest conceivable degree of expenditure.' Many prisoners of war, particularly Soviets, were compelled to work in munition factories and even be deployed as Ack-Ack gunners.

On 4 January 1944 Hitler directed Sauckel to obtain four million *new* workers from the occupied territories. It was called the Slave Labour Programme. Albert Speer, as chief of the Organisation Todt, desperately needed these slaves not only to build the Atlantic Wall, but also military highways and to man the vast range of industries under his control.

Alan Moorehead noted:

> As soon as we crossed the Rhine *we were confronted by a problem almost as big as Germany herself* [author's emphasis], the millions upon millions of semi-slave workers. With every mile we went into Germany they grew more numerous on the roads: little groups of Frenchmen, then Dutch, then Belgians and Czechs and Poles and Italians and finally, in overwhelming majority, the Russians in their bright green uniforms with 'S.U.' – Soviet Union – painted in white on their backs. Half the nationalities of Europe were on the march, all moving blindly westward along the roads feeling their way by some common instinct towards the British and American lines in the hope of finding food and shelter and transportation there. These millions lived a vagabond life. At every bend of the road you came on another group, bundles on their shoulders, trudging along the ditches in order to avoid the passing military traffic. The Germans were terrified of the Russians.

About a million captured Soviet soldiers out of the 5.7 million in total who surrendered joined some form of service with Germany. The Russian general Andrei Andreivich Vlasson, who was captured in July 1942, was persuaded to accept command of the Russian Liberation Army but the enrolled men were either working in the Todt organisation (Fritz Todt was Speer's predecessor) or in separate auxiliary units until March 1945. Because Hitler was scraping the barrel for 'bodies', Vlasson found himself in command of two renegade Russian divisions on the Eastern Front. Eventually captured by the Russians, Vlasson was hanged and the

German refugees walk westward along one of Hitler's pre-war motor roads.

Ostflucht. Not waiting to be expelled, a flood of Germans from East Prussia and other eastern provinces took to the road.

survivors of the Russian Liberation Army almost certainly never got as far as the gulags. As a result, *all* the Russian prisoners of war in Germany were decreed by Stalin to be 'traitors'. So of the original 5,754,000 Russians captured, 3,700,000 died in captivity – many simply were starved to death and in May 1945 there were more than two million Russian soldiers and slaves at large.

After the German surrender Russian commissars were allowed – they were still Allies – to supervise repatriation of their unfortunate compatriots.

By 1953, 5,457,856 Soviet citizens had been returned to the Soviet Union. Russian historians estimate that at least 20 per cent were executed or given a life sentence – 25 years imprisonment in the gulags. Some three million served shorter sentences.

An estimated nine and a half million people were on the roads of Europe in the week following VE Day, most – not all – longing to get home. Among those leaving the rubble-strewn cities of Germany in the immediate aftermath of the war were more than eight and a half million people: 2,400,000 Russians, 2,100,000 Frenchmen, 1,500,000 Poles, 600,000 Lithuanians, 570,000 Belgians, 560,000 Latvians, 420,000 Italians and 400,000 Dutchmen. Tens of thousands of Danes, Yugoslavs, Greeks, Estonians, Bulgarians, Roumanians, Hungarians and Czechs were also on their way home. Fleeing in a counter-direction were nine and a half million German civilians. Half a million of these were from Roumania, Hungary and Yugoslavia: Germans who had been living outside Germany for several centuries. Two million were German citizens expelled from East Prussia.

Nothing on earth would have kept the industrial slave workers in the factories, some underground, and the mines, once their German masters were gone. First the rescued slaves rushed out into the streets to loot. Some tried to take physical revenge on German families. Part of the loot was of course, drink. Moorehead reported that liquor at the moment of liberation caused as much uproar as anything else. The Poles and the Russians especially, in their first wild moments of freedom, would run roaring on to the hated factory machines and smash them with crowbars.

Most of the war's finest journalists were travelling with the Allied armies into the Third Reich and their reports to the BBC make sad but fascinating reading.

Even some Germans welcome the British as liberators.

Matthew Halton, Canadian Broadcasting Company, sent this report to the BBC on 12 April:

Your hate rises against everything German when you see Dutchmen who have been tortured to death. And it rises again when you see the streams of freed slaves thronging down the roads. This astonishing sight is one we see every day. In the areas we've already overrun in Germany we've liberated over two million of these slaves, chiefly Russian and Polish but also French, Czechs, Yugoslavs and others. We've seen them in bands of several hundred at a time. They're not always emaciated, starving, ragged. Sometimes you wouldn't know they were slaves, except for their language, and the fact that they're laughing and chattering away, and waving and singing. But I've seen others, hungry, and even barefooted, mad with hate of the Germans, looting shops for food and clothes. What an extraordinary thing this is, in the 20th century! You see these things and wonder if you're not back in the pages of an historical novel, back in the Thirty Years War. Freed bondsmen – ten or twelve million men and women of Europe have been uprooted by the Germans and enslaved. It makes you hate all right when you question some of them, and women tell you how they were brought from Russia, put up on auction blocks, pawed and mauled by lecherous fat Germans, and sold into slavery. I've seen women on

Retribution on a German foreman by forced foreign workers.

their knees, tears running down their cheeks as British tanks rolled past and they knew they were free. What a story that told, millions of Ruths sick for home, who stood in tears amid the alien corn, and even now many of them will go back and find their homes destroyed and their families dead or gone. Is there any measure for the rivers and tides of sorrows and tears that the Nazis have set flowing in Europe?

Halton's countrymen, the gallant Canadian Army, had been struggling in the *verdronken* land of the Scheldt delta in the autumn of 1944. Now he was over the Rhine. And a few days later Wynford Vaughan-Thomas wrote this report for the BBC:

22 April 1945. The basis of German agricultural prosperity was slave labour, and as soon as the Allied armies swept by these prosperous farms, the slaves, very naturally, stopped working. We've opened the floodgates of a dam, and every single person who can get away is off. The roads of Germany today are one of the unforgettable sights of the war. You can walk a few hundred yards from the transmitter from which I'm speaking and you'll see for yourself the wealth of the German farmlands flowing away to the west. There go the farm tractors, towing the German farmers' carts, filled with jubilant Poles or Yugoslavs; there go his farm horses ridden by Russian prisoners of war, there

go his bicycles and his lorries, and his eggs and his chickens and his pigs. This great flood goes steadily on day after day, and now in the semi-deserted fields the German farmer has got to work himself; you see him with his wife and his daughter and the young children, for his sons have long since left for the army, maybe they'll never be coming back to this farm. You see him working to salvage something out of the wreck. It's impossible he can salvage enough to feed the townsfolk of Germany, for the labour with which he cultivated these rich fields is gone or is living on his farm as self-invited guests. Yes, the Germans are in for a grim winter. But then, they might have thought of that before they based their agriculture on slave labour.

George Blake, who was 'embedded' with 52nd Lowland Division, encountered dreadful conditions as the battle for Bremen ended:

The civilian population of Bremen was beyond resisting. It was, in the physical sense, bomb happy after the terrible pounding it had received from the Lancasters a few nights before; it was psychologically in the desperate state of crazy abandonment that so often comes on people who cannot bring themselves to stare the bleak face of defeat in the face. They had gone wild, looting, drinking, fighting among each other for what are called consumer goods; their frenzy was complicated by the presence among them of large numbers of utterly demoralised displaced persons from internment camps in the countryside round about. For two or three days towards the end of April 1945 Bremen was probably among the most debauched places on the face of God's earth: all sanctions broken down among those Germans who rioted in their shocking inability to accept the consequences of their own political stupidity.

The control of this bear-garden was a heavy responsibility on the cool and terribly tired Scottish soldiers who had taken the city after such a long and gruelling battle. It was immensely complicated by the litter of smashed and fallen masonry left by the bombers. A central area of the city, some four miles by one, had ceased to exist. All who have seen something of Germany since the war ended have their own pet notions as to degrees of degradation among the smashed German towns – Essen, Munster, Halle, Cologne, Berlin or what you will. The present writer thought that the ruins of Hamburg, seen from a draughty jeep through the drizzle of a darkling January evening, was as much as he ever wished to see of destruction; but Bremen on a bright February afternoon seemed even more calamitous, its undoubtedly handsome, metropolitan air all sullied and humbled by the bombs.

Mass graves of slave workers were found in the woods near Soltau. Desert Rats made local civilians disinter the bodies and give them proper burial.

Policing and patrolling the great, smashed seaport and its bewildered population was continuous work for at least a brigade. Some units left the area to mount guard over groups of DP camps.

What the DPs urgently needed were registration cards (new identity cards), soup kitchens, medical aid, and DDT dustings to combat the filth and squalor of their initial interim abodes. They wanted some kind of security, law and order, without threats of violence and death.

Every German woman feared rape as the Red Army plundered, pillaged, looted and raped its way through the German regions they overran in late April 1945. As the British armour moved up to and over the river Elbe the vast, moving, sad human frieze kept pouring down the roads increasing in numbers with every new town or village that was captured and liberated. Moorehead again: 'One began to get a new picture of Nazi Germany. What we were seeing was something from the Dark Ages, the breaking up of a medieval slave state. All the Nazi flags and parades and conquests in the end were based on this one thing – slave labour. There was something monstrous about the wired-in workers' compounds and sentry boxes round each factory, something that was in defiance of all accepted ideas of civilisation … we had only begun to glimpse the extent and depth of the Nazi terror system, but already one sensed the utter disregard of the value of human life in Germany. And now the Reich was collapsing at its roots because the slaves were melting away.'

By mid-May ten million German soldiers had become prisoners in the hands of the Allies. The Russian NKVD reported they were holding 1,464,803 Germans including 93 generals in camps in their conquered sector of East Germany. As a result nearly all the German men were either prisoners, wounded or dead.

The military achievement of conquest was backed by an equally remarkable ordering of the chaos that followed the Reich's implosion. Hard on the heels of troops fighting through cities, Allied military government officers moved in to take control. Their task was to set up administrations to restore law and order, to secure water, food and fuel supplies, and shelter. Riots in cities such as Hannover and Osnabruck – total anarchy – needed force to restore some order.

Public order was the essential prerequisite of any revival of a proper social existence. In many towns, order was admirably enforced, and tensions defused by imperturbable public safety officers – mostly bobbies drawn from British police forces.

The Allied military administrators directed Germans to dig, build and clear wreckage, insisting that only by work could they feed and shelter themselves. They had expected some hostility, but often found people willing to co-operate; for most civilians the arrival of a military government signalled the welcome ending of the war. The new military governments sought out local leaders, preferably of anti-Nazi sentiment, and installed them as mayors to help get basic services going. The military authorities provided tent camps for thousands of displaced persons and, wherever possible, made Germans feed them.

Overall, Germany was in a worse mess than planners had envisaged, millions were homeless. The breakdown of transport, local government and communications was almost total.

Food was an urgent problem. The Allies were determined that the Germans, who had eaten well by ransacking conquered territories, should not have more than newly liberated peoples.

However, a balance had to be struck. Famine would bring catastrophic disorder and disease. The Allies drew calorie scales and rations: not so high as to enrage the liberated countries, not so low as to make the black

German refugees, trudging westward, pass a Soviet poster, July 1945.

market worse. Ordinary people were rationed to 1,550 calories a day, men doing heavy work to 2,800 calories. The Allies set a daily ration of 12.7 oz of bread and 10.5 oz of potatoes. In reality many people had much less.

Even before the surrender of German forces it was seen that there would be disaster if the harvest were not gathered. The military government launched Operation Barleycorn and half a million German servicemen were ordered to bring in the corn.

The British had a particular difficulty in the industrial powerhouse of the Ruhr, which was under their control. Ruhr miners needed more food if they were to hew coal to power the factories. Feeding them was a matter of economic necessity, so the Allies sent them food.

In November 1943 a conference took place in Atlantic City, New Jersey USA for the founding of the United Nations Relief and Rehabilitation Administration (UNRRA). This was dedicated to the welfare of refugees and the distressed population of liberated countries in the warfare of the future. In the wake of Operation Torch in North Africa the first UNRRA help was deployed. In the next four years, 1943–47, it was to dispense US$44 billion of radical, practical help to refugees in 17 countries. UNRRA was mainly funded by the USA, Canada and Britain and was a gigantic global relief effort.

In December 1944 President Roosevelt's key advisers, Harry Hopkins and Dean Acheson, realised: 'The war can be lost in the liberated countries. It cannot be won with success in the liberated countries. Liberated people are the most combustible material in the world. They are fighting people. They are violent and restless. They have suffered unbearably ... to win the war requires that we win the battle of the liberated countries.'

More than 100 UNRRA teams were soon in the field after VE Day, assisted by 697 Allied Liaison Officers. Field Marshal Montgomery had organised very thoroughly the division of the British Army of the Rhine into 'fiefs' with his soldiers responsible for law and order until the German police had been disbanded from their duties fighting alongside the Wehrmacht. The UNRRA teams would always find the military very helpful. Accommodation had to be found for the multitude of displaced persons in former military barracks, summer camps for children, hotels, castles, hospitals, private homes, even partly demolished houses. A Central Tracking Bureau was started in conjunction with the International Red Cross to identify individuals and trace their families. Soon one million names were on the register. Soon ethnic and religious groups tended to concentrate in certain camps. German universities were compelled to take a quota of DP students.

By the end of 1945 AMGOT, UNRRA, the Red Cross and other aid agencies had repatriated six million DPs, but it was evident that a hard core of well over one million could not, or would not be repatriated. Few DPs *wanted* to return to Stalin and the Communist dictator of Yugoslavia, Tito. Most of the free world grieved for these dispossessed souls. By 1950 Israel had taken 650,000 Jews; USA eventually accepted 600,000; Australia 182,159; Canada 157,000; Belgium 20,000, mainly coal miners; France 30,000. The Latin American countries accepted 80,000. The UK instituted Operation Westward Ho and accepted 86,000 DPs plus 115,000 Polish Army veterans and 12,000 of the Ukranian Halychyna Division.

CHAPTER 30

Retribution:
War Crimes Tribunals

A United Nations War Crimes Commission was set up in London in 1943. In November the British, Americans and Russians declared that Germans responsible for abominable deeds would be sent back to where they had committed them to be tried by the liberated countries. The massacres of many American soldiers at Malmédy during the German Ardennes offensive in December 1944 convinced America of the need to punish the guilty. It was agreed by May 1945 that an international tribunal should sit with American, British, French and Russian judges and prosecutors. In August it was decided that Nuremberg should be the location for the trials because it had been the site of the great Nazi party rallies. There would be four possible counts: crimes against peace (planning and making war); war crimes (responsibility for crimes during warfare); crimes against humanity (to cover racial persecution); and conspiracy (to commit crimes alleged in other courts). The teams of prosecutors would come from the Allies, and the defence lawyers would be German. The tribunal also put Third Reich organisations on trial. If an organisation was declared criminal, any member of it could be tried on that count alone. The SS and the Waffen SS, the Gestapo, the SD (Sicherheitsdienst, the Nazi Party's own intelligence and security body) were all declared guilty organisations, as were the senior ranks of the Nazi Party from the rank of kreisleiter upwards.

The whole world followed the great trial, which sat from November 1945 to September 1946. Twenty-one defendants were tried. The sentences were: death for Frank, Frick, Göring, Jodl, Keitel, Kaltenbrunner, Ribbentropp, Rosenberg, Saukel, Seyss-Inquart and Streicher; life imprisonment for Funk, Hess and Raeder; 20 years for

Twenty-four Nazi leaders on trial.

von Schirach and Speer; 15 years for von Neurath; 10 years for Dönitz. Those condemned to death were hanged in October 1946.

Smaller war crimes tribunals were set up in various places where major crimes had been committed. In 1939 the British government published a White Paper on the German concentration camps and a widely read Penguin book on international affairs (1939) listed Dachau, Buchenwald, Oranienburg and Papenburg. There were two categories of camps. Between 1933 and 1945 a total of 1,600,000 people were sent to concentration *work* camps, and over one million died. In the even more infamous *extermination* camps, such as Auschwitz, Sobibor, Treblinka and Chelmno, where upwards of 18 million people were sent, up to 11 million were killed. There were camps outside Germany, many in Poland, and also into Austria and Czechoslovakia. Most camps were commanded by an SS officer of the rank of colonel or major and were divided into military style companies. Each camp block was under the charge of a senior prisoner or *kapo*. The SS charged industrial companies four to eight Deutschmarks per day for the use of prisoners working a full 12-hour day. The average survival of a prisoner in a work camp was nine months. The SS could count on a net gain of 1,431 marks per labourer for their short life.

In the war crimes tribunals set up in the post-war period in Poland, where there were seven camps, 631 war criminals were executed; in the US zone of Germany 278; in the British zone 240; in Hungary 149; and in the French zone of Germany 104; a total of 1,402. In Auschwitz camp under Commandant Höss, between two and four million inmates were murdered. The majority of the dead were Jewish.

Nearly two million German soldiers and civilians had to be screened in the British zone at the end of the war. German bureaucratic records were fortunately excellent. There were five categories to be identified from their Nazi records:

Above: Court room at Nuremberg.

Left: Ruins of Nuremberg in 1945: more than half of the city had been destroyed by Allied bombing, but the survival of its courthouse and prison determined the trial's value. (*Getty Images*)

1) *Hauptschuldige* (offender)
2) *Belastete* (an active military record involved in war crimes)
3) *Minderbelastete* (a minor offender, a Party member, not known to have committed any crime)
4) *Mitlaufer* (person who joined the Nazi Party to keep a job)
5) *Entlastete* (innocent, proved anti-Nazi)

Since the liberation of the Bergen-Belsen concentration camp on 15 April by the author's battlegroup of 11th Armoured Division, the British press were justifiably baying for blood. *The Illustrated London News* described Josef Kramer, the camp commandant, as: 'a typical German brute – a sadistical, heavy-featured Nazi. He was quite unashamed.' Raymond Phillips, a barrister who edited the official published transcript of the Belsen trial, wrote afterwards: 'To many it seemed superfluous that there should be a trial at all, and the popular cry was for a summary identification and execution of the offenders.' In some of the camps liberated by American forces, SS guards were simply lined up and shot. Some guards were lynched by the prisoners immediately after they were freed. On 27 April, twelve days after the liberation, a team of war crimes investigators consisting of two majors, a captain and some NCO translators, plus another team of fifteen who joined in May, were allotted to a camp of nearly 60,000 witnesses, two-thirds of them Polish, Hungarian and Roumanian Jews.

The Belsen trial opened on 17 September 1945. The defendants were sixteen male members of the SS, including Josef Kramer, commandant, Dr Fritz Klein, camp doctor, and Franz Hössler, commandant of Camp 2. Also accused were sixteen female SS guards, including Irma Grese, who commanded a compound, and Elizabeth Volkenrath, the camp overseer of the women's camp. Grese, twenty-one, with long blond hair, high leather boots and a short whip for her guard dogs, was what the tabloid press wanted. Also on trial were a dozen *kapos* accused of mistreating their fellow prisoners.

The British authorities were determined to follow the practices being laid out by the UN War Crimes Tribunal. 'Arch' criminals would be tried at Nuremberg: 'ordinary war criminals in the custody of Allied military authorities could be dealt with by military courts'. Kramer and his fellow guards fell into the 'ordinary' category and faced a court made up of five British military officers. Colonel T. M. Backhouse led the prosecution team as senior Judge Advocate General of the legal staff of the new British Army of the Rhine (BAOR). The forty-four accused were represented by eleven British regimental officers, including Captain Lionel Cranfield, who was the author's solicitor post war, and one Polish officer.

The trial took place in a specially built dock in a gymnasium on the outskirts of Luneburg, a town 40 miles north-east of Belsen. The army painstakingly gathered evidence, produced witnesses, provided the accused with defence counsel, allowed the defence to answer the charges against them and treated the prisoners with a degree of respect.

The Belsen defendants were not on trial for crimes against Jews, not for genocide, but for mistreating and abusing *Allied nationals*. This included Jews and others from Allied nations such as Poland and Russia. The insistence on correct and traditional British justice was immediately criticised by the Russian and French press as being 'unnecessarily attentive to the rights of the defendants'.

Twelve of the accused had appalling track records and had worked in Auschwitz previously; these included Kramer, Klein, Hössler, Grese and Volkenrath. Kramer had spent his *entire* career in camps. He had joined the SS in 1932 aged twenty-six, and then worked in Dachau, Sachsenhausen, Malthausen, Auschwitz, was commandant at Natzweiler, back to Auschwitz, commandant of Birkenau in Poland, the extermination camp for Russian officers, then in December 1944 to Belsen. Grese had started at Ravensbruck, then Auschwitz, then back to Ravensbruck and finally Belsen.

Two of the star witnesses were Brigadier Llewelyn Glyn Hughes, who gave precise medical details of the camp upon its liberation, as did Captain Derek Sington. The court watched a film made of the camp in April by the British and the court toured the camp grounds, which were burned by Crocodile-tank flame-throwers after the trial. The defence counsel did their best. Colonel H. A. Smith argued that concentration camps had been legal in Germany since 1933, therefore what went on there was legal by German law. Most of the evidence was witness statements. Another theme was that Kramer and the others were simply taking orders from their superiors in Berlin, Richard Glücks and Oswald Pohl, who was Heydrich's No. 2, but was remarkably similar to Oskar Schindler, as in *Schindler's Ark* by Thomas Keneally.

Colonel Backhouse, in his closing summary, went over the details of the transport, beatings, shaving, tattooing, forced labour, starvation, selections and crematoria. The only difference between Auschwitz and Belsen was that the latter had no gas chambers. He also stated that: 'the martyrdom of the Jews ... was a war crime which has never been equalled.'

On 16 November 1945 the court adjourned and six hours later delivered the verdicts. Thirty out of forty-four defendants were declared guilty on one or both counts of mistreating Allied nationals at Auschwitz and Belsen. Eleven defendants: Kramer, Klein, Hössler, Grese, Bormann, Volkenrath and five others were sentenced to death and hanged on 12 December. Nineteen others received sentences from life in prison to a mere one year in jail.

Belsen was, in effect, the first war crimes trial in the British zone. There were several others and the author was involved in two of them: in Hamburg and also in Oldenburg. In each case a British Judge Advocate General supervised and made sure that the same high legal standards applied. There was an interpreter for the Crown and another for the defence who had to agree on the accuracy of the witnesses' testimony. The judges and jury were a lt colonel, a major and the author, a lieutenant who always had to give his verdict first for obvious reasons.

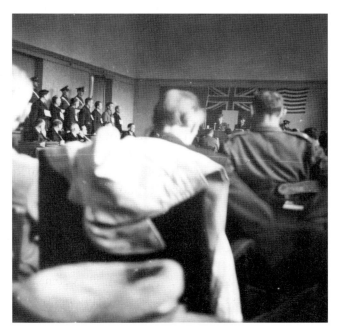

Oldenburg War Crimes Tribunal: September 1946. The author was a junior member of the three man court (judge and jury) seen back to the camera with two gleaming RHA stars (Lieutenant). Trial of Willi Erold and eleven others charged with the murder of 300 persons (POWs and DPs) at a 'people's camp' in April 1945. The verdict was death by hanging for Erold and six others. The remaining persons on trial received lesser sentences.

The Oldenburg trial in September 1946 was of Willi Erold and eleven others charged with the murder of 300 at a 'People's Camp' in April 1945. Erold and six others were found guilty and sentenced to death by hanging. The other five faced other lesser charges.

The author was Intelligence Officer of 3rd Regiment Royal Horse Artillery at the time of both trials. On 13 December 1945 he was one of fifty officers of BAOR who witnessed Mr Albert Pierrepoint, the official British hangman, execute thirteen convicted war criminals in Hameln.

It is true to say that thousands of war crimes went untried and unpunished. For instance when the SS units left Belgium in a hurry in early September 1944, they or the Hitler Jugend, and some Wehrmacht, committed undeniable war crimes in Ghlin, Jemappes, Quaregnon, Quevaucamps, Sovet, Anhée, Godinne, Bouillon, Hun, Warnant, Rivière, Faillon and Bonsin.

This author and separately Alan Moorehead, the journalist, witnessed the SS camp at Breendonck, just south of Antwerp, an absolute charnel house of butchery of civilians who might, or might not, have been members of the Belgian Resistance.

Alfred Pierrepoint (1905–1992) first flew to Germany on 11 December 1945 and the next day executed eleven Belsen guards, plus two more Germans convicted of murdering a RAF pilot on 11 March. Altogether Pierrepoint made twenty-five visits to the British zones in Germany and Austria and hanged over 200 war criminals in a four-year period.

The Holocaust and the Death Camps

As soon as Hitler took power in the Third Reich in January 1933 his SA (Sturm Abteilung), tough brownshirts, unemployed ex-soldiers, began rounding up all possible enemies and putting them under guard, initially in Dachau, Oranienburg, Buchenwald, Gross-Rosen, Mautausen and Sachsenhausen. In 1939 and 1940 came Flossenburg, Ravensbruck, Neuengamme, Theresienstadt (Czechoslovakia), and Auschwitz 1, 2 and then 3 in Poland. In 1941 Stutthof, Natzweiler (Alsace) and a batch of five more in Poland: Birkenau, Chelmno, Belzec, Sobibor, Treblinka and Lublin-Majdanek. Bergen-Belsen opened as late as 1943. All the camps were run by the SS Death's Head Formation, camp colonels, under the overall chief inspector Theodor Eicke (1892–1943). He was succeeded by Richard Glucks (1889–1945). The whole system was supervised by the infamous Reichsführer SS Heinrich Himmler (1900–1945).

The two main types of camp, excluding POW and work camps, were concentration and extermination or death camps. The former included Dachau, Belsen and Sachsenhausen, which were defined as penal camps under a very harsh regime. There was no release and the average life expectancy was six months before death from overwork, starvation, diseases such as typhus, and of course intense brutality. If a concentration camp held 60,000 inmates, then the deaths would be about 100 a day. The SS defined them as 'camps of protective custody'.

A typical concentration camp like Dachau had five departments: 1 for the commandant and his staff; 2 was the political office run by the Gestapo; 3 was for the SS officers responsible for work schedules and discipline; 4 was the camp administration – initially there were *totenbuch* or death registers identifying the victims and cause and date of death;

The main concentration, extermination camps and prisoner of war camps.

5 was the medical section who often caused severe medical problems, theoretically for research, besides a minimum of aid for sick prisoners.

Towards the end of the war, usually in 1944, camps were being overwhelmed as Himmler's SS rounded up victims for *schutzhaft* (protective custody): trade unionists, communists, homosexuals, petty criminals, dissenters of all kinds. Coloured patches were worn: green for criminal, black for anti-social, pink for homosexuals, red for politicals, blue for stateless or potential escapees from the Third Reich, and violet for religious fundamentalists. Bergen-Belsen, according to Josef Kramer, was overwhelmed, but starvation, typhus and SS brutality caused the scenes that were photographed and shown round the world. Most of the concentration camps were in the centre of a circle of cheap labour industries. At the end of 1944, 13 parent camps in Germany had 500 sub-camps.

The second category of extermination or death camps were limited to reception areas, often railways, temporary accommodation, gas chambers and crematoria, used exclusively for the Holocaust and genocide. Killing people by gas was perfected in December 1941 after the use of zyklon B gas at Chelmno (Kulmhof) near Lodz west of Warsaw. It is estimated that 320,000 Jews were killed there 1941–45. The three purpose-built

Above left: A concentration camp victim is buried in a mass grave.
Right: The scene at one concentration camp.

death camps in Poland were constructed in 1942. Sobibor killed over 300,000 Jews, Belzec 600,000 and Treblinka over 700,000.

Rudolf Höss, Commandant of Auschwitz, told the Nuremberg Tribunal that in the period 1 May 1940 to 1 December 1943 he estimated that 2,500,000 were exterminated and a further 500,000 died from disease and starvation. In that last month the Red Army were getting close, so the SS dynamited the main installation and drove 60,000 prisoners on a march of death. The Judgement of Nuremberg 1946, details Höss's testimony of the screening and the actual killing. Adolf Eichmann, who was put in charge of 'The Final Solution' by his Führer, estimated that his policies killed six million Jews, four million of them in the extermination camps. Poles accounted for three million, Russians for two million, and Germans one million.

From January 1945 when 750,000 concentration camp prisoners were driven from the eastern camps into western Germany, at least 250,000 of them died on the way.

Hitler's Nuclear Option

The Nazis had been the leaders in the race for technology that could produce V weapons: V for Victory or Vengeance. They produced the world's first operational jet fighters (ME 262s), ballistic missiles, electro high-speed submarines, flying bombs, infra-red gun sights, rocket planes and dangerous new chemical weapons such as Sarin and Tabun. Hitler was devoted to the development of new battlefield weapons.

In 1920 Hitler had a great respect for Professor Philipp Lenard of Heidelberg University, a Nobel Prize laureate in physics. Lenard joined the Nazi Party in its early days and told Hitler that: 'science, like every other human product, is racial and conditioned by blood'. Lenard attacked Einstein and the theory of relativity and persuaded Hitler that: 'the Jew conspicuously lacks understanding for the truth ... being in this respect in contrast to the Aryan research scientist with his careful and serious will to truth ... Jewish physics is thus a phantom and a phenomenon of degeneration of fundamental German physics.' Professor Wilhelm Müller of Aachen Technical College and Professor Ludwig Bierback of Berlin University were unanimous in their agreement: modern physics and this included nuclear physics, was in reality a bid for 'Jewish world rule'. So to Hitler nuclear physics were Jewish physics. Thus Alfred Rosenberg, later Minister of Education, took his cue from his master and failed to support nuclear research. Nevertheless work and research did continue and Dr Hans Süss began searching in 1940 for a nuclear 'moderator' to control an atomic reactor, and the physical characteristics of heavy water, which has the chemical formula of D_2O rather than the usual H_2O. German War Office planners estimated that they needed five *tons* of heavy water to control chain reaction in a uranium pile. None was available in Germany

Copenhagen Physics Conference, June 1936. First row (left to right): Pauli, Jordan, Heisenberg, Born, Meitner, Stern, Franck; second row: Weizsäcker and Hund behind Hiesenberg, Otto Frisch (second from right); third row: Kopfermann, Euler, Fano; fourth and fifth rows, second from left: Peierls and Weisskopf; standing along wall: Bohr and Rosenfeld.

but Norsk Hydro plant at Vemork in Norway was producing ten kilograms of heavy water per month. In January 1940 a representative of the great I. G. Farben, which held shares in Norsk Hydro, visited the plant and offered to buy their stock of 185 kilograms of heavy water and would start purchasing 100 kilograms per month. The sensible Norwegians, however, sold this stock to a French group which included the renowned physicist, Frédéric Joliot-Curie. They were experimenting with an atomic pile and took delivery in February. After that blow a batch of German scientists descended on the plant during 1940, urging that output should be increased to an annual output of 1,364 kilograms. Then Lt Commander Eric Welsh, head of the Norwegian section of British Intelligence, the SOE and RAF sprang into action for Operations Swallow, Grouse, Freshman and Gunnerside to destroy Norsk Hydro. Many brave Norwegians, such as Knut Haugland, Helberg, Kjelstrup, Ronneberg and finally, Knut Haukelid, eventually completely sabotaged the heavy water project.

Göbbels' diary of 21 March 1942 noted: 'Research into the realm of atomic destruction has now proceeded to the point where results may possibly be used in the present war. It is essential that we should keep ahead of everybody.'

General Friedrich Fromm, Chief of Army Armaments, suggested to Albert Speer in April that the only chance of Germany winning the war lay in developing a weapon with totally *new* effects. So Speer chaired a meeting at Harnack House, the Berlin centre of the Kaiser Wilhelm Gesellschaft, with General Fromm, Admiral Witzell, Field Marshal Milch and various scientists including Nobel Prize-winners Otto Hahn and Werner Heisenberg. The latter was bitter about the lack of support for nuclear research in Germany. He also tabled a report on 'atom smashing', and the development of the cyclotron, a particle accelerator or atom-smashing machine. Heisenberg stated that Germany had found the scientific solution to nuclear fission and that theoretically building an atom bomb was possible given time, money and more scientific staff.

In the same way that secret personal armies were developed in the Third Reich, such as Göring's huge land-based parachute army, unbeknownst to others, so it was with scientific research. All three branches of the armed forces, also the SS, even the postal service, had separate research facilities. Thus progress on the development of nuclear fission was negligible. Speer in 1942 had immense power as Armaments Minister. He could have, perhaps, centralised all the key research facilities and asked Hitler for funds to continue and develop a nuclear missile.

T-Force, the 'thieving magpies', had a rather important role in tracking down and politely capturing scientists involved in nuclear research. They included Professor Wilhelm Groth, Dr Paul Harteck, an associate who had used an ultra-centrifuge at Celle on the separation of uranium 235 and 238 (FO 1032/205) and Professor Otto Hahn, head of physics at the Hannover Technische Hochschule, who was perhaps the most famous, with his discovery of fission or uranium and thorium in medium-heavy nuclei.

Operation Alsos was the American secret group searching for evidence of the Nazis' atomic research programme. In October 1945, the movements of ten nuclear scientists (three in particular) were vital in case they fell into the hands of the Soviets: Heisenberg, Gerlach, Diebner, Hahn, von Laue, von Weizsäcker, Wirtz, Bagge, Korshing and Harteck were 'persuaded' to live on parole in East Anglia, although British authorities initially wanted them to go to Bonn University *en masse*.

T-Force discovered the Mega Research Association, anti-military, anti-industrial, pure researchers; an alliance of physicists devoted to pure atomic and nuclear research who knew 'everybody' in Germany connected with nuclear research.

Above left: Farm Hall, where ten German physicists were detained in 1945.
Above right: Max von Laue resisted the Nazis while remaining in Germany during the war.
Below left: Carl Friedrich von Weizsäcker, Heisenberg's younger colleague in the Nazi bomb project.
Below right: Paul Harteck solicited funding for atomic-bomb research from Army ordnance in 1939.

Alsos picked up several leads: Professor Fleischmann, a leading physicist working at Strasbourg University, and in November 1944 a group of scientists hidden in a wing of Strasbourg Hospital masquerading as medical officers. Professor Samuel Goudsmit, the scientific head of Alsos, later concluded that: 'their pile work was still in a very early state, and had been unable to produce a chain reaction'. In February 1945 the Auer factory at Oranienburg, north of Berlin, was manufacturing uranium metals and thorium ore for atomic energy.

When Carl Friedrich von Weizsäcker's obituary was published in the *Daily Telegraph* it mentioned that he and fellow scientists were briefly interned near Cambridge where their conversations were *secretly* recorded. In one Weisensäcker, on hearing that the USA had dropped atom bombs on Hiroshima and Nagasaki, remarked: 'If they were able to finish it by summer '45 then with a bit of luck we could have been ready in winter '44–45.' At the end of the war the scientists had been interned at Farm Hall, Godmanchester after Cambridge. The taped transcripts revealed that Weizsäcker had taken the lead in arguing for an agreement among the group that they would claim they had *never* wanted to develop a German bomb. This story, which they knew to be untrue, was known within their circle as *die lesart* (the version).

After Dresden was battered and burned between 13 and 15 February 1945 by the RAF and USAAF, Hitler was beside himself with fury and spoke to Dr Giesing in the Berlin Chancellery: 'I'm going to start using my Victory weapon [*siegwaffe*] and then the war will come to a glorious end. Some time ago we solved the problem of nuclear fission and we have developed it so far that we can exploit the energy for armaments purposes [*rüstungszwecke*]. They won't even know what hit them! It's the weapon of the future. With it Germany's future is assured.'

Albert Speer had visited the Krupp armaments works and was shown parts of Germany's first cyclotron. And at Heidelberg in the summer of 1944 he was shown 'our first cyclotron splitting an atomic nucleus' by Professor Walter Bothe. Professor Walther Gerlach was the Reich chief of nuclear research; Professors Werner Heisenberg and Carl Friedrich von Weizsäcker were developing an experimental atomic pile at Haigerloch. Hitler's boast was valid. In his memoirs Speer wrote that he was convinced that Hitler would have used the atomic bomb on London and Moscow.

The seminal book on this subject is John Cornwell's *Hitler's Scientists*. He recounts the agonised conversation in the Farm Hall 'camp' where

Werner Heisenberg, Otto Hahn, Paul Hartech, Max von Laue, Erich Bagge, Kurt Diebner, Walter Gerlach, Karl Wirtz and, of course, von Weizsäcker were benevolently imprisoned. He describes their secret (so they thought) conversations and their agreement to *lesart*. The conspirators drew up a detailed memorandum but carefully omitted: (1) Paul Harteck's approach to their key minister, Bernhard Rust for funding to push forward uranium research with the aim of creating weapons of mass destruction; (2) Weizsäcker's 1940 report on the neptunium path to a bomb; (3) Fritz Houterman's speculations about plutonium; and (4) no mention was made of the theoretical research on graphite as a moderator.

Perhaps the Allies were fortunate after all.

Operation Unthinkable

Winston Churchill was deeply angry and also extremely gloomy about the fate of Poland and evidence of Soviet barbarism in the territories which they had 'liberated'. On 13 May 1943, he cabled President Truman in Washington:

> Our armed power on the continent is in rapid decline. Meanwhile what is to happen about Russia[?] I have always worked for friendship with Russia but, like you, I feel deep anxiety because of their misinterpretation of the Yalta decisions, their attitude towards Poland, their overwhelming influence in the Balkans excepting Greece, the difficulties they make about Vienna ... and above all their power to maintain very large armies in the field for a long time. What will be the position in a year or two, when the British and American armies have melted ... and when Russia may choose to keep two or three hundred [divisions] on active service? An iron curtain is drawn down upon their front ... Surely it is vital now to come to an understanding with Russia, or see where we are with her before we weaken our armies mortally, or retire to the zones of occupation. I should be most grateful for your opinion or advice ... To sum up, this issue of a settlement with Russia before our strength has gone seems to me to dwarf all others.

Truman answered: 'From the present point of view, it is impossible to make a conjecture as to what the Soviets may do when Germany is under the small forces of occupation and the great part of such armies as we can maintain are fighting in the Orient against Japan.' The President agreed with Churchill that a tripartite meeting with Stalin had become urgently necessary.

On 24 May Churchill instructed the chiefs of staff to consider the military possibilities of pushing the mighty Red Army back eastwards *before* the Anglo-American armies were demobilised: 'impose upon Russia the will of the United States and British Empire to secure a square deal for Poland'. The target date for Operation Unthinkable – the launching of an assault would be – 1 July 1945. It was a marvellous pipe-dream story – but true – and recounted with Max Hastings' usual brio in his book *Finest Years*.

Joseph Stalin, the Russian dictator.

Bibliography

BBC War Report, Despatches: D-Day to VE Day (OUP, 1946)

Blake, George, *Mountain & Flood* (Jackson & Co, 1950)

Churchill, Winston, *Triumph & Tragedy* (Cassell, 1951)

Cornwell, John, *Hitler's Scientists* (Penguin, 2004)

Davies, Norman, *Europe at War* (Pan, 2007)

De Guingand, Francis, *Operation Victory* (Hodder & Stoughton, 1941)

Delaforce, Patrick, *Churchill's Secret Weapons* (Pen & Sword, 2006)

Delaforce, Patrick, *The Rhine Endeavour* (**Amberley, 2010**)

Ford, Ken, *Rhineland 1945* (Osprey, 2000)

Gilbert, Martin, *The Day the War Ended* (Harper Collins, 2001)

Gilbert, Martin, *Second World War* (Phoenix, 2009)

Hastings, Max, *Finest Years (Churchill)* (Harper Press, 2009)

Hastings, Max, *Armageddon* (Pan, 2004)

Hauge, Jens Chr, *Liberation of Norway* (Norsk Forlag, 1950)

Hitchcock, William, *Liberation, Bitter Road to Freedom* (Faber, 2009)

HMSO, *By Air to Battle (Airborne Divisions)* (1945)

HMSO, *World War 2 Collection* (2001)

Horrocks, Brian, *A Full Life* (Collins, 1960)

Longden, Shaun, *T-Force, Race for Nazi Secrets* (Constable, 2009)

Lucas, James, *Last Days of the Reich* (Arms & Armour, 1986)

Moorehead, Alan, *Eclipse* (Hamish Hamilton, 1945)

Petrow, Richard, *The Bitter Years* (Purnell Book Services, 1975)

Rosse & Hill, *Guards Armoured* (Geoffrey Bles, 1956)

Saunders, Hilary, *Red Beret* (Michael Joseph, 1950)

Shulman, Milton, *Defeat in the West* (Secker & Warburg, 1947)

Speer, Albert, *Inside the Third Reich* (Sphere, 1971)

Stacey, C. P., *History of the Canadian Army* (Queens/Ottawa, 1960)
Taylor & Shaw, *Dictionary of the Third Reich* (Penguin, 1997)
Trevor-Roper, Hugh, *Hitler's Table Talk* (Enigma Books, NY 2000)
Whiting, Charles, *Monty's Greatest Gamble* (1985)
Wilmot, Chester, *Struggle for Europe* (Collins, 1957)

Also Divisional Histories: *Red Crown and Dragon, Polar Bears, Fighting Wessex Wyverns, The Black Bull, Churchill's Desert Rats, Monty's Ironsides, Monty's Northern Legions, Monty's Highlanders* by Patrick Delaforce.

Acknowledgements

Special thanks to Cathy Pugh and Ernest Tate of the Second World War Experience Centre; to Jens Anderson, Curator of Museumscenter Hanstholm, Denmark; to Becks Skinner of Airborne Assault Museum; to Frode Færoy, Curator of Norwegian Armed Forces Museum, Oslo; to Leif Thingsrud, Archivist, Riksarkivet, Oslo; to Craig Murray, Imperial War Museum, London, and to the Imperial War Museum Photographic Archive.

Glossary

German and Dutch Terms

Abteilungen	Combat Units
Abwehr	Military intelligence department of the OKW
Festung	German Garrison designated only by Hitler
Flak Units	German anti-aircraft units
Hitler Jugend	Young and highly indoctrinated Nazis, fanatically loyal to Hitler
Kampfgruppe	Impromptu German battle group
Kranken	Wounded convalescent formation
Kriegsmarine	Members of the German Navy
Landsturm Nederland	Dutch Nazi volunteers
Luftwaffe	German Air Force
Minnenwerfer	German mortars known by the Allies as 'Moaning minnies'
Nebelwerfer	Mortar that fired chemical or HE shells
OKW	Oberkommando der Wehrmacht
Panzerfaust	Cheap German one-shot anti-tank weapon
Panzergrenadier	German motorised or mechanised infantry
Panzerjaeger	Armoured units designed to fight tanks, usually SP guns
Schmeisser	German submachine-gun, also known as the MP-40
Schu mine	Wooden cased anti-infantry mine

Schwerpunkt	Concentrated method of advance upon a focal point with co-ordinated armour and infantry and appropriate flank protection
Spandau	German machine-gun
Stonk	German word for a sudden artillery bombardment, also used by the British
Teller	Cylindrical, powerful anti-tank mine
Verdronken land	Flooded region in Holland
Volksgrenadier Divisions	Emergency divisions created in 1944 to combat the German manpower crisis
Wehrmacht	The unified armed forces of Germany

Military Abbreviations

AA	Anti-Aircraft
ADC	Aide-de-camp
AFV	Armoured fighting vehicle
AVRE	Armoured Vehicle Royal Engineers; special Churchill tank
BAOR	British Army of the Rhine
BEF	British Expeditionary Force
BLA	British Liberation Army
CAS	Close Air Support, usually by RAF planes
CIGS	Chief of the Imperial General Staff
CO	Commanding Officer
CRA	Commander Royal Artillery
CRE	Commander Royal Engineers
Crocodile	Churchill tank with flame-thrower
CSM	Company Sergeant-Major
DCLI	Duke of Cornwall's Light Infantry
DCM	Distinguished Conduct Medal
DD Tanks	Duplex Drive Tanks
DLI	Durham Light Infantry
DP	Displaced Person
DSO	Distinguished Service Order

DUKW	Wheeled amphibious landing craft
DZ	Drop zone for paratroops
FOO	Artillery Forward Observation Officer
GOC	General Officer Commanding
HAA	Heavy anti-aircraft gun
HLI	Highland Light Infantry
Kangaroo	Armoured infantry carrier on selfpropelled tank-type chassis
KOSB	King's Own Scottish Borderers
KOYLI	King's Own Yorkshire Light Infantry
KRRC	King's Royal Rifle Corps
KSLI	King's Shropshire Light Infantry
LAA	Light Anti-Aircraft artillery
LCA	Landing Craft Assault
LZ	Landing zone for glider troops
MC	Military Cross
MM	Military Medal
MMG	Medium Machine Guns
NAAFI	Navy, Army and Air Force Institutes
NCO	Non-Commissioned Officer
OBE	Order of the British Empire
OC	Officer commanding
PBI	Poor Bloody Infantry
PIAT	Projector Infantry Anti-Tank
PIR	Parachute Infantry Regiments
RA	Royal Artillery
RAC	Royal Armoured Corps
RAMC	Royal Army Medical Corps
RB	Rifle Brigade
RE	Royal Engineers
REME	Royal Electrical and Mechanical Engineers
RHA	Royal Horse Artillery
RSF	Royal Scots Fusiliers
RTR	Royal Tank Regiment
RWF	Royal Welch Fusiliers
SHAEF	Supreme Headquarters Allied Expeditionary Force

SOE	Special Operations Executive
TCV	Troop Carrying Vehicle
VE Day	Victory in Europe Day
UNRRA	United Nations Relief & Rehabilitation Administration

Index

Adair, Major General Allan 7, 295, 403
  on German marine defenders 241-2
Allied Commission (AMGOT) 18, 417-8

Barr, Robert 179-181
Bellamy, Major Bill
  on St Joost battle 78-9
Bergen-Belsen 219, 223-32
  horrors 341
  concentration camps 423-8
Bittrich, SS Obergruppenführer Wilhelm 12
Blake, George
  Lowland division advance 212
  Bremen battle 253, 259
Blaskowitz, General Johannes von 202
  i/c Holland 337-59
Blumentritt, General Günther
  on defence orders 202-3
Brett-Smith, Lt 100
  on ruined Moerdijk 323
  on Berlin victory parade 327
British Liberation Army (BLA) 100-1, 194-7,
  312-20, 368
  on tribulations ahead 16
  bringing peace to victims 18
  battles to the Baltic 19
Bormann, Martin 261, 300-1, 332, 362, 384,
  425

Carver, (later Field Marshal) Michael 12, 74,
  247
Canadian Army
  Cinderella War 46
  tribute to 103
  role in Operation Veritable 111
  earn VCs 129
  Hochwald breakthrough 146
  Operation Anger plan 147
  in Operation Dutch Cleanser 160
Churchill, Winston 11
  waning influence 15
  begs Stalin for help 24, 45, 63
  cruise on Rhine 79
  visits Siegfried Line 112, 128, 142
  praises Stalin 167, 171, 178-81, 190-2
  heated exchange with Stalin 278
  wants BLA to get to Lubeck before
  Russians 279
  memo re Dönitz's power 280-2, 305
  on Hitler's death 322
  speech re Desert Rats 328
  on the task ahead 329
  on Danish surrender 362-5
  sends force into Denmark 379
  interest in Norway 384
  'iron curtain' cable to Truman 436-7

Dimbleby, Richard 32
  with Airborne troops in Varsity 184-5
  visits Bergen-Belsen 230-2
Displaced persons (DPs) 18, 217, 258, 321, 328
  statistics and help 408-25
Dönitz, Grand Admiral Karl 269-71, 368, 376,
  387, 397, 421
  new U-boats 24-5
  surrender of 'Fourth' Reich 300-17

Eisenhower, General Dwight 191-4, 244, 346,
  350, 370, 380, 389
  decision not to capture Berlin 9, 15, 18, 45
  broad front strategy 62-4, 103
  on Reichswald & Operation Grenade plans
    110-12
  on Airborne casualties 135, 146, 179, 181-4
  taken in by Göbbels' hoax 264
  SHAEF policy 281-3
  instructs Montgomery to accept German
    surrender 306-10, 314
  orders Operation Manna 341
Evans, Major John
  on Susteren battle 77

Festungs (fortresses) 12, 27
  Holland 149, 330-61
  Norwegen 381-97

Göbbels, Dr Josef 29-30, 261-4, 300-1, 338,
  431
Göring, Field Marshal Hermann 27-9, 46-7,
  300-1, 420, 422
  fanatical parachute army 14
  private army 47

Hamilton, Lt Colonel C. D.
  at Arnhem 155
  heading for Rotterdam 159
  disarming German troops in Holland 349-
    55

Hastings, Max
  on German leadership 36
  on Operation Varsity 195
  Finest Years 437
Halton, Matthew (CBC)
  on capture of Arnhem 157-8
  on liberation of 2 million slaves 413-14
Hibbert, Major Anthony
  on 'capture' of Kiel 292-4
Himmler, SS Reichsführer Heinrich 55, 243-5,
  269, 271, 283-4, 367-8, 427-8
  propaganda 29-30
  'rivers of blood' 48
  negotiations with Count Bernadotte 300
  rejected by Dönitz 302
Hitler, Adolf 6, 9-15, 20, 134, 191-2, 200-2
  Mein Kampf 24
  Victory weapons 25, 434
  and *festung* commanders 27
  upped bombing stakes 46
  counter-attack in Ardennes 47
  Volksgrenadier divisions 48
  Operation Bodenplatte 53
  secret weapons 162-7
  jet planes 163-7
  designates Bremen a *festung* 245
  orders Höfer's plan 262-4
  orders Wolz to defend Hamburg 271
  inspired by Roosevelt's death 278
  key appointments in Holland 331
  Table Talk on Holland 332
  Table Talk on Denmark 362-3
  meeting with Quisling 381-2
  on Norwegian campaign 383
  confidence in Terboven 384
Hobart, Lt General Percy 334, 346
  Army history 65-74
  magnificent 'zoo' 72-3
  in Elbe crossing 287
Horrocks, Lt General Brian 135, 138, 140-2
  on PBI 7, 39

guilt about RAF bombing 43-4

result of Ardennes battle 50, 52-3, 64

Reichswald battle plan 86, 103

on Operation Veritable 111-14, 119-21

capture of Goch 126, 128-9

Operation Plunder 171-3

on his armoured divisions 195

plans for capture of Bremen 246

benevolent dictator 322

visits Sandbostel camp 403

Infantry patrols 95

Joyce, William (Lord Haw-Haw) 31, 273

Liberation

Velp 156

Arnhem 158

Lunteren 159

unpleasant aspect 161

enthusiasm in Utrecht 352-3

Liddel Hart

on superior German generals 12

Lunghi, Hugh

on Stalin's fury at Reims surrender 317

Maxted, Stanley

on Airborne bravery 185-6

Model, Field Marshal Walther 12

order of the day 27-8

determination to capture

Nijmegen 90, 95

Montgomery, Field Marshal Bernard 15, 50,

73, 124, 134, 142

set-piece attacks 33, 43

'cracking around' in Germany 39

grand-slam operation 43

generalship 52, 195

rash interviews 62-3

'Monty's Moonlight' 80

attributes 168

Operation Plunder 192-9

Gazette article 281

Elbe crossing 283-4

signal to War Office 299

German forces surrender 313-16

civilian operation orders in Germany 322

hero's welcome in Copenhagen 380

Moorehead, Alan

German morale 10

German civilians 31

von Runstedt plan 49-50

British commanders 168

Rhine battle 181

Operations Plunder & Varsity 186-7

post-war Germany sordid life 309-10

V-weapons in Holland 340

Copenhagen visit 373-4

Oslo visit 389-90

DP slave workers 410

break-up of medieval state 416-17

Pierrepoint, Albert

official British hangman 19

in action in Germany 425-6

Roosevelt, President Franklin D. 11, 15, 24,

190-1, 194, 278, 325, 419

Royal Navy 15, 25, 152, 218, 294-5, 300,

319, 330, 334

'strange manoeuvres' 170

Operation Deadlight 305

grand tour of Scandinavia 372

Norwegian sea-battles 382

returns to Norway 391-3

Rundstedt, Field Marshal Gerd von

defence of Germany's sacred soil 27-8

commands Ardennes attack 49

Order of the Day 126-7

Shirer, William

on Hitler characteristics 21-3

Shulman, Milton
  Göbbels propaganda 30
  Siegfried Line defences 101-2
  General Schlemm 109
  German paratroops 131-2
  Wesel bridgehead 144
  Nazi brutalities in Holland 338
Speer, Albert 25, 162, 307-8. 408-10, 432-4
  production miracles 27
  Inside the Third Reich 163
  A-4 weapon development 166
  bombing of Hamburg 268-9
  Dönitz 302
Stacey, Colonel C. P.
  Reichswald battle 110-111
  The Victory Campaign 141
Stalin, Marshal Joseph 24, 64, 264, 278, 323
  revenge on Operation Barbarossa 15
  cynical quotations 16
  orders capture of Berlin 45
  Yalta conference 190-1, 194
  fury at German surrender to Allies 317

Thompson, R.W. (*Sunday Times*)
  on Ardennes battle 62
  on Reichswald battle 117

Vaughan-Thomas, Wynford
  11th Armoured Division actions 41, 220-2
  Operation Varsity 187-8
  Bremen battle 254-5
  capture of Hamburg 272
  DP slaves 414-15
Victoria Crosses
  Private Donnini 83
  Sgt Cousins & Major Tiltson 129
  Private Joseph Stokes 138-9
  Corporal Topham 185
  Corporal Chapman 208
  Guardsman E. Charlton 242

Vince, Lt A. A.
  winter campaign in Holland 97-9
  capturing Arnhem 153
  static battle 159

War Crimes Tribunals 19, 232, 277, 333, 378, 395, 420-6
War Office reports
  German views on British tactics 33
  German report 36
  casualty statistics 43
  Target Force brief 215
  Target Force in Holland 358
  British-Soviet relations 371
  Target Force in Denmark 377
  uranium discovery 432
Watson, Jack
  Ardennes battle 54-6
Whistler, Major General 'Bolo'
  most successful battle 140
  Bremen battle 250
Wilmot, Chester
  struggle for Europe 25
  Ardennes battle 52
  praise for Red Berets 188-9
  Teutoburger Wald battle 206
  battle for Bremen 246-50
  German navy 283
  Dönitz 'defeat & despair' 304-5
  two German armies surrender 312-13
  final surrender to Montgomery 314-15
Wilson, Andrew
  Crocodile flame-thrower 67-8
  flame-thrower in action 201

ALSO BY PATRICK DELAFORCE